This volume represents a major contribution to the emerging literature on litigation costs. It should be of value to academic lawyers, economists and others, as well as those interested in, or responsible for, policy formulation on the funding and management of litigation.

Paul Fenn, *Emeritus Professor, Nottingham University Business School, UK*

This book contains a wealth of information about litigation costs in different jurisdictions. It explores economic dimensions, as well as legal aspects, and discusses various ways of funding collective actions including third party funding.

Adrian Zuckerman, *Emeritus Professor of Civil Procedure, Oxford University, UK*

Modern commercial litigation is marked by a growing number of lawsuits in which considerable amounts of money are claimed. Strategies not only look at the performance and quality of the available court systems but also focus on the possibilities of financing large-scale litigation by third-party funders or by contingency fees, the possibilities of getting their own costs reimbursed and the risk of paying the costs and fees of the other party. This volume takes up these developments and provides for thoughtful insights into an area of procedural and commercial law which has been neglected for a long time. It is highly recommended to all stakeholders in legal practice and science who are involved and interested in these fascinating developments.

Burkhard Hess, *Director, Max Planck Institute, Luxembourg*

Litigation, Costs, Funding and Behaviour

This collection explores the practical operation of the law in the area of litigation costs and funding, and confronts the issue of how exposure to cost risks affects litigation strategy. It looks at the interaction of the relevant legal regime, regulatory framework and disciplinary rules with the behaviour of litigants, courts and legislatures, examining subjects such as cost rules and funding arrangements. The book discusses a wide range of topics such as cost-shifting rules, funding and mass tort litigation, cost rules and third-party funding (TPF) rules in specific areas such as intellectual property (IP) litigation, commercial arbitration, investment arbitration, the role of legal expense insurance arrangements, fee regulation and professional ethics. The contributors include renowned scholars, experts in their respective fields and well-versed individuals in both civil procedure and the practice of litigation, arbitration and finance. Together, they present a broad approach to the issues of costs, cost-shifting rules and third-party funding. This volume adds to the existent literature in combining topics in law and practice and presents an analysis of the most recent developments in this fast developing area.

Willem H. van Boom is Professor of Civil Law at the Institute for Private Law, Leiden Law School, the Netherlands. His research interests include contracts, torts and insurance, consumer law and civil procedure and he has published widely on these and related areas.

First published 2017 by Routledge

2 Park Square, Milton Park, Abingdon, Oxfordshire OX14 4RN
711 Third Avenue, New York, NY 10017

Routledge is an imprint of the Taylor & Francis Group, an informa business

First issued in paperback 2018

British Library Cataloguing in Publication Data
A catalogue record for this book is available from the British Library

Library of Congress Cataloging in Publication Data
Names: Boom, W. H. van, editor.
Title: Litigation, costs, funding and behaviour : Implications for the law / Willem H van Boom.
Description: Abingdon, Oxon ; New York, NY : Routledge, 2017. | Includes bibliographical references and index.
Identifiers: LCCN 2016024998 (print) | LCCN 2016025479 (ebook) | ISBN 9781472482891 (hardback) | ISBN 9781315592701 (E-book) | ISBN 9781317104230 (Web PDF) | ISBN 9781317104223 (ePub) | ISBN 9781317104216 (Mobipocket)
Subjects: LCSH: Lawyers – Fees. | Contingent fees. | Third party litigation funding. | Practice of law – Economic aspects.
Classification: LCC K130 .L58 2017 (print) | LCC K130 (ebook) | DDC 347/.057–dc23
LC record available at https://lccn.loc.gov/2016024998

ISBN: 978-1-4724-8289-1 (hbk)
ISBN: 978-0-367-02420-8 (pbk)

Typeset in Galliard
by Cenveo Publisher Services

Contents

Figures

Tables

Contributors

Eric De Brabandere is Professor of International Dispute Settlement, Grotius Centre for International Legal Studies, Leiden University, the Netherlands and attorney-at-law, member of the Ghent Bar, Belgium.

Jef De Mot is Senior Research Fellow, Research Foundation Flanders, at the Department of Interdisciplinary Study of Law, Private Law and Business Law, Ghent University, Belgium.

Michael Faure is Professor of Comparative and International Environmental Law at Maastricht University and Professor of Comparative Private Law and Economics at Erasmus University Rotterdam, the Netherlands.

Vince Morabito is Professor of Law at the Department of Business Law and Taxation Monash University, Caulfield, Australia.

John Peysner is Emeritus Professor of Civil Justice, Lincoln Law School, University of Lincoln, England and Programme Associate of the Swiss Re/CMS Research Programme on Civil Justice Systems, Centre for Socio-Legal Studies, University of Oxford, England.

Astrid Stadler is Professor of Civil Law, Civil Procedure, Private International Law and Comparative Law at the University of Konstanz, Germany.

Ilja Tillema is PhD Candidate at Erasmus School of Law, Erasmus University Rotterdam, under supervision of Professor SD Lindenbergh (Erasmus University Rotterdam) and Professor WH van Boom (Leiden University). The findings in her chapter are part of her ongoing PhD research project 'Third-party funding of mass litigation'.

Willem H. van Boom is Professor of Civil Law at at the Institute for Private Law, Leiden Law School, the Netherlands.

Ben van Velthoven is Associate Professor of Law & Economics at Leiden Law School, the Netherlands.

Peter van Wijck is Associate Professor of Law & Economics at Leiden Law School, the Netherlands.

Louis Visscher is Professor of Legal Economic Analysis of Tort and Damages at Erasmus University Rotterdam, the Netherlands.

Charlotte Vrendenbarg is PhD Candidate at the Institute for Private Law, Leiden Law School, the Netherlands.

Vicki Waye is Foundation Professor of Law at the School of Law, University of South Australia, Adelaide, Australia.

Preface

This volume brings together contributions that were originally presented at a research conference at Leiden Law School (December 2015). I am grateful to the contributors for participating and delivering such excellent papers. Furthermore, kind support by Leiden Law School and its staff in organising the conference is acknowledged with gratitude. The excellent editing assistance by Mariska Hoppers is also highly appreciated. The volume was prepared in Spring 2016. Later developments were not included.

Leiden, Spring 2016
Willem H. van Boom

List of Abbreviations

ADR	Alternative Dispute Resolution
ALF	Association of Litigation Funders
ASIC	Australian Securities & Investments Commission
ATE	After the event
ATE LEI	After the event legal expenses insurance
B2B	Business to business
BGB	Bürgerliches Gesetzbuch (German Civil Code)
BIS	Department for Business, Innovation & Skills
BTE	Before the event
BTE LEI	Before the event legal expenses insurance
CAT	Competition Appeal Tribunal
CDC	Cartel Damage Claims
CF	Contingency fees
CFA(s)	Conditional fee arrangement(s)
CFE	Claims Funding Europe
CJC	Civil Justice Council
DBA(s)	Damages-based agreement(s)
DCC	Dutch Civil Code
DCCP	Dutch Code of Civil Procedure
ECJ	The European Court of Justice EU
e.g.	Exempli gratia (for example)
et al.	Et alia (and others)
EWCA	Court of Appeal of England and Wales
GDP	Gross domestic product
HF	Hourly fees
ICSID	International Center for the Settlement of Investment Disputes
i.e.	Id est (that is)
IP	Intellectual property
IPR	Intellectual property rights
LEI	Legal expenses insurance
Ltd	Limited
NERA	National Economic Research Associates
NGO	Non-governmental organization
QPL	Quota pars litis
SME(s)	Small and medium-sized enterprise(s)

SPV(s)	Special-purpose vehicle(s)
TPF	Third-party funding
TTIP	Transatlantic Trade and Investment Partnership
UK	United Kingdom
UNCITRAL	The United Nations Commission on International Trade Law
US(A)	United States (of America)
v.	versus
WCAM	Wet Collectieve Afwikkeling Massaschade (Collective Settlement of Mass Damage Act)

1 Introduction

Willem H. van Boom

In litigation and other forms of dispute resolution, parties usually incur substantial costs. Apart from the time spent in court and the so-called 'opportunity cost' involved in litigation, civil proceedings give rise to attorney fees, expert and witness costs, court fees and reimbursements. Some of these costs may be recouped; others may remain where they happen to fall. How does the exposure to cost risks affect litigation strategy? And to what extent does the opportunity to shift costs on to the adversary influence these strategies? Does the legal framework for litigation cost allocation (cost-shifting rules) further influence the litigants' behaviour? And how do private financing arrangements such as insurance and third-party funding (TPF) fit into this picture? Do funders exercise specific powers over parties and their lawyers? Do they introduce certain dynamics to the proceedings that would otherwise not exist? And, if so, is that bad? Should there be a legal framework in place to restrain these third parties or should this best be left to market forces?

In this volume 'Litigation, Costs, Funding and Behaviour: Implications for the Law', experts from various jurisdictions confront these issues by presenting their legal, economic and policy-oriented perspectives. Their contributions include topics such as cost-shifting rules and the behavioural response they elicit; the insurance, financing, sale and commodification of claims; and specific case studies in areas such as intellectual property (IP) litigation, personal injury litigation, investment arbitration and class action litigation.[1]

With this introduction, a brief overview of the themes and contributions to this volume is given. The contributions can be divided into three themes: *general perspectives* (Chapters 2, 3 and 4), *specific case studies* (Chapters 5, 6 and 7) and *mass litigation* (Chapters 8, 9 and 10).

General perspectives

Chapters 2, 3 and 4 offer general perspectives on litigation, costs, third-party funding and the behavioural implications for litigants.

By means of general introduction, Chapter 2 titled 'Litigation costs and third-party funding' offers an in-depth comparative analysis of the issues, developments and regulatory choices concerning costs of litigation and funding arrangements. It also reflects on the behaviour of litigants and others involved in the business of litigating, adjudicating and settling private disputes. This chapter thus paints the background against which the following chapters are to be understood.

1 This volume focuses on private funding arrangements. Hence, public legal aid remains mostly outside the scope of the contributions.

Chapter 3, titled 'TPF and its alternatives', authored by Jef De Mot, Michael Faure and Louis Visscher, offers an economic analysis of third-party funding and its alternatives. From an economic perspective, TPF can be considered as a remedy for cases where individuals do not bring claims because they do not possess sufficient funds to bring the claim, and do not have access to other ways of financing their claim. TPF can also mitigate rational apathy in cases of so-called dispersed losses. The authors explain why TPF emerges and how it can help cure the failures that result from incomplete access to justice. However, they acknowledge that TPF has both advantages and disadvantages in terms of effects on the behavioural incentives of the parties involved in litigation. By means of comparison, the authors explore viable alternatives for TPF, namely legal expenses insurance (LEI) and attorney contingency fee arrangements.

In Chapter 4, 'Playing the man not the ball', John Peysner reviews recent developments concerning the financing of access to justice in England and Wales. It seems that since the recoverability of conditional fees and after-the-event insurance has been effectively abolished, TPF agreements may act as potential fuel for a range of corporate and individual claims. Such arrangements may bring sufficient reward for investors in the context of limited returns on investments in an era of low interest rates and the need for balanced portfolios. However, concerns are voiced that TPF in the English context may in fact herald an era of frivolous claims, unfettered financial speculation and predatory practices. Against this background, Peysner analyses a recent attempt by the 'Justice Not Profit' organisation sponsored by the US Chamber of Commerce Institute for Legal Reform to convince English policymakers to rein in TPF. However, Peysner's analysis cautions policymakers not to discard the *evidence*, which in fact indicates that in the English context TPF may well be a useful addition to the existing funding options.

Specific case studies

Chapters 5, 6 and 7 are devoted to specific case studies concerning the interplay of costs, cost rules and funding of litigation.

In Chapter 5, Charlotte Vrendenbarg explores 'Legal costs awards and access to justice in Dutch intellectual property cases'. In Dutch civil litigation, the conventional rules on recoverable costs hold that the loser pays the prevailing party's legal costs according to a simple system of predictable tariffs. The 2007 statute implementing the European IP Enforcement Directive 2004/48/EC introduced a completely different set of rules for IP litigation in the Netherlands. There, a full cost-shifting regime was introduced in support of IP right holders to enforce their rights before the courts. Vrendenbarg explores the effects of this new regime on litigants' behaviour. Based on the available literature on the effects of costs shifting in general, she conducted a survey among Dutch IP practitioners and found that the effects of the new regime seem to be mixed at best. Obviously, the decision to litigate or to settle depends on many variables but practitioners do report irrefutable changes in litigation behaviour under the influence of the new regime. For example, the introduction of the full cost-shifting regime seems to reinforce the tendency of risk-averse parties to settle rather than to litigate, regardless the merits of their case.

In Chapter 6, '"Mercantile adventurers?" The disclosure of third-party funding in investment treaty arbitration', Eric De Brabandere takes us into the domain of investment treaty arbitration. There, the function of arbitration is different from normal commercial arbitration between commercial parties since one of the parties involved is a sovereign state at the receiving end of foreign investments on the basis of international investment treaties.

As part of these treaties, receiving states agree to dispute resolution by independent arbitral tribunals rather than by their domestic court system. This system of investment treaty arbitration has both advantages and limitations. One of the issues is whether the presence of a TPF covertly covering and fuelling an investment claim or group of claims should be disclosed to the tribunal. What could be good reasons and less well founded reasons for favouring such a 'duty to disclose'? Eric De Brabandere weighs the arguments pro and con, in light of the specific functions of arbitration in the context of international investment treaty law.

In Chapter 7, 'Experimenting with conditional fees in the Netherlands', Ben van Velthoven and Peter van Wijck test whether a recent experiment set up by the Dutch Bar Association allowing conditional *quota pars litis* (QPL) agreements between client and solicitor is fit for purpose. The overall aim of this fee regulation experiment is to increase access to justice for victims of personal injury. The experiment therefore allows solicitors to abandon the hourly fee rule and opt for a conditional QPL fee. In a sense, the solicitor acts as 'venture funder' of his client's claim. The question is whether this experimental scheme can be of mutual benefit to both parties and lawyers, in comparison to hourly fees, and whether the experiment actually succeeds in improving access to justice. In order to address these questions, the authors develop an economic model and then run a simulation to gauge the behavioural effects of the regulatory experiment. The good news is that their simulation method seems apt to generate rough predictions on real-life effects of the regulatory experiment. Less comforting is the finding that it seems unlikely that claimants and lawyers have the capacity to compare the suitability of the available fee options. This lack of overview alone may be a good reason for parties to stick to the traditional and well-known remuneration rule of hourly fees.

Mass litigation

The three final chapters are concerned with costs and funding of mass litigation procedures.

In Chapter 8, 'Financial arrangements with litigation funders and law firms in Australian class actions', Vicki Waye and Vince Morabito analyse the development of TPF in Australian class actions. The chapter examines the Australian class action landscape and considers the growth of class actions funded by third-party investors. After outlining evolution and various business models, the tension points for claim governance are identified. Moreover, the response of the Australian regulators and judiciary to TPF models in class actions is analysed and compared with developments in other jurisdictions. One of the interesting problems with the Australian class action is that law firms are only allowed to charge a success fee by means of a capped mark-up over regular lawyer fees, whereas TPF QPL remuneration by third parties is neither regulated nor scrutinized. Against this background, the authors consider the problems posed by close relationships between funders and class legal representatives and they examine whether regulation could address these problems.

In Chapter 9, titled 'Funding of mass claims in Germany: Caught between a rock and a hard place?', Astrid Stadler analyses the response by the German legislature and judiciary to the involvement of funders in mass damages claims. For instance, German courts are reluctant to embrace mass claim litigation by 'special-purpose vehicles' (SPVs) to whom claims are assigned. These SPVs are in fact unable to sue on their own behalf without facing obstacles that normal plaintiffs would not face. For example, to prevent their case from being thrown out of court without judgement on the merits, they will have to offer security for costs more or less automatically, which is contrary to existing rules and makes litigation more expensive. Stadler argues that in Germany, as in many other European countries, a clear statutory framework for litigation funding and the activities of SPVs should be introduced. This should ensure that SPVs are not banned outright but rather that they are regulated so that they can offer true added value to access to justice for individual claimants.

Finally, in Chapter 10, 'Entrepreneurial motives in Dutch collective redress: Adding fuel to a "compensation culture"?', Ilja Tillema explores the often used argument that the involvement of TPF in collective damages actions encourages an unethical 'compensation culture' detrimental to society. The chapter maps the evolution of Dutch collective redress and the ensuing funding practices over the past ten years. Some say that there has been a surge in commercially driven collective redress cases, thus fuelling a Dutch 'compensation culture'. Indeed, Dutch policymakers and courts have introduced hardly any legal restrictions on investing in collective redress actions. Tillema asks whether this has caused a change in the commercial landscape and whether we can find evidence that this liberal stance has fuelled, as some feared it would, a Dutch 'compensation culture'. These questions are highly relevant, given recent plans to further extend the Dutch legislative framework for collective redress. Tillema surveys the incidence of collective damages claims in recent years and she finds no evidence that the (slow) rise in the number of collective damages actions is related to entrepreneurial funding. Moreover, leaving aside the occasional incident, there is no evidence either of a rise of frivolous lodging of collective damages claims. Tillema thus exposes the 'compensation culture' argument as unfounded rhetoric.

Outlook

The contributions to this volume revolve around costs, cost rules, funding arrangements and behaviour of litigants. Costs matter, as do cost allocation rules and the opportunities offered by legal systems to third parties to act as funders of the litigants. How does the risk of having to bear the brunt of such cost as legal expenses, attorney fees, legal experts, court fees and so forth affect litigation strategies and the willingness to settle? Do cost-shifting rules influence litigants' behaviour in this regard? And do third-party funding arrangements cause further changes in this behavioural pattern? Insight in these questions is vital to our understanding of the interaction of the relevant legal regime, regulatory framework or disciplinary rules with the behaviour of litigants, courts and legislatures. These issues are addressed in this volume.

One conclusion can already be drawn here. None of the contributors is outright hostile towards TPF or speaks against the clever design of cost rules as a means to achieve optimal levels of access to justice or to evoke certain behavioural responses. What is clear, however, is that the devil is in the details; for instance, in certain markets for legal services the introduction of unfettered TPF agreements could disrupt an existing market balance or could lead to unfair practices. Therefore, if anything, this volume shows that the design of cost (allocation) rules and the dynamics caused by the involvement of TPF in civil litigation merit careful consideration from both the legislature and the judiciary against the background of the legal system and legal culture of the country at hand.

2 Litigation costs and third-party funding

Willem H. van Boom[1]

1. Introduction

Most often, the private costs of conducting civil litigation are high. Litigants face court fees and charges, disbursements, fees for legal representation and costs of witnesses and experts, not to mention internal business costs, opportunity costs and psychological costs.[2] Obviously, the fact that civil litigation imposes costs on both sides is, in itself, justified. In an imaginary universe where litigation came free of charge, perhaps the number of spurious summons and vexatious claims would impose excessive burdens on both courts and defendants. It could also give rise to the growth of a culture of litigiousness and reluctance to settle and reconcile. If, however, the costs of litigation are set too high or distributed unfairly, this may actually stand in the way of adequate 'access to civil justice'. Therefore, the costs of litigation and how these are financed are fundamental to access to justice and the quality of legal services.[3]

The institutional legal framework for the public or private funding of civil litigation is closely related to the cost rules framework. If costs prevent access to justice, the rule of law is at risk of being undermined. Several developments have made this relationship more apparent than before. In Europe, the gradual but certain demise of public legal aid has made alternative, market-based solutions for funding claims possible and perhaps even necessary. In post-World War II Europe, governments developed comprehensive policies to enhance access to civil justice for the impecunious. In doing so, markets for legal services were dovetailed with public funding. The soaring costs of these legal aid systems have made cuts and overhauls unavoidable and have made facilitating private financing of civil litigation a more attractive option to policymakers than before.[4]

A second, more recent development concerns the proliferation of mass claims for damages in Europe. In some form or other, European countries have adopted or are in the process of introducing special legislation for the efficient amalgamation of individual claims into collective actions. The exact scope and practicability of these procedural rules differ hugely; nevertheless, the fact remains that European jurisdictions are on the road to

1 Parts of this chapter were loosely based on earlier work by the author in this field (Van Boom 2010, 2011).

2 CJS Hodges, S Vogenauer and M Tulibacka (eds), *The Costs and Funding of Civil Litigation: A Comparative Perspective* (Oxford: Hart Publishing 2010) 12ff.

3 P Fenn, A Gray and N Rickman, *The Funding of Personal Injury Litigation: Comparisons over Time and across Jurisdictions* (London: Department for Constitutional Affairs 2006) 1.

4 Cf RD Kelemen, *Eurolegalism – The Transformation of Law and Regulation in the European Union* (Cambridge: Harvard University Press 2011) 63ff.

collectivising damages claims. This trend is also causing an upsurge of various new business models for private financing of litigation originating from countries such as the USA and Australia. Inevitably, these developments will lead to debate on the financing of such collective actions and whether the existing legal framework for claims financing is adequate for the governance of these actions.

Against this background, this chapter reviews various models of cost rules in civil litigation and analyses the various legal frameworks pertaining to cost shifting and funding of civil litigation by others than the litigants themselves. First, an overview of the main cost rules is provided, followed by some remarks on the behavioural responses associated with these rules (para 2). Thereafter, an analysis of various forms and techniques for financing civil litigation is presented (para 3). Following this general analysis, a closer look is taken at assignment, sale and third-party funding (TPF), for which these terms are broadly defined (para 4). This then allows an inventory to be made of the challenges faced by policymakers, posed by cost rules and TPF financing (para 5). A brief review of solutions (para 6) concludes this chapter.

2. Costs and cost allocation

Who bears the private costs of litigation? Usually, the two contrasting principles are referred to as the 'English rule' and the 'American rule'.[5] In a no-costs jurisdiction, the 'American rule' indicates that each side should bear its own legal costs.[6] By contrast, under the 'loser pays rule' or 'English rule', courts award costs to the prevailing party, such that the losing side requires to compensate these costs.[7] As Peysner rightly notes elsewhere in this volume: 'these approaches to the cost of litigation are at best approximations of a complex reality'.

In European legal systems, the English rule (also known as the 'costs follow the event' rule[8]) is applied in one form or another. In its pure form, the 'English rule' encompasses a full shift, on an indemnity basis, of all of the prevailing party's legal costs and court fees. If courts have discretion over cost shifting, their decision to award costs to the prevailing party may depend on the circumstances of the particular case. Sometimes, the procedural behaviour of the prevailing party may justify that they bear (part of) the costs incurred by the opposing party, such as, for instance, obstructive behaviour or wasteful tactics.

Where there are no fixed methods for assessing quantum of costs, courts may be inclined to adopt a broad-brush approach to awarding costs or, instead, may take pride in developing intricate and complex structures for costs calculation. In both instances, the exact exposure to the cost-shifting risks may be fairly unpredictable for litigants.

In more diluted forms, costs may be capped or tariffs may apply. In ordinary court procedure in jurisdictions such as Germany, the costs of the prevailing party are shifted to the

5 Hodges, Vogenauer and Tulibacka (2010) 17ff.

6 On the American rule, its provenance and scope, see JC Coffee, *Entrepreneurial Litigation – Its Rise, Fall and Future* (Cambridge: Harvard University Press 2015) 22ff.

7 RH Smit and TB Robinson, 'Costs Awards in International Commercial Arbitration: Proposed Guidelines for Promoting Time and Cost Efficiency' (2010) 20 *American Review of International Arbitration (ARIA)* 267, 271.

8 JY Gotanda, 'Awarding Costs and Attorneys' Fees in International Commercial Arbitrations' (1999) 21 *Michigan Journal of International Law* 1, 5. Generally on the development of both English and American rules, see W Pfennigstorf, 'The European Experience with Attorney Fee Shifting' (1984) 47 *Law and Contemporary Problems* 37ff.

losing party according to a fixed tariff and/or a percentage proportional to the claim.[9] Therefore, the risks of cost shifting are very predictable in litigation in Germany.

Hence, it would be more accurate to subdivide the 'loser pays rule' into a proper English rule and a German rule, where the former stipulates that the loser pays both his own expenses and all costs of the opponent, in so far as these adverse costs are deemed reasonable by the court and the latter holds that the loser bears his own costs and compensates those of the opponent according to a fixed tariff and/or a fixed percentage, proportional to the claim.[10] Usually, the 'loser pays' system operates on a *two-way cost-shifting* basis since either party may lose and thus face both his own costs and an adverse costs order. To protect certain categories of litigants, qualified one-way costs shifting could be considered.

One of the major costs of litigation is the payment of fees for legal services and representation. In civil litigation of some substance, litigants do not usually appear in person but instead are represented by a lawyer (a qualified solicitor, barrister, attorney etc.). The lawyer's legal services consist mostly of case preparation, meetings, strategy preparation, appearances in court and composition and submission of written court documents.

Rules on remuneration for legal services and representation are different throughout the world. In some legal systems, there is no regulation whatsoever, leaving market forces to dictate form and substance of retainer arrangements. Most jurisdictions, however, do seem to have some sort of regulatory regime in place and below some examples of bases on which lawyers are retained, are provided:

- a fixed fee not conditional on success in court or settlement;
- an hourly fee not conditional on success in court or settlement;
- an hourly fee variable with complexity, claim value and so forth (lodestar method);
- a basic hourly fee with mark-up or uplift fee conditional on outcome;
- an hourly fee conditional on outcome (*conditional fee arrangement*) (CFA);
- a contingency fee arrangement: an agreement where the lawyer representing the claimant is retained on *a quota pars litis* (QPL) remuneration (damages-based recovery percentage) contingent on success in court or settlement.

In some legal systems, charging fees that are conditional on outcome is considered unethical or illegal. In such circumstances, the reasoning is typically that lawyers should not have a stake in the outcome of the cases they accept since this could compromise their professional judgement or could be in violation of the core values of the legal system. In other legal systems, the fee regulation is such that lawyers may only charge fixed statutory tariffs or hourly fees for certain services. The concern here is to curb excessive remuneration *ex post* rather than *ex ante*. Indeed, the legal history of both remuneration for legal services and

9 Gotanda (1999) 6ff. Cf Pfennigstorf (1984) 44ff; B Hess and R Hübner, 'General Overview and Trends in the German Civil Litigation Costs System' in CJS Hodges, S Vogenauer and M Tulibacka (eds), *The Costs and Funding of Civil Litigation: A Comparative Perspective* (Oxford: Hart Publishing 2010) 351ff, 365ff; M Jäger, *Reimbursement for Attorney's Fees* (Den Haag: Eleven International Publishing 2010) 4ff, 21ff. Generally on German costs law, see R Jackson, *Review of Civil Litigation Costs – Preliminary Report* (London: TSO (The Stationery Office) 2009) 555ff.

10 Note that the reference to English and German is a stereotypical reference rather than an actual reference to that particular legal system. Even the English legal system does not allow for full shifting of costs on an indemnity basis but, in some forms of litigation, the detailed cost assessment (see Jackson (2009) 53ff) is applied. This detailed indemnity-based assessment comes closer to the English rule than any of the other costs rules.

representation and third-party involvement in litigation shows that fundamental notions concerning the preservation of litigants' autonomy, the authority of both the State and the court, as well as the preservation of societal values are at the heart of these considerations.

It is important to note that the rules applicable to remuneration for legal services and representation may have two sides: first, rules pertaining to the remuneration for rendering the service (costs for the client vis-à-vis the lawyer) and, second, rules for the application of a cost-shifting regime. For instance, the agreement between a client and his lawyer may be subject to one form of remuneration regulation while the lawyer's fee may be subject to a different form of tariff for the purposes of cost shifting. For instance, under French disciplinary rules, lawyers are not permitted to offer their contentious services under a contingency fee arrangement. However, a success fee, supplementary to a basic hourly fee, is permitted.[11] As far as cost shifting rules are concerned, French law operates a moderated loser pays rule.[12] The court has the discretionary power to award the costs of litigation to the successful litigant (notably, *dépens* (fees), pursuant to art. 696 Code of Civil Procedure, and *frais* (expenses), pursuant to art. 700 Code of Civil Procedure).[13] Although parties can consent to a prearranged division of costs, courts are autonomous in their decision in respect of costs. The amounts awarded are generally modest.[14]

In civil litigation, cost allocation rules go a long way to explain and to predict strategic litigation behaviour.[15] For instance, the lack of clarity and the predictability of cost-shifting rules in litigation send mixed signals to claimants and may cause inefficiencies.[16] It seems that the American rule removes the threat of adverse costs and thus lowers the threshold for access to justice and may be justified by a policy aimed at granting access to the impecunious. However, the English rule is better at deterring parties from pursuing weak claims.[17] By the same token, the English rule may also reduce the likelihood of pre-trial settlement

11 M Bonnell, P Megens, S Finizio, D Speller, P Dunham, S Nataf, P Starr, D Bateson, G Alon, A Yeo, S Yen Koh, N Radjai, C Miles and S Zagata Vasani, 'Case Notes on Third-party Funding' (2008) 3 *Global Arbitration Review* 35, 36; MG Faure, FJ Fernhout and NJ Philipsen, 'No Cure, No Pay and Contingency Fee' in M Tuil and L Visscher (eds), *New Trends in Financing Civil Litigation in Europe – A Legal, Empirical, and Economic Analysis* (Cheltenham: Edward Elgar 2010) 45. Note that there does seem to be some room for a contingency-fee arrangement as part of a success fee; see MG Faure, FJ Fernhout and NJ Philipsen, *Resultaatgerelateerde beloningssystemen voor advocaten* (Den Haag: Boom Jurische Uitgevers 2009) 67–68.

12 Cf Y Desdevises, 'France – Theoretical Perspectives' in CJS Hodges, S Vogenauer and M Tulibacka (eds), *The Costs and Funding of Civil Litigation: A Comparative Perspective* (Oxford: Hart Publishing 2010) 331; AL Villedieu, 'France – The Rules On Funding and Costs' in CJS Hodges, S Vogenauer and M Tulibacka (eds), *The Costs and Funding of Civil Litigation: A Comparative Perspective* (Oxford: Hart Publishing 2010) 345ff; Jäger (2010) 29ff. Generally for French costs rules, see Jackson (2009) 566ff.

13 Jäger (2010) 151f; Faure, Fernhout and Philipsen (2009) 65–66.

14 Jäger (2010) 36f; Villedieu (2010) 345ff.

15 Note that the existing empirical evidence is patchy, sometimes contradictory and extremely context-bound. Generally R Moorhead and P Hurst, *Contingency Fees – A Study of their Operation in the United States of America (A Research Paper Informing the Review of Costs)* (London: Civil Justice Council 2008) 28ff; E Helland and SA Seabury, 'Contingent-fee Contracts in Litigation: A Survey and Assessment' in J Arlen (ed.), *Research Handbook on the Economics of Torts* (Cheltenham: Edward Elgar 2013) 383ff. For that reason, J Peysner argues in *Access to Justice: A Critical Analysis of Recoverable Conditional Fees and No-Win No-Fee Funding* (London: Palgrave Macmillan 2014) that policies in this area should be firmly evidence-based.

16 Cf Hodges, Vogenauer and Tulibacka (2010) 81ff, 97f.

17 JW Hughes and EA Snyder, 'The English Rule for Allocating Legal Costs: Evidence Confronts Theory' (1990) 6 *J.L. Econ. & Org.* 345ff; Pfennigstorf (1984) 65ff, 76ff; PJ Mause, 'Winner Takes All: A Re-examination of the Indemnity System' (1969) 55 *Iowa L. Rev.* 26, 32ff. Cf S Shavell, 'Suit, Settlement, and Trial: A Theoretical Analysis Under Alternative Methods for the Allocation of Legal Costs' (1982) 11 *J. Legal Stud.* 55, 59.

or abandoning the claim mid-proceedings.[18] This is partially explained by the fact that expenditure on claims brought to court may be relatively high because of 'raising the stakes' [19] as this may result in inefficient 'cost wars', a *sunk cost auction*: as the costs of losing are unpredictable, litigants may be tempted to invest just a little more than the opposing side at every stage of the litigation process.[20] On the other hand, uncertainty in respect of these costs may constitute a countervailing psychological force: unpredictability may enhance willingness to settle at an early stage, even if contesting the claim may, in itself, seem reasonable.[21]

3. Financing models generally

Financing is not readily available for defendants in civil litigation given that, unlike a claim, the position of the defendant does not represent a potential positive value. Therefore, the defendant does not own an asset and can therefore only enjoy protection from risk deflection and spreading instruments such as *before the event* liability insurance and legal expenses insurance.[22] Obviously, both claimants and defendants may decide to make financial reservations and thus self-insure. They may resort to traditional commercial loans, such as bank loans with a fixed interest rate and repayment obligation not conditional on outcome. Obviously, in such cases the investment in the claim or in their defence is theirs and not the lender's. Whether the case is won or lost, the lender will only be entitled to payment of the loan, with or without interest. Obviously, the claimant retains full control over the claim and the conduct of the procedure, as does the defendant.

For claimants, in economic terms, there are alternative instruments available because their claim represents value and is therefore a commodity. Therefore, if permitted under the law, the claimant can enter into a *sales contract* and thus fully transfer ownership in the claim to a buyer against a purchase price. The price reflects the perceived chances of successfully pursuing and collecting the claim. The vendor (assignor) legally transfers the claim and thus assigns the right to conduct any litigation or arbitration procedure to the purchaser

18 Hughes and Snyder (1990) 377: optimistic litigants anticipate shifting their fees to their opponent. However, see also JJ Donohue, 'Opting for the British Rule, Or If Posner and Shavell Can't Remember the Coase Theorem, Who Will?' (1991) 104 *Harv. L. Rev.* 1093 (arguing that the level of settlement would not be different).

19 A Katz, 'Measuring the Demand for Litigation: Is the English Rule Really Cheaper?' (1987) 3 *J.L. Econ. & Org.* 143, 171ff; Mause (1969) 31ff. Cf L Visscher and T Schepens, 'A Law and Economics Approach to Cost Shifting Fee Arrangements and Legal Expense Insurance' in M Tuil and L Visscher (eds), *New Trends in Financing Civil Litigation in Europe – A Legal, Empirical, and Economic Analysis* (Cheltenham: Edward Elgar 2010) 11–12. The 'sunk-cost auction' theory basically conjectures that if a litigant perceives that if the opponent invests a unit of resources in the proceedings, his chances of winning the case increase, and he will be willing to counter that investment by adding a unit of his own in order to protect the prior investment. This prior investment in the procedure is a sunk cost. Therefore, raising the stakes resembles an auction of sunk cost. He who invests just that little extra is perceived to increase his chances of winning the procedure and then offload the sunk cost onto the opponent. Cf the concept of the Tullock-type contest.

20 Cf F Cabrillo and S Fitzpatrick, *The Economics of Courts and Litigation* (Cheltenham: Edward Elgar 2008) 163–164; R Bowles and N Rickman, 'Asymmetric Information, Moral Hazard and the Insurance of Legal Expenses' (1998) 23 *Geneva Papers on Risk & Insurance – Issues & Practice* 196, 200. Cf Beckner and A Katz, 'The Incentive Effects of Litigation Fee Shifting When Legal Standards Are Uncertain' (1995) 15 *International Review of Law and Economics* 205, 206.

21 A feature that German costs law seems to lack, according to G Wagner, 'Litigation Costs and their Recovery: The German Experience' (2009) 28 *Civil Justice Quarterly* 367, 382.

22 JT Molot 'A Market in Litigation Risk' (2009) 76 *U.Chi.L.Rev.* 367ff.

(assignee). Besides transferring full title to the claim, there are various contracts by which a third party is able to *invest* in the claim or otherwise share in its outcome. A *non-recourse loan* may be a contract by which a funder lends money to the claimant to pursue the claim. The claimant merely promises to repay the loan if the claim is successful. The lender shares in the risk of losing the case. The interest rate may be commensurately high to reflect a risk premium. A similar mechanism underlies *conditional-fee agreements* (CFAs) between the claimant and his lawyer (where this is permitted by law). Here, the lawyer undertakes to pursue the claim on a 'no-win no-fee' basis. This means that the lawyer will only be entitled to claim remuneration on an hourly fee basis if the case is won. The American *contingency fee agreement* or (a *quota pars litis* arrangement) is slightly different. Here, the conditionality of the remuneration is the same, however the calculation of the amount is not a reflection of the time spent on the case but rather a percentage of the proceeds.

The funding of litigation by third parties, broadly described as *third-party funding* (TPF) may come to the fore in those legal systems where lawyers are not permitted or are unable to invest in their client's claim. TPF has been defined as 'the funding of litigation by a party who has no pre-existing interest in the litigation, usually on the basis that (i) the funder will be paid out of the proceeds of any amounts recovered as a consequence of the litigation, often as a percentage of the recovery sum; and (ii) the funder is not entitled to payment should the claim fail.'[23] The TPF funder will bear specific parts of the claimant's out-of-pocket litigation expenses. The claimant will share a portion of the proceeds of the award or settlement with the funder. However, the funder is not entitled to any remuneration in cases where the claim fails. Additionally, the TPF funder may agree (in whole or part) to indemnify the claimant for adverse cost orders.

The TPF funder will typically offer to finance a claim after the dispute has arisen. It will diligently investigate the credit-worthiness of the defendant and the viability of the claim (with the help of legal opinion of a panel of lawyers who analyses the case). If the claim is accepted, the funder will provide the funding required in advance. The success fee is damages-based and contingent on the disputed amount. Success fees are said to vary between 20 and 50 per cent.[24] Fees may also be subject to a scale (for example, 20 per cent in case of pre-trial

23 Jackson (2009) viii. For an overview of terminology, see, e.g., WH van Boom, 'Financing Civil Litigation by the European Insurance Industry' in M Tuil and L Visscher (eds), *New Trends in Financing Civil Litigation in Europe – A Legal, Empirical, and Economic Analysis* (Cheltenham: Edward Elgar 2010) 92ff; S Garber, *Alternative Litigation Financing in the United States – Issues, Knowns, and Unknowns* (Santa Monica: RAND Corporation 2010) ix; M De Morpurgo, 'A Comparative Legal and Economic Approach to Third-Party Litigation Funding' (2011) 19 *Cardozo Journal of International and Comparative Law* 343, 352; M Steinitz, 'Whose Claim Is It Anyway? Third-Party Litigation Funding' (2011) 95 *Minn. L. Rev.* 1,268ff; C Veljanovski, 'Third Party Litigation Funding in Europe' (2012) 8 *Journal of Law, Economics and Policy* 405, 408ff; V Shannon and L Bench Nieuwveld, *Third-Party Funding in International Arbitration* (Alphen aan den Rijn: Kluwer Law International 2012) 3ff; R Pirozzolo, 'Third Party Funding' in R Pirozzolo (ed.), *Litigation Funding Handbook* (London: Law Society 2014) 155f. Cf the definition given by the draft Transatlantic Trade and Investment Partnership (TTIP) Preamble 10: '"Third Party funding" means any funding provided by a natural or legal person who is not a party to the dispute but who enters into an agreement with a disputing party in order to finance part or all of the cost of the proceedings in return for a remuneration dependent on the outcome of the dispute or in the form of a donation or grant.'

24 Hodges, Vogenauer and Tulibacka (2010) 27; CJS Hodges, J Peysner and A Nurse, *Litigation Funding: Status and Issues* (Research Report CSLS Oxford & Lincoln Law School 2012) 121f. For statutory caps on recovery percentages in damages-based agreements with solicitors, see s 4 The Damages-Based Agreements Regulations 2013; cf the Dutch experiment in DBA's in personal injury litigation, on which WH van Boom and M de Jong, 'Het Experiment Resultaatgerelateerde Beloning – verwachtingen over werking en doelbereiking' (2014) *Tijdschrift Vergoeding Personenschade* 69ff and Van Wijck and Van Velthoven, in this volume.

settlement, 30 per cent in case of success in court up to €500,000 and 20 per cent of amounts more than €500,000). TPF funding is mainly available for commercial claimants with high-value claims and a high probability of success.[25] All in all, TPF bears more resemblance to an investment, joint venture or even a contingency fee arrangement than it does to insurance.[26]

A different category of contracts concerns the hedging of financial risks through *insurance*.

Liability insurance contracts have a dual indemnity purpose, as they do not merely protect the policyholder against liability, but also contain elements of legal expenses insurance, as far as defending claims is concerned. Consequently, liability insurance is pivotal in defending tort claims as it indemnifies the insured in the capacity of the alleged tortfeasor, for legal costs and expenses incurred in defending claims made against the insured. Moreover, if the claimant prevails in court, the liability insurance policy may also cover the defendant's liability for the claimant's legal costs. Obviously, the extent to which such costs are actually shifted from the prevailing claimant to the defendant and his liability insurer depends on the applicable rules of civil procedure and the extent of the policy cover.[27]

Legal expenses insurance contracts (LEI; also referred to as *before the event* (BTE) LEI)[28] may finance either side of the claim. Indeed, in some European countries, LEI has matured into an extremely important branch of indemnity insurance offering a high level of service in kind, employing and educating professional panel lawyers or procuring contracts for legal services in bulk. In other countries, LEI has not (yet) gained much ground due to institutional obstacles.[29] For instance, in some countries, legal services may not be delivered by lawyers due to the existence of a statutory attorney monopoly.[30]

In some countries, institutional conditions are also at the root of the advance of so-called *after the event legal expenses insurance* (ATE LEI). This type of insurance is exactly what the name denotes: an insurance policy concluded after a dispute has arisen when litigation is imminent. In England and Wales, this type of insurance was a popular financing form, however, after the implementation of the 2013 Jackson Reform, its relevance has decreased.

Table 2.1 recapitulates the various contract forms – if and the extent to which they are permitted in any given legal system, as well as the consequences for control over the claim:[31]

25 J Veith and J Gräfe (eds), *Der Versicherungsprozess* (München: Beck 2016) 174ff. Jackson (2009) 161. In Germany, TPF is also provided for smaller claims. Cf M Coester and D Nitzsche, 'Alternative Ways to Finance a Lawsuit in Germany' (2005) 24 *Civil Justice Quarterly* 83ff. However, given that the German consumer insurance market is saturated by BTE, high penetration rates of this form of ATE seem unlikely.

26 On the (dis)similarities between insurance and TPF, see Van Boom (2010) 9ff; M Steinitz, 'The Litigation Finance Contract' (2012) 54 *William & Mary L. Rev.* 455ff; M Boardman, 'Insurers Defend and Third Parties Fund: A Comparison of Litigation Participation' (2012) 8 *J.L. Econ. & Policy* 673; C Silver, 'Litigation Funding versus Liability Insurance: What's the Difference?' (2014) 63 *DePaul L.Rev.* 617ff.

27 Cf Visscher and Schepens (2010) 7ff.

28 Before the Event (BTE) LEI can be loosely defined as an undertaking, against the payment of a premium, to bear the costs of legal proceedings and to provide other services directly linked to insurance cover. Cf. art. 198 Directive 2009/138/EC (Solvency II).

29 See, e.g., R Kirstein and N Rickman, 'Third Party Contingency Contracts in Settlement and Litigation' (2002) *German Working Papers in Law and Economics* 1ff. On LEI insurance, see also De Mot, Faure and Visscher, in this volume.

30 Cf T Schepens, 'Bridging the Funding Gap – The Economics of Cost Shifting, Fee Arrangements and Legal Expenses Insurance and their Prospects for Improving the Access to Civil Justice' (2007) *German Working Papers in Law and Economics* 1, 33.

31 See for a more extensive overview of risk transfer instruments V Waye, 'Litigation Risk Transfer and Law Firm Financial Arrangements' (2014) 17 *Legal Ethics* 107, 111f. Cf Hodges, Peysner and Nurse (2012) 84ff.

Table 2.1 Contract forms

Examples	*Consequences for control*
Loan agreement (by a bank, for example)	Claimant retains full control over claim, although claim may be collateralized for benefit of lender
Non-recourse loan, conditional-fee arrangement (CFA)	As under loan agreement though a lawyer retained under CFA will perform merit test
Legal expenses insurance (BTE or ATE): an indemnity insurance contract covering legal expenses but not covering the collectability of the claim itself	Claimant will be indemnified by insurer in respect of legal advice, court fees, and/or lawyers' costs, adverse costs order (depending on legal setting in which the insurance is used). Although the claim itself is not transferred, and both legal and economic ownership remains with claimant, the LEI insurer will typically have some control over the claim (merits test) and the litigation strategy.
Lawyer retained under contingency fee agreement TPF by third party	Claimant will be indemnified by third party in respect of legal advice, court fees, and/or lawyers' costs, adverse costs order (depending on legal setting in which the funding is used). In case the claim is sustained, the lawyer/TPF funder will recoup a proportion of the award. Economic ownership is thus shared between claimant and third party, who will typically have substantial control over the claim (merits test) and the litigation strategy. As far as legal ownership is concerned, this may depend on the legal system. The claim may be assigned/encumbered with a non-possessory security right (or a *lien*) for the benefit of lawyer/TPF funder, thus securing both compliance with the contract and covering insolvency of claimant.
Sale of claim	Original owner of the claim transfers ownership to purchaser in return for a price. Transfer is completed by full assignment of the claim with notice to debtor.

Thereafter, a more in-depth look is taken at the involvement of third parties on either side of the claim. Their roles may vary from simple moneylenders who do not share in the litigation risks to fully involved investors. In the former case, the claimant will merely take on debt. In the latter case, the claimant may accept investment in the claim in exchange for a share of ownership in the claim. In economic terms, the involvement of a third party could be classified as a pure debt instrument, a risk-avoidance instrument, an equity-based shared investment or a simple sale of the claim. In Table 2.2, funding arrangements on either side of the claim are listed to illustrate both the legal form and economic rationale. The rows in the table represent the economic classification and the columns represent the actual and legal form in which third parties may be involved in funding the claimant and defendant/respondent, respectively.[32]

4. Assignment, sale and third-party funding

4.1 A comparative review

In this paragraph, a brief survey of various European legal systems and their stance on sale and assignment of claims is undertaken. This review will provide a basis for analysing the

32 Note that risk avoidance and equity-based investment instruments may partially overlap in practice, as shown in the table.

Table 2.2 Involved third parties

	Third parties involved on the claimant side	*Third parties involved on the defendant side*
Debt instrument	Someone who lends money at interest, regardless of outcome litigation (lender, bank). The claim may be encumbered with a security right (or security assignment) for the lender's benefit	Someone who lends money at an agreed interest rate, irrespective of outcome of the litigation (lender, bank)
	E.g., loan agreement (possibly with the claim as collateral)	E.g., loan agreement
Risk-avoidance instrument	*Conditional funding*	
	Someone who lends money without recourse in case claim fails and who is repaid only if claim succeeds (non-recourse loan; conditional funding)[1]	Liability insurer (containing element of legal expenses insurance)
	E.g., lawyer working under CFA	Eg., BTE liability insurance contract, covering both legal expenses and exposure to the claim itself
	Non-recourse loan, conditional fee arrangement (CFA)	
	Insurance forms	Legal expenses insurance (BTE LEI)[2]
	Legal expenses insurance (BTE LEI)	BTE LEI is a contract of insurance, covering legal expenses and possibly also adverse costs orders but not covering the liability under the claim itself
	ATE LEI insurance	
	BTE/ATE LEI: legal expenses insurance contract covering legal expenses (including risk of cost-shifting if case is lost) but not covering the collectability of the claim itself	ATE LEI is (probably) a contract of insurance, covering either legal expenses and/or possibly adverse costs orders (depending on the legal setting in which it is used) but not covering the liability under the claim itself
Equity instrument (shared investment in the claim)	Someone who lends money without recourse if claim fails and shares in the proceeds if claim succeeds (contingency arrangement; *pactum de quota litis*; investment)[3]	Someone who lends money without recourse in case the defence fails and who gets remunerated if claim is successfully defended (defendant contingency arrangement)
	Examples: lawyer working under an alternative fee agreement such as a contingency fee; TPF by an investor	Not generally available (other than in the form of a risk-avoidance instrument)
	Claim may be collateralized for benefit of lender (where permitted)	
Sale	Full transfer of risks and potential benefits to buyer of claim (i.e., substitution of the original claim owner by sale of the claim, to the extent that such a sale is legal)	Not generally available (other than in the form of a risk-avoidance instrument)
	Assignment of claim for sale of debt, with notice to (alleged) debtor	

1 On litigation loan agreements, see McLaughlin (2007) 617ff.

2 Although there may be room for some sort of ATE LEI, as far as I know, this insurance form does not exist. On retroactive insurance, e.g, MB Abramowicz 'On the Alienability of Legal Claims' (2005) 114 *Yale Law Journal* 697, 748ff; Molot (2009) 367ff.

3 Cf the terminology used by D Waelbroeck, D Slater and G Even-Shoshan, *Study on the Conditions of Claims for Damages in Case of Infringement of EC Competition Rules – Comparative Report* (Brussels: Ashurst 2004) 93.

potential and the restrictions of third-party funding (TPF) in civil litigation. As will be evident, several issues may arise if the TPF construction resembles a regulated arrangement or contract form. The prohibition of maintenance and champerty under common law is, for instance, relevant in this respect. Other jurisdictions may impose similar restraints, by prohibiting lawyers from agreeing to remuneration or fees that are contingent on success. Likewise, third-party financing of litigation may also be hampered by restrictions on 'commodification' of claims.[33] Although one would perhaps expect modern legal systems to have abandoned doctrines of non-assignability of commercial (money) claims *in personam* (in common-law parlance, 'choses in action') a long time ago, in some jurisdictions, remains of the prohibition of commodification and financial support of litigated claims are still to be found.[34] Some of these prohibitions, rooted in ancient conceptions of the courts' role and access to their services, have survived into contemporary law. Moreover, they may have been taken over by privileged groups of lawyers to preserve their market interests.

4.2 French law

In terms of assignment of claims to third parties, French law is rather complex and unsettled.[35] Although guiding case law seems absent, as far as claims for damages are concerned, French law prohibits transfer of rights of action. Moreover, in order to maintain society's trust in the operation of this system, art. 1,597 of the *Code Civil* forbids the acquisition of specific claims by those involved in the legal system.[36] Generally speaking, the law seems suspicious of arrangements involving speculation with claims. For instance, if a contested claim is brought before a court and subsequently assigned, pending proceedings, the debtor can release the debt by paying an amount equal to the price paid for the claim by the assignee (art. 1,699 *Code Civil*, 'retrait litigieux'). This article seems to serve as a disincentive from speculating on on-going proceedings.[37] However, the article does not affect any assignment concluded before the start of proceedings.

In contrast with the *Code Civil* provisions, legal doctrine considers the contractual assignment of damages claims to be perfectly legitimate and valid.[38] On balance, there is still no firm case law concerning the validity or otherwise of TPF contracts.[39]

33 For a historical analysis of such restrictions, see, e.g., M Radin, 'Maintenance by Champerty' (1935) 24 *Cal. L. Rev.* 48ff; I Marcushamer, 'Selling Your Torts: Creating a Market for Tort Claims and Liability' (2005) 33 *Hofstra L.Rev.* 1,543, 1,550ff.

34 On the topic of legality of assignment of claims, see, e.g., AJ Sebok, 'The Inauthentic Claim' (2011) 64 *Vanderbilt Law Review* 61ff.

35 Generally, e.g., P Malaurie, L Aynès and P Stoffel-Munck, *Droit Civil – Les obligations* (Paris: Defrénois 2013) 731ff.

36 See A Pinna, 'Financing Civil Litigation: The Case for the Assignment and Securitization of Liability Claims' in M Tuil and L Visscher (eds), *New Trends in Financing Civil Litigation in Europe – A Legal, Empirical, and Economic Analysis* (Cheltenham: Edward Elgar 2010) 116.

37 Pinna (2010) 116.

38 F Terré, P Simler and Y Lequette, *Droit civil – Les obligations* (Paris: Dalloz 2013) 1,324.

39 Cf. Tribunal de commerce de Nanterre 25 January 2005, quashed on appeal for lack of jurisdiction by the Cour d'appel de Versailles, 1 June, 2006. See Bonnell et al. (2008) 36; P Pinsolle, 'Le financement de l'arbitrage par les triers' (2010) *Revue de l'Arbitrage* 385, 391.

4.3 German law

In principle, German law allows the sale and transfer of ownership of claims (either in tort or in contract) for the purpose of litigation (§ 398 BGB) unless the original parties to the claim have agreed on non-transferability (§ 399 BGB).[40] Although TPF is unregulated, there is no doctrine comparable to the common-law prohibitions of champerty and maintenance.[41] An assignment of a claim to a TPF funder either by means of sale or for mere claims collection is valid.[42]

Under German law, the legal setting for investing in claims is favourable. Lawyers are not permitted to offer their services under a contingency fee arrangement, although a certain supplementary success fee is permitted.[43] While German lawyers are heavily regulated and access to the market for legal services is legally monopolised to the benefit of the German bar, the financing of claims by those other than lawyers, is more or less unaffected by this regulatory framework.[44]

In Germany, the typical TPF product is the *Prozessfinanzierungsvertrag* (procedure-funding contract).[45] It is offered by companies with a track record in underwriting risk, as well as those with experience in capital investment.[46] TPF contracts are considered to be either a contract *sui generis* or a contract of (undisclosed) partnership.[47] The TPF provider offers to finance all costs involved in a monetary claim, against a premium, due only in the case of success.[48] The provider diligently investigates the credit-worthiness of the defendant and the viability of the claim (with the help of the lawyer who

40 Veith and Gräfe (2016) 186. Note that professional collection of claims for purposes of amalgamating these into a collective action is hampered by legal restrictions. See Hess and Hübner (2010) 360; WH van Boom, 'De Minimis Curat Praetor – Redress for Dispersed Trifle Losses' (2009) 4 *Journal of Comparative Law* 171, 176–177.

41 Wagner (2010) 172.

42 OLG Düsseldorf 14 May 2008, VI U (kart) 14/07 (Zementkartel), confirmed by BGH 7 April 2009, KZR 42/08.

43 Faure, Fernhout and Philipsen (2010) 43–44. Recently, an exception to the prohibition of result-based fees was implemented in German law for constitutional reasons. See C Duve, 'Success-Fees in Germany' in P Gottwald (ed.), *Litigation in England and Germany – Legal Professional Services, Key Features and Funding* (Bielefeld: Gieseking Verlag 2010) 217ff.

44 De Morpurgo (2011) 403. Note that TPF funders do have to resort to lawyers for both litigation and legal advice.

45 On these contracts, see, e.g., M Dimde, *Rechtsschutzzugang und Prozessfinanzierung im Zivilprozess – Eine ökonomische Analyse des Rechts* (Berlin: BWV 2003) 156ff; Wagner (2010) 172.

46 See, e.g., Veith and Gräfe (2016) 167ff; J Peysner and A Nurse, *Representative Actions and Restorative Justice – A Report for the Department for Business, Enterprise and Regulatory Reform (BERR)* (Lincoln: Lincoln Law School 2008) 28.

47 Cf on the nature of TPF under German law J Jaskolla, *Prozessfinanzierung gegen Erfolgsbeteiligung* (Karlsruhe: Verlag Versicherungswirtschaft 2004) 35ff; L Wilde, 'Prozessfinanzierung: Eine Branche auf dem Sprung – der Charme der Idee hat an Frische nicht verloren' (2010) *Anwaltsblatt* 813; Dimde (2003) 167ff; Veith and Gräfe (2016) 166f. Authors who argue that TPF is a contract of (undisclosed) partnership include B Grünewald, 'Prozessfinanzierungsvertrag mit gewerbsmäßigem Prozessfinanzierer – ein Gesellschaftsvertrag', (2000) 55 *Betriebsberater* 729ff; Jaskolla (2004) 72ff; Coester and Nitzsche (2005) 95; Wilde 2010 (813). Others argue that it is a contract, *sui generis*; cf H Buschbell, 'Prozessfinanzierung als Instrument der Anspruchsverfolgung' (2006) *AnwBl* 825, 829; F Frechen and ML Kochheim, 'Fremdfinanzierung von Prozessen gegen Erfolgsbeteiligung' (2004) 17 *Neue Juristische Wochenschrift* 1,213, 1,214; N Dethloff, 'Verträge zur Prozessfinanzierung gegen Erfolgsbeteiligung' (2000) *Neue Juristische Wochenschrift* 2,225, 2,226–2,227.

48 Dimde (2003) 159ff.

analyses the case).[49] If the claim is valid, the TPF provider will supply the required funding to fuel the court procedure. The TPF contract obliges the client to disclose all relevant information to the TPF funder and to co-operate during the procedure.[50] The TPF contract is usually considered confidential, and the parties concerned normally agree to keep the TPF arrangement undisclosed. The reason for non-disclosure of the agreement is not entirely clear. Courts may respond adversely to information on TPF and the funding itself may constitute insider information for the purposes of regulation of securities. This secrecy has been criticised.[51]

The client will typically transfer ownership of the claim for security purposes to the benefit of the TPF.[52] However, the assignment of the claim is not made public. The original claimant will continue to act as such, both in and outside the ensuing court procedure.[53] Under German law, it is possible to assign a claim (either for security purposes or for any other purpose) without giving notice to the debtor, i.e. an 'undisclosed assignment'.

The success premium is both contingent on the disputed amount and subject to a scale (for example, 20 per cent in the case of pre-trial settlement, 30 per cent in the case of success in court up to €500,000 and 20 per cent for amounts more than €500,000).[54] The TPF arrangement is available for mainly commercial claimants with high-value claims typically €50,000 or more, which also have a high probability of success.[55]

The principle of party autonomy in civil procedure and the possibility of covertly assigning claims leaves open the question of whether the defendant has a right to know of the involvement of TPF. German civil procedure does not give the defendant a right to know who actually owns the claim.[56] It is feasible that the claimant does not actually own the claim and this is not considered problematic. The general duty to disclose and co-operate with the court in civil proceedings[57] does not oblige the claimant to provide information on the TPF arrangement.

4.4 English law

In England and Wales, common-law principles against maintenance, champerty and also barratry are the main obstacles to creating a market for claims.[58] Under common law,

49 Wagner (2010) 173.
50 Jaskolla (2004) 23f.; Veith and Gräfe (2016) 172.
51 Jaskolla (2004) 25–26; Dimde (2003) 164.
52 Jaskolla (2004) 18; Dimde (2003) 163.
53 Dimde (2003) 161f.
54 Cf Dethloff (2000) 2,225–2,226; PL Murray and R Stürner, *German Civil Justice* (Durham: Carolina Academic Press 2004) 125; Van Boom (2010) 99f.
55 Veith and Gräfe (2016) 179. Jackson (2009) 161. In Germany, TPF is also provided for smaller claims. See Coester and Nitzsche (2005) 88. However, given that the German consumer-insurance market is saturated by LEI, it seems unlikely that high penetration rates of TPF will occur.
56 Veith and Gräfe (2016) 186.
57 On these duties, see, e.g., I Saenger, 'Case Management in Germany' in P Gottwald (ed.), *Litigation in England and Germany – Legal Professional Services, Key Features and Funding* (Bielefeld: Gieseking Verlag 2010) 20ff.
58 For a brief overview of the historical development of these principles, e.g., PC Choharis, 'A Comprehensive Market Strategy for Tort Reform' (1995) 12 *Yale J. on Reg.* 435, 460; V Waye, *Trading in Legal Claims* (Adelaide: Presidian Legal Publications 2008) 12; Steinitz (2011) 1286ff; Silver (2014) 631ff; DS Abrams and DL Chen, 'A Market for Justice: A First Empirical Look at Third Party Litigation Funding' (2013) 15 *U. of Pennsylvania J. of Bus. L.* 1,075, 1,082ff; Lord Neuberger, 'From Barratry, Maintenance and Champerty to Litigation Funding' (Harbour Litigation Funding First Annual Lecture, Gray's Inn, 8 May 2013) 5ff.

maintenance is defined as the 'officious intermeddling in a suit that no way belongs to one, by maintaining or assisting either party with money or otherwise, to prosecute or defend it'.[59] It is the 'assistance in prosecuting or defending a lawsuit given to a litigant by someone who has no bona fide interest in the case [or] meddling in someone else's litigation'.[60] Champerty, being a form of maintenance, involves supporting (financially or otherwise) a lawsuit, and barratry refers to stirring up a lawsuit vexatiously.[61] The prohibition of champertous agreements is essentially a prohibition against investment in claims. This is the prohibition of financial support of another's litigation in exchange for a share in any proceeds. If a contract is in contravention of the prohibition of maintenance and champerty, it is considered unenforceable.[62]

In English law, the prohibition of champerty and maintenance is chaotic and unprincipled. Although it is sometimes stated that it is plain 'that the application of the old law of maintenance and champerty is attenuating not increasing',[63] the state of affairs under English law still remains unsettled. For instance, recently a contingency fee agreement between a client and an accountant was deemed lawful, as was a conditional fee agreement between a client and a solicitor under which the solicitor agreed to indemnify the client against adverse cost orders.[64] However, as recently as 2011, the Court of Appeal held that the assignment of a cause of action for the purposes of enabling the assignee or a third party to make a profit out of the litigation would generally be void as savouring of champerty.[65]

Nowadays, TPF is increasingly available for commercial litigation.[66] Implementation of the Jackson Reforms in 2013 has starved the combined conditional fee and ATE insurance arrangement of its oxygen and seems to have paved the way for wider opportunities for genuine contingency fee arrangements (damages-based agreements (DBAs))

59 Sir W Blackstone, *Commentaries on the Laws of England in Four Books* (1753) IV 135. Cf *Unruh v Seeberger* [2007] 10 HKCFAR 31 (per Mr Justice Ribeiro PJ) at 82ff.

60 Black's Law Dictionary.

61 Choharis (1995) 460f.

62 Cf M Zander, 'Will the Revolution in the Funding of Civil Litigation in England Eventually Lead to Contingency Fees?' (2003) 52 *DePaul L.Rev.* 259, 260. Under English law, the consequence is that the funder cannot recover a fee for the assistance provided, not even on a *quantum meruit* basis (*Geraghty & Co. v. Awwad* [1999] EWCA Civ 3002); see Pirozzolo (2014) 157.

63 *Murray Lewis v. Tennants Distribution Ltd.* [2010] EWHC 90161 (Costs) at 18 (O'Hare, costs judge). The enforcement of the champerty and maintenance prohibition was attenuated and its boundaries blurred by s. 13 and 14 Criminal Law Act 1967. This Act decriminalised champerty and maintenance. In fact, what was left was the civil illegality of champertous agreements and the risk of costs orders against third-party funders. M Smith, *The Law of Assignment: The Creation and Transfer of Choses in Action* (Oxford: Oxford University Press 2007) 318ff. Moreover, the 1990s saw a drastic overhaul of civil-procedure funding. In that era, there was a move towards so-called conditional-fee arrangements (CFAs). See Zander (2003) 260ff. Much like a contingency fee, the CFA retainer operated on the result obtained on behalf of the claimant. Cf Zander (2003) 294. However, the recent decline of CFAs has again added to the muddled position of English law.

64 *R (Factortame) v Secretary of State for Transport, Local Government and the Regions (No. 8)* [2003] QB 381; *Sibthorpe v London Borough of Southwark* [2011] EWC Civ 25.

65 *Simpson v. Norfolk & Norwich University Hospital NHS Trust* [2011] EWCA Civ 1149 at 15 (per Moore-Bick LJ).

66 Jackson (2009) 160ff.

by English solicitors.[67] In that sense, recent policies have further pruned public legal aid and curtailed the champerty and maintenance doctrines in favour of private financing markets.[68] Acquiring a limited interest in a claim is basically considered legitimate and valid.[69] However, TPF funders should refrain from exerting too much influence on the day-to-day conduct of the litigation.[70] They are not allowed to control the course of litigation or unduly interfere with the solicitor–client relationship.[71] The sanction for excessive control may consist of nullity of the TPF contract.

Moreover, the TPF funder may risk a full-cost order if the claimant's case is lost. This is because English civil procedure allows the court to exercise a discretionary power to grant cost orders against non-parties.[72] A court is permitted to rule against a third party, in respect of costs, even if they are not formally one of the litigants. Thus, in *Chapman Ltd. v. Christopher*, a liability insurance company was ordered to pay the costs incurred by the prevailing claimant.[73] Although the insurer was not formally the defendant, it had determined that the claim would be defended, had funded the defence of the claim, had conducted the litigation and had fought the claim in order to defend its own interests.

Likewise, TPF funders who engage in excessive control may also run this risk if the case funded by them collapses in court. In *Arkin v. Borchard Lines Ltd and others*, the Court of Appeal essentially held that a funder with a commercial stake in the cause of action is at risk of partial exposure to costs.[74] There is another complication in English law that has some bearing on TPF involvement. It is unclear if, and to what extent, *assignment of claims*, namely, transfer of ownership is permitted.[75] Common law does not have a general framework for the transferability and survivability of claims. The claim's origin and content determines whether a claim can be transferred and survive. Generally, the common law originally forbade the transfer of claims. In equity, however, exceptions have been allowed.[76] Over the passage of time, the assignment prohibition has been

67 S 44–45 Legal Aid, Sentencing and Punishment of Offenders Act 2012 (amending s 58AA of the Courts and Legal Services Act 1990) and the Damage-Based Agreements Regulation 2013. See further J Peysner, 'Tail Wags Dog: Contingency Fees (and Part 36 and Third Party Funding)' (2013) 32 *Civil Justice Quarterly* 231ff; N Rowles-Davies and J Cousins, *Third Party Litigation Funding* (Oxford: Oxford University Press 2014) 154ff; R Merkin and J Steele, *Insurance and the Law of Obligations* (Oxford: Oxford University Press 2013) 383f, 388ff. Peysner, elsewhere in this volume, does draw attention to the fact that the use of DBAs is not yet widespread.

68 J Peysner, 'Expropriation, Access to Justice (and Wikileaks): A Comparative Study of Funding Difficult Cases in England and the United States' (2012) *Civil Justice Quarterly* 113ff.

69 G Wignall and S Green (eds), *Conditional Fees – A Guide to CFAs and Litigation Funding* (London: The Law Society 2008) 214f; Waye (2008) 104ff; Jackson (2009) 160.

70 Wignall and Green (2008) 133; cf Pinna (2010) 113ff; Jackson (2009) 163; M Friston, *Civil Costs – Law and Practice* (Bristol: Jordan Publishing 2010) 1,207.

71 Jackson (2009) 160ff.

72 Pinsolle (2010) 398ff.; S Middleton and J Rowley, *Cook on Costs 2016* (London: LexisNexis 2015) 635ff.

73 *Chapman Ltd. v. Christopher* [1998] 1 WLR 12.

74 *Arkin v Borchard Lines Ltd and others* [2005] EWCA Civ 655 at 41–42 (per Lord Phillips, MR). Cf *Dymocks Franchise Systems (NSW) Pty Ltd v Todd & Ors (No. 2) (New Zealand)* [2004] UKPC 39. See also Bonnell et al. (2008) 35; Pinsolle (2010) 399; Steinitz (2011) 1,281. There is ample discussion on whether the exposure of TPF funders (and, in England, DBA solicitors) to adverse costs should remain as it is, be expanded or reduced. I refer for further discussion to Rowles-Davies and Cousins (2014) 139; Civil Justice Council, *The Damages-based Agreements Reform Project – Drafting and Policies Issues* (London: Civil Justice Council 2015) 108ff.

75 On the procedural requirements for assignment in s 136 Law of Property Act 1925, see *Torkington v. Magee* [1902] 2 KB 427.

76 Smith (2007) 128ff; G Tolhurst, *The Assignment of Contractual Rights* (Oxford: Hart Publishing 2006) 11ff.

considerably eroded.[77] In the 1982 *Trendtex* case, the House of Lords introduced a test of genuine, commercial interest. If the assignee has a genuine, commercial interest in enforcing the claim for their own benefit, the assignment is valid.[78] Following the *Trendtex* test, it has been argued that, in principle, the proper and genuine assignment of debt, (other) contractual causes of action, most tortious causes involving pure economic loss and restitutionary causes are valid.[79]

4.5 Common themes

As the overview demonstrates, two main obstacles can be identified. The first concerns remuneration of lawyers and investment in litigated claims. The law may prohibit or restrict lawyers being remunerated other than on the basis of an hourly fee. Such a prohibition or restriction may restrain members of the bar from 'investing' in a claim by agreeing to be retained on a contingency fee basis. The law may likewise prohibit third-party investment. Some legal systems clearly distinguish between the investment prohibition for lawyers and other funders.

Second, a further problem is the legal uncertainty over the applicable rules and regulation and in some cases the lawfulness of TPF contracts. In some jurisdictions, assignment of claims is not generally accepted or restricted as far as certain transactions involving a commercial motive are concerned. This restricting of trading with claims will directly or indirectly affect TPF funding. In some legal systems, lawyers investing in their client's claim are at risk of committing a criminal or disciplinary offence. The contract with their client may be considered null and void (potentially leaving them without remuneration for their services). Likewise, a TPF contract may be void for violation of a funding prohibition. Furthermore, a TPF funder may unwillingly become part of the proceedings where civil procedure rules hold that third parties may owe duties towards the court and where the court is allowed to issue cost orders against a funding third party. Moreover, TPF contracts may be subject to regulatory requirements applicable to financial instruments such as insurance or lending: for example, in America, the practice that TPF funding may be labelled 'non-recourse loan' to avoid usury statutes.[80] In some states, however, substance rules over form and usury legislation is also applied equally to consumer 'non-recourse loans'.[81]

77 For instance, according to the English judicial interpretation of the common law, within the category of 'chooses in action' debts, fruits of an action and causes of action incidental to proprietary rights are deemed assignable. American courts seem to hold a meandering course; see Waye (2008) 120f; Tolhurst (2006) 121ff.

78 *Trendtex Trading Corp v. Crédit Suisse* [1982] AC 679 (HL).

79 Smith (2007) 321ff. Cf also the 2009 High Court decision in *Rawnsley and the Canal Dyeing Cy Ltd (in liquidation) v. Weatherall Green & Smith North Ltd and O'Hara (liquidator)* [2009] EWHC 2482 (Ch) at 73. In *Rawnsley*, the High Court held that an outright assignment of a cause of action by a liquidator for monetary consideration of 10 per cent of the net proceeds is valid.

80 D Richmond, 'Other People's Money: The Ethics of Litigation Funding' (2005) 56 *Mercer L.Rev.* 649, 665ff; cf Molot (2009) 424ff (concerning TPF fitting the definition of 'insurance' in some states) and E Chamblee Burch, 'Financiers as Monitor in Aggregate Litigation' (2012) 87 *N.Y.U. L. Rev.* 1,273, 1,301ff. See also J Kalajdzic, P Cashman and A Longmoore, 'Justice for Profit: A Comparative Analysis of Australian, Canadian and U.S. Third Party Litigation Funding' (2013) 61 *Am.J.Comp.L.* 93, 128ff.

81 E.g., in Maine and Ohio. See DR Leichty and ER Thomason, *Investing in Lawsuits: 'Litigation Financing' and the Consumer Protection Imperative* (Washington: Washington Legal Foundation 2009) 17f.

5. Issues to consider when contemplating regulation of TPF

5.1 Costs, financing and behaviour

Although there is little empirical data on the behavioural implications of the involvement of funders in civil litigation,[82] there is a strand of research on the behavioural influence of various remuneration methods in civil litigation. Based on available empirical research, the following behavioural influences on the parties involved, as a result of the TPF arrangement, seem plausible.

A funder with an interest in the outcome of the litigation will be (more) likely to:

- Gain access to information held by the claimant essential for the assessment of the viability of the claim and avoid mistakes by inserting clauses in the TPF contract to shift the risks associated with withholding information on to the claimant.[83]
- Merely take on highly meritorious claims.[84] In turn, the involvement of a TPF funder signals the quality of the claim. Therefore, if the defendant is aware of the fact that the claimant is sponsored by a TPF funder, it may increase the claimant's leverage to settle.[85]
- Emphasise the risk of (partially) losing the case or not fully disclose the chances of success to the potential client claimant.
- Prefer to take on higher value cases[86] and therefore perform a focused risk assessment of accepting the claimant's case by optimising due-diligence efforts to minimise adverse selection and moral hazard.[87]
- Try to keep the TPF arrangement undisclosed and confidential if there is uncertainty of the effect of disclosure on the court decision concerning both substantive issues such as quantum of damages, causation, contributory negligence, and procedural issues such as cost-shifting orders.
- Want to control the litigation strategy, for instance by making use of a power of attorney, if it feels that either the claimant or their counsel is not applying an appropriate strategy.
- Monitor and control the cost of legal counsel (probably strongest under the American rule, slightly less strong under the German rule and weakest under the English rule).

82 See, however, Abrams and Chen (2013) 1075ff, whose findings confirm some of the following but also report other effects of TPF in the Australian context; critical Silver (2014) 648ff. Australian Government Productivity Commission, *Access to Justice Arrangements (Productivity Commission Inquiry Report no 72)* (Canberra: Commonwealth of Australia 2014) 601ff reports that the two decades of TPF practices in Australia has not given cause for concern over adverse effects. Cf also Peysner (2014), who argues that policies concerning funding should be evidence-based.

83 See the overview of the contracting process and relevant contract clauses with Rowles-Davies and Cousins (2014) 111ff.

84 Cf HM Kritzer, *Risks, Reputations and Rewards: Contingency Fee Legal Practice in the United States* (Stanford: Stanford University Press 2004) 12; De Morpurgo (2011) 384.

85 Research has shown that knowledge of the defendant that the claimant has insurance against legal expenses increases the defendant's willingness to make settlement offers in the face of court proceedings. See, e.g., TM Swanson, 'The Importance of Contingency Fee Agreements' (1991) 11 *O.J.L.S.* 193, 209; De Morpurgo (2011) 382f.

86 Cf R Moorhead and P Hurst, *Contingency Fees – A Study of their Operation in the United States of America (A Research Paper Informing the Review of Costs)* (London: Civil Justice Council 2008) 6.

87 Cf Garber (2010) 24.

Furthermore, it seems feasible that, all else being equal, both LEI insurers and TPF funders prefer *predictable* cost allocation rules in civil procedure. Predictability adds to the containment of the cost and therefore these funding techniques are more likely to do well under cost-shifting regimes with fixed caps or clear tariffs rather than under open-ended regimes with *ex post* application of vague standards of reasonableness.[88]

As far as the behaviour of claimants is concerned, a rational and well-informed claimant will probably be (more) likely to weigh the costs and benefits of litigation more consciously before deciding to enter into an agreement with a TPF. Also, in a perfect market with an abundance of funding opportunities, the claimant will 'shop around' and compare quotes. The reality in most jurisdictions is, however, that TPF funding is a non-transparent niche market with few suppliers. Moreover, where claimants are unsophisticated, they may lack the information and legal background to fully appreciate the implications of the TPF contract.

5.2 Concerns over TPF involvement

Against this background, we can now deal with some of the concerns that critics have voiced regarding TPF involvement in litigation.[89] On more than one occasion, it has been argued that TPF funders may exploit claimants' hardship by charging excessive win fees, may misrepresent or neglect to inform the client properly regarding the relevant aspects of the contract, intermeddle in the client–counsel relationship by exercising wide powers to steer the litigation strategy and even distort the balance in civil procedure by exposing defendants to the risk of non-recoupable cost orders.

Whether these concerns are legitimate depends on the institutional jurisdictional environment in which the TPF funding operates. The fact remains that, for whatever reason, TPF funding has met with heavy resistance in several jurisdictions. At best, these voiced concerns have prompted the call for a dedicated regulatory framework for TPF funding.[90] In my view, most of these concerns have either no basis in fact or may be easily overcome by implementing a regulatory regime for TPF funding designed to curb the risks while preserving the overall benefits of TPF funding to society.

Here, we consider some of the main objections against TPF involvement. First, there is the claim that TPF fuels frivolous litigation. This claim is difficult to substantiate with

88 G Dannemann, 'Access to Justice: An Anglo-German Comparison' (1996) 2 *European Public Law* 271, 282ff; Prais V, 'Legal Expenses Insurance' in AAS Zuckerman and R Cranston (eds), *The Reform of Civil Procedure: Essays on 'Access to Justice'* (Oxford: Oxford University Press 1996) 440; N Rickman and A Gray, 'The Role of Legal Expenses Insurance in Securing Access to the Market for Legal Services' in A Zuckerman and R Cranston (eds), *The Reform Of Civil Procedure – Essays On 'Access to Justice'* (Oxford: Oxford University Press 1996) 320; N Rickman and P Fenn, 'Insuring Litigation Risk: Some Recent Developments in England and Wales' (1998) 23 *Geneva Papers on Risk & Insurance – Issues & Practice* 210ff; A Walters and J Peysner, 'Event-triggered Financing of Civil Claims: Lawyers, Insurers and the Common Law' (1999) 8 *Nottingham L.J.* 1, 6; J Flood and Avis Whyte, 'What's Wrong with Legal Aid? Lessons from Outside The UK' (2006) 25 *Civil Justice Quarterly* 80, 92; M Kilian, 'Alternatives to Public Provision: The Role of Legal Expenses Insurance in Broadening Access to Justice: The German Experience' (2003) 30 *Journal of Law and Society* 31, 42; Cabrillo F and S Fitzpatrick, *The Economics of Courts and Litigation* (Cheltenham: Edward Elgar 2008) 143; Wagner (2009) 379ff.

89 See, e.g., the overview by J Lyon, 'Revolution in Progress: Third-Party Funding of American Litigation' (2010) 58 *UCLA L.Rev.* 571, 590ff; De Morpurgo (2011) 366ff.

90 E.g., V Shannon, 'Harmonizing Third-Party Litigation Funding Regulation' (2015) 36 *Cardozo Law Review* 101ff.

evidence. If TPF is the fuel that drives the litigation, the number of cases may rise.[91] Whether or not an increase in the number of suits is good or bad, is another matter. If TPF helps *meritorious* claims to be brought to justice, which would otherwise not be pursued, that should not be considered bad.[92] Moreover, available evidence suggests that the screening and acceptance process may, in fact, filter out *unmeritorious* claims.[93] In practice, commercial TPF funders spend considerable time and resources reviewing and selecting cases. In doing so, they have every incentive to screen merits and monitor the case management diligently.[94] In short, they act as gatekeepers. Therefore, the concern that TPF would foster frivolous claims is counter-intuitive.[95] In fact, the core value of TPF lies in the equalising effect it may have on the different degrees of risk that claimants and respondents are prepared to take.[96] TPF may thus boost the claimant's position and increase settlement leverage.[97]

It should be noted, however, that the involvement of TPF funders may bring cases to court that impecunious claimants would otherwise not be in a position to bring. In those jurisdictions where litigants do not need to deposit sufficient funds with the court (or provide security in another form) to cover potential adverse cost orders, the risk exists that the TPF may run out of money during the proceedings and that a victorious defendant may be left unable to recoup costs. This is one reason why some call for capital requirements to apply to TPF funders so that they are able to meet their obligations and thus guarantee that

91 Garber (2010) 29ff. Submitting such claims for the American legal system, e.g., J Beisner, J Miller and G Rubin, *Selling Lawsuits, Buying Trouble* (Washington, DC: US Chamber Institute for Legal Reform 2009) 1ff. There is some evidence from Australian TPF litigation practice that supports this claim; see Abrams and Chen (2013).

92 Cf JD Glater, 'Investing in Lawsuits, for a Share of the Awards' *The New York Times* (New York, 3 June 2009). In the American context, it is thought to expose the legal system to inefficient additional incentives to sue, given the existing potential of class actions; see RH Rubin, 'Third Party Financing of Litigation' (Searle Public Policy Roundtable on Third Party Financing of Litigation, Northwestern University Law School, Chicago, Ill., 24–25 September 2009) 1ff. These arguments do not seem to relate to investment treaty claims.

93 Cf M Tuil and L Visscher, 'New Trends in Financing Civil Litigation in Europe: Lessons to be Learned' in M Tuil and L Visscher (eds), *New Trends in Financing Civil Litigation in Europe – A Legal, Empirical, and Economic Analysis* (Cheltenham: Edward Elgar 2010) 181. Australian evidence points towards the fact that TPF cases are cited more and reversed less often than comparable cases without TPF involvement. This could be an indication for a strong screening effect. See Abrams and Chen (2013).

94 Cf MB Abramowicz, 'A Fee Limitation Rule for Litigation Finance' (Searle Public Policy Roundtable on Third Party Financing of Litigation, Northwestern University Law School, Chicago, Ill., 24–25 September 2009) 2; D Dana and M Schanzenbach, 'How Would Third Party Financing Change the Face of American Tort Litigation? The Role of Agency Costs in the Attorney–Client Relationship' (Searle Public Policy Roundtable on Third Party Financing of Litigation, Northwestern University Law School, Chicago, Ill., 24–25 September 2009) 1ff; R Lindeman, 'Third-Party Investors Offer New Funding Source for Major Commercial Lawsuits', *Daily Reports for Executives* (Bureau of National Affairs, 5 March 2010) 4. Cf court reasoning in the case law cited by HE Loiseau, EC Lyttle and BN Benfield, 'Third-Party Financing of Commercial Litigation' (2010) 24(4) *In-House Litigator* 1, 3ff. Similar screening behaviour is elicited under influence of contingency-fee arrangements.

95 Cf the review of empirical research by P Fenn and N Rickman, 'The empirical analysis of litigation funding' in M Tuil and L Visscher (eds), *New Trends in Financing Civil Litigation in Europe – A Legal, Empirical, and Economic Analysis* (Cheltenham: Edward Elgar 2010) 131ff.

96 Cf JT Molot, 'Litigation Finance: A Market Solution to a Procedural Problem' (2010) 99 *Geo. L. J.* 65.

97 Molot (2010) 115, rightly asserts 'Where a one-time, risk-averse plaintiff accepts too little from a repeat-player, risk-neutral defendant, this is just as much a market failure as a failure of procedure.'

adverse costs against the claimant will actually be met.[98] In those jurisdictions where no advance deposit system exists, this may indeed make sense.

A second concern is that TPF involvement may discourage settlement. Again, there is no compelling evidence but it seems tenable that, in litigation, TPF funding may increase leverage for the claimant and incentives for settlement for the defendant. Provided that the defendant is aware of the TPF involvement, it may then be an indication of the funder's confidence in the quality of the claim. This, in itself, may increase leverage for settlement.[99] On the other hand, if cost-shifting rules allow the prevailing claimant to fully shift the third-party costs to the defeated defendant, there may be an incentive not to settle at all or indeed, not settle below an amount artificially inflated by the contract between the claimant and the funder. The defendant may prefer to raise the stakes instead. One may ask what the root cause is of this effect: is it the TPF involvement or is it an intrinsic flaw in the full cost-shifting paradigm?

A third concern is that clients are not well-informed before they enter into a TPF contract. For the avoidance of doubt, this does not concern savvy commercial operators who enter into TPF arrangements merely to outsource risk management. Instead, information problems and issues of unfair commercial practices may be expected to arise, primarily in retail TPF markets. Obviously, the normal rules of mistake, misrepresentation and perhaps specific consumer protection rules apply to the contract process. There may be a need for specific rules for the protection of vulnerable claimants such as consumers who lack information and experience and who are more risk-averse than business claimants.[100] In consumer claims, there are examples of claims management agencies resorting to sharp or unfair commercial practices in order to quickly corner the market for a particular claim. As the English experience with claims agencies shows,[101] the regulation of contract forms, of commercial practices and of the solvency of these agencies may be necessary.[102]

A fourth concern is whether the court and opposing side have a right to know about the TPF involvement. This issue of disclosure relates to the conception of the role of courts in civil litigation. In those legal systems (such as the English legal system) where non-litigating third parties may owe duties to the court notwithstanding the fact that they are not formally part of the proceedings, the idea that a third party has to disclose his identity and

98 E.g., R Jackson, *Review of Civil Litigation Costs: Final Report* (London: TSO 2010) 120f; Australian Government Productivity Commission (2014) 633. See also Stadler, in this volume, on the arguments used by German courts against permitting collective damages actions by means of assignment. Cf I Tillema, 'Cessie als instrument ter afwikkeling van massaschadezaken: in strijd met de openbare orde en goede zeden?' (2014) *Maandblad voor Vermogensrecht* 333ff.

99 Garber (2010) 33.

100 Australian Government Productivity Commission (2014) 629ff; J Walker, 'Policy and Regulatory Issues in Litigation Funding Revisited' (2014) 55 *Canadian Business L.J.* 85ff; T Cain, 'Third Party Funding of Personal Injury Tort Claims: Keep the Baby and Change the Bathwater' (2014) 89 *Chi.-Kent L. Rev.* 11ff; WH van Boom and LL Luiten, 'Procesfinanciering door derden' (2015) *RM Themis* 188ff.

101 In 2007, a regulatory regime was introduced for regulatory oversight of claims management agencies that had left a trail of insolvency, aggressive commercial practices, bad value for money, ambulance chasing and even staging accidents to collect fees. See Part 2 of the Compensation Act 2006, founding the MoJ Claims Management Regulator (see <https://www.gov.uk/government/groups/claims-management-regulator>). Recently, the regulator's activities were reviewed ('Independent Review of Claims Management Regulation'; Report by C Brady, March 2016).

102 Walker (2014) 85ff.; Hodges, Peysner and Nurse (2012) 119f. Cf on the experience with German claims agencies for flight delay and boarding denial P Rott, 'Claims Management Services: An Alternative to ADR?' (2016) *European Review of Private Law* 143ff.

involvement and may be prohibited from engaging in unlawful interference with the client–counsel relationship, may not sound alien.[103] Also, in investment arbitration the political implications of non-disclosure give rise to mounting pressure to introduce a general duty on claimants and TPF funders to disclose TPF involvement.[104] In other legal systems, where parties are only formally implicated in proceedings through the formal gateway of the issuance of a summons, this may be less palpable. In those jurisdictions, liability insurers also operate, albeit lawfully, in the semi-darkness that surrounds the proceedings without identifying themselves. In such cases, it does not seem to make sense for courts to be bothered with TPF involvement. Surprisingly, the European Commission, in a recent non-binding recommendation on collective redress, set forth a principle of disclosure of funding arrangements in collective damages actions: 'The claimant party should be required to declare to the court at the outset of the proceedings the origin of the funds that it is going to use to support the legal action.'[105] To some national legal systems, such a duty of third parties, not formally involved in the litigation, to make themselves known to the court constitutes an alien concept.

A fifth concern is that TPF funders will, if permitted, take over control of the claim and the litigation by, for instance, having the claimant sign and grant a full and irrevocable power of attorney to the TPF funder. Here, the claim is that TPF funders meddle in legal proceedings. It is difficult to say to what extent this really occurs. Where doctrines against maintenance and champerty are held in high regard, legal systems explicitly prohibit the steering of litigation. Moreover, in those legal systems, TPF funders prefer to keep their noses clean, as is demonstrated by Art. 9 of the voluntary Code of Conduct of the Association of Litigation Funders of England & Wales 2014: the funder 'not take any steps that cause or are likely to cause the Funded Party's solicitor or barrister to act in breach of their professional duties', nor will it 'seek to influence the Funded Party's solicitor or barrister to cede control or conduct of the dispute to the Funder'.[106]

Furthermore, rules of professional conduct may forbid the lawyer to be employed by, accept directions from or leave certain tasks to the third party.[107] In reality, however, the

103 E.g., on cost orders against third parties, Middleton and Rowley (2015) 635ff.

104 See further De Brabandere in this volume, referring to, *inter alia*, the recent draft of the Transatlantic Trade and Investment Partnership (TTIP) between the US and the EU. See also WH van Boom, *Third-Party Financing in International Investment Arbitration* (Report for the OECD 2011) <http://ssrn.com/abstract=2027114> 54f; E De Brabandere and J Lepeltak, 'Third-Party Funding in International Investment Arbitration' (2012) 27 *ICSID Review: Foreign Investment Law Journal* 379ff; several contributions to BM Cremades and A Dimolitsa (ed.), *Third-party Funding in International Arbitration* (Paris: ICC 2013); GJ Shaw, 'Third-party Funding in Investment Arbitration: How Non-disclosure Can Cause Harm for the Sake of Profit' (2016) *Arbitration International* 1ff. Cf P Puri, 'Profitable Justice: Aligning Third-Party Financing of Litigation with the Normative Functions of the Canadian Judicial System' (2014) 55 *Canadian Business L.J.* 34ff and V Shannon, 'Judging Third-Party Funding' (2016) 36 *UCLA L.Rev.* 1, 12ff for a discussion of TPF-involvement disclosure in ordinary litigation.

105 Principle 14 of Commission Recommendation 11 June 2013 on common principles for injunctive and compensatory collective redress mechanisms in the Member States concerning violations of rights granted under Union Law (2013/396/EU).

106 Code for Conduct for Litigation Funders (January 2014), undertaken by the Association of Litigation Funders of England and Wales. See further < http://associationoflitigationfunders.com/documents/> accessed March 2016. The ALF Code was originally agreed on in 2011 in the slipstream of the Jackson Review when the prospects for TPF funding took a turn for the better with the pruning down of CFA+ATE arrangements by the Jackson Review. The 2014 Code is an amended version. See further Pirozzolo (2014) 160ff.

107 Cf Richmond (2005) 669ff.

TPF funder will always need to obtain information to assess *case viability*. Hence, inevitably, the solicitor–client confidentiality may be problematic from the first contact onwards.[108] Therefore, the need for some waiver of privilege on the part of the client seems unavoidable.[109] Furthermore, whether 'steering the case' is considered unlawful or unethical depends heavily on the foundations of assignment of claims and debts. If, under a particular legal system, the law of assignment is unproblematic and fully permits such legal transfer, it is unlikely that any ethical problems will be experienced when a TPF funder is permitted to take control with the claimant's consent. It is, however, important to note that, depending on the rules of professional conduct applicable to client–counsel relationships, issues of conflict of interest may quickly arise if the lawyer is retained simultaneously by the claimant and the TPF funder.[110]

6. Solutions and conclusions

The concerns reviewed above illustrate that TPF may be in need of proper statutory regulation or self-regulation. I reiterate that the intensity of such intervention depends on the national procedural framework in place for the calculation and allocation of litigation costs as well as the rules applicable to lawyer remuneration and ethics. Funders will probably argue that self-regulation is preferable to a statutory regime for TPF funding. To be fair, a code of conduct concerning TPF funder behaviour may be a fairly inconspicuous instrument that could guarantee fundamental rights of clients and their counsel and further improve the TPF landscape.[111] However, a code is hardly ever sufficient if there is a need for protection of certain classes of clients, such as consumers. For instance, a solemn promise undertaken in a code that a funder will, at all times, maintain adequate financial resources to meet its obligations to fund all of the disputes that it has agreed to fund[112] is of little value when funders subscribing to the code are not supervised or regulated in terms of their solvency.[113] Moreover, self-regulatory codes may also serve as an instrument of strategic *deflection* rather than actual regulation if its main purpose is to ward off intrusive government regulation, preserve market autonomy, raise barriers to entry into the market and maintain a soft approach to compliance and enforcement. If the market for TPF funding in a specific jurisdiction grows and becomes a cornerstone for access to justice for consumers, surely systematic financial supervision of TPF funders will then become inevitable, as is already the case with LEI insurance business.[114]

To conclude, as far as the role of TPF is concerned, my overall assessment is that the involvement of TPF funders in commercial and consumer litigation can truly be beneficial to the access to civil justice. Where both the TPF funder and claimant are commercially

108 Cf JH McLaughlin, 'Litigation Funding: Charting a Legal and Ethical Course' (2007) 31 *Vt. L.Rev.* 616, 650ff.

109 See Lyon (2010) 604; Garber (2010) 19; ABA, *Issues Paper Concerning Lawyer's Involvement in Alternative Litigation Financing* (2010) 4. Under German law, such a waiver is allowed. See Jaskolla (2004) 24.

110 Richmond (2005) 669.

111 Cf Rowles-Davies and Cousins (2014) 208ff.

112 Art 9.4 of the 2014 Code of Conduct for Litigation Funders (Association of Litigation Funders of England and Wales).

113 Cf Jackson (2010) 120–121.

114 Cf for Australia M Legg, E Park, L Travers and N Turner, 'Litigation Funding in Australia' (2010) *University of New South Wales Faculty of Law Research Series* 1, 29ff and Waye and Morabito, in this volume.

sophisticated, have relatively equal bargaining power and have proper legal advice, there is little reason to prohibit their TPF agreement. If sophisticated claim holders wish to delegate conduct of proceedings to funders, it makes good business sense to allow this.[115] In theory, TPF should help screen and bring meritorious cases to court by the joint and convergent venture of claimant and TPF funder. Moreover, TPF is a welcome addition to the array of funding possibilities that may allow meritorious claims to be pursued and improve access to justice. Where it is feared that negative side-effects may occur such as, for instance, in consumer claims markets, further regulation is required to curb the risks while, at the same time, preserving the overall benefits of TPF funding to society.

Bibliography

American Bar Association, *Issues Paper Concerning Lawyer's Involvement in Alternative Litigation Financing* (2010).

Abramowicz M.B., 'On the Alienability of Legal Claims' (2005) 114 *Yale Law Journal* 697.

—— 'A Fee Limitation Rule for Litigation Finance' (Searle Public Policy Roundtable on Third Party Financing of Litigation, Northwestern University Law School, Chicago, Ill., 24–25 September 2009).

Abrams D.S. and D.L. Chen, 'A Market for Justice: A First Empirical Look at Third Party Litigation Funding' (2013) 15 *U. of Pennsylvania J. of Bus. L.* 1075.

Australian Government Productivity Commission, *Access to Justice Arrangements (Productivity Commission Inquiry Report no 72)* (Canberra: Commonwealth of Australia 2014).

Beckner C.F. and A. Katz, 'The Incentive Effects of Litigation Fee Shifting When Legal Standards Are Uncertain' (1995) 15 *International Review of Law and Economics* 205.

Beisner J., J. Miller and G. Rubin, *Selling Lawsuits, Buying Trouble* (Washington, DC: US Chamber Institute for Legal Reform 2009).

Blackstone W. Sir, *Commentaries on the Laws of England in Four Books* (1753).

Boardman M., 'Insurers Defend and Third Parties Fund: A Comparison of Litigation Participation' (2012) 8 *J.L. Econ. & Policy* 673.

Bonnell M., P. Megens, S. Finizio, D. Speller, P. Dunham, S. Nataf, P. Starr, D. Bateson, G. Alon, A. Yeo, S. Yen Koh, N. Radjai, C. Miles and S. Zagata Vasani, 'Case Notes on Third-party Funding' (2008) 3 *Global Arbitration Review* 35.

Bowles R. and N. Rickman, 'Asymmetric Information, Moral Hazard and the Insurance of Legal Expenses' (1998) 23 *Geneva Papers on Risk & Insurance – Issues & Practice* 196.

Burch E. Chamblee, 'Financiers as Monitor in Aggregate Litigation' (2012) 87 *N.Y.U. L. Rev.* 1273.

Buschbell H., 'Prozessfinanzierung als Instrument der Anspruchsverfolgung' (2006) *AnwBl* 825.

Cabrillo F. and S. Fitzpatrick, *The Economics of Courts and Litigation* (Cheltenham: Edward Elgar 2008).

Cain T., 'Third Party Funding of Personal Injury Tort Claims: Keep the Baby and Change the Bathwater' (2014) 89 *Chi.-Kent L. Rev.* 11.

Choharis P.C., 'A Comprehensive Market Strategy For Tort Reform' (1995) 12 *Yale J. on Reg.* 435.

Civil Justice Council, *The Damages-based Agreements Reform Project – Drafting and Policies Issues* (London: Civil Justice Council 2015).

Coester M. and D. Nitzsche, 'Alternative Ways to Finance a Lawsuit in Germany' (2005) 24 *Civil Justice Quarterly* 83.

Coffee J.C., *Entrepreneurial Litigation – Its Rise, Fall and Future* (Cambridge: Harvard University Press 2015).

115 Waye (2008) 241ff; Steinitz (2011) 1326ff; WB Wendel, 'Alternative Litigation Finance and Anti-Commodification Norms' (2014) 63 *DePaul L.Rev.* 655ff.

Cremades B.M. and A. Dimolitsa (ed.), *Third-party Funding in International Arbitration* (Paris: ICC 2013).

Dana D. and M. Schanzenbach, 'How Would Third Party Financing Change the Face of American Tort Litigation? The Role of Agency Costs in the Attorney-Client Relationship' (Searle Public Policy Roundtable on Third Party Financing of Litigation, Northwestern University Law School, Chicago, Ill., 24–25 September 2009).

Dannemann G., 'Access to Justice: an Anglo-German Comparison' (1996) 2 *European Public Law* 271.

De Brabandere E. and J. Lepeltak, 'Third-Party Funding in International Investment Arbitration' (2012) 27 *ICSID Review: Foreign Investment Law Journal* 379.

De Morpurgo M., 'A Comparative Legal and Economic Approach to Third-Party Litigation Funding' (2011) 19 *Cardozo Journal of International and Comparative Law* 343.

Desdevises Y., 'France – Theoretical Perspectives' in C.J.S. Hodges, S. Vogenauer and M. Tulibacka (eds), *The Costs and Funding of Civil Litigation: A Comparative Perspective* (Oxford: Hart Publishing 2010) 327.

Dethloff N., 'Verträge zur Prozessfinanzierung gegen Erfolgsbeteiligung' (2000) 31 *Neue Juristische Wochenschrift* 2225.

Dimde M., *Rechtsschutzzugang und Prozessfinanzierung im Zivilprozess – Eine ökonomische Analyse des Rechts* (Berlin: BWV 2003).

Donohue J.J., 'Opting for the British Rule, Or If Posner and Shavell Can't Remember the Coase Theorem, Who Will?' (1991) 104 *Harv. L. Rev.* 1093.

Duve C., 'Success-Fees in Germany' in P Gottwald (ed.), *Litigation in England and Germany – Legal Professional Services, Key Features and Funding* (Bielefeld: Gieseking Verlag 2010) 217.

Faure M.G., F.J. Fernhout and N.J. Philipsen, *Resultaatgerelateerde beloningssystemen voor advocaten* (Den Haag: Boom Jurische Uitgevers 2009).

—— 'No Cure, No Pay and Contingency Fee' in M. Tuil and L. Visscher (eds), *New Trends in Financing Civil Litigation in Europe – A Legal, Empirical, and Economic Analysis* (Cheltenham: Edward Elgar 2010) 33.

Fenn P., A. Gray and N. Rickman, *The Funding of Personal Injury Litigation: Comparisons over Time and across Jurisdictions* (London: Department for Constitutional Affairs 2006).

Fenn P. and N. Rickman, 'The Empirical Analysis of Litigation Funding' in M. Tuil and L. Visscher (eds), *New Trends in Financing Civil Litigation in Europe – A Legal, Empirical, and Economic Analysis* (Cheltenham: Edward Elgar 2010) 131.

Flood J. and Avis Whyte, 'What's Wrong With Legal Aid? Lessons From Outside The UK' (2006) 25 *Civil Justice Quarterly* 80.

Frechen F. and M.L. Kochheim, 'Fremdfinanzierung von Prozessen gegen Erfolgsbeteiligung' (2004) 17 *Neue Juristische Wochenschrift* 1213.

Friston M., *Civil Costs – Law and Practice* (Bristol: Jordan Publishing 2010).

Garber S., *Alternative Litigation Financing in the United States – Issues, Knowns, and Unknowns* (Santa Monica: RAND Corporation 2010).

Gotanda J.Y., 'Awarding Costs and Attorneys' Fees in International Commercial Arbitrations' (1999) 21 *Michigan Journal of International Law* 1.

Grünewald B., 'Prozessfinanzierungsvertrag mit gewerbsmäßigem Prozessfinanzierer - ein Gesellschaftsvertrag', (2000) 55 *Betriebsberater* 729.

Helland E. and S.A. Seabury, 'Contingent-fee Contracts in Litigation: A Survey and Assessment' in J. Arlen (ed.), *Research Handbook on the Economics of Torts* (Cheltenham: Edward Elgar 2013) 383.

Hess B. and R. Hübner, 'General Overview and Trends in the German Civil Litigation Costs System' in C.J.S. Hodges, S. Vogenauer and M. Tulibacka (eds), *The Costs and Funding of Civil Litigation: A Comparative Perspective* (Oxford: Hart Publishing 2010) 349.

Hodges C.J.S., S. Vogenauer and M. Tulibacka (eds), *The Costs and Funding of Civil Litigation: A Comparative Perspective* (Oxford: Hart Publishing 2010).

—— J. Peysner and A. Nurse, *Litigation Funding: Status and Issues* (Research Report CSLS Oxford & Lincoln Law School 2012).

Hughes J.W. and E.A. Snyder, 'The English Rule for Allocating Legal Costs: Evidence Confronts Theory' (1990) 6 *J.L. Econ. & Org.* 345.
Jackson R., *Review of Civil Litigation Costs – Preliminary Report* (London: TSO 2009).
—— *Review of Civil Litigation Costs: Final Report* (London: TSO 2010).
Jäger M., *Reimbursement for Attorney's Fees* (Den Haag: Eleven International Publishing 2010).
Jaskolla J., *Prozessfinanzierung gegen Erfolgsbeteiligung* (Karlsruhe: Verlag Versicherungswirtschaft 2004).
Kalajdzic J., P. Cashman and A. Longmoore, 'Justice for Profit: A Comparative Analysis of Australian, Canadian and U.S. Third Party Litigation Funding' (2013) 61 *Am.J.Comp.L.* 93.
Katz A., 'Measuring the Demand for Litigation: Is the English Rule Really Cheaper?' (1987) 3 *J.L. Econ. & Org.* 143.
Kelemen R.D., *Eurolegalism – The Transformation of Law and Regulation in the European Union* (Cambridge: Harvard University Press 2011).
Kilian M., 'Alternatives to Public Provision: The Role of Legal Expenses Insurance in Broadening Access to Justice: The German Experience' (2003) 30 *Journal of Law and Society* 31.
Kirstein R. and N. Rickman, 'Third Party Contingency Contracts in Settlement and Litigation' (2002) *German Working Papers in Law and Economics* 1.
Kritzer H.M., *Risks, Reputations and Rewards: Contingency Fee Legal Practice in the United States* (Stanford: Stanford University Press 2004).
Legg M., E. Park, L. Travers and N. Turner, 'Litigation Funding in Australia' (2010) *University of New South Wales Faculty of Law Research Series* 1.
Leichty D.R. and E.R. Thomason, *Investing in Lawsuits: 'Litigation Financing' and the Consumer Protection Imperative* (Washington: Washington Legal Foundation 2009).
Lindeman R., 'Third-Party Investors Offer New Funding Source for Major Commercial Lawsuits' *Daily Reports for Executives* (Bureau of National Affairs, 5 March 2010) 1.
Loiseau H.E., E.C. Lyttle and B.N. Benfield, 'Third-Party Financing of Commercial Litigation' (2010) 24(4) *In-House Litigator* 1.
Lyon J., 'Revolution in Progress: Third-Party Funding of American Litigation' (2010) 58 *UCLA L.Rev.* 571.
Malaurie P., L. Aynès and P. Stoffel-Munck, *Droit Civil – Les obligations* (Paris: Defrénois 2013).
Marcushamer I., 'Selling Your Torts: Creating a Market for Tort Claims and Liability' (2005) 33 *Hofstra L.Rev.* 1543.
Mause P.J., 'Winner Takes All: A Re-examination of the Indemnity System' (1969) 55 *Iowa L. Rev.* 26.
McLaughlin J.H., 'Litigation Funding: Charting a Legal and Ethical Course' (2007) 31 *Vt. L.Rev.* 616.
Merkin R. and J. Steele, *Insurance and the Law of Obligations* (Oxford: Oxford University Press 2013).
Middleton S. and J. Rowley, *Cook on Costs 2016* (London: LexisNexis 2015).
Molot J.T., 'A Market in Litigation Risk' (2009) 76 *U.Chi.L.Rev.* 367.
—— 'Litigation Finance: A Market Solution to a Procedural Problem' (2010) 99 *Geo. L. J.* 65.
Moorhead R. and P. Hurst, *Contingency Fees – A Study of their Operation in the United States of America (A Research Paper Informing the Review of Costs)* (London: Civil Justice Council 2008).
Murray P.L. and R. Stürner, *German Civil Justice* (Durham: Carolina Academic Press 2004).
Lord Neuberger, 'From Barratry, Maintenance and Champerty to Litigation Funding' (Harbour Litigation Funding First Annual Lecture, Gray's Inn, 8 May 2013).
Peysner J., 'Expropriation, Access to Justice (and Wikileaks): A Comparative Study of Funding Difficult Cases in England and the United States' (2012) *Civil Justice Quarterly* 113.
—— 'Tail Wags Dog: Contingency Fees (and Part 36 and Third Party Funding)' (2013) 32 *Civil Justice Quarterly* 231.
—— *Access to Justice: A Critical Analysis of Recoverable Conditional Fees and No-Win No-Fee Funding* (London: Palgrave Macmillan 2014).
—— and A Nurse, *Representative Actions and Restorative Justice – A Report for the Department for Business, Enterprise and Regulatory Reform (BERR)* (Lincoln: Lincoln Law School 2008).
Pfennigstorf W., 'The European Experience with Attorney Fee Shifting' (1984) 47 *Law and Contemporary Problems* 37.

Pinna A., 'Financing Civil Litigation: The Case for the Assignment and Securitization of Liability Claims' in M. Tuil and L. Visscher (eds), *New Trends in Financing Civil Litigation in Europe – A Legal, Empirical, and Economic Analysis* (Cheltenham: Edward Elgar 2010) 109.

Pinsolle P., 'Le financement de l'arbitrage par les tiers' (2010) *Revue de l'Arbitrage* 385.

Pirozzolo R., 'Third Party Funding' in R. Pirozzolo (ed.), *Litigation Funding Handbook* (London: Law Society 2014) 155.

Prais V., 'Legal Expenses Insurance' in A.A.S. Zuckerman and R. Cranston (eds), *The Reform of Civil Procedure: Essays on 'Access to Justice'* (Oxford: Oxford University Press 1996) 431.

Puri P., 'Profitable Justice: Aligning Third-Party Financing of Litigation with the Normative Functions of the Canadian Judicial System' (2014) 55 *Canadian Business L.J.* 34.

Radin M., 'Maintenance by Champerty' (1935) 24 *Cal. L. Rev.* 48.

Richmond D., 'Other People's Money: The Ethics of Litigation Funding' (2005) 56 *Mercer L.Rev.* 649.

Rickman N. and A. Gray, 'The Role of Legal Expenses Insurance in Securing Access to the Market for Legal Services' in A. Zuckerman and R. Cranston (eds), *The Reform Of Civil Procedure – Essays On 'Access To Justice'* (Oxford: Oxford University Press 1996) 305.

—— and P. Fenn, 'Insuring Litigation Risk: Some Recent Developments in England and Wales' (1998) 23 *Geneva Papers on Risk & Insurance – Issues & Practice* 210.

Rott P., 'Claims Management Services: An Alternative to ADR?' (2016) *European Review of Private Law* 143.

Rowles-Davies N. and J. Cousins, *Third Party Litigation Funding* (Oxford: Oxford University Press 2014).

Rubin P.H., 'Third Party Financing of Litigation' (Searle Public Policy Roundtable on Third Party Financing of Litigation, Northwestern University Law School, Chicago, Ill., 24–25 September 2009).

Saenger I., 'Case Management in Germany' in P. Gottwald (ed.), *Litigation in England and Germany – Legal Professional Services, Key Features and Funding* (Bielefeld: Gieseking Verlag 2010) 15.

Schepens T., 'Bridging the Funding Gap – The Economics of Cost Shifting, Fee Arrangements and Legal Expenses Insurance and their Prospects for Improving the Access to Civil Justice' (2007) *German Working Papers in Law and Economics* 1.

Sebok A.J., 'The Inauthentic Claim' (2011) 64 *Vanderbilt Law Review* 61.

Shannon V., 'Harmonizing Third-Party Litigation Funding Regulation' (2015) 36 *Cardozo Law Review* 101.

—— 'Judging Third-Party Funding' (2016) 36 *UCLA L.Rev.* 1.

—— and L. Bench Nieuwveld, *Third-Party Funding in International Arbitration* (Alphen aan den Rijn: Kluwer Law International 2012).

Shavell S., 'Suit, Settlement, and Trial: A Theoretical Analysis Under Alternative Methods for the Allocation of Legal Costs' (1982) 11 *J. Legal Stud.* 55.

Shaw G.J., 'Third-Party Funding in Investment Arbitration: How Non-Disclosure Can Cause Harm for the Sake of Profit' (2016) *Arbitration International* 1.

Silver C., 'Litigation Funding versus Liability Insurance: What's the Difference?' (2014) 63 *DePaul L.Rev.* 617.

Smit R.H. and T.B. Robinson, 'Costs Awards in International Commercial Arbitration: Proposed Guidelines for Promoting Time and Cost Efficiency' (2010) 20 *American Review of International Arbitration (ARIA)* 267.

Smith M., *The Law of Assignment: The Creation and Transfer of Choses in Action* (Oxford: Oxford University Press 2007).

Steinitz M., 'Whose Claim Is It Anyway? Third-Party Litigation Funding' (2011) 95 *Minn. L. Rev.* 1268.

—— 'The Litigation Finance Contract' (2012) 54 *William & Mary L. Rev.* 455.

Swanson T.M., 'The Importance of Contingency Fee Agreements' (1991) 11 *O.J.L.S.* 193.

Terré F., P. Simler and Y. Lequette, *Droit civil – Les obligations* (Paris: Dalloz 2013).

Tillema I., 'Cessie als instrument ter afwikkeling van massaschadezaken: in strijd met de openbare orde en goede zeden?' (2014) *Maandblad voor Vermogensrecht* 333.

Tolhurst G., *The Assignment of Contractual Rights* (Oxford: Hart Publishing 2006).

Tuil M. and L. Visscher, 'New Trends in Financing Civil Litigation in Europe: Lessons to be Learned' in M. Tuil and L. Visscher (eds), *New Trends in Financing Civil Litigation in Europe – A Legal, Empirical, and Economic Analysis* (Cheltenham: Edward Elgar 2010) 175.

Van Boom W.H., 'De Minimis Curat Praetor – Redress for Dispersed Trifle Losses' (2009) 4 *Journal of Comparative Law* 171.

—— 'Financing Civil Litigation by the European Insurance Industry' in M. Tuil and L. Visscher (eds), *New Trends in Financing Civil Litigation in Europe – A Legal, Empirical, and Economic Analysis* (Cheltenham: Edward Elgar 2010) 92.

—— *Third-Party Financing in International Investment Arbitration* (Report for the OECD 2011) <http://ssrn.com/abstract=2027114>.

—— and M. de Jong, 'Het Experiment Resultaatgerelateerde Beloning – verwachtingen over werking en doelbereiking' (2014) *Tijdschrift Vergoeding Personenschade* 69.

—— and L.L. Luiten, 'Procesfinanciering door derden' (2015) *RM Themis* 188.

Veith J. and J. Gräfe (eds), *Der Versicherungsprozess* (München: Beck 2016).

Veljanovski C., 'Third Party Litigation Funding in Europe' (2012) 8 *Journal of Law, Economics and Policy* 405.

Villedieu A.L., 'France – The Rules on Funding and Costs' in C.J.S. Hodges, S. Vogenauer and M. Tulibacka (eds), *The Costs and Funding of Civil Litigation: A Comparative Perspective* (Oxford: Hart Publishing 2010) 335.

Visscher L. and T. Schepens, 'A Law and Economics Approach to Cost Shifting, Fee Arrangements and Legal Expense Insurance' in M. Tuil and L. Visscher (eds), *New Trends in Financing Civil Litigation in Europe – A Legal, Empirical, and Economic Analysis* (Cheltenham: Edward Elgar 2010) 7.

Waelbroeck D., D. Slater and G. Even-Shoshan, *Study on the Conditions of Claims for Damages in Case of Infringement of EC Competition Rules – Comparative Report* (Brussels: Ashurst 2004).

Wagner G., 'Litigation Costs and their Recovery: The German Experience' (2009) 28 *Civil Justice Quarterly* 367.

—— 'Litigation Costs Recovery – Tariffs and Hourly Fees in Germany' in P. Gottwald (ed.), *Litigation in England and Germany – Legal Professional Services, Key Features and Funding* (Bielefeld: Gieseking Verlag 2010) 149.

Walker J., 'Policy and Regulatory Issues in Litigation Funding Revisited' (2014) 55 *Canadian Business L.J.* 85.

Walters A. and J. Peysner, 'Event-triggered Financing of Civil Claims: Lawyers, Insurers and The Common Law' (1999) 8 *Nottingham L.J.* 1.

Waye V., *Trading in Legal Claims* (Adelaide: Presidian Legal Publications 2008).

—— 'Litigation Risk Transfer and Law Firm Financial Arrangements' (2014) 17 *Legal Ethics* 107.

Wendel WB, 'Alternative Litigation Finance and Anti-Commodification Norms' (2014) 63 *DePaul L.Rev.* 655.

Wignall G. and S. Green (eds), *Conditional Fees – A Guide to CFAs and Litigation Funding* (London: The Law Society 2008).

Wilde L., 'Prozessfinanzierung: Eine Branche auf dem Sprung – der Charme der Idee hat an Frische nicht verloren' (2010) *Anwaltsblatt* 813.

Zander M., 'Will the Revolution in the Funding of Civil Litigation in England Eventually Lead to Contingency Fees?' (2003) 52 *DePaul L.Rev.* 259.

3 TPF and its alternatives

An economic appraisal

Jef De Mot, Michael Faure and Louis Visscher

1. Introduction

In many legal systems there is increasingly a variety of techniques that are developed to promote access to justice. It can be argued that from society's perspective, promoting access to justice fulfils an important goal, not only from the point of view of social justice (providing victims-plaintiffs with the opportunity to enforce their rights), but also from an economic angle. Limits on access to justice may lead to a situation whereby social costs are thrown on society at large and not sufficiently internalized. It is therefore no surprise that in many legal systems a variety of techniques has been developed or is in full development in order to encourage access to justice, particularly for plaintiffs who may have meritorious claims but who simply are not in the financial position to bring their claim.[1] Moreover, encouraging access to justice is also a way of stimulating private enforcement of laws, which is high on the policy agenda in many jurisdictions.[2]

It is in this context also that third-party funding of litigation has emerged. From an economic perspective, third-party funding can be considered as a remedy for cases where individuals do not bring claims because they do not possess sufficient funds to bring the claim, and do not have access to other ways of financing their claim. It can also mitigate the market failure that can occur in cases of so-called dispersed losses, where rational apathy may occur.

So far third-party funding (TPF) has mainly been developed in the US, the UK and Australia. A variety of different models exists. In some cases, TPF firms invest in commercial lawsuits; in others they provide loans or credit to law firms that represent plaintiffs and in yet a third situation funding is provided directly to individual plaintiffs.[3] Usually TPF focuses on supporting plaintiffs' claims; it is so far not (or rarely) focused on funding defendants, although that may develop in the future as well.

The goal of this chapter is to discuss TPF and (some of) its alternatives from an economic perspective. We start by explaining why TPF emerges and by illustrating that TPF can to a large extent cure the market failure that would result from incomplete access to justice

1 For an overview of the literature, *see inter alia* the contributions in M Tuil and L Visscher (eds), *New Trends in Financing Civil Litigation in Europe – A Legal, Empirical and Economic Analysis* (Cheltenham: Edward Elgar 2010).

2 See further F Weber and M Faure, 'The Interplay between Public and Private Enforcement in European Private Law: Law and Economics Perspective' (2015) 4 *European Review of Private Law* 525–550.

3 See further D Mayers and CW Smith, 'On the Corporate Demand for Insurance' (1982) 55(2) *Journal of Business* 281.

(Section 2). As we will argue, there are a number of different effects of TPF, which could be formulated in terms of advantages and disadvantages. Those relate strongly to the effects of the funding by a third party on the incentives of the parties involved in the litigation. We will attempt to illustrate those effects on the behaviour of the litigants (Section 3). Of course we do realize that TPF may not be the only solution to the problems with which plaintiffs are confronted. An interesting alternative is legal expenses insurance (LEI). A comparison of TPF and LEI will be undertaken in Section 4. Yet another alternative would be to make the remuneration of the lawyer (or another party representing the plaintiff) dependent upon the outcome of the case. The latter is typically known as a contingency fee arrangement and could equally protect plaintiffs against their risk aversion. There are, however, particular differences in the way that TPF and contingency fees function and more particularly how they affect the behaviour of the litigants (Section 5). Section 6 concludes.

2. Why TPF emerges and obstacles for its growth

In this general section we will sketch why, from the perspective of society and plaintiffs, one could expect a demand for TPF. Hence, we will focus on the gaps concerning access to justice that TPF could fill (2.1). At the same time, it is surprising that, as we mentioned in the introduction, TPF is still largely a common-law phenomenon, notwithstanding increasing interest in many European jurisdictions as well. It is also common in international investment arbitration. That raises the question of whether, from a law and economics perspective, there could be particular features that explain the slow development of TPF (2.2).

2.1 Why TPF emerges

As we mentioned in the introduction, there are many cases in which a civil lawsuit will not be filed although the potential damage could be large. First and foremost, the plaintiff may simply lack sufficient funds to initiate a lawsuit. Second, the total damages may be large but dispersed. One may think of environmental harm potentially leading to large social losses. However, if the loss is spread over a large number of victims, some may even consider environmental harm as 'victimless'. The result is that no one will bring a lawsuit. Another example could be the one where someone concludes a contract with a bank, receives poor advice and, as a result, suffers a loss of, say, €4,000.[4] In such a case the plaintiff could start proceedings against the bank, but the outcome is highly uncertain. Moreover, it is also unknown how much the procedure would cost in legal fees and there is a large probability that the lawyers' fees could be higher than the total benefit in the event of winning the trial (€4,000).

In such cases the plaintiff will often take the rational decision not to bring a lawsuit. In the first case it may simply be because he or she is not able to do so. In the second case the reason may be that no victim feels sufficiently harmed in order to bring a suit. In the third case the plaintiff may be discouraged from bringing a lawsuit, given the relatively high costs involved in litigation. In addition to the fees that would have to be paid to the lawyer, the plaintiff will also take into account the time involved in the case. From an economic

4 The example comes from M Faure, 'CADR and Settlement of Claims – A Few Economic Observations' in C Hodges and A Stadler (eds), *Resolving Mass Disputes, ADR and Settlement of Mass Claims* (Cheltenham: Edward Elgar 2013) 39–40.

perspective those are opportunity costs that will have to be taken into account as well. In the second case no lawsuit will be filed at all because the damage is felt collectively but not (or barely) by one individual plaintiff. In the third instance a consumer may take the rational decision not to pursue the case given high aversion against the risk of being confronted with high costs. The problem is, moreover, that the plaintiff will have to incur the costs of a trial before he can obtain compensation. The possibilities for the plaintiff to obtain financing for these costs may be limited, so he would not be able to bring a lawsuit simply because he cannot afford to pre-finance the costs of the trial. As such the decision of the plaintiff not to bring suit is rational and in the literature described as the problem of 'rational disinterest' or 'rational apathy'.[5]

The result is therefore that, in those examples, plaintiffs will not bring a lawsuit, even though a serious social loss is produced. From an economic perspective this is a problem for the simple reason that an externality is created: a cost is thrown on society and not borne by the one who causes the loss (the polluter in the second example; the bank in the third). Since the externality is not internalized, the social costs created will not be incorporated in the prices of the products or services brought on the market by those producers, leading to a market failure.

These simple examples show that barriers to justice can create a market failure. The flipside is obviously that lowering barriers to justice can be socially beneficial as this will lead to a potential internalization of an externality.

It is precisely here that TPF can potentially play a role. The first example speaks for itself. The second example is clearly not one where (only) the problem of risk aversion against high costs (or simply the lack of funds on the side of plaintiffs) plays a role. In the second example (where the damage is widespread), no victim suffers damage large enough to have an incentive to bring a lawsuit. These cases thus provide a strong argument for another type of solutions, being some form of collective action or representative action whereby another organization (e.g. a trustee or a non-gonvernmental organization (NGO)) would bring a suit and represent those who have been harmed. This would also provide the justification for class actions, for example, in the case of consumer suits.[6] One possibility for solving the abovementioned problem is thus to collectivize the interests and to bundle them into one claim. TPF may still play a role in that context, for example when financing is sought for a group litigation that could otherwise not be brought.[7] But the primary solution in the case of the second example (widespread environmental losses) is clearly to allow some kind of bundling of claims or to allow someone to represent the damaged (environmental) interest.

In the third example (the misleading bank case), TPF may be a way of dealing with the aversion of the plaintiff against bringing a suit. For the risk-averse consumer, the major advantage of TPF would be that the TPF organization finances the litigation and takes over the risk, of course in exchange for a part of the proceeds in the case where the litigation is successful. In that sense it is relatively easy to argue that TPF may be beneficial both from

5 For details see HB Schäfer, 'The Bundling of Similar Interests in Litigation. The Incentives for Class Actions and Legal Actions Taken by Associations' (2000) 9 *European Journal of Law and Economics* 183.

6 See further on class actions A Stadler, 'Group Actions as a Remedy to Enforce Consumer Interest' in F Cafaggi and HW Micklitz (eds), *New Frontiers of Consumer Protection – The Interplay between Private and Public Enforcement* (Antwerp: Intersentia 2009) 305–317.

7 See further DR Hensler, 'Financing Civil Litigation: The US Perspective' in M Tuil and L Visscher (eds), *New Trends in Financing Civil Litigation in Europe – A Legal, Empirical and Economic Analysis* (Cheltenham: Edward Elgar 2010) 153.

society's perspective and for potential plaintiffs. For the plaintiff, TPF may provide a remedy for risk aversion and thus allow the plaintiff to bring a suit that he otherwise would not bring. This is at the same time also advantageous for society: a meritorious claim that would otherwise not be brought can now be successful. Hence the market failure resulting from the high barrier to justice, and consequently lacking internalization of an externality, is solved.

Obviously TPF is not the only instrument that can deal with this particular problem. An alternative may be legal expenses insurance (LEI) or a contingency fee arrangement. Although both LEI and contingency fees can indeed remove barriers to justice as well, the discussion of those two instruments (in Sections 4 and 5) will show that there are particular reasons why TPF may be relatively attractive and so can have an added value compared to LEI and contingency fees. One problem is that many individuals may not take LEI for a variety of reasons; also, contingency fees may not provide a solution in all cases. Another problem is that lawyers themselves can in some cases be risk averse, especially when large up-front financing would be required with an uncertain outcome.

2.2 *Obstacles*

Although we have just argued that TPF may have substantial advantages both for individual plaintiffs as well as for society, it is striking that, as we mentioned in the introduction, TPF is, at least in the European context, hardly developed and has so far merely remained a common-law phenomenon. One reason is that many legal systems are opposed to third parties funding a claim. Obviously, there may always be interest group explanations that could be examined when one notices that particular potentially beneficial instruments and institutions do not emerge. However, at this stage we will not examine which interest groups may be behind raising barriers to introduce TPF in Europe; we will rather use law and economics to examine whether there may theoretically be public interest reasons that could explain why TPF has not emerged to the extent that one would imagine. Obviously, with litigation sponsored by a third party, the question will always arise of whether such a funding mechanism could lead to the well-known problems of adverse selection, moral hazard or free riding. These are generally examined within the context of insurers taking over risks, but obviously play a role at a more general level as well, when a third party finances litigation. We will hence examine these issues in turn; in Section 4 we will examine how these issues (more particularly adverse selection and moral hazard) compare in the case of TPF to LEI.

2.2.1 *Adverse selection*

Adverse selection generally refers to the danger that a particular instrument that transfers risk (such as insurance or TPF) would be especially attractive for high-risk individuals. If that were the case and if the TPF funder were not able to adequately distinguish good risks from bad risks, the danger could emerge that the TPF funder remains with only the high-risk cases. This could endanger the financial viability of the TPF system. This problem could normally be resolved if TPF funders were to carefully screen the plaintiffs seeking TPF and so would only finance meritorious suits. The problem may, however, arise that the marginal costs of screening are relatively high compared to the value of litigation, as a result of which the TPF funder would refrain from a detailed screening. This can, for example, be the case in some consumer cases.

Adverse selection is, as has been stressed by Nobel Prize winner Akerlof, the result of an information asymmetry, here between the consumer seeking TPF and the TPF funder.[8] The problem will thus emerge particularly when it is difficult for the TPF funder to assess the quality of the claim and consumers have better information but do not communicate their information to the TPF funder. This may be an issue in small consumer loans. However, if TPF funders have a substantial number of claims that they finance, they could come to a reasonable spreading of the risk.

An additional problem in this respect in the European context is that in most European legal systems contingency fees (see below under Section 5) are prohibited.[9] A combination of TPF and contingency fees may be beneficial to cure adverse selection. The fact that an attorney accepts a case on a contingency fee basis indeed implies that the attorney as gate keeper has verified the merits of the case.[10] The fact that the attorney accepts the case on a contingency fee basis could thus provide a positive signal to TPF funders and could remedy adverse selection. The fact that contingency fees are largely prohibited in Europe could hence be one of the explanations for the relatively low occurrence of TPF, because of the reduced possibility to signal case quality.[11] This could also lead to the policy recommendation that if a policy maker considered stimulating TPF as a valuable instrument for lowering barriers to justice, then this could be combined with a contingency fee system, as this may reduce the risk of adverse selection.

It should, moreover, be mentioned that this adverse selection risk may be relatively high in the market for funding consumer claims where information asymmetry between the potential plaintiff and the funder may be high. As we mentioned in the introduction, TPF can also apply to commercial firms where the value at stake can be substantially larger. This implies at the same time that the relative benefits of detailed screening increase as well. As soon as the amounts at stake are larger, TPF firms would have a stronger incentive to screen *ex ante* and thus reduce adverse selection.

2.2.2 *Moral hazard*

Moral hazard in litigation can refer to the phenomenon that the behaviour of the litigant (plaintiff) will change as a result of him no longer being exposed to risk. The problem could more particularly emerge that when the litigation is integrally funded by a third party on the one hand, the incentives to bring also unmeritorious suits may increase (which is largely a problem of adverse selection), but the problem could equally arise that during litigation the plaintiff will show behaviour that is no longer welfare-maximizing, since he is no longer exposed to any risk. This could then, for example, refer to reduced incentives for cooperating optimally during the trial, for example, with a view on truth finding.

Just as with insurance also, in this case the classic remedies for moral hazard could apply. The remedy for moral hazard could on the one hand constitute control of the behaviour of the litigant by the TPF funder through adequate monitoring. That detailed monitoring

8 See generally G Akerlof, 'The Market for "Lemons": Quality, Uncertainty and the Market Mechanism' (1970) 84 *Quarterly Journal of Economics* 488–500.

9 For details see M Faure, F Fernhout and N Philipsen, 'No Cure, No Pay and Contingency Fees' in M Tuil and L Visscher (eds), *New Trends in Financing Civil Litigation in Europe – A Legal, Empirical and Economic Analysis* (Cheltenham: Edward Elgar 2010) 33–56.

10 As under a contingency fee arrangement the attorney in fact has to pre-finance the claim.

11 Disregarding for the moment the fact that some legal systems may have formal prohibitions.

is, however, costly. The cheaper solution is still to expose the litigant partially to risk. Consequently, the litigant will always have incentives to cooperate with the TPF funder to some extent.[12]

As a result, one can hold that TPF, like any other mechanism that removes risk from a plaintiff may create moral hazard, but that on the other hand adequate remedies are advanced in the literature to cure moral hazard.[13] As long as those remedies are applied (either monitoring or still exposing the litigant to risk, or a combination of the two), moral hazard could in principle be adequately remedied.

2.2.3 Free riding through TPF?

Another problem advanced in the literature is that TPF, like other forms of funding litigation, could lead to the situation whereby positive externalities are created for third parties, more particularly society at large. Other individuals would benefit from TPF since TPF can additionally lead to more deterrence of potential tortfeasors (since more claims will be brought) but the other individuals will not have to pay for TPF. They could therefore enjoy this positive externality without paying for it. That could in theory create a free-riding problem as a result of which TPF would not emerge. This refers to the problem that people other than the litigant may benefit from the deterrent effect created through TPF.[14] Under TPF, a problem may arise if TPF were focusing on a particular category of claims. If those claims were successful, the result would be that internalization takes place, but that fewer claims would take place in the future, as a result of which TPF companies may lose business. If that scenario was realistic, there would be a danger that TPF companies would provide a sub-optimal amount of TPF, out of the fear that TPF would precisely have the socially beneficial effects of reducing the need for claims, thus reducing the business of TPF companies. However, this story may only be true in a monopolistic market. One could eventually expect that if this problem were real the TPF companies would prefer to invest in those types of claims that are difficult to deter, because that would in the end not affect the possibilities of future claims (and hence more business) for the TPF industry.

Obviously, the extent to which the TPF industry would really adapt its behaviour in that sense is an empirical matter; it may in the end be rather theoretical that TPF companies would act in this way (funding fewer claims in order to keep future income streams). It is an issue that also to some extent plays a role in the insurance industry. Insurers on the one hand may have incentives to reduce moral hazard and keep accident rates down. On the other hand, the higher the liability, the higher the demand for liability insurance is as well. This brought Kip Viscusi to note that 'in the long run the insurance industry will profit from a high level of liability since that will increase the degree of coverage it can write'.[15]

12 Of course the plaintiff only bears a part of the costs and may weigh this against the efforts of cooperating. The incentives to cooperate may therefore be less than when the plaintiff was exposed to the full costs. Still, a partial exposure to costs can at least partially remedy the moral hazard risk.

13 See in this respect more particularly S Shavell, 'On Moral Hazard and Insurance' (1979) 93 *Quarterly Journal of Economics* 541–562.

14 For a more detailed account see M Faure and J De Mot, 'Comparing Third-Party Financing of Litigation and Legal Expenses Insurance' (2012) 8(3) *Journal of Law, Economics and Policy* 765–768.

15 See WK Viscusi, 'The Dimensions of the Product Liability Crisis' (1991) 20 *Journal of Legal Studies* 147–148.

2.2.4 Summary

Summarizing: there may be a danger of adverse selection with TPF, but screening by the funder will reduce this problem. Also, a system of contingency fees could ameliorate this, since contingency fees could signal the quality of the case to the TPF funder. Moral hazard could theoretically play a role, but adequate remedies against moral hazard can be employed by TPF funders, as a result of which this should not be a major issue. Also the danger that positive externalities and free riding may reduce the demand for TPF does not seem to be a serious danger. The only issue that (again theoretically) could arise is that TPF funders would select the cases in such a way that they still could guarantee a future income stream.

However, as indicated, most of those obstacles can to a large extent be remedied through adequate measures and could in that sense not seriously limit the development of TPF. So, from an economic perspective, there are no serious arguments against employing TPF on a larger scale. The reasons why TPF is not used more than it could be (at least in Europe) may therefore possibly be due to resistance for other reasons.

We will now proceed to a more detailed analysis of TPF, analysing the effects of TPF on the behaviour of the litigants. That will also shed some light on the potential advantages and disadvantages of TPF.

3. Advantages and disadvantages of TPF

We will first analyse the potential influence of TPF on the volume of litigation (3.1). Next we will examine how TPF could affect the quality of litigation and settlements, given the different incentives generated through TPF (3.2). We further proceed with the question of how the incentives provided through TPF affect the timing of settlement (3.3). Finally, we examine the influence of TPF on the costs of (individual) disputes (3.4).

3.1 The volume of litigation

It is often claimed that TPF will increase the number of lawsuits.[16] For example, in the context of business litigation disputes, without TPF a business-plaintiff will compare the internal cost of capital with the expected return from filing a lawsuit. Only if the expected return is large enough will the plaintiff be willing to file the suit. If the expected cost of TPF is lower than the internal cost of capital, then the amount of litigation instigated by business-plaintiffs will increase.[17] This cost-reducing effect may also reduce the settlement surplus: when the plaintiff's or defendant's costs of trial decrease, the settlement surplus becomes smaller. This leads to more trials, given that one of the reasons that parties settle is to avoid the costs associated with litigation.

Obviously, also when plaintiffs are individuals, TPF can increase the volume of litigation. This is true even for countries like the United States where plaintiffs can often rely on contingency fees to finance litigation. There are cases with positive expected value that individual attorneys or law firms are unwilling to take on a contingency fee basis because

16 See J Beisner, J Miller and G Rubin, *Selling Lawsuits, Buying Trouble: Third-Party Litigation Funding in the United States*, U.S. Chamber Inst. for Legal Reform (2009) 2–3.

17 See PH Rubin, 'Third-Party Financing of Litigation' (2011) 38 *Northern Kentucky Law Review* 676.

of the large risk involved (e.g., large class actions).[18] Furthermore, due to limits on economies of scale, litigation in many very large cases is not feasible. In this context, third-party financing can fill a gap[19] since there are larger economies of scale in finance than in litigation.[20] An empirical study found that the volume of litigation increased in Australia after it allowed the free sale of lawsuits,[21] which may give some credibility to the economies of scale theory.

Others are more sceptical that the volume of litigation will necessarily increase.[22] First, the fact that TPF allows more claims to be brought or to be fought more intensely increases the deterrence of socially undesirable behaviour that could lead to lawsuits. Hence, TPF could lead to less unlawful behaviour and hence fewer grounds for lawsuits. As a consequence, the *ability* to pursue litigation does not unequivocally increase *actual* litigation.[23] Second, the existing empirical study mentioned above relies on small sample sizes (five to seven observations), so more empirical research is absolutely necessary. Third, whether TPF will significantly increase litigation may differ from country to country, depending on the (other) instruments presently available in that country to increase access to justice, and on the predictability of legal costs. For example, the resulting increase in litigation could be substantially larger in Europe than in the US if the reason why some lawsuits are at present not filed, is not because of a lack of capital, but because of a lack of additional potential claims that contingency fee lawyers are willing to litigate,[24] given that contingency fees are prohibited in many European countries (and public support for legal aid is being reduced in some European countries and many households do not have legal expenses insurance).

The conditions needed for TPF to increase litigation may strongly depend on the type of TPF segment involved.[25] In the context of loans to plaintiffs' law firms, an increase in the volume of litigation is plausible if firms use the funds to take on more clients rather than smoothing their cash flow or working more on the cases in their portfolio.[26] With respect to investments in commercial claims, the number of claims may increase substantially where the economics of a claim are interesting to a TPF supplier, but companies are not able, or do not want, to use internal capital to pay hourly legal fees and cannot find a law firm willing to represent them in exchange for a contingency fee. Because there are many

18 The risk can be so vast that losing such a case could lead to bankruptcy of the law firm.

19 See M Abramowicz, 'On the Alienability of Legal Claims' (2005) 114 *Yale L.J.* 697, 739.

20 See Rubin (2011) *supra* note 17, 677, writing, 'Limits on economies of scale will constrain the size of plaintiff-oriented law firms, which in general seem to be smaller than defendant-oriented firms, so that litigation of many very large cases simultaneously is not feasible. It is in this situation that third-party financing would be most useful. This is because such financing can separate the financial decision from the decision to litigate. Large financial investment firms could invest in several high-value, high-risk cases and have the cases litigated by separate law firms. In other words, there are greater economies of scale in finance than in litigation.'

21 See DL Chen and DS Abrams, 'A Market for Justice: The Effect of Third Party Litigation Funding on Legal Outcomes' (2011) 9–11.

22 See S Garber, *Alternative Litigation Financing in the United States: Issues, Knowns and Unknowns* (Santa Monica CA: Rand Corporation 2010) 29.

23 See also D Dana and M Schanzenbach, 'How Would Third Party Financing Change the Face of American Tort Litigation? The Role of Agency Costs in the Attorney-Client Relationship' (Searle Public Policy Roundtable on Third Party Financing of Litigation, Northwestern University Law School, Chicago, Ill., 24–25 September 2009).

24 See e.g., HM Kritzer, 'Contingency Fee Lawyers as Gatekeepers in the Civil Justice System' (1997) 81 *Judicature* 22.

25 See Garber (2010) *supra* note 22, 29–30.

26 Obviously, this will increase the costs of individual cases.

uncertainties surrounding these conditions, the force of the effect in this segment is difficult to forecast. For example, it is not known whether the level of demand for legal services based on contingency fees in commercial litigation is larger than the supply or not. If it is, there could be a substantial demand for TPF in this segment.

3.2 *The quality of litigation and the quality of settlements*

Some scholars think that TPF will increase the number of lawsuits with no or dubious legal merit,[27] because plaintiffs (and their lawyers) are more willing to bring such lawsuits if they are not fully paying for these cases themselves. However, it is not very plausible that consumer legal funding will substantially increase the number of cases without merit. Such loans are typically less than ten per cent of the estimated recoveries in the lawsuits at hand.[28] With respect to loans to law firms, TPF suppliers do not want to lend to firms who hold many claims with a small probability of victory, given that the suppliers do not share in the upside potential of these claims. The exact effect on the quantity of lawsuits with low probabilities will depend on the due diligence processes. The situation of investments in commercial claims could be different. For these claims, TPF suppliers do share in the upside potential of the claim. Since some low-probability suits have high expected profits, TPF suppliers may be willing to invest in some of these cases.

Not all scholars agree that the effect on the amount of low-probability cases will be substantial.[29] First, TPF suppliers seem to find plenty of investment opportunities among claims with quite high chances of recovery. Second, investing in claims with high probabilities of recovery may be a good strategy from a risk-management perspective. It seems that the TPF investors are not sufficiently capitalized to have enough cases so that their portfolio risk is negligible. Juridica, for example, reportedly does not accept claims 'that raise novel legal questions or that will probably end up before a jury'.[30] Naturally, this could change in the future. For now, large capital providers such as banks and insurance companies often have stayed away because of the legal uncertainty associated with litigation funding.[31] If this uncertainty fades, investing in nuisance suits may become a profitable business model for these corporations. Also, because of the high rates of return that TPF companies currently receive, new capital may be attracted into the market. Meritless lawsuits will increase if suppliers without the necessary knowhow to evaluate complex cases enter the market. It can be expected, however, that these suppliers will eventually leave the market, because investing in meritless cases will lead to substantial losses in the long run.

Asymmetric risk preferences may distort settlement amounts. A defendant who faces many suits from different plaintiffs can expect to settle many cases below the average damages award. While the repeat player defendant can pool the litigation risks, the one-time plaintiff will be more fearful of the worst-case scenario. The problem may be especially relevant in personal injury lawsuit litigation, where the spread of possible damages is large and the difference between the ability of the parties to manage litigation risk is vast.[32]

27 See e.g., Beisner, Miller and Rubin (2009) *supra* note 16, 2–3.
28 See Garber (2010) *supra* note 22, 30.
29 See ibid. 32.
30 See JD Glater, 'Investing in Lawsuits, for a Share of the Awards' *The New York Times* (New York, 3 June 2009) B1.
31 See JT Molot, 'A Market Approach to Litigation Accuracy' (2009) Geo. Univ. L. Ctr.
32 See JT Molot, 'Litigation Finance: A Market Solution to a Procedural Problem' (2010) 99 *Geo. L.J.* 85.

Thus, settlements may more often reflect bargaining power than actual legal merit. Third-party financing levels the playing field between plaintiffs and defendants and thus leads to more accurate settlements.[33] However, it is uncertain to what extent the availability of TPF presently has an effect on the accuracy of settlement amounts. For example, investment funds only invest in large commercial claims, and refuse smaller claims or personal injury claims held by individuals. Regarding consumer loans, high interest rates and the fast accumulation of interest may take away much of the value of this type of TPF.[34]

3.3 The timing of settlements

With TPF, a defendant may be more willing to settle a claim at an earlier stage.[35] There are a number of reasons for this. First, the defendant's bargaining power may decrease because a defendant who knows that the plaintiff's claim is financed may become conscious that certain threats made during the negotiations are not credible any longer. Also, the fact that a TPF supplier has agreed to fund a case can be seen by the defendant as a signal that the case is of relatively high quality. An empirical study by Fenn and Rickman has shown that meritorious cases settle earlier. They found that the more the defendant thinks he is liable, the shorter the settlement delays.[36] They also established that cases, in which insurers believe that their policyholder is fully responsible, lead to faster settlements.[37] Finally, they discovered that cases in which a hospital at first believes it is not liable are settled much slower compared to cases where the hospital originally believes it is liable.[38] Furthermore, when new information arrives that weakens a hospital's case, the settlement process is accelerated. That signal may be especially important for investments in commercial claims because of the scrupulous due diligence processes.[39] TPF would, however, cease to signal case quality if investing in nuisance suits were to become an attractive business model for TPF companies. In the context of consumer legal funding, TPF may decrease the incentive of a plaintiff to settle early, because the loans allow plaintiffs to pay their bills in the interim. Also, TPF may sometimes cause a plaintiff to be unwilling to settle late in the life of the claim, because the amount owed to the funder can ultimately exceed what the defendant is willing to offer as a settlement amount. The plaintiff may then favour going to trial, hoping that the court will grant an award that is larger than the one owed to the funder. During the time between the start and the later stages of the settlement process, consumer legal funding may lead to faster settlements due to the fast rate at which a plaintiff's debt to the funder grows. Likewise, a law firm paying interest on a loan may want to settle relatively early so it can repay its debt from the proceeds.

33 Ibid.

34 Under these loans, consumers pay interest, not a part of the judgment they receive in the case of a plaintiff victory.

35 See Garber (2010) *supra* note 22, 32–34.

36 P Fenn and N Rickman, 'Delay and Settlement in Litigation' (1999) 109 *Econ. J.* 487.

37 P Fenn and N Rickman, 'Asymmetric Information and the Settlement of Insurance Claims' (2001) 68 *J. Risk & Ins.* 627.

38 P Fenn and N Rickman, 'Legal Liability and the Timing of Settlement in Medical Malpractice' (2005) American Law & Economic Association Annual Meetings, Paper No. 44 <http://law.bepress.com/cgi/viewcontent.cgi?article=1543&context=alea>.

39 See Garber (2010) *supra* note 22, 26.

3.4 *The costs of (individual) disputes*

One important effect of TPF is the relaxing of budget constraints.[40] At first sight, one may think that TPF will always increase the costs of individual disputes because cash-constrained plaintiffs tend to invest less in out-of-pocket expenses (e.g., expert consultants and witnesses). However, when one uses rent seeking theory to examine how the relaxing of budget constraints influences the litigation expenditure of the parties, this result becomes less obvious.[41] In contrast to what intuition may suggest, relaxing budget constraints does not always increase litigation expenditure. Due to strategic interaction between the parties, expenditure under TPF may either decrease or increase. Interestingly, expenditure is more likely to decrease for meritorious suits and more likely to increase for relatively weak cases. The reasoning behind this result is the following. For weak claims, when the plaintiff spends more due to vanishing budget constraints, the case becomes closer,[42] and it becomes more valuable for the defendant to spend additional resources as well. For relatively strong claims, when the plaintiff spends more, the case becomes even less close[43] and it becomes less worthwhile for the defendant to spend more.

Furthermore, the extent to which TPF will influence the costs of individual disputes depends on whether funders are able to influence how cases are pursued. Unfortunately, much is unknown here.[44] With respect to investments in commercial litigation, the influence on expenditure depends to a considerable extent on the share of the recovery and the costs for the funder.

4. A comparison with legal expenses insurance

As we have already mentioned in the introduction, TPF is one technique of funding litigation and removing risk from risk-averse litigants, especially plaintiffs. However, alternatives exist. One prominent example is legal expenses insurance (LEI). The question arises of whether TPF may have some advantages compared to LEI. We will try to analyse this question by focusing on the same issues analysed before, namely how LEI affects the volume of litigation (4.1), the quality of litigation and settlements (4.2), the timing of settlements (4.3) and the costs of individual disputes (4.4).

40 See, e.g., DS Abrams and DL Chen, 'A Market for Justice: A First Empirical Look at Third Party Litigation Funding' (2013) 15 *U. Pa. J. Bus. L.* 1,075.

41 Rent seeking models are increasingly used to study the behaviour of litigants during trial. See, e.g., A Katz, 'Judicial Decision-making and Litigation Expenditure' (1988) 8 *International Review of Law and Economics* 127–143; A Farmer and P Pecorino, 'Legal Expenditures as a Rent-seeking Game' (1999) 100 *Public Choice* 271–288; J Hirshleifer and E Osborne, 'Truth, Effort and the Legal Battle' (2001) 108 *Public Choice* 169–195; J De Mot, 'Comparative versus Contributory Negligence: A Comparison of the Litigation Expenditures' (2013) 33 *International Review of Law and Economics* 54–61; F Parisi and B Luppi, 'Litigation as Rent-seeking' in RD Congleton and AL Hillman (eds), *A Companion to Rent Seeking: Theory and Practice* (Cheltenham: Edward Elgar 2015); J De Mot, B Luppi and F Parisi, 'Are Sequential Trials Really Better than Unitary Trials?' (Second International Meeting in Law and Economics, Paris, 11–12 June 2015); J De Mot and TJ Miceli, 'Comparing All-or-Nothing and Proportionate Damages: A Rent Seeking Approach' (2015) 11(1) *Review of Law & Economics* 1–17. These models add reality to the economic theory of litigation. They have delivered several theoretical results that have been empirically confirmed.

42 The total arguments in favour of the plaintiff are moving closer to the threshold of the standard of proof.

43 The total arguments in favour of the plaintiff are moving further away from the threshold of the standard of proof (in the direction favourable for the plaintiff).

44 See Garber (2010) *supra* note 22, 35.

4.1 The volume of litigation

Legal expenses insurance can increase the amount of litigation for several reasons. To start with, an insured person may face more justiciable incidents due to moral hazard. However, empirical research has shown that the effect of moral hazard in this context is relatively small.[45] Second, given a justiciable incident, LEI makes it easier to undertake legal action. A victim may now be willing to pursue a claim with negative expected value because the insurer pays (a part of) the cost.[46] Note, however, that not all costs are externalized to the insurer (e.g. psychological costs and the opportunity cost of time). Third, LEI allows risk-averse plaintiffs to file suits they would otherwise not have filed, as they now bear only part of the litigation cost risk. Fourth, plaintiffs with insufficient funds may now bring a suit. Dutch empirical research has examined whether LEI holders react differently from non-insured individuals when they encounter a justiciable problem.[47] Among the uninsured individuals who faced a justiciable problem, 7.5 per cent did nothing, 47.4 per cent sought to resolve the problem without help and 45.1 per cent sought advice from one or more experts or organizations. In comparison, insureds seek more advice and are less prone to resolve the problem without help: 4.8 per cent did nothing, 37.7 per cent sought to resolve the problem without help and 57.5 per cent sought advice from one or more experts or organizations. The difference between holders and non-holders of LEI particularly holds for the higher income classes. Lastly, an insured plaintiff may act tougher during settlement negotiations because he does not bear all of the costs of a trial. This decreases the settlement surplus and consequently increases the frequency of trial. However, one should not forget the active role that legal expenses insurers play in the settlement stage. In countries in which lawyers enjoy monopoly rights for representation in court but not for out-of-court work (e.g. Belgium), an insurer can reserve the right to take all necessary steps to settle the case.[48] He may have a large incentive to settle the case given that he bears most or all of the costs. This finds some support in the fact that the settlement frequency of claims covered by legal expenses insurance – 80 per cent – is seemingly higher than the settlement frequency of claims not covered by LEI.[49] Note that this could also be the result of selection effects. For example, according to the relative optimism model of litigation, the settlement rate is larger for smaller claims.[50] And empirical research shows that LEI stimulates the settlement of some of these smaller claims.[51] In contrast, in countries like Germany, where lawyers enjoy monopoly rights both for representation in court and for out-of-court work, the insurer's role in the settlement stage may be more restricted. German empirical research shows that the incidence of trial for claims covered by LEI is a bit larger than for

45 See e.g. E Blankenburg and J Fiedler, *Die Rechtsschutzversicherung und der steigende Geschaftsanfall der Gerichte* (Legal Insurance and the Growing Demands on the Courts) (Tübingen: Mohr, 1981); W Jagodzinski, T Raiser and J Riehl, *Rechtsschutzversicherung und Rechtsverfolgung* (Legal Insurance and the Recourse to the Court) (Köln: Bundesanzeiger 1994).

46 See e.g., R Kirstein, 'Risk Neutrality and Strategic Insurance' (2000) 25 *The Geneva Papers on Risk & Ins.* 260.

47 See BCJ van Velthoven and CM Klein Haarhuis, 'Legal Aid and Legal Expenses Insurance, Complements or Substitutes? The Case of the Netherlands' (2011) 8(3) *Journal of Empirical Legal Studies* 600–601.

48 See P Colle, *Handboek Bijzonder Gereglementeerde Verzekeringscontracten* (Antwerp: Intersentia 2005) 304.

49 Ibid.

50 See e.g., S Shavell, 'Suit, Settlement, and Trial: A Theoretical Analysis under Alternative Methods for the Allocation of Legal Costs' (1982) 11 *J. Legal Stud.* 59.

51 See V Prais, 'Legal Expenses Insurance' in AAS Zuckerman and R Cranston (eds), *Reform of Civil Procedure: Essays on 'Access to Justice'* (Alderley: Clarendon Press 1995) 439.

claims not covered by LEI.[52] Dutch research points out that court proceedings were initiated in 4 per cent of problems for uninsured individuals compared to 6.5 per cent of problems for insured individuals.[53] The difference is larger for higher income classes. As with third-party financing, the presence of insurance may increase deterrence, and this in turn can have a mitigating effect on the amount of litigation. Consequently, one should always be cautious in interpreting these numbers: it is not necessarily socially undesirable if the volume of cases increases. It may be undesirable if LEI stimulates claims with a so-called nuisance value, but because access to justice is costly without insurance, too few claims may be filed, leading to under-deterrence.

4.2 The quality of litigation and the quality of settlements

It is often claimed that LEI causes a flood of cases without merit.[54] As the argument goes, a plaintiff may be interested in filing a claim with virtually no chance of victory, solely because someone else bears the costs. However, it is doubtful that a legal expenses insurer will provide coverage for obviously weak claims. Insurers have a rather strong incentive to cautiously screen cases before providing coverage, given that they bear all or most of the costs of a trial but obtain no direct monetary benefits.[55] In practice, legal expenses insurers reject weak cases in several ways. For example, LEI policies often include a deductible.[56] Evidently, a deductible will not only weed out some weak cases, but will also inhibit some strong cases with small stakes. In addition, LEI policies often incorporate a merits test. And even if such a clause has not been included in the contract, doctrines of contract law may give insurers the right to refuse coverage for unreasonable claims, for futile claims, and for claims that lack evidence.[57] A study from Germany shows that insured litigants win their cases a little more often (3 per cent) than uninsured litigants who paid their attorneys a fixed fee at every stage of the litigation process.[58] While this could be a reflection of more careful case screening, this can also be explained by a selection effect (LEI encourages the filing of some strong claims with stakes that are relatively small but still outweigh the deductible).

4.3 The timing of settlements

Fenn et al. (2005) find evidence that claims funded by legal expenses insurance in England and Wales settle sooner than claims funded by other means.[59] The reasoning behind this is straightforward. The insurer has an incentive to settle quickly because he internalizes all or

52 See ibid.

53 See Van Velthoven and Klein Haarhuis (2011) *supra* note 47.

54 See e.g., M Kilian, 'Alternatives to Public Provision: The Rule of Legal Expenses Insurance in Broadening Access to Justice: The German Experience' (2003) 30 *J.L. & Soc'y* 45.

55 One can expect legal expense insurers to have a stronger incentive to screen cases than hourly fee lawyers or contingency fee lawyers.

56 Kilian (2003) *supra* note 54, 46.

57 For example, the contractually implied obligation of good faith.

58 See Prais (1995) *supra* note 51, 439.

59 P Fenn, A Gray, N Rickman and Y Mansur, *The Funding of Personal Injury Litigation: Comparisons over Time and across Jurisdictions* (Report to the Department for Constitutional Affairs, 2006) <www.dca.gov.uk/research/2006/02_2006.pdf>.

a big part of the cost of the settlement. This effect will be most pronounced if the insurer is in charge of the settlement negotiations.[60] [61] Even if an independent lawyer is in charge of the negotiations, the case may still be settled faster than cases that are not funded through insurance, because the insurer is most likely in a better position to control lawyer opportunism. A lawyer monitored by an insurer will be able to shirk less and will, on average, settle cases sooner.

4.4 The costs of (individual) disputes

LEI can clearly lead to an increase in the costs of individual disputes. While an uninsured plaintiff has to pay for each additional hour his lawyer spends on the case, an insured plaintiff can use the staff of the insurer, or, if necessary, a lawyer at no cost or a fraction of the true cost. Dutch empirical research corroborates this, at least for the high-income class.[62] Once insured, the intensity of the contacts with legal advisors is significantly higher for this income class (2.09 contacts versus 1.73 contacts).[63] The impact of LEI is mainly by substitution for lower income classes.[64] The assistance of the staff of the insurer comes, to a large extent, in place of the subsidized lawyer.[65] Of course, other factors could have influenced the use of legal advisers.[66] After controlling for other relevant factors like the sort of problem, the complexity of the problem and expected revenue, multivariate analysis confirms these findings.[67] If a person actively responds to a justiciable problem, being insured heightens the chance that a person will ask for more legal advice.[68] Income is an important element when people are uninsured: the number of contacts with legal advisers varies in relation to income.[69] When individuals are insured, the effect of income is not significant.[70]

5. A comparison with contingency fees

Not only TPF and LEI exist as techniques of funding litigation and removing risk from risk-averse litigants, but also fee arrangements between clients and lawyers can, to a certain extent, play this role. The relationship between a client and his lawyer can be analysed as a principal–agent relationship. The lawyer may have different goals than the client, and the latter is not able to fully monitor and evaluate the behaviour of the former. This may lead

60 In Belgium, for example, the monopoly rights of lawyers only encompass representation in court. In the context of LEI, legal services are often provided by in-house personnel.
61 Of course, an important limitation is that policyholders have the right to free choice of counsel from the moment they are involved in judicial or administrative proceedings. See art 4(1)(a) Directive 87/344/EEC on the Coordination of Laws, Regulations and Administrative Provisions relating to Legal Expenses Insurance, official reporter *OJ* 1987 L185/77, available at <http://eurlex.europa.eu/LexUriServ/LexUriServ.do?uri=CELEX:31987L0344:en:NOT>.
62 See Van Velthoven and Klein Haarhuis (2011) *supra* note 47, 597.
63 Ibid.
64 Ibid.
65 Ibid.
66 Ibid. 598.
67 Ibid.
68 Ibid.
69 Ibid.
70 Ibid.

to moral hazard of the lawyer (he does not exert enough effort) and/or to adverse selection (the client is not able to distinguish between high- and low-quality lawyers).[71] In agency-relationships the contract between principal and agent may be used to (try to) better align the interests of both parties.[72] The most studied aspect in this respect is the payment scheme of the lawyer.

Especially contingency fees ('CF') are an interesting topic in this respect. With CF, we mean a situation where if the case is lost, the lawyer receives no compensation ('no cure, no pay'). If the case is won, the fee is often a percentage of the obtained award ('*quota pars litis*'). In this section we will analyse CF from an economic perspective, focusing on the issues that are by now familiar to the reader. However, the structure of this section differs a little from the structure of Sections 3 and 4. This is caused by the fact that the economic insights regarding CF are made most clear when comparing CF to hourly fees ('HF'). Such a comparison warrants a slightly different structure than in the previous sections. We investigate how CF affects the volume and quality of claims (5.1), the settlement process (5.2) and the costs of individual disputes (5.3).

5.1 The volume and quality of claims

CF are a way to finance the lawyer's costs of bringing a claim, because of the 'no cure no pay' aspect. The lawyer in a sense pre-finances the case. Therefore, the plaintiff can also bring a suit in cases where the costs of HF would have prohibited him from so doing. In addition, CF shifts the financial risk regarding the attorney costs from the client to the lawyer. Lawyers can diversify their portfolio and are repeat players, so that they are likely to be less risk averse than their clients. CF therefore allows a form of risk allocation that is not possible under HF, enabling risk-averse plaintiffs to also bring a claim.[73]

These two effects may increase the volume of litigation, but only if there is over-capacity in the market for legal services. Without such over-capacity, a shift from HF to CF could even reduce the volume of litigation, if lawyers spend more time on a case under CF than under HF.[74] The choice between HF and CF is likely indeed to affect the time a lawyer spends on a case. Under HF, the lawyer is remunerated for every hour he spends on the

71 The informational advantage of the lawyer over the client concerning the legal issues at stake may result in a situation where the lawyer does not always act in the best interest of the client, e.g. by providing more legal services than are actually required. See BL Hay, 'Contingent Fees and Agency Costs' (1996) 25(2) *The Journal of Legal Studies* 504ff; BL Hay, 'Contingent Fees, Principal-Agent Problems, and the Settlement of Litigation' (1997) 23 *William Mitchell Law Review* 44ff; DA DeMott, 'The Lawyer as Agent' (1998) 67(2) *Fordham Law Review* 301–326. L Sacconi, '"The Case against Lawyers" Contingent Fees and the Misapplication of Principal-agent Models' (2011) 32 *European Journal of Law and Economics* 263–292 on the other hand argues that agency theory is not well equipped to study the lawyer–client relationship dues to bounded rationality and incomplete contracts.

72 KM Eisenhardt, 'Agency Theory: An Assessment and Review' (1989) 14 *The Academy of Management Review* 61.

73 RA Posner, *Economic Analysis of Law* (6th ed, New York: Aspen Publishers 2003) 584; HSE Gravelle, 'Conditional Fees in Britain' in P Newman (ed.), *The New Palgrave Dictionary of Economics and the Law* (Palgrave Macmillan 1998) 383. This argument is less important in situations where the client is a well-informed repeat player himself.

74 LT Visscher and T Schepens, 'A Law and Economics Approach to Cost Shifting, Fee Arrangements and Legal Expense Insurance' in ML Tuil and LT Visscher (eds), *New Trends in Financing Civil Litigation in Europe – A Legal, Empirical and Economic Analysis* (Cheltenham: Edward Elgar 2010) 18.

case, so that he may be induced to spend more time than necessary. Under CF it is not attractive for the lawyer to spend more time on the case than necessary, because this does not yield additional income. On the contrary, under CF the lawyer may rather spend *too little* time on the case, because he compares the full costs of spending an additional hour with only a percentage of the expected benefits of this time investment. Empirical research suggests that CF lawyers spend more time on cases with a high value and less time on cases with a low value than HF lawyers.[75]

The agreed CF percentage can also impact the volume of litigation, because it affects the expected award of the plaintiff after covering the attorney costs. Litigation entails more costs than only the lawyer's remuneration and in as far as those costs are not covered by the CF arrangement, a striking difference as compared to TPF and LEI may occur.[76] In theory, a higher CF percentage may lead to a lower volume of litigation because the expected benefits of litigation for the plaintiff decrease. On the other hand, if the higher percentage induces the lawyer to spend more effort on the case, and if this increases the probability of prevailing, the expected benefit can increase. The overall effect cannot be predicted theoretically.

CF and HF give different incentives to lawyers to act as gatekeeper and this may affect both the volume of litigation and the quality of the claims. A client with full information about the law and about the value of the legal services provided by a lawyer could hire an HF lawyer and instruct him only to invest additional time in the case if the marginal benefits (which the fully informed client could perfectly assess) exceed the hourly fee of the lawyer.[77] In reality, clients may not be fully informed and this information asymmetry may affect the behaviour of the lawyer. As mentioned above, an HF lawyer, whose remuneration does not depend on the outcome of the case, may spend more time on a case than a fully informed client would want him to. The HF lawyer may even advise to litigate, also if the expected value of the case would be lower than the costs of legal aid.[78] This problem is caused by the fact that the HF lawyer is rewarded for the number of hours spent on the case, irrespective of whether these hours yield higher benefits than costs to the client.

CF provide better incentives to the lawyer because he only receives a reward if the case is won. He will therefore be incentivized to provide better legal advice to his

75 This can be explained by the *quota pars litis* characteristic of contingency fees: whether or not it is worthwhile to spend more time on a case depends on the marginal benefits of this additional time investment. For cases with a higher value, the agreed percentage yields more benefits than for cases with a lower value, inducing lawyers to spend more time on cases with a higher value. After all, in low-value cases, the costs of an additional hour will relatively soon outweigh the expected benefits to the lawyer, but investing an additional hour in a high-value claim is worthwhile much longer. See HM Kritzer, WLF Felstiner, A Sarat and DM Trubek, 'The Impact of Fee Arrangement on Lawyer Effort' (1985) 19 *Law & Society Review* 266–267. Also see HM Kritzer, 'Lawyer Fees and Lawyer Behaviour in Litigation: What Does the Empirical Literature Really Say?' (2002) 86 *Texas Law Review* 1,968–1,969.

76 Of course it depends upon the specifics of the legal system to what extent this is the case. In legal systems where TPF and LEI would also cover costs other than the lawyer's remuneration (such as court fees and costs for expert witnesses), those costs would then be covered under the financing arrangement while that is usually not the case under CF.

77 AM Polinsky and DL Rubinfeld, 'Aligning the Interests of Lawyers and Clients' (2003) 5 *American Law and Economics Review* 166.

78 See e.g. E Johnson Jr., 'A Theoretical Appraisal of Litigation Investment Decisions' (1980) 15 *Law & Society Review* 576ff; PM Danzon, 'Contingent Fees for Personal Injury Litigation' (1983) 14 *The Bell Journal of Economics* 215; JD Dana and KE Spier, 'Expertise and Contingent Fees: The Role of Asymmetric Information in Attorney Compensation' (1993) 9 *The Journal of Law, Economics, & Organization* 349, 352.

client regarding whether or not to start a case. Accepting or refusing a case on a CF basis therefore provides a signal to the client regarding the quality of the case, which is lacking under HF. The CF lawyer acts as a gatekeeper, because he will refuse cases with a too low probability of success. This screening effect may have a decreasing impact on the volume of litigation, because low-quality claims are refused.

This characteristic of CF obviously also affects the quality of the claims. Relatively weak cases will not be litigated, because the expected reward for the lawyer is too low. The fact that the lawyer is a repeat player with better information than the client implies that the lawyer is better able to screen the cases on quality.[79] This would imply that the average quality of the cases that *are* brought increases. This hypothesis fundamentally differs from the often-expressed fear that CF would encourage meritless litigation due to the fact that the plaintiff does not bear a financial risk when bringing a claim.

Empirical research corroborates the gatekeeper-hypothesis. Based on a survey of more than 500 lawyers from Wisconsin, Kritzer concludes that CF lawyers indeed act as gatekeepers. Cases with a low success probability are not accepted, because the expected reward for the lawyer is too low. Lawyers try to create a portfolio that contains enough cases yielding enough profits to compensate for lost cases. However, besides the quality of the case, the possible outcome is also relevant in this respect. High-quality cases regarding a low amount are therefore also regularly refused.[80]

Helland and Tabarrok measure case quality by the probability that the plaintiff terminates his case rather than continuing until a settlement or a verdict has been reached. If CF result in better screening, fewer cases should be terminated because the relatively weak cases would not have been brought in the first place. The authors compare the difference in the probability of terminating certain types of cases in States where they are tried on a CF basis with States where they are tried on an HF basis. They check their results by studying whether introducing restrictions on the use of CF in Florida in 1985 resulted in a discontinuity in the probability of terminating certain types of cases in American states.[81] They conclude that restricting the use of CF results in more terminated cases, which suggests that CF indeed result in better screening of cases.[82] This conclusion corroborates the earlier finding of Danzon and Lillard that limitations on CF result in a higher drop-out rate.[83]

79 KM Clermont and JD Currivan, 'Improving the Contingent Fee' (1978) 63 *Cornell Law Review* 571–572; Dana and Spier (1993) *supra* note 78, 349, 350. Also see TJ Miceli, 'Do Contingent Fees Promote Excessive Litigation?' (1994) 23 *The Journal of Legal Studies* 223 and A Shajnfeld, 'A Critical Survey of the Law, Ethics, and Economics of Attorney Contingent Fee Arrangements' (2010) 54 *New York Law School Law Review* 807.

80 Kritzer (1997) *supra* note 24, 26ff. Also see HM Kritzer, *Risks, Reputations, and Rewards: Contingency Fee Legal Practice in the United States* (Stanford: Stanford University Press 2004) 84–85.

81 E Helland and A Tabarrok, 'Contingency Fees, Settlement Delay, and Low-Quality Litigation: Empirical Evidence from Two Datasets' (2003) 19 *The Journal of Law, Economics, & Organization* 521–522.

82 Ibid. 529, 533. Shajnfeld (2010) *supra* note 79, 808, 809 is not convinced by these results, because the higher probability of terminating a case under HF can also be caused by a client running out of money during the adjudication process, so that he cannot afford the lawyer to spend more hours on it. Helland and Tabarrok reject this line of reasoning, because it would imply that the plaintiff, when deciding whether or not to start a claim, overlooked the fact that he would not have enough resources to be able to pay the lawyer long enough.

83 PM Danzon and LA Lillard, 'Settlement out of Court: The Disposition of Medical Malpractice Claims' (1983) 12 *The Journal of Legal Studies* 363.

5.2 Settlements

The choice between CH and HF may have a severe impact on settlements: whether they are reached in the first place, the time it takes to reach them and the quality thereof. On the one hand, CF lawyers may settle too quickly, because they then receive a percentage of the settlement award without much effort and without the additional costs of litigation (which the lawyer would have to bear).[84] This would imply a relatively short duration before the settlement is reached, but the quality of the settlement can be low. Another theoretical reason why CF may result in settlement quicker than HF is that an HF lawyer may advise the client not to accept a settlement offer (so that the lawyer can spend more hours on the case) while the settlement would have been beneficial to the client (due to the lower legal expenses).

On the other hand there are two possible reasons why under CF settlements could be reached less quickly and less often: (1) under the assumption that the plaintiff's CF lawyer would spend too little time on the case when it is tried (because he bears the full marginal costs of the additional time invested but only gets a percentage of the marginal benefits), the *defence* lawyer may rather litigate than settle; (2) the fact that the CF lawyer receives a percentage of the final award may induce him to reject a relatively low settlement offer, in order to try to reach a higher amount in subsequent negotiations. Such an initial rejection may be perceived by the other party as a signal that the true losses of the plaintiff justify the rejection, especially under CF, because otherwise the lawyer would have accepted the offer. Rickman labels this behaviour 'hard bargaining'.[85]

Thus theoretical literature does not yield unambiguous predictions regarding the impact of CF on settlements. Danzon and Lillard have empirically investigated the way in which about 6,000 American cases of medical malpractice have been resolved.[86] They analyse, among many others factors, the impact of restrictions on the use of CF (such as establishing a maximum percentage). They conclude that such restrictions result in more settlements and in lower settlement awards.[87]

Snyder and Hughes reach a similar conclusion in their empirical research regarding the influence of several legislative changes regarding the way in which medical malpractice claims are handled in Florida: restrictions on the use of CF results in more settlements.[88] Helland and Tabarrok investigate the impact of restrictions on CF on the time it takes to reach a settlement and they find that such restrictions result in a longer duration.[89] This, together with the results of Kritzer et al. and Danzon and Lillard, suggests that HF lawyers have more incentives to delay the settlement process,[90] but also that CF result in fewer settlements because the expected costs of the defendant decrease, and because the

84 See, e.g., H Gravelle and M Waterson, 'No Win, No Fee: Some Economics of Contingent Legal Fees' (1993) 103 *The Economic Journal* 1,215. The authors in their model can vary the extent in which the lawyer is driven by his own interests vis-à-vis the interests of the client. If a lawyer puts more emphasis on the client's interests than on his own interests (the authors label such a lawyer as 'relatively altruistic'), the effect that the lawyer settles too quickly does not appear. Also see Shajnfeld (2010) *supra* note 79, 792ff.

85 N Rickman, 'Contingent Fees and Litigation Settlement' (1999) 19 *International Review of Law and Economics* 306.

86 Danzon and Lillard (1983) *supra* note 78, 348.

87 Ibid. 363–366.

88 EA Snyder and JW Hughes, 'The English Rule for Allocating Legal Costs: Evidence Confronts Theory' (1990) 6 *The Journal of Law, Economics, & Organization* 366.

89 Helland and Tabarrok (2003) *supra* note 81, 536, 538.

90 Ibid. 540.

plaintiff's lawyer chooses 'hard bargaining'. Therefore, the line of reasoning that CF lawyers settle easily in order to receive a percentage of the award without much effort, has to be rejected. On the contrary, under CF there is a larger probability that a claim proceeds to trial than under HF. But *if* a settlement is reached under CF, it generally takes less time to reach it than under HF.

5.3 *The costs of disputes*

Above it was established that under CF there is a larger probability that a claim proceeds to trial than under HF. Given the fact that settlements are less costly than trials, this tendency may increase the costs of disputes. On the other hand, the duration of claims (during settlement but also during trial) is shorter under CF than under HF, because a CF lawyer does not gain by delaying the procedure while the HF lawyer does.[91] The better screening under CF in addition prevents low-quality claims from being tried, which also reduces the costs of disputes. It cannot be predicted theoretically which of the above-mentioned effects dominates.

However, because CF enables claims to be brought that could not be brought under HF, the volume of litigation is expected to increase, so that the costs of dispute rise. After all, such claims would not have been brought under HF and hence would not have resulted in litigation costs.

The ultimate empirical question, which brings us back to the economic *raison d'être* of CF, LEI and TPF, of course is whether the increased litigation costs are outweighed by the desirable effects of the behavioural incentives that result from the fact that the negative externality is now internalized. In that case, enough *potential* claims are avoided to make the increased litigation costs for those cases that are not avoided, worthwhile. The total effect then would be that ultimately fewer cases are tried because fewer violations occur.[92] This issue, however, lies beyond the scope of our contribution.

6. Concluding Remarks

In this chapter we aimed at providing an economic perspective on TPF. Our goal was to answer the question of why TPF emerges and what could be its economic function, especially in the light of alternative financing mechanisms such as legal expenses insurance (LEI) and contingency fees (CF). Of course, the goal of this chapter was not to dwell on the many different ways in which TPF can appear. We mainly looked at mechanisms whereby a third-party finances litigation on a 'no cure no pay' basis, whereby the remuneration for the funder will usually consist of a percentage of the proceeds of the case. However, one could well imagine (and also observe in practice) other forms of TPF, for example where a TPF funder provides a loan to a law firm. Also the institutions providing funds can differ. Theoretically, the law firms could also provide TPF (although in that case the difference

91 Not to mention the possibility that an HF lawyer bills more hours than he has actually spent on the case. See e.g. LG Lerman, 'Lying to Clients' (1990) 130 *University of Pennsylvania Law Review* 705, 706.

92 See TJ Miceli and K Segerson, 'Contingent Fees for Lawyers: The Impact on Litigation and Accident Prevention' (1991) 20 *Journal of Legal Studies* 381–399; AW Katz, 'Indemnity of Legal Fees' in B Boukaert and G De Geest (eds), *Encyclopedia of Law and Economics, Vol. 5, The Economics of Crime and Litigation* (Cheltenham: Edward Elgar 2000) 76.

with CF of course becomes very small). Instead of focusing on those different appearances of TPF, we have rather focused on the question of why it is that TPF has emerged. From an economic perspective we find a relatively straight-forward explanation in the fact that for several reasons, meritorious lawsuits are not brought. High risk aversion against costs may be a problem, but also the mere fact of lacking possibilities for pre-financing a claim. From an economic perspective, the fact that those meritorious claims are not brought is problematic, for the simple reason that tortfeasors causing externalities are not sufficiently confronted with the social costs of their activities. This is a market failure. To the extent that TPF can contribute to lowering the barriers to access to justice it can be considered as socially beneficial as it contributes to solving the market failure. Notwithstanding those beneficial aspects of TPF, we have noticed that there are quite a few legal systems that are opposed to TPF. In some legal systems TPF does not emerge (even though there are no legal objections); in others there is an outright prohibition. Although all systems where a third-party finances litigation could give rise to adverse selection (an undesirable increase in the volume of litigation where suits lacking merit would also be brought), moral hazard (as a result of which the plaintiff would no longer have adequate incentives for risk reduction during litigation) or free riding (whereby others who do not finance the claim could benefit as well), adequate remedies have been indicated in the literature and are also possible to implement in practice.

The remainder of our contribution focused on the comparative benefits of TPF, especially in the context of the alternatives CF and LEI. We have compared TPF, LEI and CF on the basis of their influence on the volume of litigation, timing, quality, settlements and total costs. As is often the case with these types of comparison, the devil is in the detail. Hence it is impossible to generally argue that one financing system would be preferred to the other as the type of influence of any specific mechanism is highly dependent on the type of cases and the particular design mechanism chosen. In fact, in all three mechanisms (TPF, LEI and CF) there is a third party that finances a claim and so that will exercise some gate-keeping function to ensure that only meritorious suits are brought. One important difference between on the one hand CF and on the other LEI and TPF is that CF only seems to cover the remuneration of the lawyer, whereas LEI and TPF could also cover other costs. If that indeed is the case, LEI and TPF are relatively attractive for the litigant and could therefore better contribute to a lowering of the barriers to access to justice.

Of course there are important differences as far as the influence of the particular funder on the course of the procedure and on the decision to settle are concerned. With CF that influence may be the largest since the funder is the lawyer himself who decides on the strategy during trial and also on the content and timing of the settlement. Both under LEI and CF, the funder (insurer or lawyer) will have considerable (but not perfect) incentives to optimize the litigation strategy in the interest of the client and also to avoid very long-lasting trials. Under LEI that would only increase the costs of the insurer (especially if the lawyer paid under LEI is compensated on the basis of an hourly fee). Also under CF, lawyers cannot benefit from investing more in a trial than would be reasonable. It is only under TPF that the question arises of to what extent funders have sufficient expertise and information in order to allow them to adequately monitor the procedure and hence the settlement process. If their intervention is limited to the *ex ante* financing and if no further monitoring takes place, TPF could create the danger of an over-long trial.

TPF, LEI and CF are all attractive mechanisms that can lower the barriers to access to justice and hence remedy the market failure caused by the fact that meritorious suits are not always brought. In that sense there is no particular reason to prefer one over the other.

The reason why these different types of financing mechanisms emerge often has to do with the fact that for one reason or another not all systems may be available. For example, as far as LEI is concerned, we have already indicated that in systems where LEI is voluntary, the number of persons concluding LEI is relatively low. The fact that LEI may create positive externalities could reduce the incentives to purchase LEI. With CF the problem is that many legal systems in Continental Europe have (in different forms) prohibitions on it. In those legal systems where CF is prohibited and individuals do not conclude a LEI before the event, TPF may often be the only financing remedy available to plaintiffs. If on the other hand LEI were to be widely used in a particular legal system and/or the system also allowed CF, the demand for TPF may be reduced or TPF would then focus on those cases where (for a variety of reasons) CF is not available.

From a law and economics perspective, the fact that many different financing mechanisms are available on the market only seems positive and beneficial. The competition between those different mechanisms can also allow an increase of quality and a diversified supply of financing mechanisms to litigants. As such there is little reason to argue in favour of any particular form of regulation, other than that the information on the specificities and contents of the various financing mechanisms is presented in a clear and transparent manner, allowing litigants an informed choice. On the contrary, much of the regulation that has intervened in this domain so far, for example, prohibiting particular kinds of TPF, LEI or CF in particular legal systems, can only be classified as inefficient. Those types of regulation often come into being in order to benefit particular interest groups but in fact only increase the barriers to access to justice rather than lowering them. Although this should undoubtedly still be subject to further research, at this stage we argue that regulation in this domain seems to have done more harm than anything else. A facilitative type of regulation stimulating the emergence of differing financing mechanisms in a competitive environment seems a better way to simulate access to justice and hence to remedy market failures.

Bibliography

Abramowicz M., 'On the Alienability of Legal Claims' (2005) 114(4) *Yale L.J.* 697.

Abrams D.S. and D.L. Chen, 'A Market for Justice: A First Empirical Look at Third Party Litigation Funding' (2013) 15(4) *U. Pa. J. Bus. L.* 1,075.

Akerlof G., 'The Market for "Lemons": Quality, Uncertainty and the Market Mechanism' (1970) 84 *Quarterly Journal of Economics* 488.

Beisner J., J. Miller and G. Rubin, U.S. Chamber Inst. for Legal Reform, Selling Lawsuits, Buying Trouble: Third-Party Litigation Funding in the United States (2009) 2–3.

Blankenburg E. and J. Fiedler, *Die Rechtsschutzversicherung und der steigende Geschaftsanfall der Gerichte* (Legal Insurance and the Growing Demands on the Courts) (Tübingen: Mohr 1981).

Chen D.L. and D.S. Abrams, 'A Market for Justice: The Effect of Third Party Litigation Funding on Legal Outcomes' (2011).

Clermont K.M. and J.D. Currivan, 'Improving the Contingent Fee' (1978) 63(4) *Cornell Law Review* 529.

Colle P., *Handboek Bijzonder Gereglementeerde Verzekeringscontracten* (Antwerp: Intersentia 2005).

Dana D. and M. Schanzenbach, 'How Would Third Party Financing Change the Face of American Tort Litigation? The Role of Agency Costs in the Attorney-Client Relationship' (Searle Public Policy Roundtable on Third Party Financing of Litigation, Northwestern University Law School, Chicago, Ill., 24–25 September 2009).

Dana J.D. and K.E. Spier, 'Expertise and Contingent Fees: The Role of Asymmetric Information in Attorney Compensation' (1993) 9(2) *The Journal of Law, Economics, & Organization* 349.

Danzon P.M., 'Contingent Fees for Personal Injury Litigation' (1983) 14(1) *The Bell Journal of Economics* 213.
—— and L.A. Lillard, 'Settlement out of Court: The Disposition of Medical Malpractice Claims' (1983) 12(2) *The Journal of Legal Studies* 345.
De Mot J., 'Comparative versus Contributory Negligence: A Comparison of the Litigation Expenditures' (2013) 33 *International Review of Law and Economics* 54.
—— and T.J. Miceli, 'Comparing All-or-Nothing and Proportionate Damages: A Rent Seeking Approach' (2015) 11(1) *Review of Law & Economics* 1.
—— B. Luppi and F. Parisi, 'Are Sequential Trials Really Better than Unitary Trials?' (Second International Meeting in Law and Economics, Paris, 11–12 June 2015).
DeMott D.A., 'The Lawyer as Agent' (1998) 67(2) *Fordham Law Review* 301.
Eisenhardt K.M., 'Agency Theory: An Assessment and Review' (1989) 14(1) *The Academy of Management Review* 57.
Farmer A. and P. Pecorino, 'Legal Expenditures as a Rent-seeking Game' (1999) 100 *Public Choice* 271.
Faure M., 'CADR and Settlement of Claims – A Few Economic Observations' in C. Hodges and A. Stadler (eds), *Resolving Mass Disputes, ADR and Settlement of Mass Claims* (Cheltenham: Edward Elgar 2013) 38.
—— F. Fernhout and N. Philipsen, 'No Cure, No Pay and Contingency Fees' in M. Tuil and L. Visscher (eds), *New Trends in Financing Civil Litigation in Europe – A Legal, Empirical and Economic Analysis* (Cheltenham: Edward Elgar 2010) 33.
—— and J. De Mot, 'Comparing Third-Party Financing of Litigation and Legal Expenses Insurance' (2012) 8(3) *Journal of Law, Economics and Policy* 743.
Fenn P. and N. Rickman, 'Delay and Settlement in Litigation' (1999) 109(457) *Econ. J.* 476.
—— 'Asymmetric Information and the Settlement of Insurance Claims' (2001) 68(4) *J. Risk & Ins.* 615.
—— 'Legal Liability and the Timing of Settlement in Medical Malpractice' (2005) American Law & Economic Association Annual Meetings, Paper No. 44 <http://law.bepress.com/cgi/viewcontent.cgi?article=1543&context=alea>.
—— A. Gray, N. Rickman and Y. Mansur, *The Funding of Personal Injury Litigation: Comparisons over Time and across Jurisdictions* (Report to the Department for Constitutional Affairs, 2006) <www.dca.gov.uk/research/2006/02_2006.pdf>.
Garber S., *Alternative Litigation Financing in the United States: Issues, Knowns and Unknowns* (Santa Monica CA: Rand Corporation 2010).
Glater J.D., 'Investing in Lawsuits, for a Share of the Awards' *The New York Times* (New York, 3 June 2009).
Gravelle H.S.E., 'Conditional Fees in Britain' in P. Newman (ed.), *The New Palgrave Dictionary of Economics and the Law* (Basingstoke: Palgrave Macmillan 1998).
Gravelle H. and M. Waterson, 'No Win, No Fee: Some Economics of Contingent Legal Fees' (1993) 103(420) *The Economic Journal* 1,205.
Hay B.L., 'Contingent Fees and Agency Costs' (1996) 25(2) *The Journal of Legal Studies* 503.
—— 'Contingent Fees, Principal-Agent Problems, and the Settlement of Litigation' (1997) 23(1) *William Mitchell Law Review* 43.
Helland E. and A. Tabarrok, 'Contingency Fees, Settlement Delay, and Low-Quality Litigation: Empirical Evidence from Two Datasets' (2003) 19(2) *The Journal of Law, Economics, & Organization* 517.
Hensler D.R., 'Financing Civil Litigation: The US Perspective' in M. Tuil and L. Visscher (eds), *New Trends in Financing Civil Litigation in Europe – A Legal, Empirical and Economic Analysis* (Cheltenham: Edward Elgar 2010) 149.
Hirshleifer J. and E. Osborne, 'Truth, Effort and the Legal Battle' (2001) 108 *Public Choice* 169.
Jagodzinski W., T. Raiser and J. Riehl, *Rechtsschutzversicherung und Rechtsverfolgung* (Legal Insurance and the Recourse to the Court) (Köln: Bundesanzeiger 1994).
Johnson E. Jr., 'A Theoretical Appraisal of Litigation Investment Decisions' (1980) 15(3/4) *Law & Society Review* 567.

Katz A., 'Judicial Decision-making and Litigation Expenditure' (1988) 8 *International Review of Law and Economics* 127.

—— 'Indemnity of Legal Fees' in B. Boukaert and G. De Geest (eds), *Encyclopedia of Law and Economics, Vol. 5, The Economics of Crime and Litigation* (Cheltenham: Edward Elgar 2000) 63–94.

Kilian M., 'Alternatives to Public Provision: The Rule of Legal Expenses Insurance in Broadening Access to Justice: The German Experience' (2003) 30 *J.L. & Soc'y* 45.

Kirstein R., 'Risk Neutrality and Strategic Insurance' (2000) 25(2) *The Geneva Papers on Risk & Ins.* 251.

Kritzer H.M., 'Contingency Fee Lawyers as Gatekeepers in the Civil Justice System' (1997) 81(1) *Judicature* 22.

—— 'Lawyer Fees and Lawyer Behaviour in Litigation: What Does the Empirical Literature Really Say?' (2002) 86 *Texas Law Review* 1943.

—— *Risks, Reputations, and Rewards: Contingency Fee Legal Practice in the United States* (Stanford: Stanford University Press 2004).

—— W.L.F. Felstiner, A. Sarat and D.M. Trubek, 'The Impact of Fee Arrangement on Lawyer Effort' (1985) 19(2) *Law & Society Review* 251.

Lerman L.G., 'Lying to Clients' (1990) 130 *University of Pennsylvania Law Review* 659.

Mayers D. and C.W. Smith, 'On the Corporate Demand for Insurance' (1982) 55(2) *Journal of Business* 281.

Miceli T.J., 'Do Contingent Fees Promote Excessive Litigation?' (1994) 23(1) *The Journal of Legal Studies* 211.

—— and K. Segerson, 'Contingent Fees for Lawyers: The Impact on Litigation and Accident Prevention' (1991) 20 *Journal of Legal Studies* 381.

Molot J.T., 'A Market Approach to Litigation Accuracy' (2009) Geo. Univ. L. Ctr.

—— *'Litigation Finance: A Market Solution to a Procedural Problem'* (2010) 99(1) *Geo. L.J.* 65.

Parisi F. and B. Luppi, 'Litigation as Rent-seeking' in R.D. Congleton and A.L. Hillman (eds), *Companion to the Political Economy of Rent Seeking* (Cheltenham: Edward Elgar 2015) 293–310.

Polinsky A.M. and D.L. Rubinfeld, 'Aligning the Interests of Lawyers and Clients' (2003) 5(1) *American Law and Economics Review* 165.

Posner R.A., *Economic Analysis of Law* (6th ed, New York: Aspen Publishers 2003).

Prais V., 'Legal Expenses Insurance' in A.A.S. Zuckerman and R. Cranston (eds), *Reform of Civil Procedure: Essays on 'Access to Justice'* (Alderley: Clarendon Press 1995) 433.

Rickman N., 'Contingent Fees and Litigation Settlement' (1999) 19(3) *International Review of Law and Economics* 295.

Rubin P.H., 'Third-Party Financing of Litigation' (2011) 38(4) *Northern Kentucky Law Review* 673.

Sacconi L., '"The Case against Lawyers" Contingent Fees and the Misapplication of Principal-agent Models' (2011) 32 *European Journal of Law and Economics* 263.

Schäfer H.B., 'The Bundling of Similar Interests in Litigation. The Incentives for Class Actions and Legal Actions Taken by Associations' (2000) 9(3) *European Journal of Law and Economics* 183.

Shajnfeld A., 'A Critical Survey of the Law, Ethics, and Economics of Attorney Contingent Fee Arrangements' (2010) 54 *New York Law School Law Review* 773.

Shavell S., 'On Moral Hazard and Insurance' (1979) 93 *Quarterly Journal of Economics* 541.

—— 'Suit, Settlement, and Trial: A Theoretical Analysis under Alternative Methods for the Allocation of Legal Costs' (1982) 11(1) *J. Legal Stud.* 55.

Snyder E.A. and J.W. Hughes, 'The English Rule for Allocating Legal Costs: Evidence Confronts Theory' (1990) 6(2) *The Journal of Law, Economics, & Organization* 345.

Stadler A., 'Group Actions as a Remedy to Enforce Consumer Interest' in F Cafaggi and HW Micklitz (eds), *New Frontiers of Consumer Protection – The Interplay between Private and Public Enforcement* (Antwerp: Intersentia 2009) 305.

Tuil M. and L. Visscher (eds), *New Trends in Financing Civil Litigation in Europe – A Legal, Empirical and Economic Analysis* (Cheltenham: Edward Elgar 2010).

Van Velthoven B.C.J. and C.M. Klein Haarhuis, 'Legal Aid and Legal Expenses Insurance, Complements or Substitutes? The Case of the Netherlands' (2011) 8(3) *Journal of Empirical Legal Studies* 587.

Viscusi W.K., 'The Dimensions of the Product Liability Crisis' (1991) 20(1) *Journal of Legal Studies* 147.

Visscher L.T. and T. Schepens, 'A Law and Economics Approach to Cost Shifting, Fee Arrangements and Legal Expense Insurance' in M.L. Tuil and L.T. Visscher (eds), *New Trends in Financing Civil Litigation in Europe – A Legal, Empirical and Economic Analysis* (Cheltenham: Edward Elgar 2010) 7.

Weber F. and M. Faure, 'The Interplay between Public and Private Enforcement in European Private Law: Law and Economics Perspective' (2015) 4 *European Review of Private Law* 525.

4 'Playing the man not the ball'

John Peysner[*]

1. The question: Apples or oranges?

In the spring of 2015 the author received out of the blue a round-robin email from an organisation called Justice Not Profit inviting me (by name) alongside other 'leading scholars' to sign a letter that it was proposed would be sent to a national newspaper. The main points of the letter were:

1. Concern over introduction of class actions on the US model.
2. Coupling of class actions with 'unregulated and predatory third-party litigation funding'.
3. These developments could increase 'meritless lawsuits' that in turn could negatively affect the economy.
4. UK litigation costs have risen at an alarming rate.
5. To deal with these issues only opt-in class actions should be allowed. Government licensing should be imposed on third-party litigation funders and disclosure rules should be imposed on them.

The overall objective was to 'prevent financial speculators from manipulating the civil justice system for profit'.[1]

In due course the letter was signed by 13 academics (although not by the author). With due respect to some distinguished colleagues, who in their reported comments make some important contributions to this debate, none of the scholars are mainstream commentators on the issue of the funding of litigation and its somewhat fraught relationship with access to justice.

This lobbying by a US group is an unusual intervention in the development of funding in England and Wales[2] and invites further study. Three main questions will be addressed in

* The research on which this chapter is based was sponsored by the Association of Litigation Funders. All opinions expressed are those of the author only

1 For full texts of the letter and covering letter see 'Legal experts warn Michael Gove about "U.S.-style abuses" threatening the English civil justice system' (<www.justicenotprofit.org>).

2 It is not the first intervention. J Ames, 'Litigation Financing Needs Crackdown' *The Times* (London, 11 December 2011) 66, reports that officials from The Institute for Legal Reform were in England in December 2011 to press the Justice Minister and the Lord Chancellor to reject the liberalisation of commercial funding, especially in multi-party litigation. However, the draft letters moved beyond internal lobbying to a public campaign. This campaign is referred to in positive terms by Lord Thomas in the House of Lord Committee stage on the Legal Aid, Sentencing and Punishment of Offenders Bill (1 February 2012) in moving an amendment to require government regulation of third-party funding.

this chapter: What is the background and position of Justice Not Profit? Are they comparing US oranges with English apples? Is there a problem in England?

2. Justice Not Profit

The Justice Not Profit organisation is part of the US Chamber Institute for Legal Reform, a not-for-profit public advocacy organisation affiliated with the US Chamber of Commerce. In effect it is part of an international advocacy arm of US-based multi-national companies and the Institute operates internationally. The US Chamber of Commerce is the world's largest business organisation representing the interests of more than three million businesses of all sizes, sectors, and regions. Its lobbying addresses government and legislators.[3] Its lobbying expenditure in 2013 in the USA was $74 million (twice as much as the next biggest).

The Institute for Legal Reform's interest in the area of third-party litigation funding and its relation to class actions is a long-term one. In 2009 it published 'Selling Lawsuits, Buying Trouble: Third-Party Litigation Funding in the United States'.[4] The paper concluded that third-party funding (TPF) by increasing the money available to litigate would increase the volume of litigation and that this would increase the number of frivolous claims. It called for TPF to be banned generally or at least in class actions.[5]

2.1 International work

While the Chamber is US-based, its international arm is powerful, reflecting the importance of international trade to the US economy. In 2015[6] world trade in goods and services reached $23,434 billion. The USA's share of this was 22.4 per cent,[7] reflecting a growth in international economic engagement since World War II that is now only matched by China.

While the Chamber states that it has three million members from 'mum and pop stores' to huge corporations, it would not be unreasonable to assume that its international agenda is led by those US companies now operating on a global scale.[8] The ICBC Bank in China is the richest company in the world,[9] according to *Forbes Magazine*'s list of the world's 100 biggest public companies as of May 2013. Coming in second was China Construction

3 The US Chamber Litigation Center outlines its 2015 policy objectives in relation to what it sees as 'lawsuit abuse'.

4 J Beisner, J Miller and G Rubin, *Selling Lawsuits, Buying Trouble* (Washington, DC: US Chamber Institute for Legal Reform 2009).

5 This paper kick-started a wave of academic and media responses. A digest is available at 'Law and Finance in the News' (<www.rand.org>, Institute for Civil Justice).

6 Figures released October 2015: data 2014 (<www.wto.org/english/res_e/statis_e/its2015_e/its15_world_trade_dev_e.pdf>).

7 The UK share of world trade was 9.5 per cent (2014 figures).

8 For completeness it should be noted that not all Fortune 500 companies follow this narrative. At the conference in London 'Third-Party Litigation and the Future of the Voluntary Code' (28 November 2012) Westminster Legal Policy Forum, Leslie Perrin, Chairman of Association of Litigation Funders pointed out that the General Counsel of Dupont in 2010 made a speech in support of litigation funding. Dupont has historically been involved in a raft of litigation internationally including aggregate actions. It saw that it could use TPF for its own cases.

9 According to *Forbes Magazine*'s list of the world's 100 biggest public companies as of May 2013. ICBC's assets totalled $2.81 trillion, and its market value was $237.3 billion.

Bank, and the remaining three spots in the top five were US companies JP Morgan Chase, General Electric and Exxon Mobile. The UK and the Netherlands each had a company in the top ten, but other than those two examples, China and the US rounded out the top ten richest companies in the world.[10]

3. Definitions and introduction to the debate in the English context: The twin elements of procedure and finance

The issues raised in the Justice Not Profit letter must be considered in the context of the current procedures in England and the financial arrangements that underpin them. In the author's view the basic elements of a modern civil justice system fit for purpose are:

- an independent, non-corrupt and competent judiciary efficient procedure in the use of resources for the state and parties;
- appropriate boundaries and co-operation with 'private methods' of dispute resolution, for example, Alternative Dispute Resolution (ADR) and arbitration with State power being essential to underpin these methods, for example, to enforce an arbitral award or an ADR contract;
- equality of arms as an objective with moves in this direction following the Woolf 'Access to Justice Inquiry' and the Jackson 'Review of Civil Costs' having been made by controlling litigation effort and expense by case and cost management;
- access to justice needs funding, including, as explained below, conditional fees, contingency fees and TPF.

The author has suggested that changes in this area and in pursuit of these objectives should be based on evidence and tested.[11] How does the Institute's lobbying meet these objectives?

3.1 Employing a lawyer

The overall menu of different products to employ legal representation whether in litigation (court-based dispute resolution) or ADR now includes: hourly pay (no risk management and the principal/agent problem); fixed fee; conditional fee (multiplier of fees); and contingency fee *quota litis* (now in effect, introduced in England as 'Damage Based Agreements' (DBAs)). All but the hourly fee are risk-managed products with different risk/reward profiles and contingencies.

3.2 Funding a case

Parties can fund cases out of their own money, borrow money or more recently utilise TPF. TPF funders may require lawyers to go on risk or they will pay them in any event. A full-blown contingency fee effectively makes the lawyer a funder.

10 *Forbes Magazine*, accessed 15 December 2015.

11 J Peysner, *Access to Justice: A Critical Analysis of Recoverable Conditional Fees and No-Win No-Fee Funding* (London: Palgrave Macmillan 2014).

4. Changing attitude of the judiciary and legislatures

The US Chamber in its round-robin letter drew attention to the need to 'prevent financial speculators from manipulating the civil justice system for profit'. This concern is far from new in legal history. The three 'sins' of champerty (sharing the profits of another's litigation), maintenance (instigating and controlling another's litigation) and barratry (stirring up litigation with a view to profit) were familiar as far back as both criminal and civil Roman Law.[12] Assignment of actions and contingency fees (quota pars limits (QPL)) were banned. While, in the USA, particularly in the early 20th century, contingency fees on the quota pars model became widely accepted, in England the judges remained firmly against the idea. However, things have rapidly changed, with some considerable bumps on the road, since the year 2000.

In his 2013 lecture Lord Neuberger, President of the UK Supreme Court, in a comprehensive review of litigation prohibitions and their reform[13]describes the abolition of the crimes of maintenance and champerty and their continued existence as 'they lived on in a public policy-based half-life'.[14] His focus is firmly on access to justice – describing 'funding as the lifeblood of the justice system'. Earlier judicial concerns over the courts and society wilting under mass litigation no longer have primacy. He sees the abolition of the prohibitions on funding support as supporting not limiting access to justice. His concluding remarks address TPF. He echoes Bentham by stating, 'For him, as long as litigation, access to the courts, remains expensive, then anyone who has a right that stands in need of vindication should be able to obtain funding from anyone willing to offer it and on whatever terms it is offered. The public policy rationale is simple in his opinion: access to the courts is a right, and the State should not stand in the way of individuals availing themselves of that right.'[15] This is particularly apposite when the state has effectively closed down the legal aid scheme. He reminds us that any form of litigation funding is not without risks both of promoting meritorious claims, particularly 'blackmail claims'.[16] He also points to the risk of ethical conflicts. However, he points out that the conflict between lawyer and client is much more acute in CFAs or DBAs than in TPF because in that case lawyers are normally fully funded win or lose or have only a partial contingency payment.[17] He raises the issue that 'commercially driven pressures from expert serial litigation funders on lawyers could be significant'.[18]

12 For an interesting and novel challenge to the very basis of the prohibitions on champerty and maintenance see AJ Sebok, 'The Inauthentic Claim' (2012) 61 *DePaul Law Review* 615. For the background to these prohibitions see CJS Hodges, J Peysner and A Nurse, *Litigation Funding Status and Issues* (Centre for Socio-Legal Studies, Oxford University and Lincoln Law School, University of Lincoln 2012) <www.law.ox.ac.uk/sites/files/oxlaw/litigation_funding_here_1_0.pdf>.

13 Lord Neuberger, 'From Barratry, Maintenance and Champerty to Litigation Funding' (Harbour Litigation Funding First Annual Lecture, Gray's Inn, 8 May 2013).

14 Para 37 of his speech. While the life was attenuated it was sufficient to cause difficulties in assessing the risk of litigation funding and in recovering costs.

15 Para 46.

16 Claims with little merit or those that would be contested but are settled because of the threat of an opponent's deep pocket. See below.

17 Para 50.

18 See Neuberger, para 51 and below, para 11.

5. Initial discussion of the role of TPF

The fee arrangements outlined above are all lawful arrangements in England and Wales. Each has its own regulatory regime. However, an increasing regime of fee arrangements still leaves four major issues unresolved:

1. Who pays for disbursements (expert reports, etc.)? The client may be unwilling or unable to put the lawyer in funds to pay these disbursements. The lawyer is normally not prepared to incur liability for disbursements without funds. (As will be seen below, the fact that TPFs are willing to advance disbursements as part of their support to a case is a key part of their offer.)
2. Some lawyers and most barristers (who can't spread their risk as easily) insist on payment in any event. A hybrid DBA (part certain/part contingent) would help but government hasn't approved this.[19]
3. In insolvency liquidators (administrators) cannot or are unwilling to use their own money to pursue claims on behalf of creditors/shareholders.
4. Most companies do not pursue profit via litigation. Thus, if they have to use their money or human resources in litigation, this is an opportunity cost. A 'good' case with a strong chance of success and recovery creates an asset class that, subject to the regulatory/legal position, can be sold just like any other asset class such as intellectual property or real property.

It is in these four areas that a space has opened up for TPFs. As will be seen, the cases that are funded and are likely to be funded by them are commercial cases with a high prospective of success (at least 60 per cent plus), and cases with high damages to which a lien can apply or are capable of being purchased.

6. The research base

What do we know about TPFs, a relatively new phenomenon in England? The 'Litigation Funding Status and Issues' report (2012) was the first and most comprehensive review of TPF in England. The empirical research that underpinned the report was conducted during 2010 and 2011. Although there have been some developments since the date of the report, its evidence and conclusions (edited here) remain broadly relevant:[20]

> Conclusions and Recommendations…
>
> **A revolution in national policy.** The rules on funding and costs of litigation are being transformed in England and Wales with implementation of most of the Jackson Recommendations. The policy favours a 'mixed economy' of methods of funding, with adoption of the principle that fees can be deducted from recoveries…the acceptance of third parties, but restriction of legal aid.

19 See below, para 9.

20 CJS Hodges, J Peysner and A Nurse, 'Litigation Funding Status and Issues' (Centre for Socio-Legal Studies, Oxford University and Lincoln Law School, University of Lincoln 2012) 153f.

> **The established state of Litigation Funding – limited to commercial cases.** Litigation funding by third party investors who are not involved as parties has been established in England and Wales as an identifiable phenomenon in the past decade. Demand for funding currently far exceeds supply, and the market is expanding...To date, most funders support claimants, who are almost entirely commercial clients and frequently SMEs [small and medium-sized enterprises]. The threshold of viability for a claim value is currently not less than £100,000, and for many funders £1 million.
>
> Such funding provides a useful function and has filled an access to justice gap. The commercial imperative to select good (and the best) investments, and to obtain best returns for the investment, currently acts as pressure to support cases with merits, to advance them strongly, and to settle them without delay.
>
> We recommend that funders should not control tactical decisions in litigation, and that the demarcation of roles between client, lawyer and funder should remain and should be set out clearly in professional ethical requirements. If that position is to change, there is an urgent need for full empirical evidence on the consequences and on what level of regulation should be introduced.
>
> We also see conflicts of interest and risks where lawyers are the sole funder of litigation and have large stake in the outcome: the current increase in DBAs gives cause for concern and should be carefully reviewed.
>
> **Confidentiality, privilege and transparency.** Litigation funding requires full disclosure between client, lawyer and funder, and confidentiality of all information outside that circle. Funders favour transparency of the existence of a funding agreement. **We recommend that these principles of full disclosure and information, confidentiality, and transparency of notification be adopted.**
>
> **The need for regulation.** Regulation will be necessary to control commercial activities, financial prudence and the reliability of the funding source, and to maintain the integrity of the legal system. In the last case, the central issue is the potential for conflicts of interest to arise.

This report gives a research base and invites the question: what has happened since? Certainly, the last five years has seen TPF move from a peripheral position in the menu of funding options to a more central position. The reasons for this development are explored below. There are multiple reasons, including changes in procedure, public funding and the attitude of the judiciary.

7. What can be concluded from the NERA research?

7.1 Changes in the cost of access: Court fees & costs

The draft letter from the Justice Not Profit organisation contains the startling claim: 'Between 2008 and 2011, UK litigation costs rose by a staggering 47 per cent. In 2011, liability cost equated to 1.05 per cent of the UK's GDP.' This claim is from a report, 'International Comparisons of Litigation Costs', prepared for the US Chamber Institute for Legal Reform by NERA economic consulting.[21] The comparison is between Canada, Europe, Japan and the United States. The econometric methodology uses proxies of

21 NERA, *International Comparisons of Litigation Costs* (2013). NERA Consulting is an internationally respected economic consultancy, particularly in competition issues, established by Irwin Seltzer.

commercial insurance (liability and property) and the number of lawyers as a control for non-litigation related factors.

There is very little by way of a research base against which this claim can be judged. The complexities of cultural and procedural differences between civil justice systems has produced a rich literature in comparison studies and the import/export of different 'killer apps' to resolve procedural difficulties.[22] While isomorphism[23] has been widely used in England in the process of developing procedural reform, this has not been against a standardised and rigorous background of analysis of domestic and international cost comparisons. One important report was published as *The Costs and Funding of Civil Litigation: A Comparative Prospective*;[24] this used a different methodology, namely reporters from different jurisdictions harvesting data from the courts, law firms and clients, giving wide coverage of both common law and civil law systems. In cost terms the most relevant differences between these two systems are that in the civil law system the judge does more of the heavy lifting; court fees are higher to reflect this split in litigation effort and civil law jurisdictions tend to have predictable, fixed or matrix cost systems.[25] The crucial difference between the USA and the rest of the world is that costs tend to follow the event – the loser pays – in every jurisdiction apart from the USA. While this is the general rule, the quantum of costs varies substantially as does the proportion of clients costs recoverable.

Both of these approaches to the costs of litigation are at best approximations of a complex reality. The paradigm of data would be the actual total fees and out payments (disbursements) that each party to an action pays out.[26]

7.2 Jurisdictional comparisons

The NERA research concludes that 'differences in costs are largely explained by features of the legal environment in each country that may affect the frequency and cost of claims. [...] The USA has the highest estimated liability costs in proportion to GDP and the UK is the most costly European country.' The statement about the UK (read as England) is not fundamentally different from the Oxford research that suggests that the highest lawyers' fees can be observed in Australia, England and Wales, and Denmark. Germany, Austria and Greece have relatively low lawyers' fees; in other words, broadly a common law/civil law split.[27]

Accepting, for the purpose of the argument, that legal costs in their widest definition (characterised as liability costs) in the USA are higher than in Europe/UK, and that UK (England) costs are higher than in Europe, where does this get us?

First, a broad comparison between civilian and English common law 'between the parties': recoverable costs would suggest that the former would invariably be lower as this system incorporates as standard fixed or tariff costs. However, this bald comparison between open and limited costs is increasingly old-fashioned, as within the English

22 For example: 'hot tubbing' of experts.

23 Comparative policy research – see p 129; Peysner (2014).

24 CJS Hodges, S Vogenauer and M Tulibacka (eds), *The Costs and Funding of Civil Litigation: A Comparative Perspective* (Oxford: Hart Publishing 2010). Part 1 deals with comparative costs.

25 For reasons explained, ibid., there is limited data from the USA.

26 As explained in the report this would be a difficult if not impossible exercise.

27 Hodges et al. (2010) 69.

jurisdiction fixed costs imposed by the court rules are spreading.[28] However, fixed costs are likely to be focused on the lower end of litigation quantum. Budgeting, now introduced for higher value cases, is far from perfect and is at an early stage in English procedure and practice but it will inevitably curb 'between the parties costs' except in the most heavy-weight commercial/international litigation where legal costs, however high, are still outweighed by the claim being contested.

Running alongside the comparison in cost recovery between England/Europe and the USA are procedural differences which suggest that US procedure is likely to be globally more expensive (i.e. to the client *and* the state). There are many differences but to mention a few: the presence of US juries to decide damages, diversity of jurisdiction rules, the tradition of private attorney general, and punitive damages. Above all, the fact that it is widely understood, including in popular culture[29], that claimant lawyers work on a contingency fee influences juries to reflect in their damage awards the anticipated 'cut'.[30]

7.3 Inflation and the market

The Justice Not Profit campaign in its letter highlights one issue: 'Between 2008 and 2011, UK litigation costs rose by a staggering 47 per cent.' In other words there has been rapid inflation in English legal costs. As indicated this is a calculation from proxy figures. Is there any other evidence? One clear change is the switch in government policy in relation to court fees. The difference between court fees and the overall cost of running courts was made up by general taxation. In January 2015 the government made a handbrake turn by increasing court fees above the level of general inflation in a move that was explained as a need for the Ministry of Justice to pull its weight in the general austerity programme. The implication on commercial cases was profound: a 1,000 per cent increase on claims more than £200,000.

Another possible driver of legal fees is high and increasing demand. The demand for legal services in the commercial sphere has a long history:

> In the 1660s and 1670s English ships still had to be insured in Amsterdam. Marine insurance developed in England from the eighties; in 1688 we first hear of Lloyd's. Modern fire insurance dates for after the fire of London. The stock exchange was incorporated in William III's reign. Before the end of the century there was a highly organised stock and share market in London and newspapers carried stock exchange news.[31]

International trade rocketed during the 20th century and London as a centre of commercial law has grown rapidly, pulling ahead of other centres such as New York. With such a strong demand it is unsurprising that fee rates for commercial work are high and inflating. The NERA analysis does not break down the fees into different types of work but it can be assumed that commercial work drives these high numbers.

28 D Regan, 'The Future is Fixed' *Litigation Funding* (London: December 2015) 8.

29 Hollywood films such as *Erin Brockovich, A Civil Action* and many others are premised on a contingency fee lawyer in a 'David and Goliath' struggle with corporate America.

30 Under the US rule the winner does not normally get his costs unlike under the 'English Rule'.

31 C Hill, *The Century of Revolution 1603–1704* (Oxford: Routledge 2001).

Following the Civil Procedure Rules 1988 a system of exchanged estimates of costs was found wanting and has been superseded by the preparation and court approval of budgets – but not in cases over £10 million. It is hoped that this system will eventually suppress over inflated costs, but it is relatively early days and it would not affect the proxy calculations used by NERA for some time.

7.4 Number of claims issued

The NERA Report (at page 5) states:

> Differences between countries' legal systems may result in more frequent, weaker or unfounded claims, unusually high compensation or higher legal costs. Having selected countries with similar scopes of civil redress, similar regulatory protections and deterrence, and adjusted liability cost estimates for differences in government benefits, the cost differences we measure are most likely explained by more frequent claims or higher claim costs, or both.

Accepting this argument and having to consider the costs (fees and disbursements) per case we turn to frequency of claiming. Of course, the number of issued cases bears only an indirect relationship with the number of issues.[32] The abolition of recovery of 'additional liabilities has reduced the number of cases and this reduction in this demand side is reflected in the judicial statistics'.[33]

The latest complete statistics at the time of writing (2014 report) show '[a]nnually, there was a general downward trend in the number of claims between 2006 and 2012 from 2.1 million to a low of 1.4 million – since then, the trend has reversed, with a slight increase in 2013 and a further increase to 1.6 million claims being made in 2014'.[34]

These figures suggest a decrease across the board with some increases in specialised jurisdictions. There are multiple reasons for this overall trend. There have been changes in the jurisdictional borders between the County Court and the High Court with many Multi-Track cases proceeding in the County Court rather than the High Court. There has been an increase in ADR.

7.5 Are the number of cases going to increase?

The NERA analysis, adopted by Justice Not Profit, suggests that increases in the frequency of claiming would be a potential problem for the UK. The statistics outlined above suggest that such an increase, other than gentle, would be against the trend.[35] In fact, there is a decline from historic highs. Accepting, for the purposes of the argument, that more cases are a 'bad thing' is it possible to identify changes in the dispute resolution scene that may

32 For a definition of 'justiciable issues' see H Genn, *Paths to Justice: What People Do and Think about Going to Law* (Oxford: Hart Publishing 1999).

33 'Additional Liabilities', i.e. the cost of insurance and the lawyer's reward (success fee), were recoverable in addition to normal costs until abolished by the Legal Aid Sentencing and Punishment of Offenders Act 2012. See Peysner (2014).

34 Judicial Statistics, <www.gov.uk/government/organisations/ministry-of-justice/about/statistics>.

35 See the chapter by A Stadler herein. Increasing access to TPF does not necessarily lead to increased volume of lawsuits.

pump prime such an increase. There are three prime candidates, of which the last two are specifically referred to in the Justice Not Profit draft letter: contingency fee funding, aggregated cases and third-party funding.

8. Contingency fee funding

While the specific Justice Not Profit campaign addressed here does not refer to contingency fees, the Institute of Legal Reform in many papers and interventions blames this model of funding for what they describe as the ills of litigation in the USA. As described above,[36] the historical opposition of the judiciary (and governments) to contingency fees in England has latterly declined. This development came to a head in Lord Justice Jackson's Review of Costs, which proposed a model called a 'damage based agreement' (DBA). This form of contingency fee on the 'Ontario model' incentivises the lawyer (normally acting for the claimant) on a no-win no-fee basis by giving the successful lawyer a percentage of damages. The unsuccessful party (normally the defendant) pays costs in the normal way, which are discounted against what the client pays to the lawyer.[37] There are different rules for the percentage that a lawyer can take from damages. In personal-injury cases the maximum is 25 per cent. In commercial cases the maximum is 50 per cent. DBAs are available alongside conditional fee agreements where the lawyer's reward is not a percentage of damages but a multiplier of the lawyer's fees.

What has happened to contingency fee funding in England? In the context of TPF the Swiss Re report on litigation funding had suggested that there was a 'current increase in DBAs'.[38] This was written in the context of the Jackson proposals. Research work carried out by the author for the Civil Justice Council and published in 2014[39] discussed introduction of the reforms in costs proposed by Lord Justice Jackson. In relation to contingency fees/DBAs the conclusion was much less sanguine than the earlier Swiss Report:

> Damage Based Agreements (DBAs). A Damp Squib…DBAs appear to be like the Yeti: they are believed to exist in practice but hardly any sightings have been made.[40]

Anecdotally, nothing seems to have changed since. The reason for the lack of take-off of DBAs is described as complex in the CJC report. Ultimately, the reward to the lawyer against the risk was felt to be too low.

In commercial cases the potential damage pot may be higher and the potential 'cut' (up to 50 per cent subject to agreement) may also be higher. However, there is another fatal flow in the Jackson scheme – the continuing existence of CFAs. A cost regime that rewards litigation effort by a multiplier for success (albeit now not recoverable from the other side) is more appealing.

A potential solution to this conundrum identified by Jackson was a hybrid DBA. The findings of 'Impact of the Jackson Reforms: Some Emerging Themes' was that a model that

36 Above para 4.

37 The Damages-Based Agreements Regulations came into force on 1 April 2013.

38 CJS Hodges, J Peysner and A Nurse, *Litigation Funding Status and Issues* (Centre for Socio-Legal Studies, Oxford University and Lincoln Law School, University of Lincoln 2012) 166.

39 J Peysner, *Impact of the 'Jackson' Reforms: Some Emerging Themes* (London: Civil Justice Council 2014) <www.judiciary.gov.uk/related-offices-and-bodies/advisory-bodies/cjc/>.

40 Ibid. 15.

allowed the risk/reward equation to be salami sliced would be very attractive to commercial litigators. The whole case may be conducted on a part hourly paid/part DBA basis. Despite being an obvious solution to the needs of both clients and lawyers, it has been blocked by the government. Lord Justice Jackson blamed, without identifying them, 'powerful vested interests'.[41] Interviews and further research for this report suggests there is a strong suspicion across the litigation funding industry that there has been lobbying by domestic defendant interests.[42]

8.1 Comparison with the USA

Whether or not the Institute for Legal Reform exaggerates the malign influence of contingency fees in the USA, what they are highlighting is a very different beast than the mixed model that has emerged in England. Damages are higher, lawyer rewards can be higher, and the idea of contingency fees is central to US litigation. The analysis above indicates that absent major changes in procedure, which are unlikely, contingency fees are likely to remain a somewhat marginal funding model in England. The Institute is confusing apples with oranges.

9. Aggregated cases

To quote from the Justice Not Profit letter:

> [W]e are concerned that recent proposals – such as the introduction of U.S.-style class action lawsuits – coupled with unregulated and predatory third-party litigation funding, pose a serious threat to the effective administration of justice. Whilst well-intended, we believe recent Government reforms could lead to a proliferation of meritless lawsuits and have an adverse impact on the UK economy.

The Institute's attitude to contingency fees is intimately bound up with its approach to aggregated cases – class actions – in the USA. These may be 'retail' actions involving individuals with businesses as defendants. They may also involve numbers of businesses, often SMEs, in dispute with a large corporation or group of corporations, the classic 'David and Goliath' situation. There is unlikely to be a shortage of potential clients in an increasingly globalised world where communications between claimants and the lawyers in different countries are increasing apace.

9.1 Australia

Outside the USA and apart from Hong Kong and Québec province (Canada) – backed by state funds – and Ontario province (Canada) with funding arrangements and procedure influenced by the USA, the most sophisticated activity in aggregating cases is in the

41 R Rothwell, 'Jackson Warns against "Vested Interests" on DBAs' (*Law Society Gazette*, London, 21 October 2014) <www.lawgazette.co.uk/law/jackson-warns-against-vested-interests-on-dbas/5044478.fullarticle>.

42 There have been some suggestions that the National Health Litigation Authority, which has the responsibility for dealing with clinical negligence cases against the NHS, was concerned that a hybrid DBA would allow more cases to be brought as the investigation stage could be funded separately from the litigation.

jurisdictions of Australia.[43] Because of the similarities of procedure, judicial arrangements and professional organisation between Australia and England, they present a useful comparator. A comprehensive and up-to-date analysis of the position in Australia was presented in the paper 'Class Actions: Financial Arrangements with Litigation Funders and Law Firms' by V Waye (University of South Australia) (co-written with V Morabito, Monash University) at the Leiden conference. New South Wales, Victoria and the Federal Court have opt-out class-action regimes, while in other jurisdictions there are a variety of opt-in or hybrid schemes. However, this has not led to many class actions. From 2002 to 2015 there were five class actions in the Federal Court (0.03 per cent of all Federal Court matters).

Despite this limited number of class actions, they are important because of the issues involved and the procedurally disproportionate burden on claimants if they could only proceed one by one. The point of aggregated actions is that the number of specific cases issued is less important than the numbers of claimants involved and the potential damages.[44] From the defence side, potential corporate targets consider that class actions and a more litigious environment is the greatest business threat.[45]

How are these cases funded? Australian law firms cannot charge on a contingency fee basis and as such have had to rely on their own limited funds to support cases. The judiciary is broadly supportive of aggregate actions and the Australian Productivity Commission has proposed introduction of contingency fees.[46] The prospect for class actions rests on TPF.

9.2 England

The history of aggregated actions in the England has been a sorry one.[47] What if there are a large number of claimants with relatively small claims or larger claims that are difficult to prove? For example, in pharmaceutical cases where the allegation is that the drug caused harm but causation is contested. The costs of mounting such claims are breath-taking and not to be lightly undertaken or funded. Since 1947 the potential solution in England was to use the resources of the state through the legal aid system. This was not just to offer access to justice to groups of individuals but in suitable cases to form part of regulatory overview whether this involves drugs, mass casualty accidents, or consumer issues. Unfortunately, many of the most expensive of these cases were unsuccessful and thus cast doubt on the funding model. Also, the procedures ultimately adopted under the Civil Procedure Rules 1998 – the group litigation order and the representative action – were not found to be effective. In a group action individual claimants would join the action taking their share of the costs: *opting in*. However, the funding model developed to replace legal

43 For a general comparative view see Kalajdzic J, P Cashman and A Longmoore, 'Justice for Profit: A Comparative Analysis of Australian, Canadian and U.S. Third Party Litigation Funding' (2013) 61 *Am.J.Comp.L.* 93.

44 Examples given in Waye and Morabito's chapter herein include an $A 500 million settlement against a power company in relation to bushfires, $A 200 million settlement in relation to disclosure, and an $A 120 million settlement in relation to price-fixing.

45 Newspaper article quoted at fn 20 in the Waye and Morabito chapter.

46 Australian Government Productivity Commission, *Access to Justice Arrangements (Productivity Commission Inquiry Report no 72)* (Vol 2, Canberra: Commonwealth of Australia 2014) 612–613.

47 See generally M Hvid and J Peysner, 'Comparing Economic Incentives to Pursue Private Actions across EU Member States' in B Rodger (ed), *Competition Law. Comparative Private Enforcement and Collective Redress across the EU* (Alphen aan den Rijn: Kluwer Law International 2014).

aid – conditional fees with additional recoverable liabilities – was not fit for this purpose.[48] As of 15 November 2015, there have only been 94 group action orders since 2000 with two in 2015.[49]

In purely operational terms the solution adopted in the USA and, as described above, in certain jurisdictions of Australia is a much more logical solution: the opt-out model. The second difficulty – funding – is resolved by the ubiquitous contingency fees and a business model of lawyers banding together to split the risk and reward. This bald statement of how the system operates should not disguise the extreme binary view in the United States of its validity, in particular, the alleged danger of a nuisance value suit and an allegation that they benefit lawyers rather than class members.[50]

The solution adopted by the government in England was to introduce collective action[51] in this area of anti-trust under the Consumer Rights Act 2015 (amending the Competition Act 1998).[52] The new rules will allow the Competition Appeal Tribunal in both 'stand alone' and 'follow on' cases to certify as suitable for collective proceedings the proposed class representative that cannot be a law firm or a special-purpose vehicle (as is common in Europe). Certification by the Tribunal will allow the case to proceed on an opt-out basis. The tribunal will also certify settlements. However, the Act bans exemplary damages and DBAs (contingency fees). While the tribunal may well hold the representatives harmless as to costs, if the case is lost the problem is that this funding model does not look very attractive and is very different indeed to class actions mounted by entrepreneurial US or Australian lawyers. It is not certain which organisations, if any, will step forward to be representatives and whether they will have the funding clout and organisational experience to manage large and complex cases with hundreds or thousands of claimants. For reasons discussed below, while it may make sense for TPFs to manage cases, as happens in other jurisdictions, a general 'hands off' approach in England tied to the continuing risk of maintenance would give TPFs pause.

It is clear that the government has responded to lobbying and dipping its toe in the water by steering what it saw as a middle course between compensating victims and generating litigation. Justice Not Profit in its letter overstates the position about class actions – *the introduction of US-style class action lawsuits.* This implies a major general adoption of opt-out procedure whereas in fact the adoption is limited to the competition area and hedged about with exceptions.

This does not look like the starting gun for a revolution in claiming, and even if successful, it seems highly unlikely to generate procedural changes in other areas where individual

48 For group actions generally see CJS Hodges, *Multi-Party Actions* (Oxford: Oxford University Press 2000). For funding issues see J Peysner, 'Access to Justice in a Multi-Party Context' in P Odell and C Willet (eds), *Global Governance and the Quest for Justice: Volume III* (Oxford: Hart Publishing 2008).

49 <www.justice.gov.uk/courts/rcj-rolls-building/queens-bench/group-litigation-orders>.

50 See the chapter of Waye and Morabito herein, p 9 and references there for a comprehensive overview of the literature.

51 A Higgins and A Zuckerman, 'Class Actions Come to England – More Access to Justice and More of a Compensation Culture, but They Are Superior to the Alternatives' (2016) 35(1) *Civil Justice Quarterly* 1. See also Z Juska, 'The Future of Collective Antitrust Redress: Is Something New under the Sun?' (2015) *Global Competition Litigation Review* 14.

52 For a full analysis and discussion of the limitations of the new procedure see B Rodger, 'The Consumer Rights Act 2015 and Collective Redress for Competition Law Infringements in the UK: A Class Act?' (2015) 3(2) *Journal of Antitrust Enforcement* 258. See also A Mozetic, 'Collective Redress: A Case for Opt-Out Class Actions in England and Wales' (2016) 35(1) *Civil Justice Quarterly* 29.

citizen or businesses are victims of generalised misconduct.[53] The Justice Not Profit attack looks like a pre-emptive strike.

10. The current status and position of third-party funding

To quote from the Justice Not Profit letter:

> New measures – including statutory licencing for third-party litigation funders and disclosure rules to enhance transparency – should also be introduced to prevent financial speculators from manipulating the civil justice system for profit.

If DBAs are not available in the limited foray into competition class actions, then history suggests that these actions will not happen. Either prospective claimants (including businesses) will be unable or unwilling to risk their capital, or it will be difficult to identify suitable and willing representatives who cannot be incentivised in this new scheme by a profit motive. As Rodger and others have pointed out it seems most likely that only third-party funders are likely to step forward, albeit with some trepidation.[54] As such these cases will form a part of a select group of cases funded on a TPF basis. To examine the current situation, against the claims above, this paper will consider two areas: the number and type of cases currently and in the future funded by TPF and, second, the current regulatory structure of TPFs and, in the light of their practice, whether they should be regulated on a statutory basis.

10.1 The number and type of cases currently and in the future funded by third-party funding

The 2012 report 'Litigation Funding: Status and Issues' found that the funding market shared some general approaches.[55] These could be summed up as a 'good case', a 'good client', and a 'good team'. Funders will normally pay lawyers and for disbursements as the case proceeds, and in the event of failure will be liable for the opponent's costs under the 'pound for pound' *Arkin* judgment.[56] This risk-management profile predicates a reward of between 40 and 60 per cent as each case exists in a silo and must stand or fall on its own. This is contrary to the position of lawyers operating a caseload of DBAs or conditional fees where it is the overall result of many cases that counts. As will be demonstrated below, TPF is essentially a risk business and there have been failures.

53 There is increasing interest in models such as regulators or ombudsmen with powers to order authorities and businesses to compensate individuals. The discussion of this is outside the scope of this report. In any event, in the author's view, the boundaries of ADR, regulatory control, and deterrence/compensation through the litigation system are fluid and it is unlikely that a 'one size' or 'one approach' solution is the answer.

54 Rodger (2015) 283: 'The uncertainty on cost recovery suggests a potentially crucial role, particularly in relation to class claimant representative actions, for external investment in the form of Third Party Funding. There was an attempt to amend the legislation in Parliament to exclude such third-party litigation funding agreements (…) The Government stressed during the passage of the Bill that blocking access to third party funding would unnecessarily constrain competition law private enforcement by limiting access to larger businesses and discouraging organizations such as *Which?* from fully participating as a lead representative organization' (author's edit).

55 See Chapter 4.

56 *Arkin v Borchard Lines Ltd and others* [2005] EWCA Civ 655. See p 25.

TPFs do not back personal injury cases. The cases that reach or exceed the quantum required are a combination of general damages and additional long-term financial damages such as aids and adaptations and nursing care. A funder's 'cut' of 40 per cent plus would bite into these additional items. Funders remain queasy at the prospect of media headlines about depriving victims of care. A similar analysis might apply in divorce cases. While the particular menu of cases taken on varied from funder to funder, they were all essentially commercial cases such as insolvency,[57] shareholder disputes, contract disputes, intellectual property disputes, employment cases, tax appeals, and so on.[58]

The journal *Litigation Funding*, the 'journal of record' of litigation funding, has a table of TPFs. The December 2015 issue shows those TPFs currently active in the market and details of their business model. As might be expected in a dynamic market environment, there are now a variety of approaches to claim values. Potentially, seven will only fund claims worth over £1 million – sometimes substantially more than this. The rest might fund considerably less than this that in every case the damages will need to justify the funding offered. One funder's minimum is £5 million, but higher for group actions. No funder sets its stall out to do personal injury or family work, although, of course, such work might be introduced to a funder by broker for consideration.

Rachel Rothwell[59] has reported that the TPFs Augusta and Burford have 'moved into the low value claims arena'. She recalls that Lord Justice Jackson 'was broadly supportive of funding, and believed funders could help small businesses achieve access to justice despite losing the ability to recover success fees and insurance premiums'. While both are prepared to consider applications without a minimum figure of damages, both stress that they are interested in commercial cases. Augusta's website identifies a focus on commercial disputes with examples of breach-of-contract, professional negligence, shareholder disputes, contentious probate, commercial agency disputes, insurance disputes, compulsory acquisition and marine disputes. Burford identifies its interest in monetising legal claims as assets.

Current research suggests no major change in the 2012 report conclusion that TPF was targeted on the whole on 'heavyweight' commercial cases with clients.

There are a number of reasons why it is unlikely in the short-term that funders will change their focus from such 'heavyweight' cases. These reasons all, in essence, derive from the need for risk management:

1. Cases with more limited damages may be covered by commercial BTE often through a trade association.
2. TPFs carry out a risk-management analysis that can be expensive in resources and it isn't worth doing except in cases where the quantum is high.[60]
3. It follows that the percentage taking in cases by the funder will be high, and the numbers of cases supported by funders will be in tens, not hundreds. Given the choice between small numbers of high-value claims and large numbers of small claims, the TPF industry at the moment is unlikely to adopt the latter as a business plan.

57 See A Jay, 'Funding Insolvency Litigation: A New Dawn' (2015) 8(5) *Corporate Rescue and Insolvency* 183; which refers to TPF as one of the methods now available to assist pursuit of chose in action.

58 An interesting but limited edition to the menu of TPF is crowdfunding. See H Spendlove, 'I'm in with the "In Crowd"' (2015) 112(15) *L.S.G.* 20.

59 Editorial, 'Litigation Funding' *The Law Society of England and Wales* (London, October 2015) 3.

60 Augusta offers a product, presumably for a specific fee, which can cover the pre-investigation stage of the claim and allow both sides then to assess the risk for future funding.

4. Funders are vehicles for that part of investors' risk profile that looks to more risky investments with a high reward. The rest of the portfolio will be in (normally) less risky investments such as equities, property or the bond market. The need to manage a spread means that the money available to TPF is necessarily limited and targets high returns.
5. An important element in a client's decision to approach litigation funders, whether TPF or a lawyer offering a DBA, is the question of opportunity cost. An efficiently run commercial enterprise should not have the spare resources of time and capital to invest in litigation as those assets should find a more profitable use in the business. As such, risk-management strategy might suggest that getting a third party to fund the case may be more profitable than using internal funding. Even if the client has in-house counsel, they are likely to be too stretched, or not specialised enough in litigation, and not to use an external law firm, and funding then enters the picture.[61] Of course, some clients do not fall into this category. For example, liquidators do not have or cannot use their own funds to pursue assets of the liquidated company. Individual clients pursuing contentious probate cases may not have financial opportunity costs. However, for the vast majority of clients currently in the TPF marketplace opportunity cost is a factor.
6. All contractual and business relations depend on an exchange of information. The most robust and sustainable arrangements involve parties who have a profile of symmetrical information. One of the problems of TPF in the 'retail' (normally single consumer) field is that consumers, victims of accidents, or parties to divorce are likely to be 'one shot players'. There is risk but as important is the *perception* of the risk that the more economically powerful and knowledgeable party may persuade the other party to enter into a bad bargain. Jackson recognised this risk by proposing that before parties enter into a DBA they take independent advice.[62] In commercial funding the risk is less, as the entity seeking funding is likely to be more savvy.[63]

10.2 Funders can lose

No matter how experienced the funder is, nor how tight their risk management, it must never be forgotten that TPF is a risk business and the business model inevitably links high risk to high reward. Juridica, a large Guernsey-based litigation funder and overseas member of the Association of Litigation Funders (ALF), announced in June 2015 it was writing down $30 million in a price-fixing case. In November 2015 the funding it had provided in a trade dispute case that resulted in a $2 million jury verdict left it with a booked loss despite winning the case.

10.3 What will the future market look like?

The 2015 International Arbitration Survey: Improvements and Innovations in International Arbitration (Queen Mary University of London/White and Case) confirms that the vast

61 S Dluzniak, 'The (Other) Benefits of Third Party Funding for In-House Counsel' (2015) 230(May) *The In-House Lawyer* 37.

62 The government did not take up this proposal. It is similar to the requirement that before employees sign a voluntary severance agreement in employment, they must obtain a solicitor's advice and sign off.

63 This is not inevitable as has been demonstrated in the scandal in England involving banks requiring commercial borrowers to take inappropriate hedging products. A mixture of asymmetrical information, an impossibly complex product, and a measure of financial necessity worked against the interests of the borrower.

majority of all participants in cross-border commerce, including investment treaties, believe that the most appropriate mechanism for resolving any disputes arising out of such arrangements is international arbitration and the most popular seats are London, Paris, Hong Kong, Singapore, and Geneva. It is therefore not surprising that research for this report suggests that funding such arbitrations is for many TPFs a growing part of their portfolio.[64]

What international arbitration – at least under the English Arbitration Act 1996 – shares with most other commercial cases (with some employment cases being an exception) is that the funder has to take into account the fees and disbursements of the client and *also* the risk of paying the other side's fees and disbursements if the case is lost. Some of these risks can be 'reinsured' through after-the-event insurance and other forms of layering. However, the tentative arrangements for budgeting – still not available for cases over £10 million in the commercial court – leave considerable uncertainty.

Nothing in this analysis or the 2012 report or recent interviews suggests that TPF is likely to expand beyond the commercial world of heavyweight cases. This suggests that the number of cases handled by most TPFs at any one time will continue to be in tens or hundreds rather than thousands. This is the context through which the continuing debate over regulation should be viewed.

11. Regulation

To quote extracts from the Justice Not Profit letters:

> New measures – including statutory licensing for third party litigation funders and disclosure rules to enhance transparency – should also be introduced to prevent financial speculators from manipulating the civil justice system for profit.[65]

11.1 Principles of regulation

The issue of regulation is canvassed in detail in the 2012 report at Chapter 11. This was in the context of a nascent industry, that met a need, that was largely business-to-business (B2B) was developing generally welcomed voluntary regulation. A flag was put up that if the nature of the business model altered – if it became a retail operation – then it was unlikely that the industry could remain 'unregulated', although, as explained below, a better description would be a patchwork of regulation rather than unregulation. The earlier reports do not

64 F Blavi, 'Towards a Uniform Regulation of Third Party Funding in International Arbitration' (2015) *International Law Review* 143, suggests that the use of TPF is becoming a standard feature of international arbitration and that harmonisation of arbitral rules is needed; security for costs can be ordered in some jurisdictions and TPFs can provide this. See also *RSM Production Corp v Saint Lucia* unreported 8 April 2015 (ICSID) (2015) 81(3) *Arbitration* 304; E Chua and N Patmore, 'Singapore: Third Party Funding – An Emergent Reality' (2015) 10(5) *G.A.R.* 43. For a more concerned view see European Union Preparatory Acts 2015/C332/06 'Opinion of the European Economic and Social Committee on Investor Protection and Investor to State Dispute Settlement in EU Trade and Investment Agreements with Third Countries' OJ C332/45. The increasing use of the London legal market for international arbitration in commercial and Investment Treaty cases is supported to an extent by TPF. This is important as access to tribunal justice (which is not cheap) protects companies from having their funds/property being expropriated by governments and thus helps development and, potentially, reduces the risk of such investments.

65 Edited by author.

overtly point to the fact that the spirit of our age, for good or ill, has been to encourage voluntary regulation and limit state regulation except to egregious cases. In the area of funding in England the most graphic example is the free-for-all in the market for accident claims following the Access to Justice Act 1999.[66] Only after the excesses of the 'Cost Wars' was the government persuaded to introduce a statutory regulatory scheme for claims management companies (claims farms).[67] The scandals have virtually disappeared. While governments of whatever hue have recently been ideologically opposed to state regulation, one key issue is cost. Governments do not want to use scarce resources, including the diminishing number of civil servants, to regulate industries unless this can be done on a full cost recovery basis of registration fees. However, there is a recognition that in relation to a nascent industry this could act as a barrier to entry and inhibit new and useful developments.

11.2 The current system of patchwork regulation of TPFs

In 2010 in Chapter 11 of the Jackson Review of Civil Litigation Costs, there was judicial endorsement to litigation funding. He suggested that 'I support the approach of the CJC in trying to establish, in the first instance, a voluntary code for third-party funding. Provided that a satisfactory code is established and that all funders subscribe to that code, then at this stage, subject to my concern about capital adequacy requirements, I see no need for statutory regulation. However, if the use of third-party funding expands, there may well be a need for full statutory regulation.' Jackson does not explicitly state what he means by 'expands', but presumably this would include TPF funding a significant proportion of commercial litigation and/or moving into the retail sector. For the reasons outlined above neither has yet happened, nor is either likely to.

Following this lead in 2011 a regulatory body responsible for litigation funding and ensuring compliance with a new code was formed, the Association of Litigation Funders (ALF). Under the Code the funder will not try to take control of the litigation, has the money to pay for the costs of the funded litigation (capital adequacy), and the litigation funder will not terminate funding absent a material adverse development. This voluntary code has been approved by Lord Justice Jackson and the Civil Justice Council.[68] While the members of ALF are not the only funders in the market, they appear to represent the majority of those utilising their *own* capital.

Funders who are listed will be regulated by the Financial Conduct Authority. As well as the funders themselves, many individuals with executive positions will be bound by professional regulation whether they are solicitors, barristers, or accountants. There will normally be lawyers on both sides of the bargain: in the funding organisations; the solicitors acting for the parties, and, in many cases, in-house counsel in the client's organisation. Ensuring that these professionals act responsibly and ethically is important both to the client considering entering a funding agreement, but also the funder who will often be reliant on the case presented to it by a law firm. In recognition of this, in 2015 the Solicitors Regulation Authority published 'Walking the Line: The Balancing of Duty in Litigation'. It refers[69] to

66 See Peysner (2014).

67 The regulation is by the Claims Management Regulator (Ministry of Justice).

68 Which has a statutory monitoring role over civil justice.

69 Solicitors Regulation Authority, *Walking the Line: The Balancing of Duties in Litigation* (2015) 3 <www.sra.org.uk/risk/resources/balancing-duties-litigation.page>.

predatory litigation 'where the solicitor, in the interests of the client, uses the threat of litigation to obtain settlement, often from several opponents, on cases that have no real merit, but where the cost of the settlement is less than the financial, emotional or reputational cost of fighting the claim'. This directly deals with the question of nuisance value settlements alleged to be one of the problems of US-style contingency fees.

Finally, TPFs, to a great extent, owe the development to the supportive attitude of the judiciary exemplified by cases such as *Arkin* (*Arkin v Borchard Lines Ltd and others* [2005] EWCA Civ 655).[70] The judges might have stifled this funding option at birth but in common-law style chose to offer qualified support and keep a watching brief.

11.3 Have TPFs behaved badly?

No principle of regulation or cost–benefit analysis would stand in the way of statutory regulation if, as in a case of the claims management companies, the work of TPFs became a public scandal. It is important to note the high level of concern that would be required for this to happen.

What is the position about the activities of TPFs based or linked to England? The Institute for Legal Reform has generalised critiques of TPFs but largely directed at the USA and Australia.

A number of cases have raised issues:

The **Arkin** case. This anti-trust case is best known for the Court of Appeal establishing the principal that non-champertous funding is lawful but that there is no risk-free reward. On a pragmatic policy basis, the funder would be liable under the English rule on a 'pound for pound' basis, that is, each £1 invested in the case attracts the risk of having to pay a further £1 if the case fails. This kickstarted TPF in England as it established that liability was not open ended and that this form of funding was an important aspect of access to justice. For all the benefits that the case brought to the development of the common law, it should not be forgotten that it was described in the judgement as a 'disastrous case' that just survived a strikeout and that failed on all liability claims and had considerable difficulties on causation. However, the case did survive a strikeout application and as such was entitled to its day in court.

The **Excalibur** case. (*Excalibur Ventures LLC v Texas Keystone Inc and Ors (Rev 2)* [2014] EWHC 3436 Comm). This was a dispute between two US corporations over the ownership of oil fields in Kurdistan. It was a huge case funded by private investors and investment funds (in effect an SPV) and a leading English law firm, Clifford Chance, acting for the claimant. Lord Justice Clarke was scathing about the claim, which he found to be 'based on no sound foundation in fact or law'. He found the group of funders to be extensively liable for both the defendant's and claimant's costs. Most commentators have taken the view that the main lesson of the case was that it suffered from not having an established and experienced TPF in place so that there would be risk management flowing from both the instructed lawyer and the funder. Again, whatever the private pain to the claimant and advisors the case has established a set of legal parameters for the conduct of the industry.

70 See reference list for details.

Chevron & Texaco and Ecuador (The Lago Agrio case). In 1993 people living in the Oriente Area of Ecuador filed a class-action lawsuit in US federal court against Texaco for alleged environmental damage. Although the action was dismissed on forum grounds it was restarted in 2003 in the courts of Ecuador (by this time Chevron had taken over Texaco). In 2011 the Ecuadorian court found in favour of the plaintiffs and awarding $18 billion in damages. At the same time parallel proceedings were taking place in the permanent Court of Arbitration at The Hague and Chevron unsuccessfully attempted to use an order from that Tribunal to block further action in the Ecuadorian courts. This multi-forum, multi-jurisdictional case was funded by the plaintiffs on a contingency fee basis. However, this funding did not extend to further process in Canada and Brazil attempting to seize assets of Chevron to satisfy the judgement. As reported,[71] Woodsford Litigation Funding, based in England, became involved in funding enforcement proceedings. The defendant's argument in all these cases has included allegations that the original judgement was achieved by fraud and bribery. The original lawyer in the class action has been accused of civil racketeering by Chevron, which has won some rulings on that basis. However, it is understood that a witness who alleged fraud has partially recanted his evidence. In May 2015 Chevron and Woodford agreed that Woodford would not engage further in the case.[72]

While this arcane and apparently never ending case has been a focus of criticism of support of class actions by funders, it raises important issues.[73] Because of its multi-forum nature, a setback to a party in one jurisdiction can be countered by progress elsewhere. In September 2015 the Canadian Supreme Court allowed the plaintiffs to continue enforcement proceedings against Chevron assets in Canada. This case illustrates the lawful steps available to a large multi-national to litigate (and arbitrate) each and every aspect of a claim using resources not available to many plaintiffs without financial support. Whatever the rights and wrongs of the Lago Agrio case, it is an essential part of the architecture of international dispute resolution that no matter where the forum of the original litigation or the seat of arbitration was, enforcement of a judgement can be made in any country party to the New York Convention.[74] That enforcement process may well be in a jurisdiction of which the judgment holder has little or no knowledge or experience and without funding support the award will be moot.

11.4 General conclusion on behaviour

The picture presented above, while a matter of concern, is not particularly surprising given the contentious and adversarial nature of litigation. This is not a mass-market and the number of cases funded is small but there do not appear to be generalised problems or scandals about the funding regime in England. The ALF operates a voluntary complaint

71 R Parloff, 'Chevron Sues another Funder of Ecuadorian Litigation' (*Fortune*, 24 September 2014) < http://fortune.com/2014/09/24/chevron-sues-woodsford-litigation-funding/>.

72 The Chevron website annexes the settlement agreement in full. See <http://theamazonpost.com/chevron-ecuador/wp-content/uploads/Woodsford-Settlement-Agreement.pdf>.

73 For a discussion of this case (as of 2014) and TPF generally in the USA – suggesting that it will not generate frivolous suits – see DR Hensler, 'Third-Party Financing of Class Action Litigation in the United States: Will the Sky Fall?' (2014) 63 *DePaul Law Review* 499.

74 The Convention on the Recognition and Enforcement of Foreign Arbitral Awards, 1959.

system and ALF sources indicate that they have not received any complaints against members under this voluntary code. However, if the behaviour of funders does not suggest an urgent need to regulate, there are some structural issues that need to be looked at.

11.5 Transparency

TPF is a contractual relationship and is subject to normal commercial confidentiality. At the same time the ALF and Lord Justice Jackson have promoted the need for transparency in order to reassure the public and to preserve the reputation of the model. There is a tension here that exists in other forms of funding including DBAs and After the Event Insurance Cover.

In 2014[75] a member of ALF, Argentum Capital, was discussed by the board of the Association over the sources and adequacy of its capital and the transparency of is corporate structure. (ALF rules require minimum capital requirements of £2 million.) In due course Argentum voluntarily left the association.

A second issue of transparency is the disclosure of the funding arrangement to the opponent. The existence of an external supporter might well be relevance of the details of any funding agreement – when the funding is to be reviewed, the overall level of funding and so on – would give the opponent an unfair advantage in, for example, the timing and amount of offers to settle. Currently, since the abolition of additional liabilities[76] there is no requirement to disclose the existence of DBAs or CFAs, with some narrow exceptions.[77] [78] [79]

11.6 Control

The 2012 report made it clear that while champerty was no longer a bar to external funding maintenance, *control* of the litigation remained an issue. Control in this context could in its most egregious form involve the funder stepping into the shoes of the client, effectively becoming the client, and instructing the acting lawyers on that basis. Interviews carried out for this research suggests that while many jurisdictions[80] take a robust view that the funder should have full control, there remains considerable reticence by funders operating in England to adopt this position. While funders will contractually have right of access to

75 See K Beioley, 'Funding Fail: Argentum Exits Association of Funders' (*The Lawyer*, 30 April 2014) <www.thelawyer.com/issues/online-april-2014/funding-fail-argentum-exits-association-of-litigation-funders/>.

76 Under LASPO 2012.

77 Even before 2013 when there was a generalised disclosure requirement but no requirement to disclose details. See *Pedro Emiro Florez Arroyo and Others v BP Exploration Company (Colombia) Limited* [2010] EWHC 1643 (QB).

78 In the context of Investment Treaty Arbitration see the chapter of E De Brabandere herein.

79 The 2015 International Arbitration Survey showed widespread support full disclosure of the use of third-party funding (76 per cent) and the identity of the funder (63 per cent) but not details of the funding arrangements (71 per cent).

80 E.g. South Africa, Germany. In Australia in relation to class actions 'through their strict budgetary practices and project management of class claims, funders have been identified as effective monitors of class action law firm performance'. See the chapter of Waye and Morabito herein. Funders are subject to advice from the Australian Securities and Investment Commission and in some jurisdictions explicit court control but there is no statutory regulatory scheme. See Waye and Morabito 14, 15. In the Netherlands funders can operate under a full power of attorney (a mandate) so that they are co-terminous with the client and can instruct a lawyer to act (in some cases an assignment can be taken).

information and to take a view on settlement they do not want day-to-day control. There is a risk of a court finding that the funder has strayed into unlawful maintenance and therefore become liable for a full non-party costs order outside the protection of the *Arkin* limit on liability. Equally important is the fact that funders do not have the resources to exercise day-to-day control. The business model is that by selecting cases introduced by experienced lawyers or by referring cases to such lawyers, the funder's position is protected. Moreover, by establishing some distance from the client, necessary objectivity is introduced. This analysis further reinforces the view that TPF will be reluctant to enter into the retail market, particularly class actions, where asymmetry of information would put pressure on the TPF to intervene in decision-making unless and until a model develops allowing for a representative organisation or a law firm to take the lead in managing the litigation and liaising with the client base.

11.7 The prospects for state regulation

Interviews carried out for this research suggested no particular antipathy to state regulation from funders in England and in other jurisdictions, but no expectation that it was likely to happen. This view might alter if the market expresses concern.

England remains unique internationally in having a system of self-regulation for the funding sector,[81] but this approach is not unusual across many sectors in this country, particularly in the B2B sector where asymmetry of information may be less of a problem. In effect, an organisation starting up as a litigation funder could organise itself in such a way that it is not a member of ALF, nor subject to the Financial Conduct Authority, nor have staff who are professionally regulated. In accordance with normal English law what is not unlawful or illegal is lawful and the barriers to entry in this business might seem low. However, the prospects for such a business are likely to be limited. The complexities of the funding business including legal, managerial, regulatory, project management, business development, and so on dictate a certain 'heft' to be successful and to be attractive to the market. Further, membership of the self-regulatory body, ALF, depends on a number of factors including having £2 million capital. A business that does not have that capital under its control will be unattractive to prospective claimants, likely to be businesses themselves and their lawyers, looking for funding support to be put in place that will be available if and when called for. This might suggest an entry into this market by large financial institutions such as banks or insurers who are extensively, if not always adequately, regulated. However, the experience of Allianz Litigation Funding in England, a division of Allianz ProzessFinanz GmbH in Germany, suggests otherwise.[82] It entered and left the funding market citing 'irreconcilable systemic conflict'. In other words, its core customers didn't like Allianz helping people to sue them. Absent a major scandal, an expansion into retail or changing market demand – none of which seems likely – the regulatory position, while needing to be kept under review, seems unlikely to alter.

81 R Mulheron, 'England's Unique Approach to the Self-Regulation of Third Party Funding: The Critical Analysis of Recent Developments' (2014) 73(3) *The Cambridge Law Journal* 570.

82 See CJS Hodges, J Peysner and A Nurse, *Litigation Funding Status and Issues* (Centre for Socio-Legal Studies, Oxford University and Lincoln Law School, University of Lincoln 2012) 62.

12. Overall conclusion: Playing the man not the ball

Litigation is not for the faint-hearted. To achieve a just result, parties must be able to put their case robustly and, increasingly under judicial direction, be prepared to consider mediation to resolve issues. Litigation is a central plank of human rights and just, proportionate, and efficient litigation in dispute resolution systems are fundamental to a healthy democracy. This analysis suggests that while it is entirely appropriate for opponents to thoroughly test parties' claims (playing the ball), they should be reticent in challenging the financial basis – in individual and aggregated cases – that allows the party to access justice (playing the man). The common-law principle that insurance is not relevant to a party's right to participate in a case has been somewhat abridged (see *XYZ v Various Companies (PIP Breast Implant Litigation)* [2013] EWHC 3643 in the context of case management) or, of course, in the principle that the third-party funder should partially satisfy an adverse costs order. Both courts and legislature have been careful to preserve, as far as possible and practical, the right of a party to come to court.

While it may not have felt so at the time even during the most bitter periods of the 'Cost War', there was a consensus that individuals were entitled to bring forward arguable cases and recover reasonable costs for doing so. What the insurance industry objected to was the sudden and unprecedented hike in the legal costs created by the recovery of additional liabilities under the Access to Justice Act 1999. In due course those additional liabilities were restrained and finally abolished. However, the replacement of conditional fees with recoverable additional liabilities by, for example, DBAs was intended to be mitigated by an increase in general damages.[83] In other words, there was no substantial disagreement between the claimant and defendant lobbies that a solution should be found to ensure that claimants could have effective access to court.

The campaign by Justice Not Profit appears to have entered new territory by an unprecedented generic attack on access to justice. Such an approach poses the danger of establishing a narrative in the media, outpacing the evidence. This happened after the Access to Justice Act when the trope of a 'compensation crisis' became solidly established and have not been displaced despite evidence to the contrary.[84] For example, Lord Young of Graffam's Report to the Prime Minister, 'Common Sense Common Safety: Following a Whitehall-Wide Review of the Operation of Health and Safety Laws' and the Growth of the Compensation Culture'[85] established that no such culture existed but there was a *perception* that it did and so there should be action to curb claims.

The Justice Not Profit Campaign first challenges the concept of 'class actions' and second attacks TPF – 'financial speculators...manipulating the civil justice system for profit...unregulated and predatory third-party litigation funding'.[86] This is a generic attack that does not display a concern for cultural sensitivities and different approaches to civil

83 If personal injury damages were increased by 10 per cent it was calculated that the client would be held harmless *after* deduction of the lawyer's 'cut'. Thus, the defendant would not pay the lawyer's 'cut' over and above costs (as in the original 'additional liabilities' scheme under the Access to Justice Act 1999) but via an increase in damages.

84 See J Peysner, *Compensation Crazy: Do We Blame and Claim Too Much Institute of Ideas?* (London: Hodder and Staughton 2002).

85 <www.gov.uk/government/uploads/system/uploads/attachment_data/file/60905/402906_CommonSense_acc.pdf>.

86 Author's edits from Justice Not Profit letters.

justice problems, including the difference between the 'English cost rule' and the 'US rule'. Certainly, the International Chamber has introduced discussion on civil justice that is to be welcomed. Most academic work on justice has, historically, been on criminal process and legal aid and there has been too little concern about civil justice and funding of access through the new market mechanisms. Certainly, the author's view is that the borders of litigation need to be explored. While the new models of ADR and ombudsmen have a vital role there are disputes – often involving individual citizens or SMEs – where unequal power relations can only be balanced by access to funding and access to appropriate procedural solutions, such as aggregate actions.

TPF forms a new and useful addition in England to the range of funding options available. To attack it (the 'Man') rather than to dispute the claims it supports (the 'Ball') is as unwelcome in the dispute resolution as it would be on the sports field.

Bibliography

Ames J., 'Litigation Financing Needs Crackdown' *The Times* (London, 11 December 2011).

Australian Government Productivity Commission, *Access to Justice Arrangements (Productivity Commission Inquiry Report no 72)* (Vol 2, Canberra: Commonwealth of Australia 2014) 612–613.

Beioley K., 'Funding Fail: Argentum Exits Association of Funders' (*The Lawyer*, 30 April 2014) <www.thelawyer.com/issues/online-april-2014/funding-fail-argentum-exits-association-of-litigation-funders/>.

Beisner J., J. Miller and G. Rubin, *Selling Lawsuits, Buying Trouble* (Washington, DC: US Chamber Institute for Legal Reform 2009).

Blavi F., 'Towards a Uniform Regulation of Third Party Funding in International Arbitration' (2015) *International Law Review* 143.

Chua E. and N. Patmore, 'Singapore: Third Party Funding – An Emergent Reality' (2015) 10(5) *G.A.R.* 43.

Dluzniak S., 'The (Other) Benefits of Third Party Funding for In-House Counsel' (2015) 230(May) *The In-House Lawyer* 37.

Editorial, 'Litigation Funding' *The Law Society of England and Wales* (London, October 2015) 3.

Genn H., *Paths to Justice: What People Do and Think about Going to Law* (Oxford: Hart Publishing 1999).

Hensler D.R., 'Third-Party Financing of Class Action Litigation in the United States: Will the Sky Fall?' (2014) 63 *DePaul Law Review* 499.

Higgins A. and A. Zuckerman, 'Class Actions Come to England – More Access to Justice and More of a Compensation Culture, but They are Superior to the Alternatives' (2016) 35(1) *Civil Justice Quarterly* 1.

Hill C., *The Century of Revolution 1603–1704* (Oxford: Routledge 2001).

Hodges C.J.S., *Multi-Party Actions* (Oxford: Oxford University Press 2000).

—— S. Vogenauer and M. Tulibacka (eds), *The Costs and Funding of Civil Litigation: A Comparative Perspective* (Oxford: Hart Publishing 2010).

—— J. Peysner and A. Nurse, *Litigation Funding Status and Issues* (Centre for Socio-Legal Studies, Oxford University and Lincoln Law School, University of Lincoln 2012).

Hvid M. and J. Peysner, 'Comparing Economic Incentives to Pursue Private Actions across EU Member States' in B. Rodger (ed.), *Competition Law. Comparative Private Enforcement and Collective Redress Across the EU* (Alphen aan den Rijn: Kluwer Law International 2014) 195.

Jay A., 'Funding Insolvency Litigation: A. New Dawn' (2015) 8(5) *Corporate Rescue and Insolvency* 183.

Juska Z., 'The Future of Collective Antitrust Redress: Is Something New under the Sun?' (2015) *Global Competition Litigation Review* 14.

Kalajdzic J., P. Cashman and A. Longmoore, 'Justice for Profit: A Comparative Analysis of Australian, Canadian and U.S. Third Party Litigation Funding' (2013) 61 *Am.J.Comp.L.* 93.

Lord Neuberger, 'From Barratry, Maintenance and Champerty to Litigation Funding' (Harbour Litigation Funding First Annual Lecture, Gray's Inn, 8 May 2013).

Mozetic A., 'Collective Redress: A Case for Opt-out Class Actions in England and Wales' (2016) 35(1) *Civil Justice Quarterly* 29.

Mulheron R., 'England's Unique Approach to The Self-Regulation of Third Party Funding: The Critical Analysis of Recent Developments' (2014) 73(3) *The Cambridge Law Journal* 570.

NERA, *International Comparisons of Litigation Costs: Canada, Europe, Japan, and the United States* (Washington: U.S. Chamber Institute for Legal Reform) (2013).

Parloff R., 'Chevron Sues Another Funder of Ecuadorian Litigation' (*Fortune*, 24 September 2014) <http://fortune.com/2014/09/24/chevron-sues-woodsford-litigation-funding/>.

Peysner J., *Compensation Crazy: Do We Blame and Claim Too Much Institute of Ideas?* (London: Hodder and Staughton 2002).

—— 'Access to Justice in a Multi-Party Context' in P. Odell and C. Willet (eds), *Global Governance and the Quest for Justice: Volume III* (Oxford: Hart Publishing 2008) 103–115.

—— *Access to Justice: A Critical Analysis of Recoverable Conditional Fees and No-Win No-Fee Funding* (London: Palgrave Macmillan 2014).

—— *Impact of the 'Jackson' Reforms: Some Emerging Themes* (London: Civil Justice Council 2014).

Regan D., 'The Future Is Fixed' *Litigation Funding* (London: December 2015) 8.

Rodger B., 'The Consumer Rights Act 2015 and Collective Redress for Competition Law Infringements in the UK: A Class Act?' (2015) 3(2) *Journal of Antitrust Enforcement* 258.

Rothwell R., 'Jackson Warns against "Vested Interests" on DBAs' (*Law Society Gazette*, London, 21 October 2014) <www.lawgazette.co.uk/law/jackson-warns-against-vested-interests-on-dbas/5044478.fullarticle>.

RSM Production Corp v Saint Lucia unreported 8 April 2015 (ICSID) (2015) 81(3) *Arbitration* 304.

Sebok A.J., 'The Inauthentic Claim' (2012) 61 *DePaul Law Review* 615.

Spendlove H., 'I'm In with the "In Crowd"' (2015) 112(15) *L.S.G.* 20.

5 Legal costs awards and access to justice in Dutch intellectual property cases

How the IPR Enforcement Directive impacts on litigation and settlement behaviour in IP disputes

Charlotte Vrendenbarg

1. Introduction

With the implementation of the IPR Enforcement Directive,[1] the Dutch legislature has introduced an exception to the civil procedure rules on recoverable costs. These rules, which currently apply to all but intellectual property rights (IPR) enforcement cases, set forth a tariff system: the losing party is ordered to compensate the winning party for legal fees according to a tariff (*liquidatietarief*). In practice, this tariff tends to be well below the actual cost of the services of a lawyer. With the introduction of article 1019h of the Dutch Code of Civil Procedure (DCCP) on 1 May 2007, this changed for IPR enforcement cases. On the basis of article 1019h DCCP, legal costs including lawyer's fees may be shifted in full to the losing party. In other civil proceedings, the conventional rule providing mitigated compensation for legal costs ('losing party pays according to a tariff') remains in effect.

In legal writing, the actual effect of this new rule laid down in article 1019h DCCP on litigation behaviour has been the subject of debate. Some have argued that the prospect of being ordered to reimburse these costs affects the behaviour of litigants in IP disputes. Particular emphasis is placed on the negative effects of the provision. It is said that the risk of being ordered to pay the larger part of the legal costs or even the total amount of the costs incurred by the opposing party deters parties to an IP dispute from bringing proceedings. Litigants may be inclined to settle rather than be exposed to the risk of having to pay these costs. The number of IP cases is said to have decreased as a result. The legislative intent of the provision was, however, the exact opposite, namely, that the rule would have a positive effect on the behaviour of litigants. In short, the legislature's reasoning was that parties to an IP dispute would be encouraged to 'claim their rights' because of the prospect of (full) compensation of the legal costs by the defendant.

These two versions of the behavioural effects of the newly introduced article 1019h DCCP are obviously incompatible. Therefore, one needs to consider the empirical evidence for guidance. Unfortunately, the empirical underpinning of both behavioural mechanisms

1 Directive 2004/48/EC of the European Parliament and the Council of 29 April 2004 on the enforcement of intellectual property rights (2004) OJ L157/32.

is lacking. In this contribution, we set out to answer which of the two mechanisms is actually dominant in current Dutch IP-practice. Does it offer incentives to IP-right holders to enforce their rights and a disincentive to infringers or does it merely deter all concerned to go to court? To answer this question, in the spring of 2015, we conducted a survey of the effects of article 1019h DCCP among expert IP lawyers. Analysis of the results of this survey, in view of the available research on the effects of costs shifting, sheds further light on the tenability of the two opposing versions of the impact of article 1019h DCCP and, in doing so, it contributes to the debate about the sense and nonsense of article 1019h DCCP legal cost awards in Dutch IP practice.

This chapter is structured as follows. First, we explain the background and aim of article 14 of the IP Enforcement Directive (2). Second, the different costs shifting rules under Dutch civil law will be described (3). A discussion of the available research on the effects of costs shifting follows (4). Thereafter, the research method is described (5). This is followed by a presentation of the main survey results concerning the influence and effects of article 1019h on the decision to litigate or to settle (6) and on the expenditure in IP litigation (7). Lastly, the results of the survey are evaluated in light of the literature on the effects of costs shifting (8), followed by our conclusion (9).

2. Article 14 IPR Enforcement Directive: Aim and intended effect

The costs of IP litigation are often said to be high, if not excessive.[2] The relatively high level of costs is explained by the high level of specialisation of lawyers in this field, the costs involved in tracking down alleged infringers as well as the gathering of evidence, high evidential burdens and the need for expert opinions in complex infringement cases.[3] Stakeholders, practitioners and scholars have expressed their concerns about the extent of IP litigation costs[4] such that these IP costs constitute an important obstacle or even a '*key deterring factor*' for initiating enforcement proceedings.[5] Particularly small and medium-sized enterprises (SMEs) are said to be deterred from engaging in litigation due to high costs.[6]

Additionally, at European legislative level it is recognised that the costs of IP litigation can be an important obstacle for the enforcement of intellectual property rights. The IPR Enforcement Directive, which aims to harmonise national legislation in the context of civil enforcement of IP rights, explicitly addresses the issue of costs. It stipulates that the

2 WIPO, 'IP Litigation Costs – Special Edition' (2010) 1 *WIPO Magazine* 2; European Commission, 'Syntheses of the Responses "Civil Enforcement of Intellectual Property Rights: Public Consultation on the Efficiency of Proceedings and Accessibility of Measures"' (Brussels 2013) 8ff; European Commission, 'Staff Working Document Accompanying the Report on IPR Enforcement Directive 2004/48' SEC (2010) 1589 final, 24.

3 European Observatory on Counterfeit and Piracy 'Damages in Intellectual Property Rights' (2010) 5ff; WIPO, 'IP Litigation Costs – Special Edition' (2010) 1 *WIPO Magazine* 2ff; SEC (2010) 1589, 24.

4 See also F Wilman, 'The Vigilance of Individuals. How, When and Why the EU Legislates to Facilitate the Private Enforcement of EU Law before National Courts' (Leiden: Wöhrmann 2014) 354 with further references.

5 European Commission (2013) 8ff.

6 Lord Justice R Jackson, 'Review of Civil Litigation Costs: Preliminary Report - Volume 1' (London: Judiciary of England and Wales 2009) 257 <www.judiciary.gov.uk>; European Commission, 'Proposal for a Directive of the European Parliament and the Council on Measures and Procedures to Ensure the Enforcement of Intellectual Property Rights' COM (2003) 46 final, 53.

measures, procedures and remedies to ensure the enforcement of the intellectual property rights covered by the directive shall not be '*unnecessarily complicated or costly*' (article 3). In article 14, Member States are required to ensure that '*reasonable and proportionate legal costs and other expenses incurred by the successful party shall, as a general rule, be borne by the unsuccessful party, unless equity does not allow this*'. The European Court of Justice EU (ECJ) ruled that this provision aims to strengthen the level of protection of intellectual property rights, by avoiding the situation in which an injured party is deterred from bringing legal proceedings in order to protect his rights.[7] According to the ECJ, this entails that the infringer '*must generally bear all the financial consequences of his conduct*' (Para. 48). In other words, the aim, as well as the intended effect of the legal costs provision, is that parties who would initially have refrained from initiating legal proceedings due to the irrecoverable legal costs, are now encouraged to go to court, enhancing the overall level of protection of IP rights within the EU.

Indeed, the Commission initially proposed a rule that would entail *full* reimbursement of all costs incurred, including legal fees.[8] The above-cited ECJ ruling seems to refer to this initial proposal. The proposed provision, however, was heavily criticised by Member States, that felt that the rather precarious issue of costs allocation is in fact a matter of national sovereignty.[9] In the final version, the explicit reference to lawyer's fees was deleted, and instead of the term 'full' the criteria 'reasonable and proportionate' were added. The result is a provision on legal costs shifting that is formulated in such a broad manner that most Member States have not implemented this provision specifically, as they considered their existing costs rules to already cover the Directive's requirements.[10] As is illustrated below, the Netherlands form a notable exception.

Although Member States are left with some leeway, they are obliged to ensure that national legislation is *effective*, meaning that the objective of the Directive is achieved.[11] In conformity with the aim of article 14 of the Directive, this entails that Member States are obliged to ensure that the national rules for allocating costs secure wide access to justice for IP right holders. In this respect, stakeholders and practitioners have drawn attention to the inability to recover the full costs in most Member States, which would constitute a disincentive to pursue IP infringements for all right holders, particularly for SMEs.[12] In several countries where the shiftable legal fees are calculated on the basis of tariffs, such as Germany and Belgium, it is debated whether these rules are commensurate to the purpose

7 ECJ 18 October 2011, C-406/09 *(Realchemie v. Bayer)*, paras 48–49.

8 COM (2003) 46 final, 24: '*Article 18 provides for the legal costs, lawyer's fees and any other expenses incurred by the successful party (for example, investigation costs, costs for expert opinions) to be borne in full by the other party, unless equity or the economic situation of the other party does not allow this.*'

9 See CJS Vrendenbarg, 'De "volledige" proceskostenveroordeling in IE-zaken: een kritische bespreking van de implementatie en interpretatie van artikel 14 Handhavingsrichtlijn in Nederland' (2013) 6 *BIE* 160ff. For a discussion and further references, see also Wilman (2014) 145.

10 SEC (2010) 1589, 24.

11 Art 288, third subpara TFEU; ECJ 18 July 2011, C-324/09 *(L'Oréal v. eBay)*.

12 European Observatory on Counterfeit and Piracy, 'Damages in Intellectual Property Rights' 5ff. <http://ec.europa.eu/internal_market/iprenforcement/docs/damages_en.pdf>; European Commission, 'Syntheses of the Responses "Civil Enforcement of Intellectual Property Rights: Public Consultation on the Efficiency of Proceedings and Accessibility of Measures"' (Brussels 2013) 9.

of the Directive.[13] Prior to the implementation of article 14 of the Directive, similar discussions took place in the Netherlands.[14]

3. Costs shifting rules under Dutch law

3.1 Costs shifting in IP enforcement cases: The implementation of article 14 of the IPR Enforcement Directive in the Netherlands.

In contrast to Germany and Belgium, the Dutch legislator interpreted article 14 of the Directive as requiring divergent and '*generous*' legal costs awards in IP cases.[15] According to the legislator the provision required even '*full*'[16] legal costs awards in cases concerning so-called counterfeit or piracy practices.[17] The legislator seemed convinced that compensation for legal fees based on liquidated tariffs could not be considered as 'reasonable and proportional' within the meaning of the IP Enforcement Directive. Since 1 May 2007, therefore, in language identical to article 14 of the Directive, article 1019h DCCP is applicable in cases concerning the enforcement of IP rights.

13 S Rojahn and JP Rektorschek, 'Europäische Harmonisierung der Kostenerstattung im Bereich des gewerblichen Rechtsschutzes – ist RVG noch EU-konform?' (2014) 1 *Mitteilungen der deutschen Patentanwälte* 8; J Deene, 'De rechtsplegingsvergoeding in procedures inzake intellectuele rechten: een sui generis-regime?' (2011) 23 *RW* 946. Recently, the Antwerp Court of Appeal referred a preliminary question to the ECJ on whether cost-capping by means of tariffs is allowed under the IPR Enforcement Directive; Hof van Beroep, Antwerpen, 26 January 2015, *IEF* 14605 *Telenet v. United Video Properties* (available via <www.ie-forum.nl>). For a discussion see CJS Vrendenbarg, 'Toelaatbaarheid van forfaitaire proceskostenvergoeding bij handhaving van IE-rechten: De proceskostenregelingen van België, Nederland en het Unified Patent Court getoetst aan de beginselen van het Unierecht' (2015) 5 *IER* 259ff.

14 C Gielen, 'De richtlijn handhaving IE-rechten' (2005) 1 *NTER* 6ff; JLRA Huydecoper, 'Nous maintiendrons – de nieuwe Richtlijn Handhaving' (2004) 4 *AMI* 117ff.

15 Kamerstukken II 2005/06, 30 392, nr 3 (MvT) 26: '*Artikel 14 van de richtlijn verplicht tot een ruime proceskostenveroordeling van de verliezende partij*'. (Translation: 'Article 14 of the directive requires a generous costs order of the losing party'.)

16 Kamerstukken II 2005/06, 30 392, nr 3 (MvT) 26: '*De rechter zal moeten komen tot een veroordeling in evenredige kosten, te toetsen aan de redelijkheid en billijkheid. Deze billijkheid zal bijvoorbeeld meespelen bij de proceskostenveroordeling van een inbreukmaker te goeder trouw. Beperking van de proceskostenveroordeling tot hetgeen onder het huidige recht gebruikelijk is, ligt dan meer voor de hand dan een volledige kostenveroordeling. Deze laatste ligt vooral in de rede wanneer het gaat om grootschalige namaak of piraterij*'. (Translation: 'It is the judge's task to order reimbursement of the proportional costs, that are to be tested against the criteria of fairness and reasonableness.. Equity may play a role in the case of a cost order against an infringer who acted in good faith. In that case, mitigation of the costs awarded toward the liquidated tariff seems more appropriate than a full costs award. Full costs awards seem more appropriate in cases of widespread counterfeit or piracy'.) The literature states that, in practice, where generous or full costs awards in all types of IP cases are the rule rather than the exception, these considerations appear to be of little significance.M Driessen, 'De willekeur van de proceskostenveroordeling' (2007) 6 *BIE* 343ff.

17 The definition of counterfeit according to the TRIPs-Agreement (Agreement on the Trade-Related aspects of Intellectual Property Rights) is: '*Counterfeit trademark goods shall mean any goods, including packaging, bearing without authorisation a trademark which is identical to the trademark validly registered in respect of such goods, or which cannot be distinguished in its essential aspects from such a trademark and which thereby infringes the rights of the owner of the trademark in question under the law of the country of importation*'. According to TRIPs, the definition of piracy is: '*Pirated copyright goods shall mean any goods which are copies made without the consent of the right holder or person duly authorised by the right holder in the country of production and which are made directly or indirectly from an article where the making of that copy would have constituted an infringement of a copyright or a related right under the law of the country of importation*'.

The terms 'generous' and 'full' were taken very literally in legal practice and lead to full costs awards becoming the rule rather than the exception.[18] By Dutch standards, costs awards in IP cases became alarmingly high. A need for clear standards by which to assess the reasonableness and proportionality of legal costs in IP cases in practice gave rise to the issuance of guidelines called *Indicatietarieven in IE-zaken* (Indicative Tariffs in IP cases) in August 2008.[19] Similar tariffs also became applicable to appeals and Supreme Court proceedings as of 1 January 2015.[20] These tariffs do not apply to patent cases. The tariffs distinguish between different types of procedures (interim proceedings and proceedings on the merits) and they also relate to the complexity of a case. The tariffs are not intended to be flat rates but merely recommendations for the maximum amount of legal costs that can generally be considered reasonable and proportional. The tariffs do not prevent the award of a higher or lower amount. In fact, '*winner takes all*' remains the starting point.[21] In the literature, it is argued that much remains unclear about the application of 1019h and the indicative tariffs. Whether the indicative tariffs are applicable (and if so, which tariff applies) depends on many factors. This would lead to difficulty in predicting the outcome of cost awards.[22] The fact that article 1019h is exclusively applicable to claims based on IP law makes the cost award in so-called mixed cases (in which IP-related claims are accompanied by other claims, such as claims under tort law, to which the mitigated costs-shifting rule applies) even more complicated and unpredictable.

In legal literature, the rule of article 1019h DCCP is heavily criticised for *impeding* access to justice. The fear of being ordered to compensate for all costs incurred by the opposing party could have a 'chilling effect' on parties involved in IP disputes, particularly, financially weaker parties.[23] Furthermore, the unpredictability of the financial risk involved in litigation may lead plaintiffs to refrain from instigating proceedings. Defendants may be more inclined to agree to settle.[24] According to some, the provision has actually led to a decrease in the number of IP cases in court.[25]

3.2 Costs shifting in 'general' civil proceedings

The conventional costs shifting rule of article 237 DCCP, which remains in effect in cases that do not concern the enforcement of IP rights, provides for predictable and low cost

18 Driessen (2007) 343ff; DJG Visser and A Tsoutsanis, 'De volledige proceskostenveroordeling in IE-zaken' (2006) 34 *NJB* 1940ff.

19 The Indicatietarieven are issued by the 'Landelijk Overleg Voorzitters van de Civiele Sectoren van de rechtbanken (LOVC)' (National Consultation of Chairs of the Civil Sectors of the Courts).

20 The *Indicatietarieven in IE-zaken* are available via <www.rechtspraak.nl>.

21 See art 10 of the *Indicatietarieven in IE-zaken Hoge Raad* (Surpreme Court).

22 P Sluijter, *Sturen met proceskosten. Wie betaalt de rekening van verstorend procesgedrag?* (Deventer: Kluwer 2011) 275; W Wefers Bettink and J Hoefnagel, 'Artikel 1019h Rv en de indicatietarieven: toepassing in de praktijk' (2010) 47 *IER* 336ff; S van Gompel and W Olieslagers, 'Het proceskostenrisico in IE-zaken - Een empirisch onderzoek naar toepassing van de indicatietarieven' (2014) 5 *AMI* 133ff.

23 See the opinion of Advocate-General Verkade in Dutch Court of Appeal case HR 3 October 2014, ECLI:NL:HR:2014:2900 *(Leo v. Sandoz)*; PMM van der Grinten, 'The Netherlands: Policy Observations' in C Hodges, S Vogenauer and M Tulibacka (eds), *Funding and Costs of Civil Litigation: A Comparative Perspective* (Oxford: Hart Publishing 2010) 421ff.

24 Van der Grinten (2010) 421ff; DJG Visser, 'Kroniek van de intellectuele eigendom' (2012) 15 *NJB* 1041ff; DJG Visser, 'Kroniek van de intellectuele eigendom' (2015) 15 *NJB* 973ff.

25 Asser procesrecht/Van Schaick 2, 130, 'Eerste aanleg, 130 Artikel 1019h' (2011); Van der Grinten (2010) 424.

awards made to the successful party.[26] While some of the costs incurred during civil proceedings, such as court fees, bailiff's costs and witness costs, are usually fully reimbursed, the pre-summons costs and lawyer's fees are mitigated. Pre-summons costs are awarded to the extent that they meet the requirement of *reasonableness*.[27] The calculation of the shiftable lawyer's fees, which are often said to be the greatest expense for litigants, is based on a liquidated tariff known as the '*liquidatietarief*'.[28] The number of procedural steps taken is multiplied by a tariff that is linked to the value of the claim, regardless of the actual hourly fees and the time and costs spent on the case. Although the liquidated tariff is a non-binding guideline issued by the courts and the Dutch Bar Association, judges tend to follow the liquidated tariff. Under exceptional circumstances, full costs may be awarded to the prevailing party. The policy objective of the mitigated and predictable cost award based on article 237 DCCP and the *liquidatietarief* is to protect the losing party against high shiftable costs.[29]

The idea that high litigation costs may unduly impede access to justice is deeply rooted in the Netherlands.[30] In fact, even at the time of implementation of article 1019h, the legislator feared that a generous award of legal costs could impair access to legal justice:

> The measures being implemented in this legislative proposal are not of such a nature that we can expect that rights holders who would previously have refrained from starting an infringement procedure, will now start a procedure. The opposite can more readily be argued. A plaintiff will run the risk of being ordered to pay all of the legal costs, his own as well as those of the opposing party, while now only certain fixed amounts can be claimed from the losing party.[31]

4. Available research on the effects of costs shifting in civil litigation

The contradictory expectations and hypotheses about the effects of article 1019h gave rise to this study. As mentioned earlier, there is no empirical research available on the effects of the introduction of article 1019h. It has occasionally been suggested that quantitative data on caseload before and after introduction of article 1019h in itself, would reveal little about the cause of any decline. In other words, it would not be possible to draw concrete causal conclusions from the figures alone.[32] Moreover, it has been stated that because of the uncertainties surrounding the application of article 1019h and the *Indicatietarieven*, the effects in the periods before and after implementation could neither be compared with each

26 See also M Tuil, 'The Netherlands' in C Hodges, S Vogenauer and M Tulibacka (eds), *Funding and Costs of Civil Litigation: A Comparative Perspective* (Oxford: Hart Publishing 2010) 401ff.

27 The pre-summons costs that are incurred with the collection are calculated based on a statutory rate schedule.

28 The *liquidatietarief* is available via <www.rechtspraak.nl>.

29 Tuil (2010) 415.

30 Tuil (2010) 404.

31 Kamerstukken II 2005/06, 30 392, nr 3 (MvT) 16: '*De maatregelen die in dit wetsvoorstel worden ingevoerd zijn niet van dien aard dat verwacht wordt dat rechthebbenden die voorheen wellicht afzagen van een inbreukprocedure, nu die procedure wel zullen starten. Het tegendeel kan eerder betoogd worden. De eiser loopt het risico veroordeeld te worden in alle proceskosten, zowel die van zichzelf als die van zijn wederpartij, terwijl nu enkel bepaalde forfaitaire bedragen verschuldigd zijn door de verliezende partij.*'

32 Sluijter (2011) 253ff.

other nor with the effects on non-IP cases in the same period.[33] Given that the practical application of 1019h and the *Indicatietarieven* is unclear and ambiguous in several respects, conducting research in this area is indeed arduous.

A first step towards studying the effects of the introduction of article 1019h would be to draw parallels with earlier theoretical and empirical studies on the effects of differing rules for awarding legal costs. In the *law and economics,* the question of the effects of legal costs shifting has received much attention.[34] The literature mainly focuses on costs shifting based on the loser pays rule, which is the predominant rule in most Western countries.[35] The recoverable amount of legal costs, however, varies substantially amongst these countries. In order to be able to predict or explain the effects of victory-based costs shifting systems, the literature often distinguishes between two extremes: the *English rule* (loser pays all) on one hand, and the *American rule* (each party bears his own costs) on the other.[36] In the 'scale' between these two, the more complex systems that provide mitigated costs awards (such as the conventional Dutch rule) should be placed somewhere in the middle.[37] Although there are differences between the English rule and article 1019h, the costs shifting rule of article 1019h, should actually be placed somewhere near the English rule. The economic literature on the English rule may thus provide valuable insights into the possible effects of article 1019h.

To examine the effects of the different costs shifting mechanisms, the standard economic theory of litigation is often used.[38] According to this, the decision to raise proceedings or to settle a dispute depends on the outcome of a cost–benefit analysis.[39] It is assumed that a party will only proceed to court if the expected value of the claim (the expected judgment multiplied by the probability of prevailing) exceeds the expected costs (the total amount of legal costs).[40] If the costs are expected to exceed the expected value of the claim (so-called negative expected value cases), the plaintiff will not have a credible threat to go to court.[41] Litigation in negative expected value cases is therefore deemed unlikely. There are exceptions, however. Kobayashi and Parker (2000) show that negative expected value cases may also be initiated in order to extract a settlement.[42] According to Visscher and Schepens

33 Sluijter (2011) 348.

34 For an overview see Katz AW and CW Sanchirico, 'Fee Shifting in Litigation: Survey and Assessment' (2010) University of Pennsylvania Institute for Law and Economics Research Paper No. 10-30 <http://ssrn.com/abstract=1714089>.

35 AW Katz, 'Indemnity of Legal Fees' in B Bouckaert and G De Geest (eds), *Encyclopedia of Law and Economics, Volume V. The Economics of Crime and Litigation* (Cheltenham: Edward Elgar 2000) 63–94.

36 It should be noted that these rules are formulated in an extreme manner, disregarding various nuances of the respective rules.

37 Sluijter (2011) 256–258.

38 S Shavell, 'Suit Settlement, and Trial: A Theoretical Analysis under Alternative Methods for the Allocating of Legal Costs' (1982) 11 *Journal of Legal Studies* 55–81; S Shavell, 'Basic Theory of Litigation' in *Foundations of Economic Analysis of Law* (Cambridge: Harvard University Press 2004) 389ff.

39 Shavell (1982) 389ff. Litigants in IP disputes indeed tend to base the decision to litigate or to settle on a cost–benefit analysis; see Wilman (2014) 354ff with further references, see also F Fischmann, 'Patent Litigation and Costs Shifting in Europe: Critical Appraisal and Proposal of Alternative Solutions' (2014) 10(2) *Journal of Intellectual Property Law & Practice* 98ff.

40 Shavell (2004) 390; L Visscher and T Schepens, 'A Law and Economics Approach to Cost Shifting, Fee Arrangements and Legal Expense Insurance' in M Tuil and L Visscher (eds), *New Trends in Financing Civil Litigation in Europe – A Legal, Empirical, and Economic Analysis* (Cheltenham: Edward Elgar 2010) 7–32.

41 Shavell (1982) 3ff; Visscher and Schepens (2010) 10.

42 BH Kobayashi and JS Parker, 'Civil Procedure: General' in B Bouckaert and G De Geest (eds), *Encyclopedia of Law and Economics, Volume V. The Economics of Crime and Litigation* (Cheltenham: Edward Elgar 2000) 1–26.

(2010), this could occur if the defendant's costs for going to court exceed the costs of settlement, even if the defendant is certain to prevail in court.[43]

The theory based on the standard model is that the greater the likelihood of prevailing in court and the higher the expected benefits, the greater the willingness to raise a court action.[44] This effect is considered to be stronger under the English rule: the higher the probability of winning, the lower the probability of having to bear the legal costs (which are expected to be shifted in full to the losing party), whereas under the American rule the prevailing party would still have to bear his own legal costs.[45] The English rule therefore encourages claims with relatively high *ex ante* probabilities of success.[46] At the same time the English rule discourages 'weak claims': the lower the probabilities of prevailing, the higher the probability of having to bear the legal costs *including* the opposing party's legal costs. [47]

Significantly, the model assumes that litigants are risk neutral, that they behave rationally and regard suit and settlement solely as a financial matter.[48] It is recognised, however, that (subjective) circumstances such as risk profile and rationality of the parties to a dispute may in fact play a decisive role. In that respect, the literature distinguishes various interrelated factors and effects that determine the likely effect of costs shifting on the decision to litigate or to settle.

First, the risk attitude of parties is recognised as an important factor in determining the effect of costs shifting.[49] Litigation entails uncertainty. The uncertainty as to the outcome of a case will weigh heavier for the risk-averse party, leading to less willingness to go to court. This effect is said to be reinforced under the English rule.[50] By increasing both the returns from success and the losses from defeat, the English rule enlarges the private risk of litigation.[51] There is literally more at stake under the English rule. In this connection, several authors argue that the English rule discourages risk-averse parties from filing or defending civil proceedings, *regardless* of the merits of their claims.[52] Notably, the factor 'costs' in the cost–benefit analysis is more unpredictable under the English rule than under the American rule. The party's own costs for legal representation are difficult to estimate and to manage. The exposure to the opposing party's costs can be entirely unpredictable and unmanageable.[53] The unpredictability of costs can have a significant, deterrent effect on a litigant who is less certain about the outcome of a case.[54] At the same time, the literature recognises a connection

43 Visscher and Schepens (2010) 10.

44 Shavell (1982) 3ff.

45 Shavell (1982) 5–6; Visscher and Schepens (2010) 12.

46 Shavell (1982) 3ff; Katz and Sanchirico (2010) 9; Visscher and Schepens (2010) 13.

47 Katz and Sanchirico (2010) 10–11; Visscher and Schepens (2010) 14; JPB De Mot and GGA de Geest, *Juridische infrastructuur: een internationale vergelijking vanuit economisch perspectief* (Den Haag: WODC 2004) 49ff.

48 Shavell (1982) 3.

49 Shavell (1982) 4; Shavell (2004) 390; Katz and Sanchirico (2010) 11; Visscher and Schepens (2010) 13.

50 Shavell (1982) 8.

51 Katz and Sanchirico (2010) 11.

52 Katz and Sanchirico (2010) 34; TD Rowe Jr., 'The Legal Theory of Attorney Fee Shifting: A Critical Overview' (1982) *Duke Law Review* 651, 656.

53 C Hodges, S Vogenauer and M Tulibacka (eds), *Funding and Costs of Civil Litigation: A Comparative Perspective* (Oxford: Hart Publishing 2010).

54 HM Kritzer, 'Fee Arrangements and Fee Shifting: Lessons from the Experience in Ontario' (1984) 47 *Law & Contemp Probs* 125, 133; see also ES Knutsen 'The Costs of Costs: The Unfortunate Deterrence of Everyday Civil Litigation in Canada' (2010) 36 *Queen's Law Journal* 113 <http://ssrn.com/abstract=1667722>.

between risk attitude and (private) wealth or financial resources.[55] Rowe (1984) emphasises '*the particularly strong effect of risk aversion and sharply changing diminishing marginal utility of income and wealth on litigants of modest means, who may be especially influenced by the threat of substantial loss introduced by fee shifting*'.[56] In this respect it was stressed that costs shifting deters middle-class litigants from exercising their legal rights.[57]

Another factor that may determine the effect of costs shifting is the legal expenditure of both the plaintiff and the defendant.[58] If the expenditure of the defendant is expected to exceed the expenditure of the plaintiff, the plaintiff will be less willing to litigate, even if they have a strong claim. This effect is said to increase under the English rule.[59] The prospect of having to bear all costs, even if there is only a minimal chance of losing, may discourage the plaintiff from proceeding to court.[60] In the case where the plaintiff is expected to spend more on court proceedings, they will be more willing to litigate under the English rule than under the American rule.[61] Meanwhile, it has been established that the English rule encourages greater legal expenditure.[62] This so-called 'greater expenditure effect' can be explained by the fact that the amount spent on litigation can be regarded as a form of private investment. A litigant may be under the impression that higher expenditure will increase the prospect of a positive outcome (marginal over-optimism). In the case of marginal (over)optimism, costs shifting is considered to lower the expected marginal costs of litigation, since these costs are expected to be recovered by the losing party.[63] Empirical research by Snyder and Hughes (1990) supports the theory that the English rule leads to increased legal expenditure.[64] Snyder and Hughes further show that the 'greater expenditure effect' is reinforced in case of marginal over-optimism.[65]

Bearing in mind that the English rule is considered to increase legal expenditure on the one hand, and that the expected expenditure of the opposing party may be a decisive factor in the decision to litigate or to settle on the other, it could be assumed that the English rule results in a lower number of cases. Snyder and Hughes (1990) indeed found that the greater expenditure effect leads to a significantly higher percentage of dropped claims.[66] Hughes and Snyder (1995) also found that the number of cases in which the plaintiff prevailed increased under the English rule, which supports the theory that the English rule discourages weak cases and encourages strong cases.[67] Visscher and Schepens (2010) show

55 Shavell (1982) 4; Visscher and Schepens (2010) 13.

56 TD Rowe Jr., 'Predicting the Effects of Attorney Fee Shifting' (1984) 47 *Law & Contemp Probs* 139, 170. See also ES Knutsen, 'The Costs of Costs: The Unfortunate Deterrence of Everyday Civil Litigation in Canada' (2010) 36 *Queen's Law Journal* 113 <http://ssrn.com/abstract=1667722> who illustrates how the everyday litigant is deterred from litigation in Canada due to the unpredictability of the outcome of the costs.

57 Knutsen (2010); Rowe (1984).

58 Visscher and Schepens (2010) 12; De Mot and De Geest (2004) 51.

59 Visscher and Schepens (2010) 12.

60 De Mot and De Geest (2004) 51.

61 Visscher and Schepens (2010) 13.

62 Katz and Sanchirico (2010) 6 with reference to literature; Visscher and Schepens (2010) 11–13.

63 Katz and Sanchirico (2010) 6–7;

64 EA Snyder and JW Hughes, 'The English Rule for Allocating Legal Costs: Evidence Confronts Theory' (1990) 6 *Journal of Law, Economics & Organization* 345–380.

65 Snyder and Hughes (1990); see also De Mot and De Geest (2004) 51.

66 Snyder and Hughes (1990); see also Sluijter (2011) 254.

67 JW Hughes and EA Snyder, 'Litigation and Settlement under the English and American Rules: Theory and Evidence' (1995) 38 *Journal of Law and Economics* 225–250.

that the greater expenditure effect leads to more settlements.[68] They note that settlement becomes more attractive under the English rule because it avoids higher litigation costs. The authors stress that risk aversion will strengthen this tendency.

In the *law and economics*, attention has also been paid to the so-called 'over optimism effect' of the English rule. Litigants can be relatively optimistic as to the outcome of a case, which may be caused, for instance, by an overestimation of the chances of prevailing or by inaccurate information.[69] Under the English rule, the over optimism effect is said to be higher since the over optimism extends to litigation costs.[70] In other words, if a litigant expects to have a fair chance of winning, he will equally consider his chances to have all costs recovered to be fair. Under these circumstances, a litigant will be more inclined to litigate. According to the theory, the over optimism effect in fact leads to less settlements under the English rule.

The question arises with regard to the overall effect of English rule: does it lead to more or to fewer settlements? This seems to depend on the relative size of the greater expenditure effect on one hand and the over optimism effect on the other.[71] Empirical research by Snyder and Hughes (1990) seems to suggest that the over optimism effect prevails, since they have established that a decrease in the settlement rate occurs under the English rule.[72] However, in view of the inherent limitations of the available theoretical and empirical research,[73] several authors emphasise that the results are too ambiguous to draw definite conclusions regarding the effects of the English rule on litigation and settlement behaviour.[74] Given that the aforementioned factors are interrelated and the effects depend on the circumstances of the case, any general statement about the overall effect of the English rule should be made and taken with caution.[75]

Nonetheless, among others Katz and Sanchirico (2010) are convinced that based on the available research, a few robust conclusions can be drawn about the overall effect of costs shifting. First, they conclude that it increases the legal expenditure per case. Second, they conclude that costs shifting discourages weak cases and that it has the same effect on risk-averse litigants, regardless of the merits of their case.[76] In any case, as Shavell noted, the results of these and other studies should be of use for the purposes of explanation or prediction of the effects of different costs shifting mechanisms.[77]

5. The survey

The theoretical and empirical studies discussed above provide insights that can be used to affirm (or to reject) certain asserted effects of article 1019h. It should be emphasised that this has to be done carefully. The English rule and article 1019h are different in several

68 Visscher and Schepens (2010) 15.
69 Sluijter (2011) 220.
70 Visscher and Schepens (2010) 15.
71 Visscher and Schepens (2010)15.
72 Snyder and Hughes (1990) 366; Visscher and Schepens (2010) 15.
73 De Mot and De Geest (2004) 54 and Sluijter (2011) 255 discuss several limitations to the available theoretical and empirical studies on the effects of costs shifting.
74 Katz and Sanchirico (2010) 34; Sluijter (2011) 255; Visscher and Schepens (2010) 13–15; De Mot and De Geest (2004) 54.
75 Visscher and Schepens (2010) 13.
76 Sluijter (2011) draws similar 'hard' conclusions based on the available research on the effects of the English rule, 255; idem Knutsen (2010).
77 Shavell (1982) 16.

respects. Specific research on the rule of article 1019h is required to make more accurate statements about the effects of this specific rule.

Given the absence of readily usable data, the many ambiguities concerning 1019h and the *Indicatietarieven*, as well as the contradictory hypotheses about the effects, this study chose an explorative approach, namely a survey among lawyers practising IP law. The goal was to gather information from the practical operation of article 1019h by means of an open-textured survey. It was expected that the survey method would yield not only information about the effects intended by the legislature but would also reveal information on potential side effects. In addition, it was also expected that the respondents would take the opportunity to share their experiences with and their opinions of the provision of 1019h. To a considerable extent, these expectations were met.

5.1 The respondents

The request to participate in our online survey was sent to 490 Dutch practising lawyers with an Internet profile indicating work activity in the area of IP.[78] No less than 170 respondents participated; the number of answers varies per question. In the following, where applicable we report the number of actual responses ('n').

The group of respondents can be described as diverse, with varying backgrounds and levels of experience. The spread across the practices is as follows:[79]

Table 5.1 Practices

Practice	*Number of respondents*	*Number of respondents in %*
Soft IP	94	55
Patent/Pharma	19	11
Combination of soft IP and patent/pharma	25	15
General practice (including IP)	16	9.5
Other	16	9.5

With respect to the years of experience in IP litigation:

Table 5.2 Years of experience

Years of experience (YoE)	*Number of respondents*	*Number of respondents in %*
< 5	40	24
5–9	42	25
10–15	47	28
>15	40	24
YoE not indicated	1	0.6

78 The data were provided by VIEPA, the Dutch Association of Intellectual Property Litigators (<www.viepa.nl>).

79 Soft intellectual property is used to refer to trademarks, copyright, design rights and passing off, in contrast to 'hard intellectual property', which is used to refer to patents. Source: Wikipedia.

5.2 The questions

The respondents were essentially asked the following questions with respect to the possible effects of article 1019h on the decision to litigate or to settle:

1. Have you observed changes in your practice that have occurred due to the influence of article 1019h?
2. In the case that you have observed changes, could you explain the relationship between article 1019h and those changes?
3. If you think that article 1019h can have a deterrent ('chilling') effect, what circumstances do you believe would give rise to such an effect?
4. If you think that article 1019h can have an encouraging effect, what circumstances do you believe would give rise to such an effect?
   The answers to these questions are reported and analysed together in para 6. Finally, we asked:
5. Has litigation in IP cases become more expensive under the influence of article 1019h? (para 7).

6. The respondents' views of the influence and effects of article 1019h on the decision to litigate or to settle

The first two questions posed to the respondents were whether they have observed changes in their practices under the influence of article 1019h and, if so, what the relationship is between those changes and 1019h. The emphasis was thereby placed on the causal relationship between 1019h and the possible changes. Respondents could choose one or more of the following answers: 'more or less writs of summons issued', 'more or less settlements in the pre-litigation phase', 'more or less settlements pending litigation', 'no changes' or 'other'.

When asked 'Have you observed changes?' (n=164), 31 respondents reported no change (19 per cent). A total of 133 respondents (81 per cent) reported changes in their practices and/or checked the answer 'other'. A majority reported a decrease in writs of summons, as well as an increase in settlements in the pre-litigation phase and an increase in settlements pending litigation (Table 5.3).

In para 6.1 below we discuss the comments from respondents who observed changes in their practice; in para 6.2 we discuss the comments of respondents who checked the answer 'no changes'.

6.1 The effects of 1019h according to the respondents

The answer 'more settlements in the pre-litigation phase' was chosen by 75 respondents (56 per cent) while 59 respondents (44 per cent) chose the answer 'less writs of summons

Table 5.3 Observed changes

N=133	*More %*	*Less %*
Writs of summons	13	44
Settlements in pre-litigation phase	56	8
Settlements pending litigation	26	5

Other 26%

issued'. Several respondents checked both answers, which is understandable; in cases that are settled in the pre-litigation phase, a writ of summons is generally not issued. Other combinations, such as more writs of summons issued/less settlements, also occurred. The answer 'other' was selected by 35 respondents (26 per cent), of which nearly half indicated that they were unable to provide an answer to the question given their limited years of experience in IP practice. 'Other' was also selected a number of times to indicate *other* possible causes of observed changes in IP practice, such as the economic climate changes and judges more often pushing towards settlement. Some respondents who checked the answer 'other' remarked that they found it difficult to attribute certain observed changes to 1019h.

We invited respondents to provide additional comments with their answers. According to some respondents, 1019h plays an 'important', 'decisive', 'compelling but improper' and even an 'independent' role in the decision to litigate or settle. Further text analysis of the answers to questions 2–4 above led to the conclusion that respondents identify four major variables that determine the effect of article 1019h. Note that that these variables ensue from our text analysis of the answers provided by the respondents and that, therefore, they are indicative rather than exhaustive. Nonetheless, as will become apparent, they are highly plausible in light of the literature on the effects of costs shifting. The four variables are:

I. The assessment of the chances of success.
II. The (un)predictability of the award of costs.
III. The 'size' or financial capacity of a party.
IV. The (pre-)litigation phase of the dispute.

I. The assessment of the chances of success

From the answers to questions 2-4 of the survey, it follows that respondents believe that 1019h may be an incentive to litigate in case of a strong claim, and the opposite, to refrain from litigation, where a weak claim is concerned. Most respondents did not define or explain the terms 'weak claim' and 'strong claim'. Several respondents mentioned percentages varying from a minimal chance of success at 60 per cent up to 90 or even 100 per cent. Few respondents drew comparisons with the mitigated cost-shifting rule: under this rule a 50 per cent chance of success could be worth taking a gamble and going ahead with litigation while a 50 per cent chance of success would not be worth the gamble under 1019h due to the financial risk involved. These comments are in conformity with the theory based on the standard economic model of the litigation process: by increasing the factor 'costs', the benefits of litigation also need to increase. Cases with little chance of succeeding are less likely to be brought to court under a more extensive costs-shifting regime. In view of the literature about the effects of costs shifting, it is also plausible that the acceptable minimum chance of success (%) may depend *inter alia* on the risk profile of the plaintiff.

It is noteworthy that a number of respondents who mentioned the factor 'chance of succeeding' also pointed out that a characteristic of litigation in IP enforcement cases is that the outcome either cannot be predicted or is difficult to predict. According to these respondents, in most IP cases, the risk of losing a case and having to pay the legal costs of the opposing party can never be ruled out entirely:

> 'I think 1019h may deter one from starting litigation in case the outcome is uncertain. This is par excellence the case in IP cases. After all, the assessment of the infringement is mainly a

subjective issue. Even though we try to objectivise the question whether or not the subject-matter looks too much alike, this is often subject to the respective judge's opinion.'[80]

'After all the outcome of litigation in IP cases cannot be predicted, which holds especially true in enforcement matters since the total impression, risk of confusion, degree of similarity, the overall impression etc. are in fact subjective concepts.'[81]

Occasionally, the comment was made that the deterrent effect would be even more pronounced in legally or factually complicated IP cases, on the one hand, because they require greater expenditure, and on the other because the outcome is even more uncertain.

Some respondents mentioned that only cases involving counterfeiting or piracy could be characterised as 'clear-cut'.[82] In this connection reference was made to cases regarding online copyright infringements (relatively small claims, but high *ex ante* probabilities of successful outcomes).[83] In these cases it is possible to predict the outcome, so that 1019h would in fact form an extra incentive to litigate since the legal costs can be fully reclaimed from the infringer. The 'over optimism effect' as described above may play a role in this context, in that relative optimism regarding the outcome of a case may extend to the recoverability of the legal costs. Some respondents stated that 1019h is a 'good remedy' in counterfeit and piracy cases. A few felt that 1019h should in fact only be applied in those cases.

> Clear-cut infringement cases (counterfeit, 1-on-1 copyright infringements) are being solved quicker because of 1019h – which is in my view in accordance with the initial ratio of the provision. 1019h relates in a negative way to the many dubious cases in our field of practice. IP is no exact science – a litigant takes a gamble to a greater or lesser extent, while the stakes are higher because of 1019h.[84]

In view of the theory discussed above, the question whether or not a litigant dares to take a gamble in cases that do not concern piracy or counterfeit (i.e., cases with an uncertain outcome), is likely to depend on the risk attitude of the litigant. While some respondents have experienced a greater tendency to litigate in 'strong cases', others noted that in such cases parties are more willing to settle. If a plaintiff appears to have a strong claim, he will be more likely to litigate, according to a respondent. If the plaintiff has a strong case, 'the defending party will cut his losses and be more willing to agree to an amicable settlement',

80 Soft IP practice, six years of experience.

81 Soft IP practice, 16 years of experience.

82 The definition of counterfeit according to the TRIPs-Agreement (Agreement on the Trade-Related aspects of Intellectual Property Rights) is: '*Counterfeit trademark goods shall mean any goods, including packaging, bearing without authorisation a trademark which is identical to the trademark validly registered in respect of such goods, or which cannot be distinguished in its essential aspects from such a trademark and which thereby infringes the rights of the owner of the trademark in question under the law of the country of importation*'. According to TRIPs, the definition of piracy is: '*Pirated copyright goods shall mean any goods which are copies made without the consent of the right holder or person duly authorised by the right holder in the country of production and which are made directly or indirectly from an article where the making of that copy would have constituted an infringement of a copyright or a related right under the law of the country of importation*'.

83 This type of case is said to have increased over the past years, see: KA Sandvliet and A Engelfriet, 'Vaststellen van schade bij online auteursrechtinbreuk' (2015) 5 *AMI* 204ff.

84 Soft IP practice, six years of experience.

said another respondent. There were also respondents who felt that settlements are generally reached more quickly due to the influence of 1019h, as both parties then have certainty as to the costs.

> 'The stakes are higher and parties often prefer to buy-off the uncertainty of a high costs award.'[85]
>
> 'The due to article 1019h DCCP increased litigation risk leads to less willingness to litigate. Clients usually prefer the certainty provided by an amicable settlement.'[86]

Bearing in mind that it is said that the risk of losing is inherent in most IP cases, no case can in fact be considered to be 'strong', except perhaps for piracy and counterfeit cases. In view of this inherent uncertainty, risk aversion is likely to lead to less willingness to litigate (and more willingness to settle), a tendency that is described in the literature on costs shifting and also seems to be reflected by Table 5.3.

II. The (un)predictability of the award of costs

The unpredictability of the outcome of a decision to award costs based on 1019h was mentioned a number of times as an independent, deterrent factor. Various respondents noted that due to 1019h, the financial risk of litigation has increased. The financial risk was defined a few times as the risk of double costs, or 'double or nothing'. According to some, the uncertainty of what litigation can end up costing has also become greater. It was mentioned that under the influence of 1019h the stakes are higher and the interest in succeeding is greater. More nuanced statements were also made, such as: 'litigants see the possibility of compensation for legal costs as an opportunity, but also as a risk'.

It was stated several times that it would be difficult for lawyers to advise their clients properly in advance in respect of the financial consequences of losing. The 'reasonable and proportionate costs' of 1019h would often be explained as meaning 'all costs', while the costs of the opposing party are said to be unmanageable and unpredictable. It was also noted that judgments about 1019h and application of the *Indicatietarieven* could differ per case and even per court.

> Despite the Indicatietarieven it is impossible to indicate in advance what litigation in a worst-case scenario will end up costing (unless an agreement on the recoverable costs is made). Judges deal with the tariffs in different ways. Even judgments show different motivations regarding different amounts. Obviously if you win the case this is not an issue, but you never know whether you will win.[87]

As discussed above, according to the theory, uncertainty of costs may have a strong deterrent effect on litigants who are less certain about the outcome of a case. It follows from the survey that this is recognised in practice by a number of respondents.

85 Soft IP practice, 25+ years of experience.
86 Combined practice, nine years of experience.
87 Soft IP practice, nine years of experience.

III. *The 'size' or financial capacity of a party*

SMALL PARTY / CHANCE OF SUCCESS

The chance of success, in combination with the size or the financial capacity of a party, was mentioned as a relevant factor regularly. It was often mentioned that the deterrent effect of 1019h is more pronounced for smaller or less affluent parties in cases where there is a chance of defeat. According to several respondents small, less affluent parties that are uncertain about the outcome are less likely to allow matters to progress as far as court proceedings. For larger, more affluent parties the financial risk is said to play a less significant role. These comments seem compatible with the theory that there is a relationship between risk attitude and (private) wealth or financial resources.

> 'In practice 1019h has a deterrent effect on both infringers as right holders, especially when it concerns small parties and the outcome is uncertain.'[88]
>
> 'If the chances of winning are uncertain and the respective party is not very wealthy, one is more readily inclined to settle.'[89]
>
> 'The risk of having to compensate for the opposing party's full legal costs is especially for SME's a reason to refrain from starting or proceeding with litigation. This has mainly to do with the fact that the outcome of litigation in IP cases is often uncertain.'[90]

At the same time, a number of respondents remarked that, indeed, small parties that are 'convinced' of the strength of their case, that 'rate their chances highly' or that believe that an infringement is 'evident', are able to litigate under 1019h because their costs will be recovered. Article1019h is even thought to provide an incentive under these circumstances. In the same situation in the past, the mitigated cost-shifting rule would constitute a hurdle, according to one of the respondents.

> 'In promising cases of clients with lesser budget, [the provision] has a stimulating effect both in the offensive as the defensive modus.'[91]
>
> '1019h in particular has an encouraging effect on smaller companies, when the chances of winning are larg(er).'[92]

The encouraging effect of 1019h for smaller parties that are confident of the outcome is a reminder of the over-optimism effect, which according to the theory is stronger under fuller costs-shifting mechanisms, since the optimism extends to cover the costs. The fact that no more than 13 per cent of the respondents felt that *more* writs of summons are issued under influence of 1019h, as is shown in Table 5.3, puts this asserted effect in perspective.

In fact, other respondents said that 1019h has a deterrent effect on small parties in all cases, regardless of the chance of winning.

88 General practice including IP, 12 years of experience.
89 Soft IP practice, 18 years of experience.
90 Soft IP practice, six years of experience.
91 Soft IP and ICT practice, 28 years of experience.
92 Soft IP practice, nine years of experience.

> '1019h prevents small independent parties from submitting an appeal at the Supreme Court.'[93]
>
> 'Less affluent parties will settle sooner anyway due to the alleged double or nothing effect.'[94]

This ambiguity may be explained by difference in risk profile. As outlined above, for risk-averse parties, the prospect of having to pay the majority of the costs can, even if the chances of losing are negligible, bear considerable weight in the costs/benefit-analysis. As we know from the theory, costs shifting may have a deterrent effect on risk-averse parties *regardless* of the merits of the case. This theory seems to be supported by several respondents who noted that 1019h causes small, less wealthy parties to refrain from litigation even when their case is strong.

> '1019h is a reason to settle for smaller parties, even if the legal position is fairly promising. One simply does not want to run the risk of being ordered to compensate for the opposing party's legal costs.'[95]
>
> 'The costs risks are that high, that many (smaller) entrepreneurs do not want to run the risk, despite the fact that it is likely their IP rights are being infringed. Consequently, many refrain from issuing a writ of summons.'[96]
>
> 'They [SMEs and private persons] would rather disregard the infringement than be confronted with high legal costs.'[97]
>
> 'A party with an arguable claim but not a lot of money would rather step down, particularly in patent cases.'[98]

SMALL VERSUS LARGE PARTY

According to some respondents, the deterrent effect of 1019h on a 'small' party would be reinforced if the opposing party were to be a 'large' party. In this context, it was observed that the level of unmanageable costs of the opposing party could increase considerably if the opposing party was a 'large' party with expensive lawyers. In such a case the financial risk could be considerable.

> 'In particular smaller and medium-sized parties will be more inclined to settle, to meet the writ of summons and to refrain from litigation, because of the risk of a full legal costs award, especially when the opposing party is larger.'[99]
>
> 'Due to 1019h it is fairly impossible for smaller parties to summon a large party (represented by a large and expensive law firm) to court. Such smaller parties can hardly bear the financial risk of litigation under these circumstances.'[100]

93 Combined practice, nine years of experience.
94 Patent/Pharma practice, 14 years of experience.
95 Soft IP practice, 20 years of experience.
96 Other (media law practice), 19 years of experience.
97 Soft IP practice, 28 years of experience.
98 General practice (including IP), 32 years of experience.
99 Soft IP practice, 20 years of experience.
100 Soft IP practice, seven years of experience.

'The legal costs are not manageable. The costs risk is too high, especially for small enterprises that have to litigate against large parties.'[101]

This reminds us of the theory discussed by De Mot and De Geest, and Visscher and Schepens amongst others, who show that if a party expects to be outspent by the opposing party, they are less willing to litigate under the English rule. Several respondents mentioned in this connection that as a consequence of 1019h, inequality and imbalance between parties could develop. Financially well-off parties would 'exploit 1019h to the last cent' or use it as an instrument to increase the pressure on less financially well-off parties to force them to settle.

'1019h contributes to a deep pocket approach by large players. It enhances the inequality of parties.'[102]

'It is a risk that "deep pockets" which can bear the risk of losing are unjustly placed in an advantageous position, enabling them to force smaller parties on their knees even if the chances of winning are limited.'[103]

'Infringers (not being real pirates) are punished really hard by the full legal costs rule. The provision also is being misused, for example by parties setting up draconian measures against relatively small infringements.'[104]

While according to the theory, plaintiffs who expect to incur greater expenditure than their opponents are more inclined to commence court proceedings, these comments seeming to indicate that under such circumstances, plaintiffs may instead use 1019h as an instrument to press the opponent to reach a settlement.

IV. The (pre-)litigation phase

Finally, according to some respondents, the effect of 1019h also depends on the (pre-)litigation phase of the dispute. An important characteristic of IP cases was mentioned several times: IP cases are often preliminary decided in interim proceedings. After obtaining an injunction as a preliminary measure, proceedings on the merits are often the next step,[105] after which appeal and cassation are available. In all follow-up procedures, there is a risk of being ordered to pay the opposing party's costs incurred in the respective procedure.[106] For some parties the 'total financial risk' can be a reason to refrain from taking legal action at all.

It was mentioned a few times that once litigation has commenced, 1019h can in fact be a reason for pressing the case forward and not to settle it. This seems to equate to comments by other respondents that the significance of a winning case is actually enhanced by 1019h.

101 Patent/Pharma practice, 20 years of experience.
102 Soft IP practice, five years of experience.
103 Combined practice, 12 years of experience.
104 Combined practice, 15 years of experience.
105 Unless the case is settled.
106 The question of whether the losing party in the interim proceedings can reclaim their costs in the case of a contrary decision in the proceedings on the merits is subject of debate; see I Werts and Maas M, 'Wat te doen met de proceskosten uit kort geding na een andersluidend bodemvonnis?' (2015) 14656 *IEF* <www.ie-forum.nl>.

> 'Once high costs have been incurred in litigation, these costs (as well as the possibility that the opposing party will be ordered to pay them) usually constitute a reason to proceed with litigation rather than to settle while the case is pending. It is as if one is lifted over the threshold of the risk of a full cost award and thinks it is more important to have their own costs recovered.'[107]
>
> 'The risk of a substantial costs award is being weighed more carefully than before. Prior to litigation, it is more often a reason to settle and during litigation, it is a reason to proceed.'[108]

Moreover, according to some respondents 1019h has even increased the likelihood of subsequent proceedings. It was stated that if the interim proceedings are successful, it is worth the effort to litigate a decision on the merits regarding, for instance, an award of damages or a statement of law (verklaring voor recht)[109] because of the fair chance of being successful again and having the legal costs recovered from the opposing party. Another respondent experienced that this occurs even if the award of damages is relatively small. It was also noted that 1019h increases the likelihood of an appeal being lodged in an IP case as the losing party that is ordered to pay legal costs, would be even more motivated to try to recover the costs in subsequent appeal proceedings.

The over-optimism effect of costs shifting that, according to the theory, also extends to cover costs may explain the willingness to proceed with litigation. At the same time, it follows from Table 5.3 that only a few respondents seem to feel that 1019h actually leads to less settlements pending litigation, which puts these comments into perspective. Furthermore, few respondents indicated that parties settle more quickly once litigation has commenced, out of a desire for certainty about the costs or to prevent the costs from escalating. Again differences in risk attitude may be decisive in this regard.

6.2 The respondents and their answer 'no changes'

Only 31 of the 164 respondents (19 per cent) chose the answer 'no changes'. A number of these respondents indicated that in their practices the interests are often so great that the cost rule of article 1019h DCCP has hardly any influence, or 'plays only a minor role'. As one respondent reported, 'pharma litigates anyway'. Or, as another respondent stated:

> 'In my practice, the value of the claims generally is considerable. Legal costs are merely an accessory matter.'[110]

Comparable comments also came from the soft IP practice. Few respondents indicated that the decision to litigate or settle depends mainly on the likelihood of success and the interests at stake and not so much on the costs. It was mentioned several times that 1019h 'is not the deciding factor', or that the provision plays a 'secondary role'. One respondent indicated that litigation decision-making is more directed at ceasing the infringement than

107 Soft IP practice, nine years of experience.
108 Soft IP practice, 15 years of experience.
109 Under Dutch law damage compensation and statements of law can only be awarded in proceedings on the merits.
110 Patent/Pharma practice, 15 years of experience.

about the costs. Another respondent felt that there is now more awareness of the risks, however, that 1019h does not alter litigation decision-making.

7. The respondents on the question of whether litigation in IP enforcement cases has become more expensive under the influence of 1019h (n=132)

A number of respondents experienced that litigation in IP cases has become more expensive due to 1019h. Different explanations were given:

1. The increased financial risk requires a greater litigation budget;
2. Article 1019h simply entails more work for lawyers to justify a claim based on 1019h, to argue the applicability of 1019h, to specify the costs and to prepare a possible debate about the costs;
3. There is more at stake under 1019h, which means that litigants need to 'pull out all the stops';
4. Lawyers may be inclined to increase the level of costs charged to the client if it is expected that these will be recovered from the opposing party:

> 'I think lawyers are less inclined to mitigate the invoices, if there is a possibility that the costs are recovered by the opposing party.'[111]
>
> 'I think clients are told that increased lawyer's fees are justifiable because they can be reclaimed "anyway" in case of a positive outcome.'[112]

It is important to note that the reasons mentioned above under 3 and 4 are consistent with the theory of the greater expenditure effect, which may be reinforced in the case of marginal over-optimism.

Other possible causes of the increased level of costs in IP litigation were also mentioned. Occasionally, increased lawyer's fees and inflation were mentioned, as well as an asserted movement toward an Anglo-Saxon way of litigating. Others emphasised the increased complexity of IP litigation resulting from the abundance of substantive European legislation within the area of IP, which would require a higher level of legal specialisation and the increasing need to have more than one lawyer per case.

Some respondents indicated that the level of the costs claimed would depend on the estimated chances of winning the case. In solid cases, higher costs would be claimed than in weaker cases. A party who is not very certain about the chances of winning would be inclined to only claim a limited amount in order to be able to contest the reasonability and proportionality of the costs claimed by the opposing party.

> 'In strong cases a higher level of costs is claimed (towards the maximum tariff of the Indicatietarieven) whereas in weaker cases a connection with the minimum tariff is sought.'[113]
>
> '1019h influences the "costs incurred" because a litigant that does not have a strong position (or whose position is weakened during proceedings) will charge less, while the

111 Soft IP practice, nine years of experience.
112 Soft IP practice, six years of experience.
113 Soft IP practice, 15 years of experience.

> litigant with a strong position will "add up". In my opinion there is no such thing as "reasonable and proportionate costs" since the timesheets [urenstaten] will never be the "real ones".'[114]

On the other hand, a number of respondents felt that IP litigation has in fact become less expensive. The *Indicatietarieven* are said to have a mitigating effect on the level of costs claimed in litigation. In addition, the obligation of transparency was mentioned, allegedly causing lawyers to charge in a more conscious manner.

> 'Lawyers rather lower the level of costs, because of the mitigating effect of the Indicatietarieven.'[115]
>
> '[T]he fact that the narratives will be made public causes a more conscious way of charging.'[116]

Finally, there were also respondents who are of the view that 1019h has had no influence on the costs of IP litigation. The charging of fees to the client as well as the hourly fees are said to be isolated from 1019h. The costs charged are related to the hours spent on the preparation of the case, rather than to the method by which they are allocated.

8. The evaluation of the survey results in light of the literature

Essentially, based on the survey, there are indications that 1019h discourages parties to bring weak cases to court. This is in line with the standard economic theory of litigation, according to which parties are assumed to refrain from litigation if the costs are expected to exceed the benefits. It was further mentioned by a number of respondents that article 1019h might have a similar effect in cases with a fair chance of succeeding. The risk of being exposed to the larger part of (or even the full) costs of the opposing party, even if the chances of defeat are small, was said to cause certain parties to refrain from litigating in IP disputes. Similarly, the increased unpredictability of the factor 'costs' was mentioned as a deterring factor. In the literature, these effects are ascribed to the risk attitude of parties. Costs shifting is held to reinforce the deterrent effect of uncertainty of the outcome and unpredictability of the costs on risk-averse parties. Compared with the mitigated costs shifting rule of article 237 DCCP, article 1019h increases both the returns from success and the losses from defeat, considerably enlarging the private, individual risk of the parties. It therefore seems plausible that 1019h causes risk-averse parties to settle rather than to litigate, regardless of the merits of their case.

At the same time, it was stated by several respondents that in fact all IP cases inherently have a risk of losing, which would hold especially true in legally and factually complicated cases. Only 'clear cut' cases, such as counterfeit and piracy cases, would be predictable. Whereas some respondents stated that in those clear-cut cases 1019h could be an incentive to litigate, others experienced that certain parties are discouraged by 1019h regardless of the strength of their case. By contrast, some respondents noted that other parties are not

114 Soft IP practice, four years of experience.
115 Combined practice, 10+ years of experience.
116 Patent/Pharma practice, 15 years of experience.

influenced by 1019h at all. Again, differences in risk attitude (but perhaps also in relative optimism) may explain this ambiguity.

Where the literature recognises a relationship between risk attitude and (personal) wealth, based on the survey there are also indications that less affluent litigants are more affected by the financial risks imposed by 1019h than litigants with sufficient financial resources. Further, the expected legal expenditure on both sides was addressed by various respondents, who experienced that parties that expect to be outspent by the opposing parties would rather settle (or refrain from taking legal action) than be exposed to the 'unpredictable' and 'unmanageable' costs of the opposing party.

With respect to the (pre-)litigation phase of the dispute, it was mentioned, in line with the theory, that 1019h may cause parties to be more willing to proceed with litigation (by raising subsequent proceedings) once litigation has commenced. This effect seems to reflect the theory that optimistic expectations of the outcome may extend to the costs. Conversely, it was noted that litigants who prefer certainty about the costs would rather settle than proceed with litigation, to prevent costs from escalating. In view of the literature, it is plausible that risk attitude (and relative optimism) may determine whether a party decides to continue with litigation or settle during the litigation process.

Finally, there are indications that emerge from the survey regarding the question of whether IP litigation has become more expensive under the influence of 1019h. These are, however, somewhat ambiguous. In fact, respondents do not seem to agree on whether IP litigation has actually become more expensive. Respondents who believe that it has become more expensive seem divided as to the cause. The survey therefore does not point definitively in the direction of a greater expenditure effect of (fuller) costs shifting in practice, as described in the literature.

8.1 Restrictions to the survey method

Obviously, the chosen research method has its disadvantages and limitations. The opinions, observations and experiences of lawyers were investigated but not their numerical underpinning. Statistical analysis of the results is not possible. Furthermore, IP lawyers may not be equally risk-adverse as their clients and may assess the 'chance of succeeding' in a case and the financial consequences of losing differently. A wide range of factors may have influenced the answers, such as the type of clients the respondent represents (right holders or infringers, plaintiffs or defendants), the average financial resources of the clients or even the particular issue on any given day. A distorted view may therefore result. In addition, possible biases are mentioned in the context of interpretation of the questions, however this is also relevant to our interpretation (and even translation) of the answers. On a final note, we emphasise that the research results cannot be generalised to apply to all IP lawyers, let alone to the entire practice of IP law.

Furthermore, what the *overall* effect of 1019h is and whether it increases the likelihood of settlement and decreases the likelihood of litigation, cannot be established based on the studies discussed in this paper. Follow-up research, for example, in the form of longitudinal analyses of the number of cases in which the plaintiff succeeds and the amounts claimed in IP cases, could help to draw more robust conclusions. Unfortunately, such data is hard to come by. However, if the lack of available data and other challenges are overcome, a further exploration of potential differences in developments and tendencies between patent/pharma cases on the one hand and soft IP cases on the other, could be undertaken. The same applies for piracy/counterfeit cases versus 'regular' IP cases.

9. Conclusion

As yet, the mirrored versions of the behavioural effects of the newly introduced article 1019h DCCP in IP enforcement cases have not been underpinned by (empirical) evidence. Based on our analyses of available theoretical and empirical studies on the effects of costs shifting as well as an open-texture survey among IP practitioners, we found that it is difficult to draw definite conclusions regarding the effects of article 1019h. The decision to litigate or to settle depends on many different, interrelated factors and effects and these can vary from case to case. Subjective factors such as rationality, relative optimism and risk attitude may play a role, as well as, probably many, many other factors. There are simply too many variables involved, which may determine the (likely) effect of costs shifting to be able to draw general conclusions on the overall effect.

At the same time, the survey yielded several insights about the practical operation of article 1019h that appeared to correspond with the *law and economics* literature about the effects of costs shifting, enhancing the plausibility of several effects that are ascribed to 1019h in the literature. It is feasible that article 1019h reinforces the tendency of risk-averse parties to settle rather than to litigate, regardless of the merits of their case. It may also be that this effect is even stronger in cases where the opposing party is expected to have greater legal expenditures. Overall, while article 1019h aims to provide incentives to IP right holders to enforce their rights before the courts, it is possible that, to a number of litigants in IP disputes, these incentives are largely overruled by the uncertainty and the potential high costs awards that seem inherent in the provision.

Further research is required to be able to draw more robust conclusions about the effects of article 1019h on the decision to litigate or to settle in IP disputes. Nevertheless, this contribution has shown that a majority of IP-practitioners reported changes in litigation behaviour under the influence of article 1019h. This, in itself, is an indication that the right to access to justice as well as the right to (intellectual) property are potentially affected by this new cost rule. Since both rights are fundamental rights under the European Convention of Human Rights and the Charter of Fundamental Rights of the European Union,[117] such an indication that the very essence of these rights might be impaired should be taken seriously.

Bibliography

Deene J., 'De rechtsplegingsvergoeding in procedures inzake intellectuele rechten: een sui generis-regime?' (2011) 23 *RW* 946.

De Mot J.P.B. and G.G.A. de Geest, *Juridische infrastructuur: een internationale vergelijking vanuit economisch perspectief* (Den Haag: WODC 2004).

Driessen M., 'De willekeur van de proceskostenveroordeling' (2007) 6 *BIE* 343.

European Commission, 'Proposal for a Directive of the European Parliament and the Council on Measures and Procedures to Ensure the Enforcement of Intellectual Property Rights' COM (2003) 46 final, 53.

—— 'Staff Working Document Accompanying the Report on IPR Enforcement Directive 2004/48' SEC (2010) 1589 final.

—— 'Syntheses of the Responses "Civil Enforcement of Intellectual Property Rights: Public Consultation on the Efficiency of Proceedings and Accessibility of Measures"' (Brussels 2013).

117 Art 6 of the European Convention of Human Rights, art 47 of the Charter of Fundamental Rights of the European Union.

European Observatory on Counterfeit and Piracy, 'Damages in Intellectual Property Rights' (2010) <http://ec.europa.eu/internal_market/iprenforcement/docs/damages_en.pdf>.

Gielen C., 'De richtlijn handhaving IE-rechten' (2005) 1 *NTER* 6.

Fischmann F., 'Patent Litigation and Costs Shifting in Europe: Critical Appraisal and Proposal of Alternative Solutions' (2014) 10(2) *Journal of Intellectual Property Law & Practice* 98.

Hodges C., S. Vogenauer and M. Tulibacka (eds), *Funding and Costs of Civil Litigation: A Comparative Perspective* (Oxford: Hart Publishing 2010).

Hughes J.W. and E.A. Snyder, 'Litigation and Settlement under the English and American Rules: Theory and Evidence' (1995) 38 *Journal of Law and Economics* 225.

Huydecoper J.L.R.A., 'Nous maintiendrons – de nieuwe Richtlijn Handhaving' (2004) 4 *AMI* 117.

Jackson Lord Justice R., *Review of Civil Litigation Costs: Preliminary Report – Volume 1* (London: Judiciary of England and Wales 2009).

Katz A.W., 'Indemnity of Legal Fees' in B. Bouckaert and G. De Geest (eds), *Encyclopedia of Law and Economics, Volume V. The Economics of Crime and Litigation* (Cheltenham: Edward Elgar 2000) 63.

—— and C.W. Sanchirico, 'Fee Shifting in Litigation: Survey and Assessment' (2010) University of Pennsylvania Institute for Law and Economics Research Paper No. 10-30 <http://ssrn.com/abstract=1714089>.

Knutsen E.S., 'The Costs of Costs: The Unfortunate Deterrence of Everyday Civil Litigation in Canada' (2010) 36 *Queen's Law Journal* 113 <http://ssrn.com/abstract=1667722>.

Kobayashi B.H. and J.S. Parker, 'Civil Procedure: General' in B. Bouckaert and G. De Geest (eds), *Encyclopedia of Law and Economics, Volume V. The Economics of Crime and Litigation* (Cheltenham: Edward Elgar 2000) 1.

Kritzer H.M., 'Fee Arrangements and Fee Shifting: Lessons from the Experience in Ontario' (1984) 47 *Law & Contemp Probs* 125.

Rojahn S. and J.P. Rektorschek, 'Europäische Harmonisierung der Kostenerstattung im Bereich des gewerblichen Rechtsschutzes – ist RVG noch EU-konform?' (2014) 1 *Mitteilingen der deutschen Patentanwälte* 1–15.

Rowe T.D. Jr., 'The Legal Theory of Attorney Fee Shifting: A Critical Overview' (1982) *Duke Law Review* 651.

—— 'Predicting the Effects of Attorney Fee Shifting' (1984) 47 *Law & Contemp Probs* 139.

Sandvliet K.A. and A. Engelfriet, 'Vaststellen van schade bij online auteursrechtinbreuk' (2015) 5 *AMI* 204.

Shavell S., 'Suit, Settlement, and Trial: A Theoretical Analysis under Alternative Methods for the Allocating of Legal Costs' (1982) 11 *Journal of Legal Studies* 55.

—— 'Basic Theory of Litigation' in *Foundations of Economic Analysis of Law* (Cambridge: Harvard University Press 2004) 389.

Sluijter P., *Sturen met proceskosten. Wie betaalt de rekening van verstorend procesgedrag?* (Deventer: Kluwer 2011).

Snyder E.A. and J.W. Hughes, 'The English Rule for Allocating Legal Costs: Evidence Confronts Theory' (1990) 6 *Journal of Law, Economics & Organization* 345.

Tuil M., 'The Netherlands' in C. Hodges, S. Vogenauer and M. Tulibacka (eds), *Funding and Costs of Civil Litigation: A Comparative Perspective* (Oxford: Hart Publishing 2010) 401.

Van der Grinten P.M.M., 'The Netherlands: Policy Observations' in C. Hodges, S. Vogenauer and M. Tulibacka (eds), *Funding and Costs of Civil Litigation: A Comparative Perspective* (Oxford: Hart Publishing 2010) 421.

Van Gompel S. and W. Olieslagers, 'Het proceskostenrisico in IE-zaken – Een empirisch onderzoek naar toepassing van de indicatietarieven' (2014) 5 *AMI* 133.

Visscher L. and T. Schepens, 'A Law and Economics Approach to Cost Shifting, Fee Arrangements and Legal Expense Insurance' in M. Tuil and L. Visscher (eds), *New Trends in Financing Civil Litigation in Europe – A Legal, Empirical, and Economic Analysis* (Cheltenham: Edward Elgar 2010) 7.

Visser D.J.G., 'Kroniek van de intellectuele eigendom' (2012) 15 *NJB* 1041.

—— 'Kroniek van de intellectuele eigendom' (2015) 15 *NJB* 973.

—— and A. Tsoutsanis, 'De volledige proceskostenveroordeling in IE-zaken' (2006) 34 *NJB* 1,940.
Vrendenbarg C.J.S., 'De "volledige" proceskostenveroordeling in IE-zaken: een kritische bespreking van de implementatie en interpretatie van artikel 14 Handhavingsrichtlijn in Nederland' (2013) 6 *BIE* 160.
—— 'Toelaatbaarheid van forfaitaire proceskostenvergoeding bij handhaving van IE-rechten: De proceskostenregelingen van België, Nederland en het Unified Patent Court getoetst aan de beginselen van het Unierecht' (2015) 5 *IER* 259.
Wefers Bettink W. and J. Hoefnagel, 'Artikel 1019h Rv en de indicatietarieven: toepassing in de praktijk' (2010) 47 *IER* 336.
Werts I. and M. Maas, 'Wat te doen met de proceskosten uit kort geding na een andersluidend bodemvonnis?' (2015) 14656 *IEF* <www.ie-forum.nl>.
Wilman F., *The Vigilance of Individuals. How, When and Why the EU Legislates to Facilitate the Private Enforcement of EU Law before National Courts* (Leiden: Wöhrmann 2014).
WIPO, 'IP Litigation Costs – Special Edition' (2010) 1 *WIPO Magazine* <www.wipo.int/export/sites/www/wipo_magazine/en/pdf/2010/wipo_pub_121_2010_01.pdf>

6 'Mercantile adventurers'?

The disclosure of third-party funding in investment treaty arbitration

Eric De Brabandere[1]

The founders of the Convention could not have foreseen in any way the emergence of a new industry of mercantile adventurers as professional BIT claims funders. It is no reach to find that, as strangers to the BIT entitlement, such funders also should remain at the same real risk level for costs as the nominal claimant. In this regard, the integrity of the BIT regimes is apt to be recalibrated in the case of a third party funder, related or un-related, to mandate that its real exposure to costs orders which may go one way to it on success should flow the other direction on failure.[2]

1. Introduction

Investment treaty arbitrations are known for the potentially important amounts of compensation requested (and sometimes granted), but also for the high costs involved in the initiation and conduct of such arbitral proceedings. These two facts are at the same time the main reasons why investor–State disputes are a very lucrative field for third-party funders and why such disputes are increasingly being financed[3] by third-party funders.

The use of third-party funding in investment treaty arbitration has increased rapidly over the past years, resulting in amplified – but albeit relatively limited – attention

1 The term 'Mercantile Adventurers' is taken from the separate opinion of Gavan Griffith in the case *RSM Production Corporation v. Saint Lucia* ICSID Case No. ARB/12/10, Assenting Reasons of Gavan Griffith, 12 August 2014, para 14. This chapter draws in part on research previously published as E De Brabandere and J Lepeltak, 'Third-Party Funding in International Investment Arbitration' (2012) 27(2) *ICSID Review* 379–398; E De Brabandere, 'Derde Partij Financiering en de onafhankelijkheid en onpartijdigheid van arbiters in internationale investeringsarbitrage' (2013) 1 *b-Arbitra – Belgian Arbitration Review* 101–122; and E De Brabandere, *Investment Treaty Arbitration as Public International Law: Procedural Aspects and Implications* (Cambridge: Cambridge University Press 2014).

2 *RSM Production Corporation v. Saint Lucia*, ICSID Case No. ARB/12/10, Assenting Reasons of Gavan Griffith, 12 August 2014, para 14.

3 The vast majority of publicly available decisions that have discussed the issue of third-party funding, because one of the parties had in those cases obtained funding from a third-party, have all been rendered after 2009. While it cannot be excluded that third-party funding of investment treaty claims occurred prior to 2009 as well, the absence of any discussion by arbitral tribunals of issues related to third-party funding in decisions prior to that date does indicate that occurrences were in all likelihood rather limited. See JC Honlet, 'Recent Decisions on Third-Party Funding in Investment Arbitration' (2015) 30(3) *ICSID Review* 699.

from scholars.[4] The limited attention can be explained by the fact that, beyond questions of principle relating to the question of whether third-party funding is acceptable in investment arbitration as such and/or in relation to the specificities of investment treaty arbitration, third-party funding had until recently not posed any significant problems. However, the recent decision of an International Center for the Settlement of Investment Disputes (ICSID) Arbitral Tribunal in *RSM Production Corporation v. Saint Lucia* in August 2014,[5] a case in which the claimant had obtained funding from a third party, has fuelled the debate. The Tribunal in that case ordered *RSM* to post a guarantee of US$750,000 to ensure that it could pay Saint Lucia's legal costs if it was ordered to do so by the arbitral tribunal.[6] The decision had been preceded by an earlier decision of the tribunal in which *RSM* was ordered to post security for the costs to be incurred by ICSID in the arbitration.[7] While ICSID tribunals ordering security for costs in general are a very rare phenomenon, a ruling ordering security for costs partly on the basis of the presence of a third-party funder – one can well imagine – has resulted in a small upheaval in the third-party funder community and scholarship.[8]

The ruling indeed is important for a couple of reasons, which are as such alien to the question of third-party funding, such as the question of whether absent any express provision to that effect, ICSID tribunals can order security for costs based on a tribunal's general power to order provisional measures, and whether provisional measures can be ordered based on the need to preserve a procedural right (such as the contingent right to claim a reimbursement of the costs incurred), which the Tribunal accepted in this case.[9] But more importantly for the purposes of this chapter, the ruling has fuelled the already existing debate in investment arbitration as to whether third-party funding should be disclosed or not.[10]

The link between third-party funders and security for costs has been examined in relation to international commercial arbitration.[11] Yet, little or no research has been done in this

4 See amongst others, WH van Boom, *Third-Party Financing in International Investment Arbitration* (2011) <http://papers.ssrn.com/sol3/papers.cfm?abstract_id=2027114>; S Khouri, K Hurford and C Bowman, 'Third-Party Funding in International Commercial and Treaty Arbitration – A Panacea or a Plague? A Discussion of the Risks and Benefits of Third-Party Funding' (2011) 8(4) *Transnational Dispute Management* 1; JM Matthews and M Steinitz, 'Editorial: TDM Special Issue: Contingent Fees and Third Party Funding in Investment Arbitration Disputes' (2011) 8(4) *Transnational Dispute Management* 1; and E De Brabandere and J Lepeltak, 'Third-Party Funding in International Investment Arbitration' (2012) 27(2) *ICSID Review* 379–398.

5 *RSM Production Corporation v. Saint Lucia*, ICSID Case No. ARB/12/10, Decision on Saint Lucia's Request for Security for Costs with Assenting and Dissenting Reasons, 13 August 2014.

6 Ibid. para 90.

7 LE Peterson, 'In a Novel Ruling, ICSID Tribunal Orders that Impecunious Third-Party Funded Claimant Should Cover All Advance-Costs of Proceedings' (*IA Reporter*, 10 January 2014) <www.iareporter.com/articles/in-a-novel-ruling-icsid-tribunal-orders-that-impecunious-third-party-funded-claimant-should-cover-all-advance-costs-of-proceedings>.

8 See, e.g., the various contributions, including by third-party funders, in a special issue of the *Global Arbitration Review*, 'A Storm over St Lucia' (2014) 9(5) <http://globalarbitrationreview.com/news/article/32932/should-funded-claimants-pay-security>; D Kalderimis, C Tripp and P Gibbs, 'Third Party Funding in International Arbitration – Lessons from Litigation?' (*Kluwer Arbitration Blog*, 15 December 2015) <http://kluwerarbitrationblog.com/blog/2014/12/15/third-party-funding-in-international-arbitration-lessons-from-litigation/>; and R Weeramantry and M Ferrer, 'RSM Production Corporation v Saint Lucia: Security for Costs – A New Frontier?' (2015) 30(1) *ICSID Review* 30–33.

9 See *RSM Production Corporation v. Saint Lucia*, *supra* note 5, paras 63ff.

10 See, amongst others: E De Brabandere, 'Derde Partij Financiering en de onafhankelijkheid en onpartijdigheid van arbiters in internationale investeringsarbitrage' (2013) 1 *b-Arbitra – Belgian Arbitration Review* 101–122.

11 W Kirtley and K Wietrzykowski, 'Should an Arbitral Tribunal Order Security for Costs When an Impecunious Claimant Is Relying upon Third-Party Funding?' (2013) 30(1) *Journal of International Arbitration* 17–30.

respect in the context of investment treaty arbitration, which presents unique characteristics, notably in relation to transparency and publicity and the selection and qualification of arbitrators, and that warrants perhaps a different approach. Indeed, the *RSM* case raises the more general and paramount question as to whether or not third-party funding agreements should be disclosed, and, if so, how to balance such an obligation with the possible influence of the presence of a third-party funder on the conduct of the proceedings and orders for security for costs. This chapter addresses this central research question.

I will first briefly explain the specificity of investment treaty arbitration, as compared to international commercial arbitration. I will next briefly discuss the concept of third-party funding and its use in investment treaty arbitration. The third section will then analyze the question as to whether or not third-party funding agreements should be disclosed. This analysis will address disclosure, first in relation to the specific features of investment treaty arbitration, notably the rules on transparency of the procedure, second in relation the need to maintain the independence and impartiality of arbitrators, which is generally considered to be a fundamental principle of arbitration,[12] and third, in relation to the question of whether third-party funding poses any problems in relation to the identification of the 'real party' to the dispute. Disclosure will then be discussed in relation to cost allocation and security for costs, in which the following questions will be analyzed: 1) whether disclosure is required, 2) whether the resort to third-party funding says anything about the financial situation of one of the parties, and 3) whether or not, in function of that, the mere existence of a third-party funding agreement should result in a tribunal ordering security for costs against the funded party, as was proposed by Gavan Griffith in his dissenting opinion in the case *RSM Production Corporation v. Saint Lucia*.

2. Characteristics of investment treaty arbitration and the ICSID Convention

This chapter focuses on treaty-based investment arbitrations, that is, investment disputes that are based on the alleged violation by a State of an international investment treaty, which contains the State's consent to arbitrate such disputes.[13] Contemporary treaty-based investment disputes relate to the international responsibility of States for alleged violations of international legal obligations contained in international legal instruments. The existence of two distinct layers of obligations – a contractual and a treaty level – does not imply that assessing the responsibility of a State for alleged violations of the State's international investment obligations ceases to be an exercise in applying public international law rules and principles. The use of the international commercial arbitration model to settle investment disputes has not altered the fact that investment tribunals are in contemporary investment disputes mandated to assess breaches by States of their obligations under public international law, which are laid down in international treaties granting protection to foreign investors. In other words, the examination of the international legal responsibility of a State for breaches of its international investment obligations, a matter regulated by public international law and not domestic law, is the principal object of investment treaty arbitration.[14]

12 See on this De Brabandere and Lepeltak (2012) *supra* note 4, 379–398.

13 This section draws on research previously published as E De Brabandere, *Investment Treaty Arbitration as Public International Law: Procedural Aspects and Implications* (Cambridge: Cambridge University Press 2014).

14 A Newcombe and L Paradell, *Law and Practice of Investment Treaties: Standards of Treatment* (Alphen aan den Rijn: Kluwer Law International 2009) para 2.19.

The use of the method of international commercial arbitration to settle investment disputes that have a public international law character naturally results in a certain tension between the public international law nature of the dispute – because such disputes are concerned with the assessment of the exercise by a State of its sovereign powers under international law – and the private character of the dispute settlement method.[15] Yet, it is beyond doubt that the characteristics of the dispute do influence the arbitral proceedings. Because of the involvement of a State acting in its sovereign capacity and the obligations it has contracted under treaties regulated by public international law, the review of the acts of the host State by arbitral tribunals is subjected to certain specific rules, such as the transparency of the proceedings, and the challenge criteria for appointed arbitrators.

The arguments developed in this chapter are valid for investment treaty arbitration generally, that is, investment arbitration based on an international investment *treaty*. But particular attention will be given to the ICSID Convention, since, besides the possibility of having investment treaty arbitration conducted under the Permanent Court of Arbitration, or ad hoc, by the application of existing sets of procedural rules such as the United Nations Commission on International Trade Law (UNCITRAL) Arbitration Rules, the majority of investor–State disputes based on an investment treaty are settled through the facilities of the ICSID.[16] And it is precisely the ICSID Convention, and the specific rules it contains in relation to the enforcement of ICSID arbitral awards, that are particularly appealing for third-party funders (see *infra* section 2).

It is beyond the scope of this chapter to analyse all the procedural aspects and implications that derive from the specific nature of investment treaty arbitration. I shall, therefore, focus only on those procedural features that are necessary to better understand the specific implications that third-party funding has on such arbitral proceedings, namely the rules on the independence and impartiality of arbitrators. This, as explained in the introduction, will be balanced against the possible negative effects on the procedure, and more specifically the question of security for costs.

3. Third-party funding in investment treaty arbitration: Concept and basic principles[17]

Third-party funding can be described as the financing, by a third party, of a part or all of the costs of the arbitral proceedings for one of the parties to the dispute.[18] In return for this financial liability, the funder receives a certain percentage of the compensation obtained by award or settlement. The percentage varies in function of the nature of the dispute and ranges between 15 and 50 per cent of the awarded compensation.[19] Conversely, if the claim

15 See De Brabandere (2014) *supra* note 13, 7ff.

16 See for an overview of the various Model BITs and the dispute settlement forum made available to the parties: Z Douglas, *The International Law of Investment Claims* (Cambridge: Cambridge University Press 2009) 3–5.

17 This section draws on research previously published as E De Brabandere and J Lepeltak, 'Third-Party Funding in International Investment Arbitration' (2012) 27(2) *ICSID Review* 379–398.

18 See generally on the concept and various understandings of the notion of 'third-party funding', WH van Boom, 'Financing Civil Litigation by the European Insurance Industry' in M Tuil and L Visscher (eds), *New Trends in Financing Civil Litigation in Europe – A Legal, Empirical, and Economic Analysis* (Cheltenham: Edward Elgar 2010) 92–108, 92; M de Morpurgo, 'A Comparative Legal and Economic Approach to Third-Party Litigation Funding' (2011) 19 *Cardozo Journal of International and Comparative Law* 352; and M Steinitz, 'Whose Claim Is It Anyway? Third-Party Litigation Funding' (2011) 95 *Minn. L. Rev.* 1,267.

19 Khouri, Hurford and Bowman (2011) *supra* note 4, 3.

fails, the funder will usually receive no compensation and will remain liable for the client's legal fees, as well as for any other adverse costs.[20] Third-party funding essentially is an investment in a judicial or arbitral procedure. A formal definition has been included in the recent draft Transatlantic Trade and Investment Partnership (TTIP).[21] It defines third-party funding as follows:

> 'Third Party funding' means any funding provided by a natural or legal person who is not a party to the dispute but who enters into an agreement with a disputing party in order to finance part or all of the cost of the proceedings in return for a remuneration dependent on the outcome of the dispute or in the form of a donation or grant.[22]

This definition, while covering the main aspects of third-party funding described in the previous paragraph, is relatively broad, in that it covers not only traditional forms of third-party funding but also donations and grants.[23] Also, its broad formulation results in the inclusion of funding arrangements with parties' counsel, which may not necessarily have been the purpose of the inclusion of such a clause in the TTIP.

Before entering in a third-party funding agreement, a funder will usually engage in a thorough due diligence of the claim, not only to assess the facts of the case, but also the legal merits of the claim.[24] One of the elements also taken into account is the likelihood of an effective enforcement of a possible future successful award and the time of recovery. Finally, it goes without saying that the estimated value of the claim will play a fundamental role in deciding whether or not to invest in a claim.[25]

The amounts of compensation awarded in investment treaty arbitration are widely known to be relatively significant, with an average of US$492 million.[26] Second, while the enforcement of international arbitral awards against a State usually are a source of concern because of the sovereign immunity of States, it should be reminded, is not waived in case of investment treaty arbitration, arbitration under the ICSID Convention is particularly appealing to third-party funders. One of the specific benefits of ICSID arbitration indeed

20 Khouri, Hurford and Bowman (2011) *supra* note 4, 3.

21 Draft Transatlantic Trade and Investment Partnership (TTIP) (12 November 2015), at <http://trade.ec.europa.eu/doclib/docs/2015/november/tradoc_153955.pdf> accessed 18 November 2015.

22 Preamble, Draft TTIP, *supra* note 21, 10.

23 Donations and grants were involved, for example, in *Philip Morris Brand Sàrl (Switzerland), Philip Morris Products SA (Switzerland) and Abal Hermanos SA (Uruguay) v. Oriental Republic of Uruguay*, ICSID Case No ARB/10/7, in which the Bloomberg Foundation and its 'Campaign for Tobacco-Free Kids' decided to help the Uruguayan Government by partly financing the legal costs. See the Press Release by Uruguay's Counsel, Foley Hoag LLP, 'Government of Uruguay Taps Foley Hoag for Representation in International Arbitration Brought by Philip Morris to Overturn Country's Tobacco Regulations' (8 October 2010), <www.foleyhoag.com/news-and-events/news/2010/october/uruguay-taps-foley-hoag-for-representation> accessed 2 December 2015.

24 See M Smith, 'Mechanics of Third-Party Funding Agreements: A Funder's Perspective' in L Bench Nieuwveld and V Shannon, *Third-Party Funding in International Arbitration* (Alphen aan den Rijn: Kluwer Law International 2012) 19–37.

25 See S Seidel, 'Third-Party Investing in International Arbitration Claims' in BM Cremades and A Dimolitsa (eds), *Third-Party Funding in International Arbitration* (Dossier X of the ICC Institute of World Business Law) (Paris: ICC 2015) 16–49.

26 See D Rosert, 'The Stakes Are High: A Review of the Financial Costs of Investment Treaty Arbitration', *International Institute for Sustainable Development Research Report* (July 2014) 2, <www.iisd.org/sites/default/files/publications/stakes-are-high-review-financial-costs-investment-treaty-arbitration.pdf> accessed 1 December 2015.

is that awards can easily be recognized and enforced through the ICSID Convention itself, especially if compared to enforcement of arbitral awards under the New York Convention. Article 54(1) of the ICSID Convention imposes an obligation on all States that are parties to the Convention to enforce an ICSID award 'as if it were a final judgment of a court in that State',[27] with no possibility of review by the national courts of the States in which enforcement is sought. The New York Convention thus simply does not apply to ICSID awards, but only to non-ICSID investment treaty arbitrations.[28] Although it facilitates enforcement, the New York Convention contains several possibilities for review by domestic courts and may render enforcement more difficult, or at least more time-consuming.[29] But even without the automatic enforcement of the ICSID Convention, investment treaty arbitration remains an appealing and lucrative market for third-party funders, because of the high amounts of compensation.

These elements explain, at least in part, why the market of investment treaty arbitration has attracted much attention from third-party funders over the past years. Yet, third-party funding has not increased in that area of litigation only because of the amounts of compensation awarded. Indeed, there needs to be a demand for third-party funding. Because of the complexity of the claims, the high stakes involved, and the length of the cases, the legal costs, including those for expert witnesses, for parties involved in investment arbitrations are very high.[30] Foreign investors, who wish to initiate an investment treaty claim against a State, may therefore shy away from doing so because they either do not have the financial means to invest in such a claim, are not willing to invest their own funds in the arbitration, or simply do not want to take the risk inherent in an investment treaty arbitration, which after all is a procedure with an uncertain outcome.[31] Third-party funding thus can enhance access to justice, which has traditionally been seen as one of the main advantages of third-party funding. As noted by the Australian High Court in *Campbells Cash and Carry Pty Ltd v. Fostif Pty Limited Limited*[32]:

> [b]y 'organising' persons into a legal action for the vindication of their legal rights, representative proceedings are not creating controversies that did not exist. Controversies pre-existed the proceedings, even if all those involved in them were

27 Convention on the Settlement of Investment Disputes Between States and Nationals of Other States (ICSID Convention), 18 March 1965, entered into force 14 October 1966, 575 UNTS 159, Article 54(1).

28 At the same time, the annulment mechanism set forth in Article 52 of the ICSID Convention, which is the counterpart of the absence of judicial review by domestic courts, may delay the arbitral procedure. It should also be added that because of the involvement of a State acting in its sovereign capacity, and the fact that State immunity is not waived under the ICSID Convention, the effective execution of ICSID awards may prove difficult, despite the relatively favourable provisions in respect of recognition and enforcement or awards in the ICSID Convention. See VO Nmehielle, 'Enforcing Arbitration Awards Under the International Convention for the Settlement of Investment Disputes (ICSID Convention)' (2001) 7(1) *Annual Survey of International & Comparative Law* 29ff; and CL Goodman, 'Uncharted Waters: Financial Crisis and Enforcement of ICSID Awards in Argentina' (2007) 28(2) *U. Pa. J. Int'l Econ. L.* 449ff.

29 See E Baldwin, M Kantor and M Nolan, 'Limits to Enforcement of ICSID Awards' (2006) 23(1) *Journal of International Arbitration* 1, 4–5.

30 Rosert (2014) *supra* note 26, 9–10.

31 See A Ross, 'The Dynamics of Third-Party Funding' (2012) 7(1) *Global Arbitration Review* 14–15. See also, more generally, L Bench Nieuwveld and V Shannon, *Third-Party Funding in International Arbitration* (Alphen aan den Rijn: Kluwer Law International 2012) 12.

32 High Court, Australia, *Campbels Cash and Carry Pty Ltd v. Fostif Pty Limited* [2006] HCA 41.

> unaware of, or unwilling earlier to pursue, their rights. A litigation funder [...] does not invent the rights. It merely organises those asserting such rights so that they can secure access to a court of justice that will rule on their entitlements one way or the other, according to law.[33]

One should of course keep in mind that there are inevitable drawbacks to third-party funding as well. Notably, because of the intervention of a funder, the arbitral proceedings can be delayed, for instance, because of a dispute between the funder and the foreign investor,[34] or as I will address in the next section, because of a request for security for costs.

4. Disclosure of third-party funding agreements

4.1 Transparency

Traditionally, international commercial arbitration is conducted in a relatively[35] confidential and private manner, even in the absence of an explicit confidentiality provision in the arbitration agreement. Neither the existence of a dispute, nor the procedural details of the settlement of the dispute are made public, nor is there any access of non-disputing parties to the proceedings.[36] The main reason behind this practice is that the dispute and the agreement underlying the dispute are of a private nature,[37] and that sensitive business and commercial information should not be disclosed.[38]

There are several practical and theoretical reasons for increasing both the transparency and non-party access to investment treaty arbitration. More generally, these arguments are related to the public international law character of investment treaty arbitration, which instils the need for transparency and public participation in investment treaty arbitration.[39] Indeed, that investment tribunals are engaged in assessing the States' exercise of their sovereign prerogatives inevitably causes tensions between the commercial and closed character of the proceeding and the public international law character of such disputes.

The public international law character of investment treaty arbitration differentiates it from international commercial arbitration as I explained in the first part. The fact that the questions put to an investment tribunal generally concern the respect by States of their

33 Ibid. para 202.

34 See, for instance, the case *S&T Oil Equipment & Machinery Ltd v. Romania*, ICSID Case No ARB/07/13, Order of Discontinuance of the Proceeding, 16 July 2010; and U.S. District Court, S.D. Texas, Houston Division, *S&T Oil Equipment & Machinery v. Juridica Investment Limited*, Civil Action No. H-11-0542, 25 April 2011. For a discussion, see BM Cremades, 'Third Party Litigation Funding: Investing in Arbitration' (2011) 8(4) *Transnational Dispute Management* 25–32.

35 There is indeed a tendency since a couple of years ago to diminish or question the confidentiality of arbitral proceedings generally. See N Blackaby, C Partasides, A Redfern and M Hunter, *Redfern & Hunter on International Arbitration* (5th edn, Oxford: Oxford University Press 2009) para 2.152; and for an extensive discussion: A Malatesta and R Sali (eds), *The Rise of Transparency in International Arbitration* (Huntington: Juris 2013).

36 Blackaby, Partasides, Redfern and Hunter (2009) *supra* note 35, paras 2.145ff.

37 ML Moses, *The Principles and Practice of International Commercial Arbitration* (Cambridge: Cambridge University Press 2008) 162.

38 C Schreuer, L Malintoppi, A Reinisch, and A Sinclair, *The ICSID Convention: A Commentary* (Cambridge: Cambridge University Press 2009) 834.

39 See De Brabandere (2014) *supra* note 13, 150–152.

international legal obligations, and that the acts complained of relate to issues of general public interest, such as environmental legislation, labour standards, or other social and economic rights, militate in favour of both transparency of and non-party access to the proceedings.[40] Because of the potential effects of this decision on the nationals of the State, there is a general interest of the public in the outcome of the procedure.[41] Moreover, since investment tribunals may award substantial damages to foreign investors for a State's exercise of its sovereign powers, secrecy of the procedure indeed is improper.[42] This feature of investment arbitration stands in sharp contrast to dispute settlement in international commercial arbitration.[43] In other words, international commercial arbitration is usually restricted to having a private function, that is, the resolution of the dispute between the parties without more,[44] while investment treaty arbitration not only has a private function, but at the same time has a very important public aspect, which exceeds the private bilateral relations between the parties. Linked to this, public reporting responsibilities may be applicable in the sense that States and State organs may be bound by principles of open government expected of public authorities, and democratically elected governments may need to report to their electorate.[45]

It is principally for these reasons that investment treaty arbitration has departed from the commercial arbitration principles of privacy and confidentiality. This is evidenced by the modification in 2006 of the ICSID Arbitration Rules and the adoption in July 2013 of specific UNCITRAL rules on 'transparency in treaty-based investor-State arbitration' by UNCITRAL.[46] It is to be noted that it is precisely and only for *treaty based* investment arbitration that the new rules have been adopted, which again shows that the public international law (treaty) foundation of investment treaty arbitration influences the conduct of arbitration.[47]

The move towards transparency in investment treaty arbitration, however, in and of itself does not suffice to claim that there is today an obligation *proprio motu* to disclose third-party funding agreements in order to fulfil any more general obligation of 'transparency'. Nevertheless, such an absence of obligation to disclose does not imply that arbitral tribunals cannot *order* disclosure for this, or any other reason the tribunal may invoke to support such an order. Such orders can be based on the tribunal's general power to preserve the integrity of the arbitral process[48] and the good faith of the proceedings.[49] The tribunal in *Muhammet*

40 C Knahr and A Reinisch, 'Transparency versus Confidentiality in International Investment Arbitration – The Biwater Gauff Compromise' (2007) 6 *The Law and Practice of International Courts and Tribunals* 97, 113.

41 See M Kinnear, E Obadia and M Gagain, 'The ICSID Approach to Publication of Information in Investor-State Arbitration', in A Malatesta and R Sali (eds), *The Rise of Transparency in International Arbitration* (Huntington: Juris 2013) 108.

42 Ibid.

43 See for a discussion N Blackaby, 'Public Interest and Investment Treaty Arbitration' (2004) 1 *Transnational Dispute Management* 1.

44 Ibid.

45 Ibid. 4.

46 UN Information Service, 'UNCITRAL Adopts Transparency Rules for Treaty-Based Investor-State Arbitration and Amends the UNCITRAL Arbitration Rules' (12 July 2013) UN Doc UNIS/L/186. See also United Nations Commission on International Trade Law (UNCITRAL), 'Report of Working Group II (Arbitration and Conciliation) on the Work of its Fifty-Eighth Session (New York, 4–8 February 2013)' (13 February 2013) UN Doc A/CN.9/765.

47 UNCITRAL, 'Report of Working Group II' (2013) *supra* note 46, para 20.

48 See MJ Goldstein, 'Should the Real Parties in Interest Have to Stand Up? Thoughts about a Disclosure Regime for Third-Party Funding in International Arbitration' (2011) 8(4) *Transnational Dispute Management* 9ff.

49 Khouri, Hurford and Bowman (2011) *supra* note 4, 10.

Çap & Sehil Inşaat Endustri ve Ticaret Ltd. Sti. v. Turkmenistan explicitly invoked this ground, by noting, in general terms, 'the Tribunal considers that it has inherent powers to make orders of the nature requested where necessary to preserve the rights of the parties and the integrity of the process. Claimants have not challenged this inherent power under the ICSID Rules'[50].

Three additional elements, which specifically relate to transparency in investment treaty arbitration, need to be mentioned here, however. First, in any case, given the lack of consent to submit disputes in respect of the funding agreement to the tribunal, the tribunal's jurisdiction does not extend to disputes between a foreign investor or a host State and a third-party funder. A fair balance will thus need to be struck between the need for transparency and the *inter partes* effect of third-party funding agreements. Second, the lack of an obligation to disclose does not, of course, prohibit any funded party to the dispute to voluntarily disclose the agreement, in order to ensure full transparency. This occurred, for instance, in the UNCITRAL arbitration *Oxus Gold plc v Republic of Uzbekistan, the State Committee of Uzbekistan for Geology & Mineral Resources, and Navoi Mining & Metallurgical Kombinat*.[51] Whether the existence of a third-party funding agreement will be disclosed to the tribunal and the other party will usually depend on the funding agreement itself,[52] but most funding agreements contain a confidentiality clause.[53] Third, States can in their investment treaty include an obligation to disclose any third-party funding arrangements. While no publicly available treaty that has entered into force contains such an obligation, the most recent version of the draft Transatlantic Trade and Investment Partnership (TTIP) between the US and the EU contains a provision requiring, *inter alia*, the mandatory disclosure of such arrangements:

> 1. Where there is third party funding, the disputing party benefiting from it shall notify to the other disputing party and to the division of the Tribunal, or where the division of the Tribunal is not established, to the President of the Tribunal, the name and address of the third party funder.
> 2. Such notification shall be made at the time of submission of a claim, or, where the financing agreement is concluded or the donation or grant is made after the submission of a claim, without delay as soon as the agreement is concluded or the donation or grant is made.[54]

The precise reason behind the insertion of this clause is not clear, although according to the European Commission it has as result that it 'widens the ethics obligations to explicitly cover funding arrangements. The disputing parties are required to disclose who is funding their claim (so called "third party funding").'[55] The broad formulation of the obligation of

50 *Muhammet Çap & Sehil Inşaat Endustri ve Ticaret Ltd. Sti. v. Turkmenistan*, *supra* note 81.

51 Oxus Gold plc, 'REG – Oxus Gold PLC – Litigation Funding' (*Reuters*, 1 March 2012) <www.reuters.com/article/2012/03/01/idUS101378+01-Mar-2012+RNS20120301#THMs64ozyJHGRig4.97> accessed 3 December 2015.

52 Khouri, Hurford and Bowman (2011) *supra* note 3, 9.

53 See for a discussion the various contributions in Ross (2012) *supra* note 31, 19.

54 Art 8 Draft TTIP, *supra* note 21.

55 European Commission, 'Fact Sheet – Reading Guide: Draft Text on Investment Protection and Investment Court System in the Transatlantic Trade and Investment Partnership (TTIP)' (16 September 2015) <http://europa.eu/rapid/press-release_MEMO-15-5652_en.htm>.

disclosure and its location in a different section than the one covering ethical standards of arbitrators indicates at the same time that it may well have been included in order to ensure a full transparency of the dispute and the entities funding the dispute.

4.2 The independence and impartiality of arbitrators

4.2.1 General principles

The independence and impartiality of international arbitrators is a fundamental principle of arbitral procedures in general.[56] And it is not different in investment treaty arbitration. Article 14 of the ICSID Convention contains the basic rule in respect of the independence and impartiality of arbitrators: 'persons designated to serve on the Panels shall be persons of high moral character and recognized competence in the fields of law, commerce, industry or finance, who may be relied upon to exercise independent judgment'. Arbitrators, either party-appointed or appointed by the chairman, need thus to possess three essential qualities: be of 'high moral character', have the necessary competence and be independent. Although Article 14 does not explicitly contain the requirement of 'impartiality', even though the Spanish official text refers to impartiality rather than independence,[57] it is generally considered that Article 14 requires arbitrators to be both independent and impartial.[58]

As concerns the challenge of arbitrators, Article 57 of the ICSID Convention provides that a party to the dispute may propose the commission or tribunal[59] to disqualify a member 'on account of any fact indicating a manifest lack of the qualities required by paragraph (1) of Article 14'. The ICSID Convention thus imposes a relatively heavy burden on a party that seeks to challenge an arbitrator, because of the use of the word 'manifest'.[60] Other arbitration rules habitually refer only to the 'justifiable doubts' standard in their rules on the challenge of arbitrators, and do not, usually, require a 'manifest' lack of independence and impartiality. Article 12(1) of the UNCITRAL Arbitration Rules, for instance, provides the possibility to challenge an arbitrator 'if circumstances exist that give rise to justifiable doubts as to the arbitrator's impartiality or independence'. The ICSID Convention conversely does not provide for a duty of disclosure, but rather requires arbitrators to sign a declaration that, in its last paragraph added in 2006, contains a disclosure obligation, which is extended to the entire duration of the arbitral proceedings.[61] These rules in and of themselves do not show a difference in requirements of independence and

56 Blackaby, Partasides, Redfern and Hunter (2009) *supra* note 35, para 4.72.

57 See for a discussion of this, G Bottini, 'Should Arbitrators Live on Mars? Challenge of Arbitrators in Investment Arbitration' (2009) 32(2) *Suffolk Transnational Law Review* 341.

58 *Suez, Sociedad General de Aguas de Barcelona S.A. and InterAguas Servicios Integrales del Agua S.A. v. Argentina*, ICSID Case No. ARB/03/17, Decision on the Proposal for the Disqualification of a Member of the Arbitral Tribunal, 22 October 2007; *Suez, Sociedad General de Aguas de Barcelona S.A., and Vivendi Universal S.A. v Argentina*, ICSID Case No. ARB/03/19, Decision on the Proposal for the Disqualification of a Member of the Arbitral Tribunal, 22 October 2007; and *AWG Group Limited v. Argentina*, UNCITRAL, Decision on a Second Proposal for the Disqualification of a Member of the Arbitral Tribunal, 12 May 2008, para 27.

59 The ICSID Convention indeed uses a system whereby the challenge by a party of an arbitrator or an *ad hoc* committee member will be decided by the remaining arbitrators or members of the *ad hoc* committee (Article 58 of the ICSID Convention).

60 For a discussion of relevant case-law in this respect, see Schreuer, Malintoppi, Reinisch, and Sinclair (2009) *supra* note 38, 1201, paras 15ff.

61 Rule 6 of the ICSID Arbitration Rules..

impartiality between investment treaty arbitration and international commercial arbitration that may be explained by the public international law character of the former. However, in practice, major differences do appear as a consequence of this, and this is why the issue of third-party funding in investment treaty arbitration poses distinct challenges.

First of all, investment treaty arbitration usually concerns relatively similar applicable laws, and even a relative similarity in the factual circumstances of disputes. Contrary to international commercial arbitration, where the legal circumstances of the cases have usually little similarity, in particular in view of the fact that the applicable law usually consists of the municipal law of a State, investment treaty arbitration requires the application of recurring principles of public international law, and is characterized by similarly worded legal instruments, which are applied in the majority of international investment disputes.[62] Second, awards of international investment tribunals are usually made public, at least under the ICSID Convention, and the 2013 UNCITRAL rules on transparency.[63] As a consequence, it becomes relatively easy to identify the standpoint of arbitrators in respect of certain rules of international investment law. This reality coupled with the *de facto* importance of the use of and references to precedents, which has become a widespread phenomenon in investment treaty arbitration,[64] implies that 'issue conflicts' in investment treaty arbitration are relatively different than those that may arise in international commercial arbitration.[65] Third, under the ICSID Convention, States are required under Article 54(1) to enforce an ICSID award 'as if it were a final judgment of a court in that State', with no possibility of review by the national courts of the States in which enforcement is sought. Because of this feature, bias challenges may not be brought at the enforcement stage, contrary to international commercial arbitration.[66] Lack of independence and impartiality also is not possible as a claim in annulment under the ICSID Convention, with the exception of cases of improper constitution of the tribunal or corruption.[67] As a consequence; particular attention should be given to the independence and impartiality rules before and during the proceedings. Finally, the need to ensure the legitimacy of the arbitral proceedings is paramount because of the public international law dimension of investment treaty arbitration.[68] For the legitimacy of the proceedings, and this is of course even more important because of the potential effects of this decision on the general public, any appearance of bias or lack of independence should be strictly avoided. Indeed, the general confidence of the public in the outcome of the procedure is without doubt guaranteed only if it is ensured that the arbitral proceedings were legitimate and that the dispute was decided by independent and impartial arbitrators.

62 T Buergenthal, 'The proliferation of disputes, dispute settlement procedures and respect for the rule of law' (2006) 22 *Arbitration International* 495, 498; and P Sands, 'Conflict and Conflicts in Investment Treaty Arbitration: Ethical Standards for Counsel' in C Brown and K Miles (eds), *Evolution in Investment Treaty Law and Arbitration* (Cambridge: Cambridge University Press 2011) 24.

63 See De Brabandere (2014) *supra* note 13, 153ff.

64 See generally: E De Brabandere, 'Arbitral Decisions as a Source of International Investment Law' in T Gazzini and E De Brabandere (eds), *International Investment Law. Sources of Rights and Obligations* (Leiden: Martinus Nijhoff Publishers 2012) 245–288.

65 S Lutrell, 'Bias Challenges in Investor-State Arbitration: Lessons from International Commercial Arbitration' in C Brown and K Miles (eds), *Evolution in Investment Treaty Law and Arbitration* (Cambridge: Cambridge University Press 2011) 479.

66 Ibid. 456.

67 Art 52(a) and (c) of the ICSID Convention, *supra* note 27.

68 See also Sands (2011) *supra* note 62, 22–24.

4.2.2 Specific challenges in investment treaty arbitration

These specificities of investment treaty arbitration give rise to particular problems. First, because of the public availability of the awards, and the *de facto* importance of precedents, one could have justifiable doubts when individuals act as counsel in one case, while at the same time being appointed as, or generally acting as, an arbitrator in other investment law cases, or vice versa. These are generally referred to as 'issue conflicts'.[69] Under those circumstances, arbitrators may be tempted to decide an issue in a way that could benefit a position adopted by that same arbitrator acting as counsel in another investment dispute.

The second consideration is related to the previous one and concerns the issue of 'repeat arbitrators'. This phenomenon denotes the case where arbitrators are appointed by the same party or the same law firm in different disputes.[70] The ICSID Convention and the arbitration rules of the other major arbitration institutions do not usually address the issue of repeat arbitrators. The matter simply falls under the general rules relating to the independence and impartiality of arbitrators. The reason why certain arbitrators are or have been repeatedly appointed by the same party, or even category of parties – foreign investors, or States – is that, because of the publicly available knowledge of the position of the arbitrator in previous cases, appointing parties may wish to designate an arbitrator who is very likely to decide the case in favour of the appointing party. This, as such, may not necessarily be *ipso facto* a problem of independence and impartiality, but a problem 'repeat arbitrators' may pose is that, taking into account the repetitive appointments by one party, the arbitrator could be considered to be no longer independent because it has created a form of financial dependence to the appointing party.[71] The IBA Guidelines on Conflicts of Interest in International Arbitration, which do not constitute a binding, nor compulsory instrument, however do mention this specific issue. The so-called 'orange list' contains several situations, which, according to the Guidelines, 'is a non-exhaustive list of specific situations that, depending on the facts of a given case, may, in the eyes of the parties, give rise to doubts as to the arbitrator's impartiality or independence'.[72] The 'orange list' *inter alia* targets the situation in which 'the arbitrator has, within the past three years, been appointed as arbitrator on two or more occasions by one of the parties, or an affiliate of one of the parties'.[73] The mere fact that it is an 'orange list' proves that the issue is not as clear-cut as it might seem.

4.2.3 Independence and impartiality of arbitrators and the disclosure of funding agreements

It is precisely in view of these considerations that third-party funding agreements should be disclosed. I argue that the rules on independence and impartiality of arbitrators, which are formulated vis-à-vis the parties to the dispute, should apply also to third-party funders in

69 See Blackaby, Partasides, Redfern and Hunter (2009) *supra* note 35, para 4.125.

70 See generally H Kuo, 'The Issue of Repeat Arbitrators: Is it a Problem and How Should the Arbitration Institutions Respond?' (2011) 4(2) *Contemporary Asia Arbitration Journal* 247.

71 See generally AS Rau, 'On Integrity in Private Judging' (1998) 14(2) *Arbitration International* 115.

72 PART II: Practical Application of the General Standards, para 3, IBA Guidelines on Conflicts of Interest in International Arbitration, Adopted by resolution of the IBA Council on Thursday 23 October 2014, <www.ibanet.org/Publications/publications_IBA_guides_and_free_materials.aspx#conflictsofinterest> accessed 14 December 2015.

73 Ibid. art 3.1.3.

light of their role in the procedure.[74] It is indeed difficult to argue otherwise. The general requirement of independence and impartiality of arbitrators in investment treaty arbitration, in view of the specific challenges of 'repeat arbitrators' and 'issue conflicts', exists to ensure the legitimacy of the arbitral procedure by avoiding any appearance of bias. This legitimacy of course principally targets the absence of any ties between the parties and their counsel, and the arbitrators, but should extend to third-party funders also in view of the impact they have on the procedure and the nomination of arbitrators. If one considers, for example, that an arbitrator that has been appointed two or more times by the same party or law firm in a period of three years creates an appearance of bias, as explained above, it is indeed difficult to argue that an arbitrator appointed two or more times in a period of three years by a third-party funder would not create an appearance of bias.

Although it has been argued that the absence of knowledge by the arbitrator that a third-party funder is actually supporting one of the parties to the dispute would eliminate the lack of independence or impartiality,[75] the principles of independence and impartiality of arbitrators – besides targeting actual independence and impartiality – also and principally cover the absence of an *appearance* of dependence or partiality.[76] As a consequence, whether the arbitrator in question is in effect dependent or partial is of little relevance for the application of the rules in this respect. In addition, because the third-party funding agreement may be disclosed after the end of the proceedings, even outside the will of the parties (for instance, in the case of a dispute between the funder and the funded party, as happened, for example, in the dispute between *Juridica* and *S&T Oil*[77]) the entire legitimacy of the arbitral process, which is even more important in international investment arbitration because of the presence of a State, may be jeopardized.[78]

While no binding rule on the obligation for the parties to disclose third-party funding agreements exists, the October 2014 version of the *IBA Guidelines on Conflicts of Interest in International Arbitration* have incorporated the recent increase of third-party funding in international arbitration generally. The Guidelines are – as the name indicates – not binding, yet they are often referred to in the practice of arbitral tribunals, including in investment treaty arbitration. The 2014 Guidelines first extend the list of entities considered to be the equivalent of the party to the dispute for the purposes of the rules on independence and impartiality: 'if one of the parties is a legal entity, any legal or physical person having a controlling influence on the legal entity, or a direct economic interest in, or a duty to indemnify a party for, the award to be rendered in the arbitration, may be considered to bear the identity of such party'.[79] Second, it provides that parties have a duty to disclose any relation between them and the funder, and a member of the tribunal:

74 Also Goldstein (2011) *supra* note 48, 2ff.

75 See the comments by R Volterra in 'The Dynamics of Third-Party Funding' (2012) 7(1) *Global Arbitration Review* 12, 20.

76 Blackaby, Partasides, Redfern and Hunter (2009) *supra* note 35, para 4.74.

77 The third-party funder, Juridica, had taken over the funding of the claim by S&T against Romania in the case *S&T Oil Equipment & Machinery Ltd v Romania case (S&T Oil Equipment & Machinery Ltd v Romania, ICSID Case No ARB/07/13 (discontinued on 16 July 2010 for lack of payment)*. Subsequently, a dispute arose between S&T and Juridica concerning the alleged misrepresentation by S&T of certain facts and the disclosure of information. The case between the funder and the funded party was brought before a US District Court (*S. District Court, S.D. Texas, Houston Division, S&T Oil Equipment & Machinery v. Juridica Investment Limited, Civil Action No. H-11-0542, April 25, 2011*), and the existence of a funding agreement was thus made public.

78 See for a discussion, Goldstein (2011) *supra* note 48, 5–7.

79 General Standard 6(b), IBA Guidelines on Conflicts of Interest in International Arbitration, *supra* note 72.

> A party shall inform an arbitrator, the Arbitral Tribunal, the other parties and the arbitration institution or other appointing authority (if any) of any relationship, direct or indirect, between the arbitrator and the party (or another company of the same group of companies, or an individual having a controlling influence on the party in the arbitration), or between the arbitrator and any person or entity with a direct economic interest in, or a duty to indemnify a party for, the award to be rendered in the arbitration. The party shall do so on its own initiative at the earliest opportunity.[80]

The ICSID rules on independence and impartiality also may be interpreted as extending to third-party funders as well. ICSID Arbitration rule 6(2), which contains the declaration arbitrators have to make upon accepting their appointment, provides not only disclosure of 'past and present professional, business and other relationships (if any) with the parties', but also 'any other circumstance that might cause my reliability for independent judgment to be questioned by a party'. The latter provision especially may require therefore a disclosure also of relationships with third-party funders. This, of course, requires knowledge of the funding arrangement, which in turn requires disclosure, but if the arbitrators have knowledge of the existence of a third-party funding agreement and the identity of the funder, they are under an obligation to disclose any relationship with the funder that may question their independence and impartiality.

It is line with this development that one should read the request for disclosure made by the Tribunal in *Muhammet Çap & Sehil Inşaat Endustri ve Ticaret Ltd. Sti. v. Turkmenistan*.[81] In that case, the Tribunal ordered full disclosure of the third-party funder's identity and the 'nature of the arrangements concluded with the third-party funder(s), including whether and to what extent it/they will share in any successes that Claimants may achieve in this arbitration', first and foremost to 'ensur[e] the integrity of the proceedings and to determine whether any of the arbitrators are affected by the existence of a third-party funder'.[82] While the disclosure of the *existence* of a third-party funding agreement does not imply a disclosure of the agreement itself, it is notable that the tribunal here ordered also disclosure of the 'nature of the arrangements concluded with the third-party funder(s), including whether and to what extent it/they will share in any successes that Claimants may achieve in this arbitration', which, however, as will be noted below, should be read in light of a request for security for costs.

The whole argument, of course, hinges on the factual reality that third-party funders do have an influence on the procedure. And while there is no general and automatic influence of the funder on the choice of the arbitrator, it regularly occurs that the funder has a certain weight in the choice of the arbitrator since the funder's decision to fund an investment claim will also – and quite logically – take into account the choice of the arbitrators.[83]

As was the case in relation to transparency, the current arbitration rules usually used in investment treaty arbitrations do not provide for any obligation for the parties to disclose third-party funding agreements. This absence of obligation of disclosure is not only lacking in relation to the need to ensure transparency, as noted above, but also in relation to the requirement of independence and impartiality of arbitrators. Here again, I should point to the recent draft TTIP that includes a (general) obligation of disclosure of

80 Ibid. General Standard (7)(a).

81 *Muhammet Çap & Sehil Inşaat Endustri ve Ticaret Ltd. Sti. v. Turkmenistan*, ICSID Case No. ARB/12/6, Procedural Order No. 3, 12 June 2015.

82 Ibid. para 13.

83 See the discussion in Ross (2012) *supra* note 31, 17–18.

third-party funding agreements, as mentioned above, and a general obligation of disclosure for arbitrators that, because of its broad formulation, covers also relationships with third-party funders.[84] The absence of any such obligation of disclosure of third-party funding agreements, however, does not imply that a tribunal cannot order disclosure. As in the case of transparency, such an order can be based on the tribunal's general power to preserve the integrity of the arbitral process and the good faith of the proceedings. The tribunal in *Muhammet Çap & Sehil Inşaat Endustri ve Ticaret Ltd. Sti. v. Turkmenistan* explicitly invoked this ground in the context of its argument in relation to the need for disclosure in relation to the independence and impartiality of arbitrators.[85]

4.3 Identification of the 'real parties to the dispute'

A third element that I will mention briefly, because it is as such alien to the specificity of investment treaty arbitration is the need for disclosure in order to make sure that the claimant in effect still owns the claim. In the case *South American Silver Limited v. Bolivia*,[86] the respondent partly based its request for disclosure of the third-party finding agreement on the fact that it was necessary to identify 'who the real interested parties in this arbitration are. Indeed, the information requested is necessary for Bolivia to confirm whether – as part of the funding agreement – Claimant has assigned some or all of its claims in this arbitration to the third-party funder'.[87]

The tribunal has not yet decided on the request at the time of finalization of the present chapter, but this argument may result in an order for disclosure, based on the tribunal's general power to preserve the integrity of the arbitral process[88] yet it is difficult to argue that a third-party funding agreement in fact results in a transfer of the claim itself, rather than the proceeds of the award. The issue has not yet been discussed much in practice until now, with the exception of the case *Teinver S.A., Transportes de Cercanías S.A. and Autobuses Urbanos del Sur S.A. v. The Argentine Republic*.[89] In the course of the arbitration proceedings, Argentina became aware that the Claimants had obtained third-party funding for the pending claim from Burford Capital, and claimed that Claimants had 'sold' their claims to a third party. As consequence, Argentina requested full disclosure of the agreement and the submission of all related documentation. In turn, Claimants refuted that they had 'sold' their claim and that they should be under the obligation to disclose such agreement. They did, however, confirm that external funding had been sought because of the dire financial situation they were in as a consequence of the refusal by Argentina to pay compensation, but that in any event, this funding did not affect the Tribunal's jurisdiction. The Tribunal refused to grant

84 Art 3, Annex II, Draft TTIP, *supra* note 21: 'Prior to confirmation of their selection as members candidates shall disclose any past and present interest, relationship or matter that is likely to affect their independence or impartiality or that might reasonably create an appearance of impropriety or bias in the proceeding. To this end, candidates shall make all reasonable efforts to become aware of any such interests, relationships or matters.'

85 Ibid. para 9.

86 *South American Silver Limited v. the Plurinational State of Bolivia*, UNCITRAL, PCA CASE NO. 2013-15, Request for *Cautio Judicatum Solvi* and Disclosure of Information, 8 October 2015.

87 Ibid. para 39.

88 See Goldstein (2011) *supra* note 74, 9ff.

89 *Teinver S.A., Transportes de Cercanías S.A. and Autobuses Urbanos del Sur S.A. v. The Argentine Republic*, ICSID Case No. ARB/09/1, Decision on Jurisdiction and Separate Opinion of Dr. Kamal Hossain, 21 December 2012. See for a discussion: E De Brabandere, 'Teinver S.A., Transportes de Cercanías S.A. and Autobuses Urbanos del Sur S.A. v. The Argentine Republic' (2014) 15 *The Journal of World Investment & Trade* 295–304.

Respondent's request for full disclosure, but retained the possibility of doing so in the future.[90] The Tribunal further discussed the issue in relation to several claims made by Argentina during the hearing on jurisdiction in relation to the funding agreement, notably that the funder (Burford Capital) was in fact the 'real' party to dispute and that, as a consequence, the tribunal had no jurisdiction. The Tribunal refuted these arguments, without engaging in a discussion of whether the various agreements indeed had resulted in a change of ownership over the claims, by arguing that the Tribunal's jurisdiction should be assessed as of the date of filing of the case, which means that events that post-date the filing of the arbitration and that could potentially affect the jurisdiction of the court are irrelevant.[91]

Here also, disclosure can be ordered by the Tribunal based on its general power to protect the integrity of the proceedings.

4.4 Negative effects of disclosure? Third-party funding, allocation of costs, and security for costs

The obligation to disclose, in any case, will need to be balanced against the negative effects of disclosing such agreements, notably in relation to the cost aspects of arbitral proceedings. Two issues are of particular importance here: the question of whether international investment tribunals can consider third-party funding agreements when deciding on the allocation of costs and, second, the implication of third-party funding on requests for security for costs.

4.4.1 Third-party funding agreements and the allocation of costs

The answer to the question of whether international investment tribunals can consider third-party funding agreements when deciding on the allocation of costs is in theory very simple: yes, they can. There are indeed no rules prohibiting such a taking into consideration. Article 61 of the ICSID Convention, in conjunction with Rule 28 of the ICSID Arbitration Rules, provides the basis for a tribunal to take a proactive approach in general and to include the third-party funding agreement in its decision on the allocation of costs.[92] However, the practice so far demonstrates that tribunals have refused to take into consideration, as a matter of law or principle, the existence of such an agreement in their decision on the allocation of costs. The main reason for such practice is that the funding agreement falls outside of the jurisdiction of the arbitral tribunal and *Ad Hoc Annulment Committees* established under the ICSID Convention. Arbitral tribunal and *Ad Hoc Committees* have thus categorically refused to consider these agreements in their decision, most notably in the decision on costs.[93]

90 *Teinver S.A., Transportes de Cercanías S.A. and Autobuses Urbanos del Sur S.A. v. The Argentine Republic, supra* note 89, paras 24–26.

91 *Teinver S.A., Transportes de Cercanías S.A. and Autobuses Urbanos del Sur S.A. v. The Argentine Republic, supra* note 89, paras 255–259.

92 See SD Franck, 'Rationalizing Costs in Investment Treaty Arbitration' (2011) 88 *Washington University Law Review* 769, 799.

93 See *Ioannis Kardassopoulos v Georgia*, ICSID Case No ARB/05/18, Award of 3 March 2010, para 680. The Tribunal stated that it 'knows of no principle why any such third-party financing arrangement should be taken into consideration in determining the amount of recovery by the Claimants of their costs'.

One of the first ICSID cases in which the question of allocation of costs was raised in the context of a third-party funding agreement was the combined cases of *Ioannis Kardassopoulos v. Georgia* and *Ron Fuchs v. Georgia*.[94] In these cases, the Claimants requested that their costs be awarded, supporting their reasoning on a number of arguments, including the fact that they prevailed on the jurisdiction and liability phases.[95] Georgia argued that since the Claimants' costs were borne by a third party, it was arguable whether the costs should be recoverable.[96] The Tribunal stated that it 'knows of no principle why any such third-party financing arrangement should be taken into consideration in determining the amount of recovery by the Claimants of their costs'.[97] Similar considerations have been noted in *RSM v Grenada*,[98] in which the Ad Hoc Committee, citing the above-referenced passage from *Kardassopoulos*, reiterated that 'it knew of no principle why any third-party financing arrangement should be taken into consideration in determining the amount of recovery' by the parties of costs incurred in the proceedings.[99] A similar decision was made by the Ad Hoc Committee in *ATA Construction, Industrial and Trading Company v. Hashemite Kingdom of Jordan*.[100] Again citing and adopting the decision of the Tribunal in *Kardassopoulos*, and referring to the decision of the Committee in *RSM*, the Committee in *ATA* rejected the claim by the Claimant that, because of the existence of a third-party funding agreement, the costs of the proceedings could not be shifted to the Claimant.[101]

In these cases, the Tribunal and the Committees did not address the (growing) influence of third-party funders, and adopted the relatively unequivocal policy of not including third-party funding in the allocation of costs, in line with the *inter partes* effect of contractual agreements and the limited jurisdiction of international investment tribunals, which clearly do not cover third-party funding agreements. Yet, it cannot be excluded that future tribunals and Committees may make a distinction between cases in which third-party funders did actually (heavily) influence or delay the proceeding and cases where the existence of a third-party funding agreement had none or very limited influence on the proceedings. Tribunals and Committees could then focus on the consequences of the interference of third-party funders and their possible negative influence on the proceeding. It is indeed only then that a tribunal may decide to take into account a third-party funder and its (influential) role and indirectly consider it in the decision on the cost allocation.

4.4.2 Third-party funding agreements and security for costs

The recent decision of the ICSID Arbitral Tribunal in *RSM Production Corporation v. Saint Lucia* in August 2014,[102] a case in which the claimant had obtained funding from a third

94 *Ioannis Kardassopoulos v Georgia*, *supra* note 93, para 680; *Ron Fuchs v Georgia*, ICSID Case No ARB/07/15, Award of 3 March 2010, para 680.
95 Ibid. para 680.
96 Ibid. para 686.
97 Ibid. para 691.
98 *RSM Production Corporation and others v Grenada*, ICSID Case No ARB/05/14, Order of the Committee Discontinuing the Proceeding and Decision on Costs (28 April 2011).
99 Ibid. para 68.
100 *ATA Construction, Industrial and Trading Company v Hashemite Kingdom of Jordan*, ICSID Case No ARB/08/2, Order Taking Note of the Discontinuance of the Proceeding (11 July 2011).
101 Ibid. paras 34–35.
102 *RSM Production Corporation v. Saint Lucia*, *supra* note 5.

party, has sparked a debate on the question of whether third-party funding agreements should be disclosed, and the influence such disclosure has on requests for security for costs. In fact, two distinct, yet interconnected issues arise here. First, can tribunals order disclosure of the third-party funding agreement in order to have a better view on the financial situation of the funded party in the event of a request for security for costs and, second, in the event of third-party funding, whether tribunals should order security for costs. The answer to the first question here also is relatively easy, since the tribunal's general power to preserve the integrity of the arbitral process here also can be used to request disclosure, as was discussed in relation to transparency and the independence and impartiality of arbitrators. The answer to the second question is more difficult, since the possible negative effects of disclosure on this ground are more profound and the question thus requires a more careful balancing exercise.

The past year has produced a couple of interesting decisions in both respects, starting with the widely commented *RSM Production Corporation v. Saint Lucia*.[103] The Tribunal in that case ordered *RSM* to post a guarantee of US$750,000 to ensure that it could pay Saint Lucia's legal costs if it was ordered to do so by the arbitral tribunal.[104] The decision had been preceded by an earlier decision of the tribunal in which *RSM* was ordered to post security for the costs to be incurred by ICSID in the arbitration.[105] The case is peculiar, because *RSM* had already built a reputation in previous investment arbitrations by not meeting its financial obligations,[106] and the Tribunal in fact principally and predominantly relied on these circumstances to conclude that the Claimant did not have sufficient financial resources.[107] Yet, the existence of a third-party funding agreement was explicitly mentioned as an additional reason for the tribunal to have doubts on the capacity for the claimant to – if need be – reimburse the costs of the Respondent.[108] The decision has been discussed widely,[109] yet the dissenting opinion of the arbitrator appointed by the Claimant, Edward Nottingham,[110] and the concurring opinion of the other party-appointed arbitrator, Gavan Griffith,[111] precisely on the question of third-party funding, has attracted even more attention.

Gavan Griffith considered the 'third party funding issue' to be the 'preferred ground' for making an order on security for costs,[112] instead of focusing on the 'defaulting history'

103 See W Kirtley and K Wietrzykowski, 'Should an Arbitral Tribunal Order Security for Costs When an Impecunious Claimant Is Relying upon Third-Party Funding?' (2013) 30(1) *Journal of International Arbitration* 17–30.

104 *RSM Production Corporation v. Saint Lucia*, ICSID Case No. ARB/12/10, Decision on Saint Lucia's Request for Security for Costs with Assenting and Dissenting Reasons, 13 August 2014, para 90.

105 LE Peterson, 'In a Novel Ruling, ICSID Tribunal Orders that Impecunious Third-Party Funded Claimant Should Cover All Advance-Costs of Proceedings' (*IA Reporter*, 10 January 2014) <www.iareporter.com/articles/in-a-novel-ruling-icsid-tribunal-orders-that-impecunious-third-party-funded-claimant-should-cover-all-advance-costs-of-proceedings/>.

106 *RSM Production Corporation and others v Grenada*, ICSID Case No ARB/05/14, Order of the Committee Discontinuing the Proceeding and Decision on Costs, 28 April 2011. See also *RSM Production Corporation v. Saint Lucia*, para 78.

107 Ibid. para 82.

108 Ibid. para 83.

109 See e.g. the various contributions, including by third-party funders, in a special issue of the *Global Arbitration Review*, 'A Storm over St Lucia', Volume 9(5), <http://globalarbitrationreview.com/news/article/32932/should-funded-claimants-pay-security/>.

110 *RSM Production Corporation v. Saint Lucia*, Dissenting Opinion of Edward Nottingham, 12 August 2014.

111 *RSM Production Corporation v. Saint Lucia*, Assenting Reasons of Gavan Griffith, 12 August 2014.

112 Ibid. para 11.

of the claimant.[113] As third-party funders only share in the 'rewards of success', and, except in case of security for costs, risk no more than their spent costs in the event of a failure, the situation is, according to Gavan Griffith, the equivalent of 'a gambler's Nirvana: Heads I win, and Tails I do not lose'.[114] Gavan Griffith further considered third-party funders to be a 'new industry of mercantile adventurers',[115] and that it 'is no reach to find that, as strangers to the BIT entitlement, such funders also should remain at the same real risk level for costs as the nominal claimant. In this regard, the integrity of the BIT regimes is apt to be recalibrated in the case of a third-party funder, related or un-related, to mandate that its real exposure to costs orders which may go one way to it on success should flow the other direction on failure'.[116] He argues that the mere presence of a third-party funder should result in an order for security for costs, and an obligation for the funded party to explain why no security for costs should be ordered and disclosing all relevant factors to that effect.[117] The concurring opinion resulted in *RSM* filing a claim to disqualify Gavan Griffith,[118] which was eventually dismissed by the two other members of the Tribunal.[119]

Edward Nottingham, on the other hand, questioned whether an order for security for costs lay within the provisional measures powers of the ICSID Convention and Arbitration Rules,[120] and also applied to contingent rights.[121] Edward Nottingham also strongly disagreed on the decision to take into consideration the existence of a third-party funding agreement.[122]

While there is indeed still much debate as to whether an order for security for costs lays within the provisional measures powers of the ICSID Convention and Arbitration Rules, as noted by Edward Nottingham, there is some practice indicating that such a ruling is possible. I will not enter into a discussion of this in the context of this chapter. Assuming that such a power indeed exists, the question is whether the existence of a funding agreement *should* result in an order for security for costs as posited by Gavan Griffith. Here also, there are no rules indicating what arbitral tribunals can or cannot take into account when ordering security for costs. The only rule commonly accepted in the practice of investment tribunals, is that such an order can only be granted 'in exceptional circumstances'.[123] It is also beyond doubt that the existence of third-party funding may be taken into account in ordering security for costs, as the majority did in this decision.[124] Claiming, as Gavan Griffith did, that the mere presence of a third-party funder *should* result in an order for security for costs and a reversal of the burden

113 Ibid. para 17.
114 Ibid. para 13.
115 Ibid. para 14.
116 Ibid. para 14.
117 Ibid. para 18.
118 *RSM Production Corporation v. Saint Lucia*, ICSID Case No. ARB/12/10, Claimant's Proposal to Disqualify Gavan Griffith, 10 September 2014.
119 *RSM Production Corporation v. Saint Lucia*, ICSID Case No. ARB/12/10, Decision on Claimant's Proposal for the Disqualification of Dr. Gavan Griffith, QC, 23 October 2014.
120 Dissenting Opinion of Edward Nottingham, *supra* note 110, in particular paras 2–5.
121 Ibid. in particular paras 6–7.
122 Ibid. paras 18–19.
123 See, for instance, *Commerce Group Corp. and San Sebastian Gold Mines, Inc. v. The Republic of El Salvador*, ICSID Case No. ARB/09/17, Decision on El Salvador's Application for Security for Costs, 21 September 2012, para 45.
124 See also W Kirtley and K Wietrzykowski, 'Should an Arbitral Tribunal Order Security for Costs When an Impecunious Claimant Is Relying upon Third-Party Funding? (2013) 30(1) *Journal of International Arbitration* 17, 18.

of proof, however, is a step too far, in that the automaticity posited by Gavan Griffith not only finds no support in the arbitration rules usually applied in investment arbitration, but also does not necessarily correspond to the economic reality of why parties seek third-party funding. As noted above, foreign investors simply may not be willing to invest their own funds in the arbitration, or do not want to take the risk inherent in an investment treaty arbitration.[125] The reversal of the burden of proof in such situations has thus no firm basis and the automaticity posited by Gavan Griffith makes abstraction of such a situation, and could in fact result in a more limited access to justice because of the financial burden imposed on funded claimants. As noted by the tribunal in *EuroGas Inc. and Belmont Resources Inc. v. Slovak Republic*: 'the Tribunal further notes that, as held in *RSM v. Grenada*, it is 'not part of the ICSID dispute resolution system that an investor's claim should be heard only upon the establishment of a sufficient financial standing of the investor to meet a possible costs award'.'[126] Also, the Tribunal in *Hamester v. Ghana*,[127] a case in which the Claimant had also received funding from a third party, refused to order security for costs, noting that 'there was a serious risk that an order for security for costs would stifle the Claimant's claims and that, in any event, it had not been shown that the measures requested were necessary and urgent. An order for security for costs would not serve its purpose without cancelling or postponing the Hearing, which was neither requested nor practicable at that stage of the proceeding.'[128]

Compared to *RSM v. Saint Lucia*, the decision of the Tribunal in *EuroGas Inc. and Belmont Resources Inc. v. Slovak Republic*,[129] reflects a more balanced and preferable approach. Confronted to a request for provisional measures, including security for costs, the Tribunal first noted that *RSM v. Saint Lucia* was an exceptional case, in that 'the claimant was not only impecunious and funded by a third party, but also had a proven history of not complying with cost orders [that] were considered cumulatively'.[130] The Tribunal refused to order security for costs, considering that 'no such exceptional circumstances have been evidenced in the instant case. The Claimants have not defaulted on their payment obligations in the present proceedings or in other arbitration proceedings.'[131] Notably, however, the Tribunal explicitly distanced itself from the automaticity posted by Gavan Griffith:

> The Tribunal is of the view that financial difficulties and third party-funding – which has become a common practice – do not necessarily constitute per se exceptional circumstances justifying that the Respondent be granted an order of security for costs.[132]

A third recent decision that has discussed the matter is *Muhammet Çap & Sehil Inşaat Endustri ve Ticaret Ltd. Sti. v. Turkmenistan*,[133] mentioned above in relation to the

125 See L Bench Nieuwveld and V Shannon, *Third-Party Funding in International Arbitration* (Alphen aan den Rijn: Kluwer Law International 2012) 12.

126 *EuroGas Inc. and Belmont Resources Inc. v. Slovak Republic*, ICSID Case No. ARB/14/14, Procedural Order No. 3 Decision on the Parties' Request for Provisional Measures, 23 June 2015, para 120.

127 *Gustav F W Hamester GmbH & Co KG v. Republic of Ghana*, ICSID Case No. ARB/07/24 Award, 18 June 2010.

128 Ibid. para 17.

129 *EuroGas Inc. and Belmont Resources Inc. v. Slovak Republic*, *supra* note 126.

130 Ibid. para 122.

131 Ibid. para 123.

132 Ibid.

133 *Muhammet Çap & Sehil Inşaat Endustri ve Ticargt Ltd. Sti. v. Turkmenistan*, *supra* note 81.

independence and impartiality of arbitrators. In that case, the Tribunal did not order security for costs, since such a request had not yet been made by the respondent, but it did order full disclosure of the third-party funder's identity and the 'nature of the arrangements concluded with the third-party funder(s), including whether and to what extent it/they will share in any successes that Claimants may achieve in this arbitration'.[134] This order was in part grounded on the fact that 'although it has not yet done so, Respondent has indicated that it will be making an application for security for costs. It is unclear on what basis such application will be made, e.g. Claimants' inability to pay Respondent's costs and/or the existence of a third-party funder.'[135] This case is remarkable, in that it preempts a future request for security for costs, and requests disclosure of third-party funding in order to be able to properly address that future request.

The preceding case-law shows a clear indeterminate relation between third-party funding and security for costs. Indeed, while it is beyond doubt that the existence of third-party funding may be taken into account in ordering security for costs, the automaticity posited by Gavan Griffith has not yet found any confirmation, quite the contrary. At the same time, it is also beyond doubt that Respondents who are aware of the existence of a third-party funding arrangement will not shy away from requesting security for costs, as is shown in both *EuroGas Inc. and Belmont Resources Inc. v. Slovak Republic* and *Muhammet Çap & Sehil Inşaat Endustri ve Ticaret Ltd. Sti. v. Turkmenistan*. This is confirmed by the recent 'Request for *Cautio Judicatum Solvi* and Disclosure of Information' made by the respondent in the case *South American Silver Limited v. Bolivia* because of the existence of a third-party funder.[136]

5. Conclusion

Third-party financing is a fast-growing industry and probably will in the future play an important role in investment treaty arbitration. In addition to the benefits of third-party financing, there is no doubt that the presence of a third party can influence the course of the procedure.

The overall issue, as has been noticed, is that investment treaty arbitration differs substantially from international commercial arbitration, because of the higher focus on the legitimacy and public nature of the dispute and its settlement. The disclosure of third-party funding agreements, despite some inevitable negative effects at least in the early stages of the development of case-law in this respect, contributes to the legitimacy of investment treaty arbitration, which, because of its public and international law dimension, is of fundamental importance. The argument that third-party funding is a private matter between the funder and the funded party does not stand in investment treaty arbitration. Because of the need for transparency in international investment arbitration, the involvement of a State acting in its sovereign capacity, and the public nature of the dispute, the confidentiality of third-party financing appears incompatible with the foundational principles of international investment arbitration. The main tension caused by third-party funding is particularly noticeable in relation to the rules on the independence and impartiality of arbitrators. The independence and impartiality of arbitrators is fundamental in investment treaty arbitration. I have argued in this chapter that this issue in particular warrants the need for a disclosure

134 Ibid. para 13.
135 Ibid. para 10.
136 *South American Silver Limited v. the Plurinational State of Bolivia*, *supra* note 86.

of at least the identity of the funder. Third, this chapter has assessed the interplay between disclosure and the allocation of costs and requests for security for costs. While tribunals and *ad hoc* committees have so far refused to take into account the existence of a financing agreement in the distribution of costs, the situation is different in relation to requests for security for costs, in light of the *RSM v. Saint Lucia* decision. I have argued that, clearly, the existence of third-party funding may be taken into account in ordering security for costs, as the majority did in *RSM v. Saint Lucia*. This balanced and preferable approach has also been adopted by the tribunal in *EuroGas Inc. and Belmont Resources Inc. v. Slovak Republic*. Indeed, claiming, as Gavan Griffith did, that the mere presence of a third-party funder *should* result in an order for security for costs and a reversal of the burden of proof, however, is a step too far and finds no support in the arbitration rules.

In general, however, and beyond the confines of the funding agreement, it is difficult to argue that there is, at this stage, a general obligation to disclose third-party funding agreements. Neither the ICSID Convention, the ICSID Arbitration Rules, nor the UNCITRAL Arbitration Rules contain any relevant provisions requiring a funded party to disclose such information to the tribunal and the other party. However, parties are free to arrange for a full disclosure of third-party funding agreements in their investment treaties. Yet, so far, the only treaty that attempts such regulation is the Draft Transatlantic Trade and Investment Partnership and it remains to be seen whether this rule will make it to the final version. It is to be expected, however, that States will include such provisions in future treaties, notably because of the need for transparency.

Second, while the IBA Guidelines contain certain provisions in relation to independence and impartiality, such provisions are not binding and cannot impose any obligation on the parties. However, the practice discussed above shows that tribunals have, in all circumstances where disclosure might be needed or is preferable, nevertheless ordered disclosure. Such orders are based on the tribunal's general power to preserve the integrity of the arbitral process and the good faith of the proceedings. Disclosure at this stage can thus only result from an order by the tribunal based on the tribunal's general power to preserve the integrity of the arbitral process.

Bibliography

Baldwin E., M. Kantor and M. Nolan, 'Limits to Enforcement of ICSID Awards' (2006) 23(1) *Journal of International Arbitration* 1.

Bench Nieuwveld L. and V. Shannon, *Third-Party Funding in International Arbitration* (Alphen aan den Rijn: Kluwer Law International 2012).

Blackaby N., 'Public Interest and Investment Treaty Arbitration' (2004) 1 *Transnational Dispute Management* 1.

—— C. Partasides, A. Redfern and M. Hunter, *Redfern & Hunter on International Arbitration* (5th edn, Oxford: Oxford University Press 2009).

Bottini G., 'Should Arbitrators Live on Mars? Challenge of Arbitrators in Investment Arbitration' (2009) 32 (2) *Suffolk Transnational Law Review* 341.

Buergenthal T., 'The Proliferation of Disputes, Dispute Settlement Procedures and Respect for the Rule of Law' (2006) 22 *Arbitration International* 495.

Cremades B.M., 'Third Party Litigation Funding: Investing in Arbitration' (2011) 8(4) *Transnational Dispute Management* 25.

De Brabandere E., 'Arbitral Decisions as a Source of International Investment Law' in T. Gazzini and E. De Brabandere (eds), *International Investment Law. Sources of Rights and Obligations* (Leiden: Martinus Nijhoff Publishers 2012) 245.

—— 'Derde Partij Financiering en de onafhankelijkheid en onpartijdigheid van arbiters in internationale investeringsarbitrage' (2013) 1 *b-Arbitra – Belgian Arbitration Review* 101.
—— *Investment Treaty Arbitration as Public International Law: Procedural Aspects and Implications* (Cambridge: Cambridge University Press 2014).
—— 'Teinver S.A., Transportes de Cercanías S.A. and Autobuses Urbanos del Sur S.A. v. The Argentine Republic' (2014) 15 *The Journal of World Investment & Trade* 295.
—— and J. Lepeltak, 'Third-Party Funding in International Investment Arbitration' (2012) 27(2) *ICSID Review* 379.
De Morpurgo M., 'A Comparative Legal and Economic Approach to Third-Party Litigation Funding' (2011) 19 *Cardozo Journal of International and Comparative Law* 352.
Douglas Z., *The International Law of Investment Claims* (Cambridge: Cambridge University Press 2009).
Franck S.D., 'Rationalizing Costs in Investment Treaty Arbitration' (2011) 88 *Washington University Law Review* 769.
Goldstein M.J., 'Should the Real Parties in Interest Have to Stand Up? Thoughts about a Disclosure Regime for Third-Party Funding in International Arbitration' (2011) 8(4) *Transnational Dispute Management* 9.
Goodman C.L., 'Uncharted Waters: Financial Crisis and Enforcement of ICSID Awards In Argentina' (2007) 28(2) *U. Pa. J. Int'l Econ. L.* 449.
Honlet J.C., 'Recent Decisions on Third-Party Funding in Investment Arbitration' (2015) 30(3) *ICSID Review* 699.
Khouri S., K. Hurford and C. Bowman, 'Third-Party Funding in International Commercial and Treaty Arbitration – A Panacea or a Plague? A Discussion of the Risks and Benefits of Third-Party Funding' (2011) 8(4) *Transnational Dispute Management* 1
Kinnear M., E. Obadia and M. Gagain, 'The ICSID Approach to Publication of Information in Investor-State Arbitration' in A. Malatesta and R. Sali (eds), *The Rise of Transparency in International Arbitration* (Huntington: Juris 2013) 108.
Kirtley W. and K. Wietrzykowski, 'Should an Arbitral Tribunal Order Security for Costs When an Impecunious Claimant is Relying upon Third-Party Funding?' (2013) 30(1) *Journal of International Arbitration* 17.
Knahr C. and A. Reinisch, 'Transparency versus Confidentiality in International Investment Arbitration – The Biwater Gauff Compromise' (2007) 6 *The Law and Practice of International Courts and Tribunals* 97.
Kuo H., 'The Issue of Repeat Arbitrators: Is It a Problem and How Should the Arbitration Institutions Respond?' (2011) 4(2) *Contemporary Asia Arbitration Journal* 247.
Lutrell S., 'Bias Challenges in Investor-State arbitration: Lessons from International Commercial Arbitration' in C. Brown and K. Miles (eds), *Evolution in Investment Treaty Law and Arbitration* (Cambridge: Cambridge University Press 2011) 479.
Malatesta A. and R. Sali (eds), *The Rise of Transparency in International Arbitration* (Huntington: Juris 2013).
Matthews J.M. and M. Steinitz, 'Editorial: TDM Special Issue: Contingent Fees and Third Party Funding in Investment Arbitration Disputes' (2011) 8(4) *Transnational Dispute Management* 1.
Moses M.L., *The Principles and Practice of International Commercial Arbitration* (Cambridge: Cambridge University Press 2008).
Newcombe A. and L. Paradell, *Law and Practice of Investment Treaties: Standards of Treatment* (Alphen aan den Rijn: Kluwer Law International 2009).
Nmehielle V.O., 'Enforcing Arbitration Awards Under the International Convention for the Settlement of Investment Disputes (ICSID Convention)' (2001) 7(1) *Annual Survey of International & Comparative Law* 21–48.
Rau A.S., 'On Integrity in Private Judging' (1998) 14(2) *Arbitration International* 115.
Rosert D., 'The Stakes Are High: A Review of the Financial Costs of Investment Treaty Arbitration', *International Institute for Sustainable Development Research Report* (July 2014) 2, <www.iisd.org/

sites/default/files/publications/stakes-are-high-review-financial-costs-investment-treaty-arbitration.pdf> accessed 1 December 2015.

Ross A., 'The Dynamics of Third-Party Funding' (2012) 7(1) *Global Arbitration Review* 14.

Sands P., 'Conflict and Conflicts in Investment Treaty Arbitration: Ethical Standards for Counsel' in C. Brown and K. Miles (eds), *Evolution in Investment Treaty Law and Arbitration* (Cambridge: Cambridge University Press 2011) 24.

Schreuer C., L. Malintoppi, A. Reinisch and A. Sinclair, *The ICSID Convention: A Commentary* (Cambridge: Cambridge University Press 2009).

Seidel S., 'Third-Party Investing in International Arbitration Claims' in B.M. Cremades and A. Dimolitsa (eds), *Third-Party Funding in International Arbitration* (Dossier X of the ICC Institute of World Business Law) (Paris: ICC 2015) 16.

Smith M., 'Mechanics of Third-Party Funding Agreements: A Funder's Perspective' in L. Bench Nieuwveld and V. Shannon, *Third-Party Funding in International Arbitration* (Alphen aan den Rijn: Kluwer Law International 2012) 19.

Steinitz M., 'Whose Claim Is It Anyway? Third-Party Litigation Funding' (2011) 95 *Minn. L. Rev.* 1,267.

Van Boom W.H., 'Financing Civil Litigation by the European Insurance Industry' in M. Tuil and L. Visscher (eds), *New Trends In Financing Civil Litigation in Europe – A Legal, Empirical, and Economic Analysis* (Cheltenham: Edward Elgar 2010) 92.

—— *Third-Party Financing in International Investment Arbitration* (2011) <http://papers.ssrn.com/sol3/papers.cfm?abstract_id=2027114>.

Volterra R., 'The Dynamics of Third-Party Funding' (2012) 7(1) *Global Arbitration Review* 12.

Weeramantry R. and M. Ferrer, 'RSM Production Corporation v Saint Lucia: Security for Costs – A New Frontier?' (2015) 30(1) *ICSID Review* 30.

7 Experimenting with conditional fees in the Netherlands

Ben van Velthoven and Peter van Wijck[1]

1. Introduction

In the Netherlands, until recently, lawyers were not permitted to provide services on a no-win, no-fee basis, nor could the amount of their fee vary in proportion to the outcome of the particular case. The traditional line of argument in support of these restrictions has been one of professional ethics. To be of most value to his client, a lawyer, when representing a client in a case, should be independent, impartial and certainly not influenced by any direct financial interest in the outcome of that case. These restrictions have, however, been under discussion for quite some time now. Conditional and contingent fee arrangements have been introduced and are actual practice in other countries such as the UK and the US, so why not in the Netherlands?

Moreover, restrictions apply to lawyers, who are members of the Dutch Bar Association. As such, they have a monopoly over advocacy in court. In personal injury cases, however, legal assistance is frequently provided by claim agents and other non-legal professionals. This is possible because the large majority of personal injury cases are settled out of court. Not bound by the rules of the Bar, claims agents have, over time, obtained a substantial share of the market for legal services in personal injury cases by offering potential clients varying no-win, no-fee arrangements. Due to this loss of business, lawyers have started to complain about this competitive disadvantage. The Dutch Competition Authority agreed with this and stated that the regulation that prohibits no-win, no-fee constitutes a violation of competition law.[2]

In 2004, the first proposal of the Dutch Bar Association to start a no-win, no-fee experiment was blocked by the Minister of Justice, who called upon the traditional line of argument referred to above. Since then, however, government budget problems have led to a sharp rise in court fees and substantial cuts to Legal Aid. A second proposal of the Dutch Bar Association for such an experiment got a more favourable reception because it was thought it might help to improve access to justice for the less well-to-do in society. So, on 1 January 2014, a five-year experiment with conditional fees in personal injury cases commenced. During this, claimants and lawyers may waive the normal hourly fee and instead opt for a no-win, no-fee arrangement. Under this arrangement, the

1 We thank AK Abhelakh, RT Bocxe, T Kremer, AM Mooyman and M Speelmans for information on the handling of personal injury cases in the Netherlands. That information was an essential input for choosing the key parameters of our simulation model.

2 For more details see MG Faure and NJ Philipsen, 'Fees for Claim Settlement in the Field of Personal Injury: Empirical Evidence from the Netherlands' (2010) 1 *Journal of European Tort Law* 75–101.

claimant does not have to pay any fee if the case is lost. However, in a successful case, the lawyer is entitled to the normal hourly fee plus a pre-specified mark-up to compensate for risk and costs. The mark-up is either 100 or 150 per cent of the hourly fee, depending on whether it is the claimant or the lawyer who bears the risk of additional costs, such as medical expertise and court fees. Further, it has been established that the claimant's payment to the lawyer cannot exceed a certain percentage: 25 or 35 per cent of the financial result.

What consequences can be expected to arise from these systems? More specifically, how does this influence the behaviour of parties involved in a dispute? This type of question has been studied extensively in the Law & Economics literature, where scholars typically develop models providing stylised representations of the relevant process. Such literature, however, does not immediately answer our question. The Dutch experiment with conditional fees takes place in a setting that is characterised by the continental way of cost shifting: the party that loses in court must, in principle, pay for the litigation costs of the successful party. Until now, such a combination of conditional fees and cost shifting has hardly been studied in the Law & Economics literature and, if so, only on a theoretical level. In the present paper, we study whether the no-win, no-fee arrangement that is currently made available in the Netherlands really improves access to justice.[3] To that end, we built our own model to discover whether the conditional fee arrangement, in comparison to hourly fees, can in fact be beneficial to claimants and their lawyers. Given that, regrettably, hard empirical evidence is not available, a simulation was made based on certain key parameters that were distilled from conversations with stakeholders in Dutch personal injury litigation.

Our paper proceeds as follows. Section 2 provides a concise review of the Law & Economics literature on contingent and conditional fee arrangements. Section 3 describes the details of the Dutch experiment for both variants. Section 4 presents the outline of our model, which is then used in Section 5 for comparative simulations of the hourly fee and conditional fee arrangements, as they are currently available in the Netherlands. In Section 6, a reflection is made on the premises of our model simulations. A conclusion is provided in Section 7.

2. Literature review

In the United States, the principal means of funding litigation in personal injury cases is through no-cure, no-pay, with, in cases of success, a direct and proportionate relationship between fees and damages (contingent fees). This fee system of damages-based arrangements (DBAs) has been studied extensively in the Law & Economics literature. General conclusions, however, cannot easily be drawn, as Gravelle and Waterson (1993, p. 1,218) have already noted: 'the move to contingent fees will create a complex web of effects because changes in the contract between the plaintiff and his lawyer influence the decisions taken at all stages of the litigation process'. Nevertheless, the following points can be said to have sufficient

3 WH van Boom and M de Jong, 'Het experiment resultaatgerelateerde beloning – verwachtingen over werking en doelbereiking' (2014) *Tijdschrift Vergoeding Personenschade* 69, interviewed various players in the personal injury field at the start of the experiment and observed that the expectations were very modest.

theoretical and empirical support.[4] First, contingent fees tend to enlarge the access to justice for cases that are relatively strong and where the amount at stake is relatively high. If capital markets are imperfect, claimants may be unable to finance hourly fees even when litigation has good prospects of success. A contingent legal fee arrangement is a device to solve this liquidity constraint. Furthermore, if claimants are more risk-averse than lawyers, a contingent fee arrangement can facilitate an increase in net utility as a result of risk sharing. Second, bearing part of the risk means that lawyers filter out cases with poorer prospects of success and lower value claims. Overall, therefore, it is not clear whether the total number of claims filed will actually be higher under contingent fees. However, the average quality of the claims definitely will be. Whether or not a lawyer is willing to take a case on a contingent fee basis thus provides a strong signal about the quality of the case. Third, lawyers who charge an hourly rate may feel tempted to work more hours on a case than might be warranted by the (additional) expected award to his client. Contingent fees align the incentives more effectively by giving the lawyer a shared interest in the claim. Hence, contingent fee lawyers will put in less effort on a case than hourly fee lawyers. Fourth, contingent fees do not create a perfect alignment of incentives, as both the lawyer and the client only get a share of the award. It will usually be to the lawyer's advantage to obtain a quick settlement even if that settlement is below the expected gain from court proceedings, because this will allow him to minimise his efforts. This tendency is reinforced as most clients lack the necessary information and knowledge needed to assess the recommendations of and actions taken by their lawyers. In consequence, lawyers have considerable control over their clients in the settlement process. There is, nevertheless, an important check on contingent fee lawyers, as Kritzer (2004, p 178) points out and that 'comes from the incentives created by the long-term need to maintain a profitable portfolio of cases: these incentives dictate both delivering outcomes for clients (to facilitate a flow of clients) and properly preparing cases (to get good offers from opposing parties)'.

Conditional fee arrangements (CFAs) were made lawful in England and Wales in 1995. Their scope was extended in 2000 by the Access to Justice Act, which abolished Legal Aid in most personal injury cases. Under a conditional fee arrangement, the lawyer receives no fee at all if the case is lost, but is paid a normal hourly fee plus a mark-up (the success fee) if the case is won. The unsuccessful claimant is thus protected from his lawyer's bill. He would, however, still be subject to the defendant's legal costs due to the English rule of cost shifting. As a result, CFAs are typically combined with after-the-event (ATE) insurance policies, purchased when the claim is initiated, to cover these costs in return for a premium.[5]

4 ML Schwartz and DJB Mitchell, 'An Economic Analysis of the Contingent Fee in Personal-Injury Litigation' (1970) 22 *Stanford Law Review* 1125–1162; H Gravelle and M Waterson, 'No Win, No Fee: Some Economics of Contingent Legal Fees' (1993) 103 *Economic Journal* 1,205–1,220; E Helland and A Tabarok, 'Contingent Fees, Settlement Delay, and Low-Quality Litigation: Empirical Evidence from Two Datasets' (2003) 19(2) *Journal of Law, Economics and Organization* 517–542; HM Kritzer, *Risks, Reputations and Rewards: Contingency Fee Legal Practice in the United States* (Stanford: Stanford Law and Politics 2004); R Moorhead, 'An American Future? Contingency Fees, Claims Explosions and Evidence from Employment Tribunals' (2010) 73(5) *The Modern Law Review* 752–784.

5 In 2000, to further safeguard access to justice, ATE premiums and success fees were made recoverable from the defendant if the case was won. This weakened the claimants' incentives to monitor their lawyers' efforts. Indeed, litigation costs increased by approximately 25 per cent after this policy change, according to P Fenn, V Grembi and N Rickman, '"No Win, No Fee", Cost-Shifting and the Costs of Civil Litigation: A Natural Experiment' (2014) BAFFI Center Research Paper Series No 2014-152, Università Commerciale Luigi Bocconi. This recoverability rule was reversed in 2012. For more details see J Peysner, *Access to Justice – A Critical Analysis of Recoverable Conditional Fees and No-Win No-Fee Funding* (Palgrave Macmillan 2014).

A comparison of the American DBA and English CFA systems must take account of the difference in cost allocation. Emons and Garoupa (2006) and Melamed (2006) study the two systems under the American rule of cost allocation. The conclusion is that contingent fees are more efficient than conditional fees. The conditional fee may solve the contingent fee's problem of encouraging lawyers to keep their work to a minimum, but it gives rise to other significant issues. The conditional fee creates an incentive for lawyers to work as many hours as possible and simultaneously, an incentive to settle as opposed to going to court. This is because upon settlement the lawyer can expect an unusually high return per hour, due to the mark-up. Alternatively, if the case proceeds to court, the lawyer not only risks losing any reward for future efforts but also the reward for the hours he has invested in the case until then. The more hours the lawyer has worked, the less incentive he has to raise civil proceedings. Hyde (2006) shows that the cost-allocation rule has no impact on the extent of legal effort under contingent and conditional fees. However, the comparison of the two fee structures depends critically on who takes the relevant decisions in the course of the litigation process, the client or his lawyer. Conditional fees result in more legal effort if litigation is determined by the lawyer and not by the client.

3. The Dutch experiment, three options

On 1 January 2014, a five-year experiment with conditional fees in personal injury cases began. During the experiment, claimants and lawyers may opt for no-win, no-fee instead of the normal hourly fee arrangement. The no-win, no-fee arrangement comes in two variants.

- *Variant 1*: The lawyer is entitled to an hourly rate with a mark-up of (at most) 100 per cent if the case is won. His total invoice cannot exceed 25 per cent of the financial result, which is defined as the sum of the damages and any legal costs that are reimbursed by the defendant as a result of cost shifting. If the case is unsuccessful, the lawyer receives no fee at all. However, the claimant bears all the specific costs such as medical expertise and court fees. Moreover, upon losing the case the claimant is responsible for any legal costs that shift from the defendant's side.
- *Variant 2*: The lawyer pays for all the specific costs such as medical expertise and court fees and for any cost shifting from the defendant's side upon losing the case. If the case is unsuccessful, the lawyer receives no fee at all. In a successful case, however, the lawyer receives an hourly fee with a mark-up of (at most) 150 per cent. His total invoice cannot exceed 35 per cent of the financial result. Moreover, he is entitled to any specific costs that are reimbursed by the defendant as a result of cost shifting.

Thus, claimants have three options to choose from, provided they can find a lawyer to represent them under each of the three fee arrangements.

4. Set-up of the model

To study the implications of the conditional fee experiment on access to justice, a simple theoretical model of the process of handling a personal injury dispute was built. That model is at the heart of our computer simulation in Section 5. To be manageable, the model is an abstract representation of the dispute handling processes that can be observed in the real world, concentrating on the key elements. In Section 6, we return to the assumptions underlying our model and reflect on how they may affect our results.

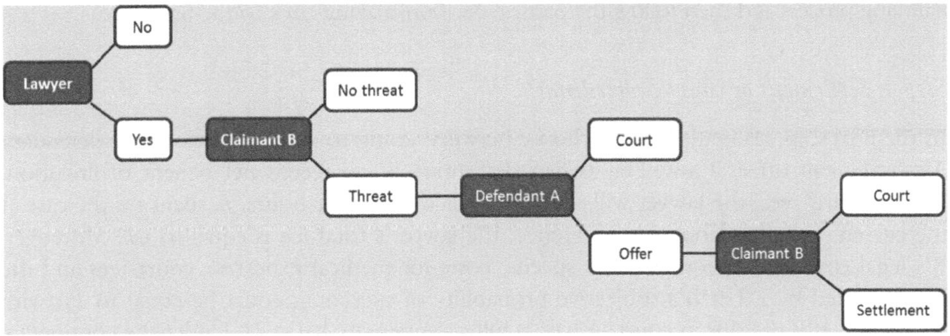

Figure 7.1 General structure of the dispute handling process

4.1 General structure

The structure of our model is illustrated in Figure 7.1.[6] Person A, the alleged injurer, has caused an accident that brought personal injury to person B, the victim. Victim B considers whether it is worthwhile to sue alleged injurer A for damages. From then on, B is the claimant and A the defendant. As a first step, claimant B needs to consult a lawyer, for information and advice and for representation in court. Therefore, he investigates whether he can find a lawyer who is willing to take his case on. Second, claimant B, duly informed by his lawyer, verifies whether the expected net benefit of legal action is positive. If so, he can credibly inform the defendant that civil proceedings may be brought. Third, defendant A may make an offer to settle, if he wishes to avoid the case being brought to court directly. Finally, it is a matter for claimant B, or his representative, to decide whether the offer made by the defendant is acceptable. Otherwise, the case will end up in court.

The model proceeds on the basis that both the claimant and the defendant are risk neutral.[7] Further, we begin with the assumption that the claimant has sufficient financial means to cover his legal costs, if any, so there is no liquidity constraint. Initially, it is also assumed that the settlement decision is controlled by the claimant. In Section 5.3, an analysis is provided with respect to what would happen, if the settlement decision were to be controlled by the lawyer. The impact of a liquidity constraint is discussed in Section 5.4.

4.2 Hourly fees

First, we address hourly fees. Suppose defendant A has caused harm H, $H > 0$, to claimant B. Claimant B wants to sue defendant A to obtain damages. To clarify the relationships of our

6 The structure of the model builds on classic papers in the field, especially WM Landes, 'An Economic Analysis of the Courts' (1971) 14 *Journal of Law and Economics* 61–107; JP Gould, 'The Economics of Legal Conflicts' (1973) 2 *Journal of Legal Studies* 279–300; RA Posner, 'An Economic Approach to Legal Procedure and Judicial Administration' (1973) 2 *Journal of Legal Studies* 399–458; and S Shavell, 'Alternative Dispute Resolution: An Economic Analysis' (1995) 24 *Journal of Legal Studies* 1–28.

7 An individual is said to be risk neutral if he is indifferent to a certain amount of money and an uncertain amount with an equal expected value. A risk-neutral individual effectively makes decisions comparing the expected values associated with choices.

model we proceed by backwards induction. That is, we start with the last step of the dispute handling process and then follow the parties' decision-making back to the first step.

Step 4: Settlement or court proceedings?

In the final step, claimant B must choose between going to court and accepting defendant A's settlement offer, if any. Let us first determine B's expected net benefit of litigation. Under hourly fees, the lawyer will send an invoice for all the hours, h, spent on the case at the current remuneration rate, w. Hence, the lawyer's total fee is equal to wh. Moreover, B's legal costs also encompass any specific costs for medical expertise, court fees and the like, denoted by s. Let B's subjective probability of success in court be equal to P_B, with $0 \leq P_B \leq 1$. If B prevails in court, A has to fully compensate harm H. Under the continental rule of cost shifting, A must also reimburse the legal costs of the claimant.[8] If B loses in court, however, he has to pay for the legal costs incurred by defendant A. These are denoted by t.[9] Claimant B's expected net benefit of litigation, L_B, is then equal to:

$$L_B = -(wh + s) + P_B(H + wh + s) - (1 - P_B)t = P_B H - (1 - P_B)(wh + s + t). \quad (1)$$

As regards the alternative option of a settlement: claimant B will only be interested in accepting a settlement offer from defendant A, if it makes him, at least, as well off as the result he can expect from court proceedings. Let us assume that the costs of bringing about a settlement are a fraction α $(0 < \alpha < 1)$ of the costs of a court action. Then, the claimant's legal costs in case of a settlement are $\alpha(wh + s)$. Hence, to be acceptable to claimant B, the settlement offer must at least amount to Z, where:

$$Z = L_B + \alpha(wh + s) = P_B H - (1 - P_B)(wh + s + t) + \alpha(wh + s). \quad (2)$$

Otherwise, the claimant will decline the offer and wait for the judge to give his final ruling in court.

Step 3: Court proceedings or settlement offer?

In this step it is up to defendant A to decide whether making an acceptable settlement offer is a good alternative to waiting for the outcome of civil proceedings.

Let A's subjective probability of success in court be equal to P_A, $0 \leq P_A \leq 1$. If A prevails, his legal costs, t, will be shifted to B. If A loses, he has to compensate claimant B for his harm, H, and his legal costs, $wh + s$. Consequently, defendant A's expected total costs of litigation are given by:

$$L_A = t - P_A t + (1 - P_A)(H + wh + s) = (1 - P_A)(H + wh + s + t). \quad (3)$$

8 We acknowledge that the Dutch rule of cost shifting is somewhat mixed in character. Court fees and expert witness costs are fully shifted; however, lawyer's costs are subject to quite a detailed tariff schedule. We pass over the specifics of that schedule.

9 There is no need to differentiate these costs in lawyer's fees and specific costs. Note that the defendants in personal injury cases are almost always represented by liability insurers.

A can also try to settle the dispute out of court. In order to be acceptable to the claimant, the settlement offer should at least amount to Z, as derived in (2). Clearly, it is not in A's interest to pay more than strictly necessary, so the offer will be equal to Z.[10] Moreover, A will incur legal costs, αt, in bringing about a settlement. Hence, defendant A's total costs in case of a settlement are given by:

$$Z + \alpha t = P_B H - (1 - P_B)(wh + s + t) + \alpha(wh + s + t). \tag{4}$$

Comparing A's expected total costs of litigation (3) and A's total costs in case of a settlement (4), it follows that A will aim for a settlement if and only if:

$$(P_A + P_B - 1)(H + wh + s + t) \leq (1 - \alpha)(wh + s + t). \tag{5}$$

Step 2: Credible threat?

In the second step, claimant B must decide whether it is credible for him to bring civil proceedings. This is the case if his expected net benefit upon doing so is positive. From the previous discussion we know that the claimant's expected net benefit of litigation equals L_B; see (1). If the case ends in a settlement, the claimant can expect to receive an amount Z, which after deduction of legal costs also yields a net benefit of L_B; see (2). Hence, the claimant will be interested in proceeding to court if L_B is positive, that is if:

$$P_B > (wh + s + t)/(H + wh + s + t). \tag{6}$$

If so, the claimant has a credible case against the defendant.[11]

Step 1: Finding a lawyer

That brings us to the first step where the claimant is looking for a legal representative. In the context of hourly fees, finding a lawyer will not be a problem given that a lawyer can send an invoice for all the hours he will spend on the case, in and outside of court, with or without success, at his current remuneration rate, w. Throughout our analysis, we assume that the remuneration rate w (at least) covers the opportunity cost of his effort, v.[12]

Summary

Table 7.1 presents an overview of the expected net benefits of the parties under an hourly fee arrangement. As the claimant can readily find a lawyer to take on the case, three possible outcomes remain: no threat, settlement and court proceedings.

10 Assuming that defendant A either knows the amount Z from his interaction with claimant B or at least has obtained sufficient information for a reliable guess.

11 Note that $Z > 0$ whenever B has a credible threat of proceeding against A. For if $L_B > 0$, then a fortiori $L_B + \alpha(wh + s) > 0$.

12 The opportunity cost of a lawyer's hour is the net return he can earn by putting the hour to its best alternative use. The opportunity cost is zero, if the lawyer, upon declining the present case, should spend his time idly due to lack of assignments. The opportunity cost is w, if the lawyer has sufficient other cases to choose from to earn him an average fee of w per hour.

Table 7.1 Hourly fee arrangement: Overview of expected net benefits

	No threat	*Settlement*	*Court proceedings*
Defendant A	0	$-Z-\alpha t$	$-(1-P_A)(H+wh+s+t)$
Claimant B	0	$Z-\alpha(wh+s)$	$P_BH-(1-P_B)(wh+s+t)$
B's lawyer	0	$\alpha(w-v)h$	$(w-v)h$

where: $Z = P_BH - (1 - P_B)(wh + s + t) + \alpha(wh + s)$

4.3 *Conditional fees, variant 1*

We now discuss the first variant of the conditional fee experiment.

Step 4: Settlement or court proceedings?

In the last step of the dispute handling process, the claimant has to choose to go to court or, rather, accept the defendant's settlement offer, provided there is one.

What can be said about B's expected net benefit of litigation? First, B has to pay for his own specific costs, s. Should the court rule in his favour, B is awarded an amount of damages H and legal cost reimbursements $wh + s$ that the defendant requires to pay. At the same time, he must pay his lawyer's invoice, which is denoted by J^C. If the court finds against B, his lawyer is not entitled to any fee. However, B still has to bear the legal costs, t, that are shifted from the defendant's side. Hence, the claimant's expected net benefit of litigation is:

$$L_B = -s + P_B(H + wh + s - J^C) - (1 - P_B)t = P_B(H + wh - J^C) - (1 - P_B)(s + t). \qquad (7)$$

Let us consider the lawyer's invoice in more detail. Under the first variant of the conditional fee experiment, the lawyer receives no fee at all if the case is lost. However, in the case of success, the lawyer can send his client an invoice for the normal hourly fees, wh, plus a mark-up of 100 per cent. The total amount of that invoice cannot exceed 25 per cent of the claimant's financial result defined as the sum of damages, H, and legal cost reimbursements, $wh + s$. The lawyer's invoice after successful court proceedings is thus given by:

$$J^C = min\{2wh,\ 0.25(H + wh + s)\}. \qquad (8)$$

Next, we turn to the settlement. Claimant B will only be interested in accepting a settlement offer if it makes him at least as well off as he would be due to the judgment in court proceedings, by yielding a net amount of L_B; see (7). To reach that goal, the settlement offer should also compensate the claimant for the legal costs in settling the case. These consist of the claimant's specific costs, αs, and the invoice from his lawyer, J^S. Upon a settlement, the lawyer is entitled to the normal hourly fee, w, for the settlement hours, αh, plus a mark-up of 100 per cent. The invoice is, however, subject to the condition that the total invoice should not exceed 25 per cent of the claimant's financial result, as given by the settlement amount Z. Thus, the settlement offer will only be successful if it is at least equal to:

$$Z = L_B + \alpha s + J^S, \text{ where } J^S = min\{2\alpha wh,\ 0.25Z\}. \qquad (9)^{13}$$

Step 3: Settlement or court proceedings?

In the third step, defendant A considers the option of settling the case instead of going to court. As before, A's expected total costs of litigation are equal to:

$$L_A = (1 - P_A)(H + wh + s + t). \qquad (10)$$

Alternatively, A might aim for a settlement. He can proceed in that direction by offering the claimant the minimum acceptable amount Z, given by (9). As defendant A also incurs legal costs αt in bringing about a settlement, he will aim for a settlement if and only if $Z + \alpha t \leq L_A$.

Step 2: Credible threat?

It follows from the previous discussion that the claimant's expected net benefit is equal to L_B, no matter whether the dispute handling process ends in litigation or a settlement. Hence, the claimant has a credible threat if and only if L_B is positive, that is if:

$$P_B > (s + t)/(H + wh + s + t - J^C). \qquad (11)^{14}$$

Step 1: Finding a lawyer

In order to be able to take his case to court, claimant B has to find a lawyer who is willing to represent him. Thereto, the lawyer's expected return must be sufficient to cover the opportunity costs of his efforts.

If the case ends up in court, the lawyer can send his client an invoice J^C if he is successful; see (8). On the other hand, the lawyer cannot charge any fee if the case is lost. *Ex ante*, the lawyer will only be interested in the case if his expected net return is positive, that is if:

$$P_B J^C - vh \geq 0, \qquad (12)$$

which boils down to $P_B \geq 0.5v/w$, as long as $2wh \leq 0.25(H + wh + s)$.

Note that the lawyer can make such a calculation on the back of an envelope, based on his subjective estimate of the claimant's probability of success in combination with the amount of harm and the expected legal costs in a case of that particular size and strength. Deciding in this way is well suited to the lawyer who has no experience with the new remuneration rule, as it has only recently been introduced as an experiment.

13 Solving the interdependency of Z and J^S yields: $J^S = 2\alpha wh$, $Z = L_B + \alpha s + 2\alpha wh$, if $\alpha wh \leq 1/6\ (L_B + \alpha s)$; and $Z = 4/3\ (L_B + \alpha s)$, $J^S = 1/3\ (L_B + \alpha s)$, if $\alpha wh > 1/6\ (L_B + \alpha s)$.

14 Note that $Z > 0$ whenever B has a credible threat. For if $L_B > 0$, then a fortiori $Z = L_B + \alpha s + J^S > 0$.

However, if the experiment runs longer and lawyers become better acquainted with its impact, they will take into account that cases can also end in a settlement. Over time, they will develop good instinct, if not expertise, to predict which cases will end up in court and which cases will be settled. Decision rule (12) still gives good guidance to determine whether it pays to accept a case that predictably ends up in court. For a case that will end in a settlement, the decision rule will be adjusted. Such a case only pays if the fee J^S, as given by (9), is sufficient to cover the opportunity costs αvh of the lawyer's efforts.

Summary

Table 7.2 provides an overview of the expected net benefits to the parties under variant 1 of the conditional fee arrangement. There are four possible outcomes: no lawyer, no threat, settlement and court proceedings.

Table 7.2 Conditional fees, variant 1: Overview of expected net benefits

	No lawyer / No threat	*Settlement*	*Court proceedings*
Defendant A	0	$-Z - \alpha t$	$-(1 - P_A)(H + wh + s + t)$
Claimant B	0	$Z - \alpha s - J^S$	$P_B(H + wh - J^C) - (1 - P_B)(s + t)$
B's lawyer	0	$J^S - \alpha vh$	$P_B J^C - vh$

where: $J^C = min\{2wh, 0.25(H+wh+s)\}$
$J^S = min\{2\alpha wh, 0.25Z\}$
$Z = P_B(H + wh - J^C) - (1-P_B)(s + t) + \alpha s + J^S$

4.4 *Conditional fees, variant 2*

Next, we address the second variant of the conditional fee experiment. As the general line of the dispute handling process does not change in comparison to the first variant, we need not repeat the four steps in full. However, the expected net returns of both the claimant and his lawyer at court and of settlement need adjustment because of the differences in the remuneration rule.

To begin, take the lawyer's expected net return in the case of court proceedings. Under the second variant of the conditional fee experiment, the lawyer has to bear the risk of the specific costs on the claimant's side, s. If the case is lost, he gets no fee, however he has to reimburse the defendant's legal costs, t, as a result of cost shifting. In a successful case, on the other hand, he can send his client an invoice for the normal hourly fees, wh, plus a mark-up of 150 per cent. The total amount of that invoice, J^C, cannot surpass 35 per cent of the claimant's financial result defined as the sum of damages payments, H, and legal cost reimbursements, $wh + s$. Upon winning the case, moreover, he is entitled to a reimbursement of the specific costs, s, he has paid in advance. In the rules of the experiment, it was further laid down that the claimant's net benefit upon winning his case should never be negative. A successful claimant should therefore never pay a larger sum to his lawyer, $J^C + s$, than his financial result, $H + wh + s$, allows. This results in an additional upper limit on the lawyer's invoice: $J^C \leq H + wh$. The lawyer's invoice after successful court proceedings is thus given by:

$$J^C = min\{2.5wh,\ 0.35(H + wh + s),\ H + wh\}. \tag{13}$$

Altogether, the lawyer's expected net return in the context of a court case is given by:

$$-s + P_B(J^C + s) - (1 - P_B)t - vh, \tag{14}$$

It can be concluded that the case only pays if:

$$P_B \geq (vh + s + t)/(J^C + s + t). \tag{15}$$

Thereafter, the claimant's expected net benefit of litigation can be assessed. If the case is won, B obtains a financial result $H + wh + s$, while his lawyer is entitled to the fee J^C, discussed above, plus a reimbursement of the specific costs, s. In the event that the case is lost, the claimant has no legal costs at all as they are all taken care of by his lawyer. The claimant's expected net benefit of litigation is thus given by:

$$L_B = P_B(H + wh - J^C). \tag{16}$$

Instead of waiting for the outcome of the proceedings in court, A can also try to settle the case by offering a settlement amount Z that would bring claimant B – net of settlement costs – into the same position as the decision of the court. B's settlement costs consist of the lawyer's fee and the specific costs, αs, he has to reimburse to his lawyer. In principle, the lawyer can claim a mark-up of 150 per cent on the normal hourly remuneration, w, for the settlement hours, αh. His invoice, J^S, is however subject to the condition that it should not exceed 35 per cent of the claimant's financial result, Z. A's settlement offer is thus equal to:

$$Z = L_B + \alpha s + J^S, \text{ where } J^S = min\{2.5\alpha wh,\ 0.35Z\}. \tag{17}$$[15]

As a consequence, B's expected net benefit of a settlement equals L_B. His lawyer's expected net return for a settlement is given by:

$$J^S + \alpha s - \alpha(vh + s). \tag{18}$$

Finally, note that claimant B's expected net benefit equals L_B, no matter whether the dispute handling process ends in litigation or settlement. From (16) and upper limit (13) on the lawyer's invoice, $J^C \leq H + wh$, it immediately follows that B always has a credible threat, if $P_B > 0$.

Summary

Table 7.3 presents an overview of the expected net benefits of the parties under variant 2 of the conditional fee arrangement. There are four possible outcomes: no lawyer, no threat, settlement and court proceedings.

15 Note that $Z > 0$ whenever B has a credible threat. For if $L_B > 0$, then a fortiori $Z = L_B + \alpha s + J^S > 0$. Solving the interdependency of Z and J^S yields: $J^S = 2.5\alpha wh$, $Z = L_B + \alpha s + 2.5\alpha wh$, if $\alpha wh \leq 14/65\ (L_B + \alpha s)$; and $Z = 20/13\ (L_B + \alpha s)$, $J^S = 7/13\ (L_B + \alpha s)$, if $\alpha wh > 14/65\ (L_B + \alpha s)$.

Table 7.3 Conditional fees, variant 2: Overview of expected net benefits

	No lawyer/No threat	*Settlement*	*Court proceedings*
Defendant A	0	$-Z - \alpha t$	$-(1 - P_A)(H + wh + s + t)$
Claimant B	0	$Z - \alpha s - J^S$	$P_B(H + wh - J^C)$
B's lawyer	0	$J^S + \alpha s - \alpha(vh + s)$	$-s + P_B(J^C + s) - (1 - P_B)t - vh$

where: $J^C = min\{2.5wh,\ 0.35(H + wh + s),\ H + wh\}$
$J^S = min\{2.5\alpha wh,\ 0.35Z\}$
$Z = P_B(H + wh - J^C) + \alpha s + J^S$

5. Model simulation

5.1 Set up

Our model covers the key aspects of the litigation process but is, in essence, still very simple. For one thing, it does not cover the choice of the level of effort by the claimant's lawyer in response to the remuneration rule. The preventative working of the legal system with respect to defendant A's choice of level of care and amount of activities are also not explicitly modelled. Yet, the model as it now stands, simple as its essence may be, is difficult to fathom by analytical means. There are many parameters that play a role. Additionally, the upper limits in the conditional fee arrangements thwart the linear structure of the model. Instead, we opt here for a computer simulation of the model. That is, the computer is used to calculate the outcomes of the model outlined in the preceding section, inserting numerical values for the key parameters. Based on various pieces of information that we obtained from Dutch publications and from conversations with Dutch lawyers, claims agents and insurers, we take the following figures and ratios for granted:

- The lawyer's costs in the case of a settlement are related to the level of harm by an increasing but concave function: $\alpha wh = 1.21 \times (46.9 + 31.10\ H^{0.5})$.
- The specific costs in the case of a settlement are 10 per cent of the lawyer's costs: $\alpha s = 0.1\alpha wh$.
- The legal costs of reaching a settlement are 25 per cent of the total legal costs of bringing a case to court and proceeding all the way to a judgment by the court: $\alpha = 0.25$.
- The legal costs on the defendant's side are 50 per cent of the legal costs on the claimant's side: $t = 0.5(wh + s)$.
- The opportunity rate of a lawyer's effort equals his remuneration rate: $v = w$. That is, if the lawyer does not agree to take on the case offered to him, he has a sufficient number of other cases to choose from to earn an average fee of w per hour.[16]

Other important parameters of our model are the degree of harm, H, and the subjective probabilities of success of the parties involved, P_A and P_B. In the literature, we found some

16 The first relationship was the outcome of a regression analysis under the authority of the Dutch Association of Insurers; see ARM Berntsen and K Nijman, 'Normering is de normaalste zaak van de wereld...' (2014) *PIV-Bulletin* December 12–13. The factor 1.21 reflects the 21 per cent VAT surcharge. The other figures and ratios were deduced from and corroborated by our conversations with different stakeholders. In Section 6, we discuss the robustness of our results for changes in these relationships.

figures with respect to payments for damages for settled cases.[17] The frequency distribution is reported to be:

≤ €5,000	38.5%
€5,000 <. ≤ €10,000	20.1%
€10,000 <. ≤ €25,000	21.3%
> €25,000	20.1%.

This distribution is skewed, with many rather small claims and relatively few large claims. However, as these figures only pertain to cases that have been settled, they do not cover the cases that have not been acted upon or were withdrawn at one point or other, nor do they cover the cases that went to court. Presumably, the former group of these cases consists of a comparatively small number of cases, while the latter group contains a comparatively large number of cases. Moreover, the figures above refer to payments of damages, which generally do not coincide with the degree of harm.

As a consequence, we do not have sufficiently reliable data on the degree of harm, H, in respect of potential cases. We also have no data on the subjective probabilities of success P_A and P_B. To solve this problem, we simulate our model with a discrete set of five values of harm, ranging from €2,000 to €1,250,000. As to P_A and P_B, we consider all values from 0 to 1, increasing by increments of 0.1.

We start in Section 5.2 with a simulation of the model as it has been specified before. In that model, the settlement decision is claimant-controlled. Furthermore, claimants are not constrained by liquidity. In Sections 5.3 and 5.4, we then address lawyer-controlled decision making and the effect of liquidity constraints.

We further distinguish between myopic and sophisticated lawyers when it comes to the decision to accept a new case under conditional fees.[18] Sophisticated lawyers are well informed and far-sighted with respect to the impact of the remuneration rule. They have sufficient expertise to predict which cases will end up in court and which cases will be settled out of court. Hence, they are able to calculate the expected net return of each case based on the predicted outcome. Myopic lawyers, on the other hand, have no extensive experience with the remuneration rule. Based on a subjective assessment of the claimant's probability of success, the amount of harm and the legal costs normally associated with a case of this strength and size, they can make an estimate of the expected net return if the case goes to court. However, they lack the information and the expertise to predict whether the case might eventually be settled with substantially less effort on their part. Therefore, they are not sufficiently equipped to accept (the risk of) a case that is not worth the effort if it ends up in court but might be if it ends in a settlement. Sophisticated lawyers would not hesitate to accept such a case.

In our simulation, we start with the assumption that lawyers are myopic. That seems to be the logical thing to do, given that the experiment in the Netherlands only started recently and lawyers have not, as yet, had much time to gain experience in dealing with

17 MG Faure and NJ Philipsen, 'Fees for Claim Settlement in the Field of Personal Injury: Empirical Evidence from the Netherlands' (2010) 1 *Journal of European Tort Law* 75–101.

18 The distinction is irrelevant under hourly fees, as lawyers know that each hour can be charged to the client in question. Hence, they will not hesitate to accept any case if the remuneration rate covers the opportunity cost, as we assume throughout the simulations.

conditional fees. Over time that may change. In Section 5.5 we see what happens if lawyers get to be sophisticated.

5.2 Simulation results: Claimant-control, myopic lawyers

Figure 7.2 presents the outcomes of our model simulation when the settlement decision is claimant-controlled and lawyers are myopic. The graphs in the first column of Figure 7.2 refer to the hourly fee arrangement, and the graphs in the next two columns are related to the first and second variant of the conditional fee experiment. In each column, comparing the graphs from the top to the bottom row shows how the outcomes are affected as the level of harm increases from a low €2,000 to a high €1,250,000.

Each separate graph illustrates how the outcome varies in relation to the subjective probabilities of success of the two parties, for a given remuneration rule and a given level of harm. The defendant's subjective probability of success, P_A, is always on the vertical axis, while the claimant's subjective success probability, P_B, is on the horizontal axis. Both range from 0 to 1 increasing by increments of 0.1. In general, there can be four different outcomes in our model: no lawyer, no threat, settlement and court proceedings. The intensity of the shading makes clear which particular outcome the computer simulation predicts will prevail for each parameter configuration. Take, for instance, the upper left graph in Figure 7.2, which informs on the outcome of the dispute handling process under hourly fees when the amount of harm is a relatively modest €2,000. The graph shows that finding a lawyer in itself is not a problem. However, the claimant has no credible threat as long as his probability of success P_B is too low. Only if the claimant's probability of success is 0.9 or higher, will the dispute end up in court or by reaching a settlement. Which of the two outcomes results, depends on defendant A's probability of success. At rather high values of P_A, the case will or is likely go to court, otherwise the dispute will be settled.

Hourly fees

Let us now address the simulation results in detail. With regard to hourly fees, we can conclude that the results in the left column of Figure 7.2 are in full accordance with the findings from the 'divergent expectations' literature.[19]

First, an increase in the level of harm, ceteris paribus, leads to an increase in the claimant's expected net benefit of litigation.[20] As the claimant has no problem in finding a lawyer under hourly fees when the remuneration rate of the latter covers his opportunity cost, the relative frequency of 'no threat' will fall. That results in an increase in the relative frequency of settlements and court proceedings.

Second, cases where the claimant has a credible threat will always end in a settlement if $P_A + P_B \leq 1$.[21] Stated differently, there will be no court proceedings if the claimant and defendant do not suffer from judicial optimism. It is then in their mutual interest to prevent the costs of a court proceedings. It should also be noted that the lawyer has no incentive

19 See, e.g., PW van Wijck and BCJ van Velthoven, 'An Economic Analysis of the American and the Continental Rule for Allocating Legal Costs' (2000) 9 *European Journal of Law and Economics* 115–125 and the references given there.

20 Cf (6).

21 Cf (5).

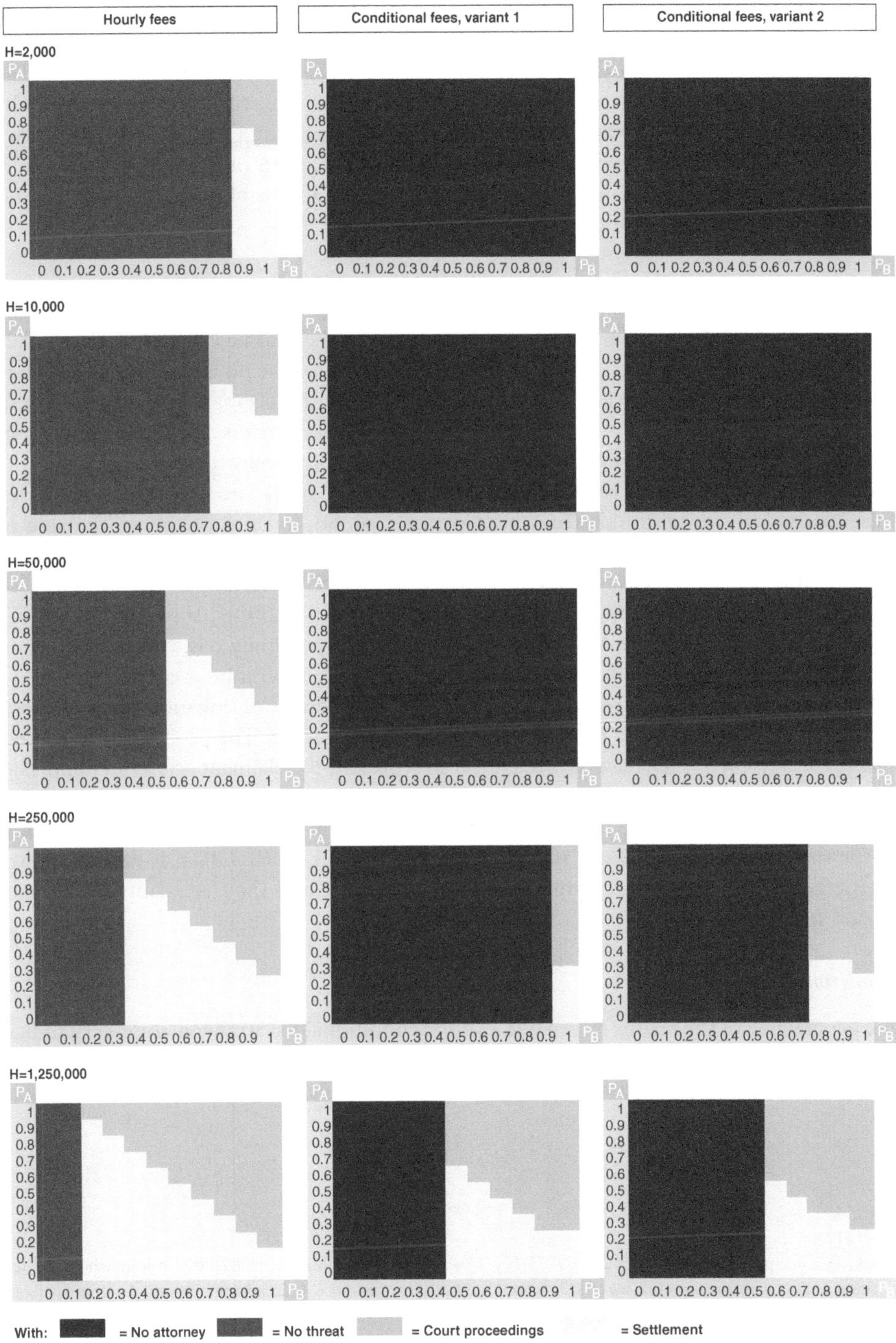

Figure 7.2 Outcome of dispute handling: Claimant-control, myopic lawyers

to act counter to the interests of his client as long as the extra hours he spends on court proceedings as compared to the hours he spends on bringing about a settlement are (just) remunerated at his opportunity cost.

Third, if there is no discussion between the parties about the cause of the harm and the liability of the defendant, such that $P_A = 0$ and $P_B = 1$, the case will always be settled. The settlement amount Z is such that the claimant is fully compensated and the defendant takes care of all his legal costs.[22] This is in conformity with Art. 6:96 of the Dutch Civil Code, stating that reasonable costs incurred in assessing damage and liability and obtaining extra-judicial payment may be claimed as patrimonial damage.

Conditional fees, variant 1

Next, we consider the first variant of conditional fees in the middle column of Figure 7.2.

First, it should be noted that there is a prominent place for the no lawyer outcome, while the no threat outcome is absent here. Under hourly fees the claimant has no problem in finding legal assistance, because the lawyer's remuneration covers his opportunity cost. Under conditional fees, however, it depends both on the probability of success, P_B, and the level of harm, H, whether a lawyer is willing to accept the case. The lawyer receives no fee if the case is lost, but a double fee if he wins the case. So, in principle he will be able to cover his opportunity cost if $P_B \geq 0.5$.[23] There is a complicating element, however, as the total amount of his invoice cannot exceed 25 per cent of the claimant's financial result. This upper limit on his invoice appears to be active for $H <$ €1,082,000.[24] If so, the probability of success must be correspondingly higher to cover his opportunity costs. As a result, until $H =$ €192,000 the lawyer will not be interested in the case even if he is certain to win.[25]

Second, it turns out that the claimant's expected net benefit of litigation is always positive once he has been able to find a lawyer to represent his case. The probability of success is large enough then.[26] The lawyer's readiness to represent the claimant acts as an important signal about the strength of the case.

Third, whether a credible threat will end in a settlement or court proceedings depends on the subjective probabilities of success of the two parties. If $P_A + P_B \leq 1$, there is always a settlement offer that is acceptable to both the claimant and the defendant, as they can save on legal costs.

Conditional fees, variant 2

The general line of the results for variant 2 of the conditional fee arrangement is very similar to variant 1 discussed above. See the right column of Figure 7.2. However, some key numerical findings need adjustment. Most notably: a lawyer will in general be able to cover

22 Cf (4).

23 Cf (12).

24 Cf (8). The upper limit is active if $2wh > 0.25(H + wh + s)$. This results in $H <$ €1,082,000 (in somewhat rounded figures) after substituting $0.25wh = 1.21 \times (46.9 + 31.10\ H^{0.5})$ and $s = 0.1wh$ from the initial settings of our simulation.

25 Note that $J^C = 0.25(H+wh+s)$ if the restriction on the lawyer's invoice is active. From (12) we know that the lawyer is only interested in the case if $P_B J^C \geq vh$. Substituting $v = w$, $s = 0.1wh$ and $0{,}25wh = 1.21 \times (46.9 + 31.10\ H^{0.5})$ tells us that the lawyer will only take the case if $H >$ €192,000, even if $P_B = 1$.

26 Cf (11).

his opportunity costs if $P_B \geq 0.52$.[27] There is a complicating element, however, as the total amount of his invoice cannot exceed 35 per cent of the claimant's financial result. This upper limit on his invoice appears to be active for $H <$ €831,000.[28] If so, the probability of success must be correspondingly higher to cover his opportunity costs. As a result, until $H =$ €71,000, the lawyer will not be interested in the case even if he is certain to win.[29]

Compensation rates

Even more interesting than the dispute handling process as such, at least from the claimant's perspective, is the (expected) compensation rate. What is the claimant's net expected return as a percentage of his original harm? Figure 7.3 presents the results.

Under each of the three fee arrangements, the compensation rate goes up as the degree of harm increases and as the claimant's probability of success increases. The reason is straightforward: both of these lead to a growth in the claimant's expected net benefit of litigation. The stronger the claimant's initial position is vis-à-vis the defendant, the better his end result will be.

The (expected) compensation rate, however, does not vary according to the defendant's probability of success. The latter parameter does affect the defendant's choice between court proceedings and settlement. Having said that, to try to reach a settlement, the defendant has no need to offer the claimant a more generous net benefit than he can expect to obtain in court.

Comparison

The stage is now set to make a mutual comparison of the three fee arrangements. It is apparent from Figure 7.2 that any of the remuneration rules may be acceptable to both the claimant and his lawyer, rather than taking no action at all, provided the degree of harm and the claimant's probability of success are high enough. However, it is also clear from Figure 7.2 that the hourly fee arrangement is acceptable to both the claimant and his lawyer for a far greater set of parameter configurations than any of the conditional fee variants. Cases that end up being settled or proceeding to court in column 1 (hourly fees) may end up as no lawyer in column 2 (variant 1) or column 3 (variant 2). In these cases, the claimant would clearly be better off under hourly fees. More specifically, no lawyer will be interested in representing the claimant under conditional fees for a level of harm below €192,000 in the case of variant 1 and €71,000 in the case of variant 2. Moreover, Figure 7.3 shows that the compensation rate under hourly fees is, in most cases, higher and never lower than under conditional fees. Hence, from the point of view of the claimant, the hourly fee arrangement is definitely the better option. As to conditional fees, neither of the two variants leads to a consistently higher compensation rate vis-à-vis the other. For some

27 Neglecting for a moment the upper limit on the invoice, the lawyer will be interested if $P_B \geq (vh + s + t)/(2.5wh + s + t)$. Cf. (15). After substituting $v = w$, $s = 0.1wh$ and $t = 0.5(wh + s)$ this boils down to $P_B \geq 1.65/3.15 = 0.52$.

28 Cf (13). The upper limit is active if $2.5wh > 0.35(H + wh + s)$. This results in $H <$ €831,000 after substituting $0.25wh = 1.21 \times (46.9 + 31.10\ H^{0.5})$ and $s = 0.1wh$.

29 Note that $J^C = 0.35(H + wh + s)$ if the restriction on the lawyer's invoice is active. The lawyer is only interested in the case if his expected net return (14) is positive. Substituting $v = w$, $s = 0.1wh$ and $0{,}25wh = 1.21 \times (46.9 + 31.10\ H^{0.5})$ tells us that the lawyer will only take the case if $H >$ €71,000, even if $P_B = 1$.

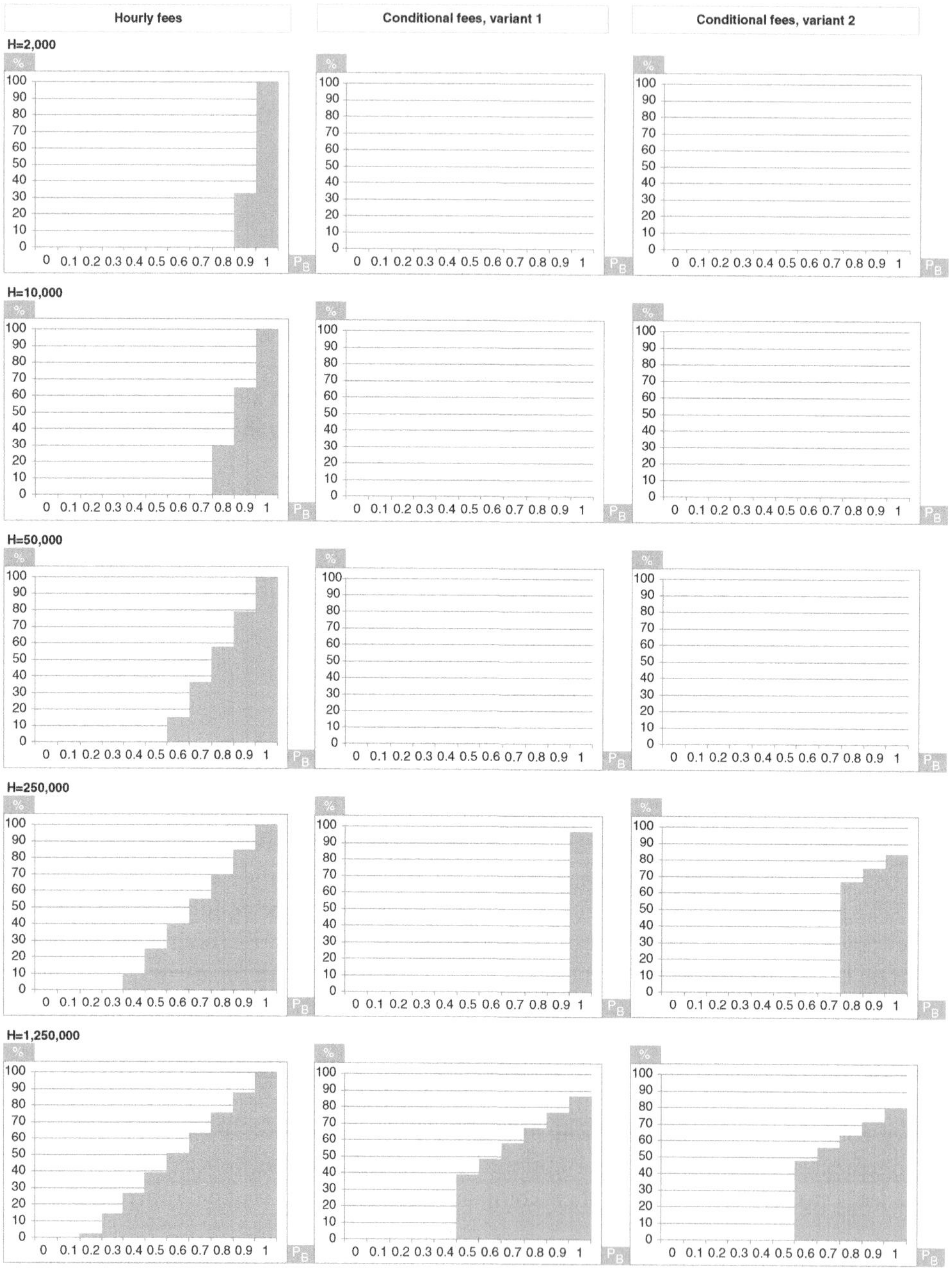

Figure 7.3 Compensation rate: Claimant-control, myopic lawyers

parameter configurations variant 1 is the better option, for other parameter configurations variant 2 will be preferred by the claimant.

5.3 Simulation results: Lawyer-control, myopic lawyers

In our literature review we noted that it is critical in the context of conditional fees whether litigation is claimant- or lawyer-controlled. The simulations in the preceding section started from the model as it was laid out before, where the settlement decision was assumed to be claimant-controlled. Let us now address lawyer-controlled decision-making.

The major change is in Step 3 of the model and only for conditional fees. Under hourly fees, the lawyer is indifferent as to whether the case settles or goes to court, provided his remuneration rate per hour equals his opportunity cost, as has been assumed. The lawyer's income does not change if he is writing hours on a new case instead of going to court and writing additional hours for the current case: an hour is an hour. The lawyer is not indifferent, however, when it comes to conditional fees. There may be cases where a settlement might be mutually acceptable to the claimant and the defendant, but where the lawyer might prefer to go to court. Court proceedings provide the scope for obtaining a 100 or 150 per cent mark-up on the additional hours in court, in return for sacrificing his opportunity cost and the certainty of obtaining a mark-up upon settling. Going to court may be worthwhile if the probability of success, P_B, is high enough. If the upper limit on the invoice does not apply, the lawyer prefers court proceedings to a settlement if $P_B > 0.62$ under variant 1, and $P_B > 0.64$ under variant 2.[30] The defendant might try to raise his settlement offer to avert court proceedings. At the end of the day, however, that will not help to change the lawyer's preference as his conditional fee does not depend on the financial result, but on the number of hours worked.

Conditional fees give the lawyer a strong incentive to go to court in respect of cases with relatively high probabilities of success. This can be seen from our simulation results. See the graphs on the right-hand side of the bottom row of Figure 7.4 (lawyer-control) in comparison to the corresponding graphs in Figure 7.2 (claimant-control). Figures 7.4 and 7.2 also indicate that the lawyer's incentive to raise a court action based on conditional fees decreases with the degree of harm. The reason is that the upper limit on the lawyer's invoice comes into effect for lower levels of harm,[31] making court proceedings less attractive.[32]

30 Cf tables 2 and 3. Leaving aside the possibility of an upper limit on the invoice, the lawyer will prefer court proceedings over a settlement under variant 1 if $P_B 2wh - vh > 2\alpha wh - \alpha vh$, which boils down to $P_B > (v + 2\alpha w - \alpha v)/2w = 0.62$, if $w = v$ and $\alpha = 0.25$. Similarly, the lawyer will prefer court proceedings over a settlement under variant 2 if $P_B(2.5wh + s + t) - (vh + s + t) > 2.5\alpha wh - \alpha vh$, which boils down to $P_B > 2.025/3.15 = 0.64$, if $w = v$, $\alpha = 0.25$, $t = 0.5(wh + s)$, and $s = 0.1wh$.

31 More specifically: for H below €1,082,000 under variant 1 and below €831,000 under variant 2. Cf Section 5.2.

32 Note that lawyer-control does not affect the claimant's (expected) compensation rate. For if the lawyer were indeed to be tempted to go to court more often, the claimant can still count on his expected net benefit of litigation, given by (7) for variant 1 and (16) for variant 2. In case of a settlement, the claimant's net result would not be better, as it is in the defendant's direct interest not to offer more than strictly necessary. If the lawyer fares better at court proceedings, it is the defendant who bears the (additional) costs.

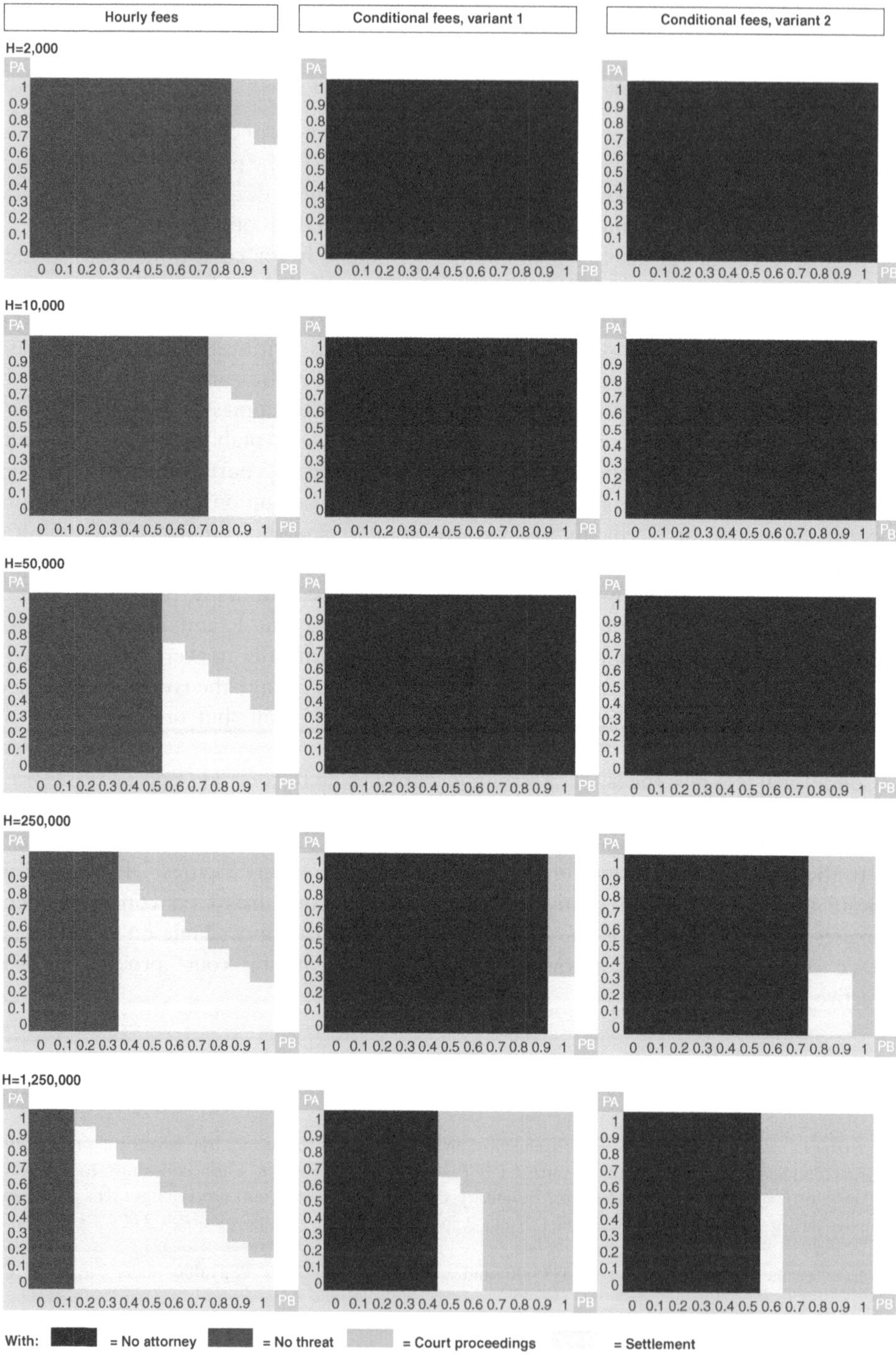

Figure 7.4 Outcome of dispute handling: Lawyer-control, myopic lawyers

5.4 *Liquidity constraint*

While presenting the model in Section 4, we noted in passing that the claimant might face a liquidity constraint upon taking judicial steps. This liquidity constraint is more stringent under an hourly fee arrangement than under each of the two conditional fee variants. Under hourly fees, the claimant faces the worst-case scenario (losing his case in court), which means that he would have to reimburse his lawyer's invoice, the specific costs and the defendant's legal costs as a result of cost shifting, a total sum of $wh + s + t$. Under conditional fees, on the other hand, the lawyer receives no fee at all if the case is lost in court. Hence, in the worst-case scenario, the claimant has only to pay for the specific costs and the defendant's costs that result from cost shifting under variant 1, a total sum of $s + t$. As far as variant 2 is concerned, the claim on the claimant's resources is nil as all legal costs are covered by his lawyer. In principle, therefore, conditional fees may provide relief to those claimants with insufficient financial means such that they cannot credibly contemplate raising court proceedings where hourly fees apply. This relief is, however, only very partial as Figures 7.2 and 7.4 point out. Lawyers only take cases on a conditional fee basis that have relatively high probabilities of success and very high levels of harm. The selection of cases with high probabilities of success may have a positive connotation, in that claimants, as well as lawyers and courts, are prevented from wasting time and financial means on (too) weak cases. On the other hand, conditional fees do not improve access to justice for the less well-to-do by very much at all if lawyers only take the few cases where a very high degree of harm is present.

5.5 *When lawyers become sophisticated*

In the simulation so far, lawyers were assumed to be myopic. The experiment with conditional fees has only recently started. Moreover, in that rather short period of time, only a few cases have been eligible for a conditional fee arrangement, if our simulation results are correct. Therefore, as yet, lawyers have not had much time and opportunity to gain experience in the new remuneration rules. This can of course change with the lapse of time.

If so, lawyers may become well-informed and far-sighted with respect to the impact of the remuneration rule. As a consequence, they may obtain sufficient expertise to predict *ex ante* whether a new case will end up in court or will settle. Sophisticated lawyers may then become able to understand whether a case that would not be worth the effort if it were to go to court, might nevertheless be interesting enough to accept if there is a prospect that it could be settled. Bringing a case to a successful settlement generally requires considerably less effort than proceeding in court. So, there is a possibility that a settlement may bring the lawyer a positive expected net return in a case where the net return of litigation would be negative. A sophisticated lawyer would accept such a case, whereas a myopic lawyer would recoil and would be reluctant to take on the risk.

What consequences can be expected if lawyers become sophisticated rather than myopic? Comparing Figures 7.2 and 7.5 can provide an answer to this question. From Figure 7.2, we know that the level of harm should be at least €192,000 under variant 1 and €71,000 under variant 2 before a myopic lawyer might even accept a case that he is certain to win in court. A sophisticated lawyer, on the contrary, is prepared to handle much smaller claims provided the prediction is that the case will end in a settlement. Our simulation therefore suggests that access to justice for claimants will improve over time under the conditional fee experiment.

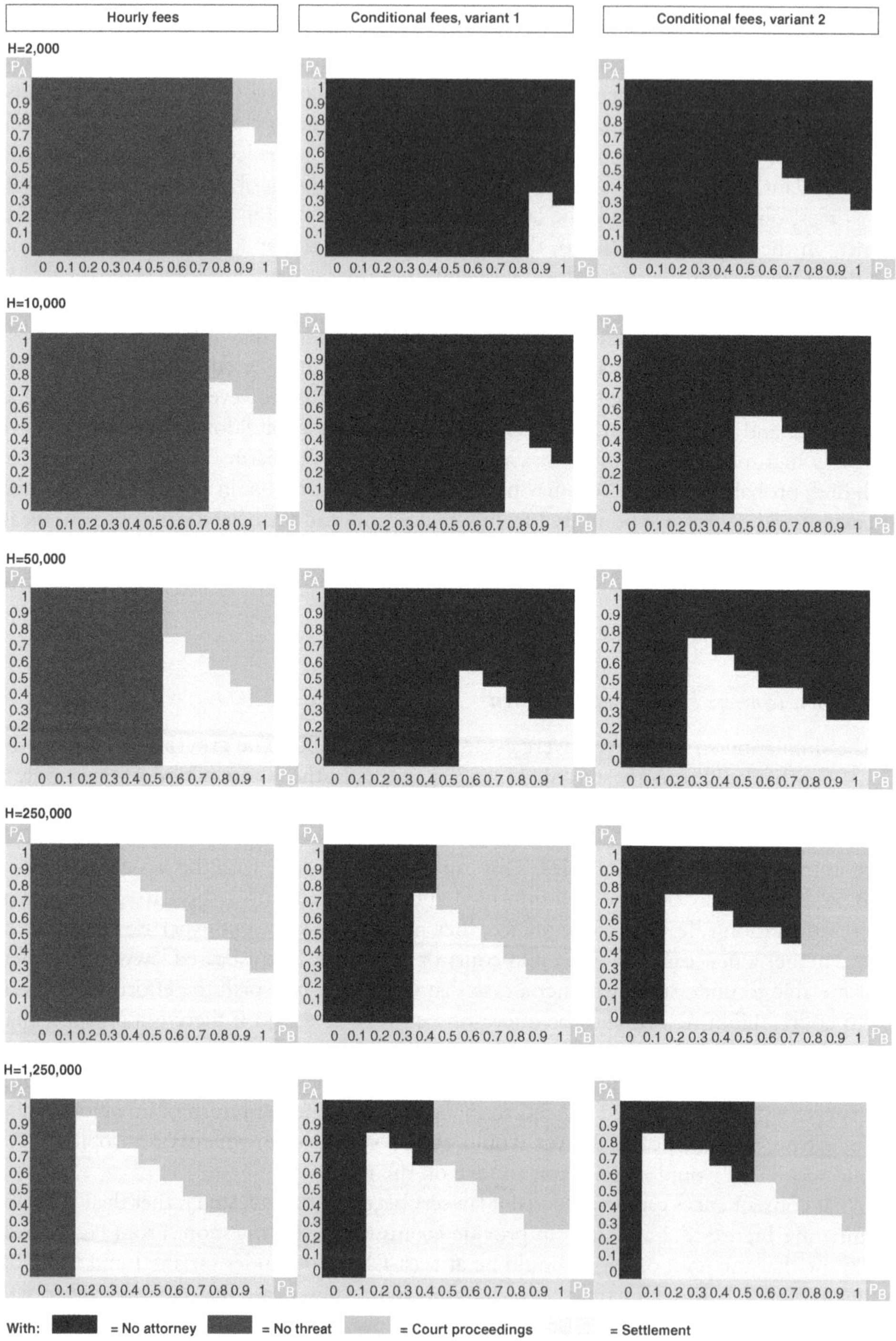

Figure 7.5 Outcome of dispute handling: Claimant-control, sophisticated lawyers

That still leaves the question as to whether the introduction of conditional fees will eventually improve access to justice when compared to the traditional hourly fees. To answer this, we focus on Figure 7.5 and compare the results in the middle and right-hand columns with those in the left-hand column. It becomes clear that hourly fees are no longer unequivocally the better option. There are cases where the combination of the degree of harm and the claimant's subjective probability of success are such that a conditional fee lawyer might accept the case and settle it, while the claimant would not have a credible threat or reasonable prospect of bringing a court case under hourly fees. There are indeed also cases where an hourly fee lawyer might take the case on and reach a settlement or proceed to a final ruling in court, while conditional fee lawyers would not be interested in representing the claimant in this case. Overall, however, the overlap is considerable.[33] Most parameter configurations that would give access to justice under conditional fees would also be handled under hourly fees and vice-versa. Our simulation, therefore, suggests that the conditional fee experiment does not really improve access to justice, not even if lawyers become sophisticated in dealing with conditional fees over the course of time. For a final verdict, however, we need more details on the relative frequency of the occurrence of the various (non-overlapping) parameter configurations.

6. Reflection on the assumptions

In our model simulations, we have made a number of assumptions with respect to the cost structure of the dispute handling process. These figures and ratios were based on information we obtained from Dutch publications and conversations with Dutch lawyers, claims agents and insurers. Hence, our simulation results are not founded on hard evidence. However, by changing the assumptions, it is possible to investigate the robustness of our results. We re-ran the model simulations under the assumptions that:

- The specific costs are, respectively, 5 and 15 per cent of the lawyer's costs, instead of the original 10 per cent.
- The legal costs on the defendant's side are, respectively, 25 and 75 per cent of the legal costs on the claimant's side, instead of the original 50 per cent.
- The legal costs of reaching a settlement are, respectively, 12.5 and 37.5 per cent of the total legal costs of bringing a case to a final ruling in court, instead of the original 25 per cent.

These changes in the legal costs do, of course, affect the details of the outcomes in our figures above.[34] The general line of the comparison of hourly fees vis-à-vis conditional fees, however, remains unaltered.

33 A similar remark holds for the compensation rate (not depicted here for reasons of space). For some parameter configurations conditional fees give a better result; for other parameter configurations hourly fees would be the better option. Overall, the differences are rather confined.

34 For instance, if $\alpha = 0.375$ instead of 0.25 we observe a decrease in 'no threat' and an increase in 'court proceedings' in the case of hourly fees, and a decrease in 'no lawyer' for variants 1 and 2. The reason is straightforward. An increase in α implies, ceteris paribus, a decrease in the overall costs of court proceedings. Hence, the claimant's expected net benefit of court proceedings goes up, giving him more often a credible threat.

To be sure, these were not the only assumptions made. It was also assumed that all those involved are risk-neutral and that the number of hours to be spent on a case varies with the degree of harm but not with the remuneration rule.

Under a conditional fee arrangement a lawyer may have an incentive to spend more hours on a case than under an hourly fee arrangement. The reason is as follows. In case of hourly fees, each extra hour generates an extra hourly fee. Since the hourly fee was assumed to be equal to the lawyer's opportunity costs, the lawyer's marginal profit of spending an extra hour on a case is zero. In the case of conditional fees, spending extra hours on a case may yield a positive expected profit. This is caused by the mark-up introduced by conditional fees. If it is true that lawyers are inclined to charge more hours that would strengthen our conclusion that an hourly fee arrangement is the better option for claimants.

Risk aversion, on the other hand, will make conditional fees relatively more attractive for claimants vis-à-vis hourly fees, as the risk of having to pay for legal costs upon losing the case is transferred, partly or completely, to the lawyer. In principle, lawyers are better equipped to carry that risk, as their portfolio may contain multiple cases where the mark-up in successful cases can compensate for the income loss in the cases with a negative outcome. Much depends on how lawyers actually handle this risk in practice. We have no information on this issue as yet.

7. Conclusion

In this paper, we studied whether the current experiment with conditional fees can be expected to improve access to justice in the Netherlands. To that end, we built a model to describe the interaction between the claimant, the claimant's lawyer and the defendant in the course of the dispute handling process. As hard empirical evidence is, as yet, unavailable, we put the model through a computer simulation, inserting numerical estimates for the key parameters. Testing the robustness of our results by varying the key parameters within a considerable band did not affect the general line of the conclusions.

First, our paper shows that simulation can be a useful method of gauging the working of new judicial policy initiatives when rigorous testing is impossible because of insufficient data.

Second, it is not that easy to fathom the elements of the two variants of the conditional fee experiment. Although the mark-up of 100 per cent or 150 per cent is clear enough in itself, the details with respect to the specific costs, the cost shifting and the upper limits on the lawyer's invoice complicate the analysis. If our model has difficulty generating an analytical solution to compare the conditional fee arrangements to hourly fees, how on Earth will claimants and lawyers in actual practice be able to do this? The problem is even greater as our model by its very nature is only an abstract representation of reality, disregarding all kinds of details and exceptions. This lack of overview alone may be a good reason for the aforementioned parties to stick to the traditional and well-known remuneration rule of hourly fees.

Third, when it comes to comparing conditional and hourly fees, it proves to be important to distinguish between myopic and sophisticated lawyers. At the start of the experiment lawyers will be myopic, in the sense that they lack the information and expertise to give an almost accurate prediction of the eventual outcome of each case. Our model simulation shows that, in the interaction between a claimant and a myopic lawyer, the hourly fee arrangement is acceptable for a much more extensive set of parameter configurations than any of the conditional fee variants. More specifically, the degree of harm should be at least

€192,000 under variant 1 and €71,000 under variant 2 before a myopic lawyer might even take on a case that he is certain to win in court. Moreover, the claimant's expected compensation rate is, in most cases, higher under hourly fees and never lower than under conditional fees. Hence, the hourly fee arrangement is definitely the better option from the point of view of the claimant, as long as lawyers are myopic.

That finding needs adjustment once lawyers become sophisticated, in the sense that they become more aware and knowledgeable of the way the new remuneration options work. With the lapse of time, lawyers will get the opportunity to gain experience with the new remuneration rules. For a full and final assessment, we need more details on the frequency distribution of the degree of harm and (the subjective perceptions of) the relative strength of the various cases at hand. However, our simulation results point out that most parameter configurations that would give access to justice under conditional fees would also be covered by hourly fees. Thus, the access to justice might grow over time under conditional fees as lawyers become sophisticated, but it would not improve on the traditional hourly fee system.

Fourth, that conclusion might only change if the conditional fee arrangements were to solve a serious liquidity constraint or risk aversion on the part of the claimants. Note, however, that the Netherlands has a system of subsidised Legal Aid for the less well-to-do, covering some 36 per cent of the population, in addition to a well-developed system of legal expenses insurance, covering some 42 per cent (partly overlapping) of households.[35] So it remains to be seen whether the liquidity constraint problem occurs frequently enough to create a non-negligible demand for conditional fees. The impact of risk aversion will depend on whether lawyers in actual practice are ready to take over the inherent risk of litigation from their clients. This presupposes that they develop a good business model to handle the increased risk on their side.[36] There is not much of a stimulus in that direction, however, as long as the market for conditional fee cases remains very limited, as our other arguments suggest.

All in all, we do not see any good reason why the experiment can be expected to be a success.

Bibliography

Berntsen A.R.M. and K. Nijman, 'Normering is de normaalste zaak van de wereld...' (2014) *PIV-Bulletin* December 12–13.

Combrink-Kuiters L., M. van Gammeren-Zoeteweij and S.L. Peters, *Monitor Gesubsidieerde Rechtsbijstand 2014* (Oisterwijk: Wolf Legal Publishers 2015).

Emons W. and N. Garoupa, 'US-style contingent fees and UK-style conditional fees: Agency problems and the supply of legal services' (2006) 27 *Managerial and Decision Economics* 379.

Faure M.G. and N.J. Philipsen, 'Fees for Claim Settlement in the Field of Personal Injury: Empirical Evidence from the Netherlands' (2010) 1 *Journal of European Tort Law* 75–101.

35 L Combrink-Kuiters, M van Gammeren-Zoeteweij and SL Peters, *Monitor Gesubsidieerde Rechtsbijstand 2014* (Oisterwijk: Wolf Legal Publishers 2015).

36 Cf Kritzer (2004) on the modus operandi of contingent fee lawyers in the US, arguing that to be successful, contingent fee lawyers must generate and manage a portfolio of cases, similar to an investment portfolio with its associated risk. In personal injury cases in the Netherlands lawyers generally operate from relatively small offices. Hence, the investment that is needed to create a portfolio may well be too high.

Fenn P., V. Grembi and N. Rickman, '"No Win, No Fee", Cost-Shifting and the Costs of Civil Litigation: A Natural Experiment' (2014) BAFFI Center Research Paper Series No 2014-152, Università Commerciale Luigi Bocconi.

Gould J.P., 'The Economics of Legal Conflicts' (1973) 2 *Journal of Legal Studies* 279–300.

Gravelle H. and M. Waterson, 'No Win, No Fee: Some Economics of Contingent Legal Fees' (1993) 103 *Economic Journal* 1205.

Helland E. and A. Tabarok, 'Contingent Fees, Settlement Delay, and Low-Quality Litigation: Empirical Evidence from Two Datasets' (2003) 19(2) *Journal of Law, Economics and Organization* 517.

Hyde C.E., 'Conditional versus Contingent Fees: Litigation Expenditure Incentives' (2006) 26 *International Review of Law and Economics* 180.

Kritzer H.M., 'Lawyer Fees and Lawyer Behaviour in Litigation: What Does the Empirical Literature Really Say' (2002) 80 *Texas Law Review* 1,943.

—— *Risks, Reputations and Rewards: Contingency Fee Legal Practice in the United States* (Stanford: Stanford Law and Politics 2004).

Landes W.M., 'An Economic Analysis of the Courts' (1971) 14 *Journal of Law and Economics* 61.

Melamed P., 'An Alternative to the Contingent Fee? An Assessment of the Incentive Effects of the English Conditional Fee Arrangement' (2006) 27(5) *Cardozo Law Review* 2,433.

Moorhead R., 'An American Future? Contingency Fees, Claims Explosions and Evidence from Employment Tribunals' (2010) 73(5) *The Modern Law Review* 752.

Peysner J., *Access to Justice – A Critical Analysis of Recoverable Conditional Fees and No-Win No-Fee Funding* (Basingstoke: Palgrave Macmillan 2014).

Posner R.A., 'An Economic Approach to Legal Procedure and Judicial Administration' (1973) 2 *Journal of Legal Studies* 399.

Schwartz M.L. and D.J.B. Mitchell, 'An Economic Analysis of the Contingent Fee in Personal-Injury Litigation' (1970) 22 *Stanford Law Review* 1125.

Shavell S., 'Alternative Dispute Resolution: An Economic Analysis' (1995) 24 *Journal of Legal Studies* 1.

Van Boom W.H. and M. de Jong, 'Het experiment resultaatgerelateerde beloning – verwachtingen over werking en doelbereiking' (2014) *Tijdschrift Vergoeding Personenschade* 69.

Van Wijck P.W. and B.C.J. van Velthoven, 'An Economic Analysis of the American and the Continental Rule for Allocating Legal Costs' (2000) 9 *European Journal of Law and Economics* 115.

8 Financial arrangements with litigation funders and law firms in Australian class actions

Vicki Waye and Vince Morabito

1. Introduction

Like the US, Australia has implemented an entrepreneurial class action regime where the identification and aggregation of claims and their subsequent prosecution is guided by the profit motives of class action law firms and, in a significant number of cases, by third-party investors.[1] This entrepreneurial regime supplements other existing systems for collective redress such as dispute resolution schemes,[2] and regulatory enforcement incorporating class wide compensation undertakings.[3] It is distinguishable from the latter more publicly oriented schemes not only because it is underpinned by profit maximisation but also because, like any entrepreneurial venture, the law firm and funder proactively identify, develop and control the exploitation of litigation investment opportunities and their concomitant risks. In the class action context, the law firm and funder are no longer simply gatekeepers to legal institutions, facilitators of value-enhancing transactions or providers of legal solutions to client-generated concerns. They are the instigators and drivers of a valuable investment opportunity. Australia's entrepreneurial form of collective redress is justified on the basis that it strengthens public law enforcement initiatives, and provides better compensation and stronger deterrence of wrongdoing than reliance upon communitarian mechanisms alone.[4] More importantly, the incentives provided by the entrepreneurial class action to law firms and funders help to fulfil the fundamental prerequisite of sufficient capital to address the scale and cost of class actions.

The advent and subsequent growth in third-party litigation investment in Australian class actions has powerfully reinforced the perception that class actions are entrepreneurial vehicles for their protagonists.[5] It has also raised concerns about the substantial transaction

1 For a discussion of the entrepreneurial nature of US class actions see JC Coffee, *Entrepreneurial Litigation: Its Rise Fall and Future* (Cambridge: Harvard University Press 2015) ch 1.

2 See, for example, V Waye and V Morabito, 'Collective Forms of Consumer Redress: Financial Ombudsman Case Study' (2012) 12(1) *Journal of Corporate Law Studies* 1.

3 For example, Australian Securities and Investment Commission Act 2001 (Cth), s 12GNC.

4 Australia, Attorney-General's Department, *A Strategic Framework for Access to Justice in the Federal Civil Justice System* (2009) 114–115; Australian Law Reform Commission, *Grouped Proceedings in the Federal Court*, Report No. 46 (1988) at [38] stating that: 'Actions by public authorities cannot be regarded as an effective substitute for private action.'

5 J Kalajdzic, P Cashman and A Longmore, 'Justice for Profit: A Comparative Analysis of Australian, Canadian and U.S. Third Party Litigation Funding' (2013) 61 *American Journal of Comparative Law* 93, 104 referring to commentators that regard the marriage of funders and class action law firms as an 'unholy alliance' leading to 'trafficking in litigation'.

costs such investment imposes upon class action members compared with other forms of collective redress.[6] More generally, third-party investment has also led to fears related to the commodification of justice.[7] These are matters worthy of serious consideration. However, the focus of this chapter is the effect of third-party litigation investment upon claim governance.

The chapter commences by examining the Australian class action landscape and considers the data related to the growth of class actions funded by third-party investors. The evolution and variability of litigation investment business models is also outlined. A model of the class action project from the perspective of the class action entrepreneur is then developed and the tension points for claim governance identified.

Australian regulatory and judicial responses to litigation investment in light of these tension points are discussed and compared with developments in other jurisdictions such as the European Union, Canada, the United States of America, and the United Kingdom. The chapter considers the efficacy of these responses and whether they are likely to facilitate optimal claim governance, and thus ultimately, the impact this may have on the entrepreneurial class action as an effective and fair means of securing collective redress.

2. Trends in Australian class actions

Three Australian jurisdictions have adopted opt-out class-action regimes: New South Wales,[8] Victoria[9] and, at the national level, the Federal Court.[10] The key feature of these regimes is that individuals falling within the class of persons the claim encompasses are bound by any judicially endorsed settlement or judgment that successful claim prosecution produces. Such a regime aims to ensure that internalisation of harm by wrongdoers is maximised.[11] Other Australian jurisdictions maintain opt-in representative proceedings[12] or hybrid opt in-opt out proceedings.[13] It is generally agreed that because of the narrow manner in which the relevant group may be defined opt-in representative proceedings are problematic, and therefore not widely used for obtaining collective redress.[14] Accordingly,

6 M Legg, 'ADR and Class Actions Compared' in M Legg (ed.), *The Future of Dispute Resolution* (Chatswood, NSW: LexisNexis 2013); Waye and Morabito (2012) above n 2.

7 WB Wendel, 'Alternative Litigation Finance and Anti-Commodification Norms' (2014) 63 *De Paul Law Review* 655; AJ Sebok, 'The Inauthentic Claim' (2011) 64 *Vanderbilt Law Review* 61, 134–139; M de Morpurgo, 'A Comparative Legal and Economic Approach to Third-Party Litigation Funding' (2011) 19 *Cardozo Journal of International and Comparative Law* 343, 407.

8 Civil Procedure Act 2005 (NSW), Part 10.

9 Supreme Court Act 1986 (Vic), Part 4A.

10 Federal Court of Australia Act 1976 (Cth), Part IVA.

11 Otherwise, through piecemeal and small-scale individual or small group actions wrongdoers avoid the full consequences of harm: R Mulheron, 'Justice Enhanced: Framing an Opt-out Class Action for England' (2007) 70(4) *Modern Law Review* 550, 556.

12 For example, Rules of the Supreme Court 1971 (WA), O 18 r 12; Uniform Civil Procedure Rules 1999 (Qld), R 75.

13 For example, Supreme Court Civil Rules 2006 (SA), Ch 5, Div 3. See further, *Proude v Visic (No. 3)* (2012) 118 SASR 444.

14 Law Reform Commission of Western Australia, *Representative Proceedings*: Discussion Paper (Perth: Quality Press 2013) 16–17; M Legg, V McBride and SS Clark, 'The Challenge of Class Actions in the Supreme Court of New South Wales' (2007) 45(8) *Law Society Journal* 56; B Murphy and C Cameron, 'Access to Justice and the Evolution of Class Action Litigation in Australia' (2006) 30(2) *Melbourne University Law Review* 399, 401; Australian Law Reform Commission, Report No. 46, *Grouped Proceedings in the Federal Court* (1988) at [93].

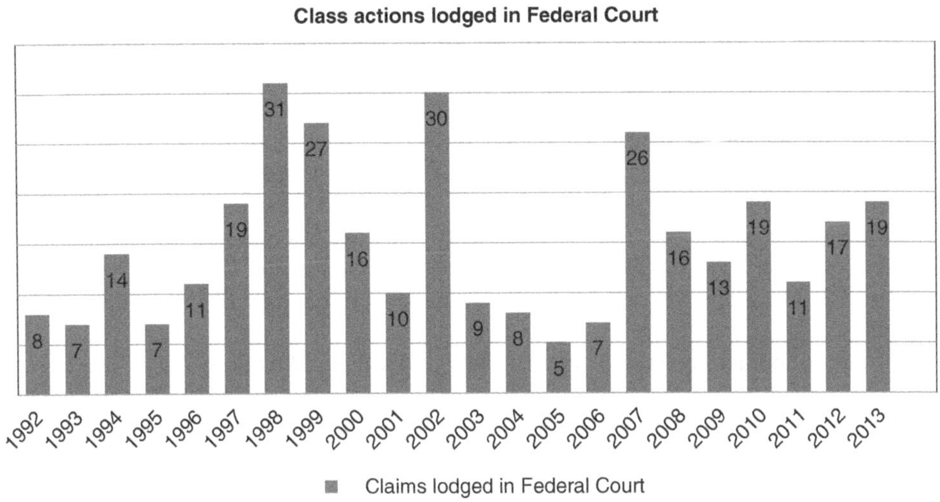

Figure 8.1 Class claims lodged in Federal Court of Australia, March 1992–March 2014

this chapter will not address opt-in representative proceedings. Rather, it is concerned with issues arising in Australia's opt-out class action regimes, commonly associated with the 'entrepreneurial litigation' moniker.

Notwithstanding their notoriety, currently there are few class actions initiated in Australian courts. An empirical study conducted by one of the authors found that between 4 March 1992 to 3 March 2014, 329 class actions were filed in the Federal Court of Australia, constituting an average of 14.9 class actions per annum.[15] On the other hand, 24,680 cases or on average of 4,936 cases per annum were filed with the Federal Court between July 2009 and July 2014.[16] Thus, over the last five years, class actions comprised only 0.03 per cent of all Federal Court matters. Figure 8.1 illustrates the pattern of class-action lodgements in the Federal Court from 1992 to 2014.

Despite their negligible number, class actions attract attention because of the large sums of money they involve. Examples include: the $500 million settlement secured for victims of the Kilmore East-Kinglake, Black Saturday bush fires from power company SP AusNet and other parties;[17] a settlement of $200 million in relation to the failure of the Centro

15 V Morabito, 'An Empirical Study of Australia's Class Action Regimes, Third Report, Class Action Facts and Figures Five Years Later' (2014) <http://papers.ssrn.com/sol3/papers.cfm?abstract_id=2523275> accessed 10 December 2015; building on the following earlier reports, *An Empirical Study of Australia's Class Action Regimes, Second Report: Litigation Funders, Competing Class Actions, Opt Out Rates, Victorian Class Actions and Class Representatives* (2010) <http://globalclassactions.stanford.edu/empirical> accessed 10 December 2015; and *An Empirical Study of Australia's Class Action Regimes, First Report: Class Action Facts and Figures* (2009) <http://globalclassactions.stanford.edu/content/empirical-study-australias-class-action-regimes-first-report-class-action-facts-and-figures> accessed 10 December 2015.

16 Federal Court of Australia, *Annual Report 2013–2014, Part 3 – The Work of the Court* (Commonwealth of Australia 2014) <www.fedcourt.gov.au/publications/annual-reports/2013-14/part-3> accessed 10 December 2015.

17 *Matthews v AusNet Electricity Services Pty Ltd & Ors* [2014] VSC 663.

group of companies to meet their continuous disclosure obligations;[18] and a $120 million settlement against Amcor-Visy as a result of price-fixing cartel arrangements.[19] Consequently, potential Australian corporate targets rank class actions and a more litigious environment as their greatest business threat.[20]

The involvement of third-party litigation funding in class actions in the Federal Court has increased from 1 per cent of matters lodged in the first decade of the Federal Court class-action regime to 39.2 per cent of matters lodged between 2009 and 2014.[21] Nonetheless, the growth of litigation funding has not opened the litigation floodgates. Over the past five years the overall number of class actions has only slightly increased. The author found that 15.8 class actions per annum were filed in the Federal Court between 2009 and 2014 compared with 14.7 per annum for the previous 17 years of the Federal regime.[22]

Analogous findings emerged in an environmental scan conducted by Allens Linklaters,[23] one of Australia's largest law firms that frequently acts on behalf of the corporate sector. The Allens Linklaters scan expanded beyond class actions filed in the Federal Court and incorporated class-action filings in the Supreme Courts of New South Wales and Victoria between 2005 and 2014. Noting that clusters of filings related to the same events confounded the statistics, the Allens Linklaters scan discerned a stronger upward trajectory in class-action filings than previously observed. However, it is important to note that in the author's trend data, the years 2004–2006 marked a nadir for Australian class actions and so the upward trajectory from that low point is not necessarily a sign of a substantial increase in class actions over the longer term. Like the author, the Allens Linklaters scan also found that the involvement of litigation funders in class actions was increasing. Between 2005 and 2009 Allens Linklaters found that approximately 20 per cent of class actions were underwritten by litigation funders. However, between 2010 and 2014 that figure rose to 35 per cent. Otherwise, class actions were largely funded by law firms.

The fact that the growth of litigation funding has coincided with a revival in Australian class actions is hardly surprising. As the data above show, up until 2007 class actions in Australia were slowly declining.[24] Class actions were simply becoming too expensive and

18 *Kirby v Centro Properties Limited (No 6)* [2012] FCA 650.

19 *Jarra Creek Central Packing Shed Pty Ltd v Amcor Ltd* [2011] FCA 671.

20 N Berkovic, 'Class Action "Main Threat" to Business' *The Australian* (Sydney, 15 May 2015); K Walsh, 'Threat of Class Actions Scaring Companies' *The Australian Financial Review* (Melbourne, 15 May 2015).

21 V Morabito, 'An Empirical Study of Australia's Class Action Regimes, Third Report, Class Action Facts and Figures Five Years Later' (2014) <http://papers.ssrn.com/sol3/papers.cfm?abstract_id=2523275> accessed 10 December 2015.

22 Ibid. 8.

23 Allens Linklaters, *Class Actions: A Ten Year Survey* (May 2015) <www.allens.com.au/pubs/ldr/cuca28may15.htm> accessed 14 June 2015. Allens Linklaters gathered their data from publicly available information including court databases, law firm and litigation funder websites, and press reports.

24 The year 2002 was an exceptional one. All Australian jurisdictions experienced a sharp increase in litigation rates in 2002 as a result of pending law reform to curb rights to recover compensation for personal injury. A perceived insurance crisis was the catalyst for this Australia wide reform, dubbed the 'Ipp Reform'. See further, EW Wright, 'National Trends in Personal Injury Litigation: Before and After "Ipp"' (2006) 33(7) *Brief* 6. It should also be noted that the figure of 30 federal class actions mentioned in Figure 8.1 in that year was 'inflated' by the filing of 19 proceedings by the same solicitors with respect to the same industrial dispute, see V Morabito, *An Empirical Study of Australia's Class Action Regimes, Second Report: Litigation Funders, Competing Class Actions, Opt Out Rates, Victorian Class Actions and Class Representatives* (2010) <http://globalclassactions.stanford.edu/empirical> accessed 10 December 2015, 21.

too risky for Australian law firms, which are prohibited from charging contingency fees, and that generally have limited access to capital markets.[25] The advent of litigation funding and its endorsement by the High Court in respect of representative proceedings in *Fostif Pty Ltd v Campbells Cash & Carry Ltd*[26] provided much needed ability to spread litigation risk[27] and to source significant volumes of capital. Consequently, in the last five years more law firms in Australia are willing to commence class actions than has previously been observed.[28] Vice versa, class actions currently constitute the prime source of revenue for the Australian litigation funding industry with market segmentation for class actions estimated at 66 per cent.[29]

IMF Bentham Ltd has been the dominant provider of litigation funding for Australian class actions. Allens Linklaters found that between 2010 and 2014 IMF Bentham Ltd funded 54 per cent of Australian class actions, 34 per cent of class actions were funded by a variety of off-shore financiers including International Litigation Funding Partners, Harbour, Omni Bridgeway and Comprehensive Legal Funding LLC, and 12 per cent were funded by a variety of small Australian funders. The findings are consistent with an analysis of the Australian litigation financing industry conducted by IBIS World, which calculated IMF Bentham Ltd's overall market share for litigation finance in Australia at 61.3 per cent.[30]

Apart from international competitors, IMF Bentham Ltd's success has encouraged a number of recent newcomers to the Australian litigation funding market, including the International Justice Fund[31] launched with a $40 million initial public offering (IPO),[32] JustKapital Litigation Partners Ltd, also engaged on a capital raising drive,[33] Epsilon Litigation Funding,[34] and Ironbark Funding.[35] In addition, although After the Event (ATE) litigation insurance has not previously been a popular funding option, insurers have begun moving into the litigation funding market targeting small- to medium-sized claims generally eschewed by Australia's mainstream litigation funders.[36] As contingency fees are currently being mooted by the Australian Productivity Commission,[37] ATE insurance may prove to be an alternative means of spreading litigation risk for class action law firms, too. These possibilities are discussed further below.

25 Although Australian law firms could incorporate from the 1990s onwards, initially membership was restricted and solicitor corporations could not be used as vehicles for raising finance from the public. Now, a small number of Australian law firms are listed on the Australian Securities Exchange and through this means are able to undertake substantial capital raising to fund growth. This phenomenon is discussed further below.

26 (2006) 229 CLR 386.

27 See *QPSX Limited v Ericsson Australia Pty Ltd (No. 3)* (2005) 219 ALR 1 at [54] per French J.

28 Allens Linklaters (2015) above n 23, 2.

29 IBIS World, *Litigation Funding in Australia: Industry Report OD5446* (IBIS World Pty Ltd 2015) <www.ibisworld.com.au> accessed 10 December 2015, 13.

30 IBIS World (2015) above n 29, 20.

31 See <http://internationaljusticefund.com.au/> accessed 18 June 2015.

32 Anon, 'International Justice Fund Pursues $40 Million IPO' *The Australian Financial Review* (Melbourne, 31 March 2015).

33 See <www.justkapital.com.au/> accessed 18 June 2015.

34 See <http://elfl.com.au/> accessed 12 July 2015.

35 See <www.ironbarkfunding.com/> accessed 12 July 2015.

36 M Papadakis, 'ATE Insurance to Open Litigation Funding Market' *Australian Financial Review* (Melbourne, 7 November 2014).

37 Australian Productivity Commission, *Access to Justice Arrangements Inquiry Report, Vol 1* (Canberra: Commonwealth of Australia 2014) <www.pc.gov.au/inquiries/completed/access-justice> accessed 16 July 2015.

Table 8.1 Types of claims: all claims vs funded claims compared 1992–2014

Type of Claim	All Claims 1992–2014	Funded Claims 1992–2014
Product Liability	18%	0%
Employee Claims	16%	4%
Investors (not shareholders)	14%	17%
Shareholders	13%	53%
Consumer Protection	9%	16%
Migration	9%	0%
Other (real estate, guarantees, franchises, cartels etc)	21%	10%

Data from the Federal Court indicates that compared with the segmentation of claim type for all class actions, litigation funders have preferred to fund shareholder and investor actions, which comprise approximately 70 per cent of all funded claims. The contrasting figures above illustrate funders' predilection for shareholder and investor claims compared with overall claim segmentation.

According to the scan conducted by Allens Linklaters,[38] shareholder and investor claims have almost doubled in the past five years and throughout Australian class action jurisdictions are the two most common forms of class action comprising 45 per cent of all class actions filed in the last five years. The scan also noted a recent increase in the number of funded class actions against large public utilities related to natural disasters such as flooding and bushfires. From a funder's perspective, these disasters, largely focused upon large-scale property and economic loss, are also attractive class-action projects.

The predominance of securities claims and the recent increase in 'disaster' claims reflects a number of interlocking factors, including funders' historical unwillingness to become involved with personal injury matters,[39] the comparative ease with which litigation risk can be quantified by funders in securities actions and other actions focused upon property and economic loss,[40] the higher probability of obtaining information of systematic wrongdoing in securities actions compared with other types of class proceedings,[41] as well as leverage

38 Above n 23, 2.

39 S Issacharoff, 'Litigation Funding and the Problem of Agency Cost in Representative Actions' (2014) 63 *DePaul Law Review* 561, 574 contending that since funders are poorly placed to assess the moral hazard associated with long-term physical injury claims they will gravitate toward claims where damages can be assessed on an aggregate basis.

40 J Walker, S Khouri and W Attrill 'Funding Criteria for Class Actions' (2009) 32(3) *University New South Wales Law Journal* 1,036, 1,053. Although personal injury claims were incorporated within the bushfire class actions, the large majority of registered claims were property or economic loss related. For example, in the Kilmore East-Kinglake bush fires class action comprised of 10,000 claims, 1,700 were personal injury claims: M Blackburn, Kilmore East-Kinglake Bushfire Class Action, Proposed Settlement Info Sheet, available at <www.mauriceblackburn.com.au/legal-services/general-law/class-actions/current-class-actions/bushfire-class-actions/kilmore-east-kinglake-bushfire-class-action/> accessed 12 July 2015. Similarly, the *Rodriguez & Sons Pty Ltd v Queensland Bulk Water Supply Authority t/as Seqwater* Brisbane flood class-action filed by Maurice Blackburn in the Supreme Court of New South Wales (and funded by IMF Bentham) expressly excludes personal injury claims: M Blackburn, Queensland Floods Class Action, available at <www.mauriceblackburn.com.au/legal-services/general-law/class-actions/current-class-actions/queensland-floods-class-action/> accessed 12 July 2015.

41 As a result of continuous disclosure obligations, securities law breach is easier to detect and investigate than anti-competition violations and latent consumer injuries.

from parallel regulatory action[42] or in the case of the 'disaster' litigation investigations undertaken by royal commissions and other inquiries.[43] In securities claims, the support of large institutional investors standing to benefit from successful litigation has also been an important facilitator of funding.[44] Similar patterns regarding the importance of institutional investors are emerging in other jurisdictions.[45]

Nevertheless, the predilection for funding securities claims and claims focused upon property and economic loss together with the scale requirements[46] imposed by litigation funders limits the scope of their impact in terms of access to justice. Increasing avenues of funding including combinations of funding that allow greater spread of litigation risk such as third-party funding combined with ATE insurance and damages-based agreements may broaden the scope of matters with which funders are willing to engage in the future. The potential of these combinations of litigation finance is discussed further below.

While of concern to Australian businesses, entrepreneurial style class actions are not as vilified in Australia as they are in the United States[47] where there is an entrenched view that class actions benefit law firms at the expense of class members[48] and fail to internalise harm

42 The interplay between actions undertaken by regulators and funded class actions is discussed in V Waye and V Morabito, 'Cultural Dimensions of Group Litigation: Australian National Report' in D Maleshin (ed.), *Civil Procedure in Cross-Cultural Dialogue: Eurasia Context* (Moscow: International Association of Procedural Law Conference Proceedings 2012). Matters discussed include the Multiplex dispute, the Amcor/Visy settlement and the Opes Prime saga.

43 See e.g. Victorian Bushfires Royal Commission Final Report 2010 available at <www.royalcommission.vic.gov.au/Commission-Reports.html> accessed 12 July 2015; Insurance Council of Australia, Flooding in the Brisbane River Catchment January 2011 (February 2011) available at <www.insurancecouncil.com.au/issue-submissions/reports/qld-floods> accessed 12 July 2015.

44 M Legg, 'The Price of Settlement? The Centro Class Action and the Divide between Public and Private Enforcement' – blog noting the significant role of institutional investors in Australian Class actions, available at <www.clmr.unsw.edu.au/article/deterrence/public-v-private-enforcement/price-settlement-centro-class-action-and-divide-between-private-and-public-enforcement> accessed 12 July 2015.

45 G Moss, 'Don't Miss Out on Class Action Payments' (September 2015) Investment & Pensions Europe Magazine <http://www.ipe.com/pensions/pensions/briefing/dont-miss-out-on-class-action-payouts/10009553.fullarticle> accessed 10 December 2015.

46 Commercial litigation funders impose monetary thresholds for funding. For example:
1. IMF Bentham Ltd – minimum claim size = $AUD 5 million
2. JustKapital Litigation Pty Ltd – minimum claim size = $AUD 10 million
3. LCM Litigation Fund – minimum claim size = $AUD 5 million
4. Harbour Litigation Funding Ltd – minimum claim size = £10 million.

47 Denigration of class actions in the US has been described as 'The "Holy War" Against Class Actions' see DR Hensler, NM Pace, B Dombey-Moore, B Giddens, J Gross and EK Moller, *Class Action Dilemmas: Pursuing Public Goals for Private Gain* (Santa Monica & Arlington: RAND 2000) 15–19.

48 E.g. US Chamber Institute for Legal Reform, 'Do Class Actions Benefit Class Members? An Empirical Analysis of Class Actions' (2013) <www.instituteforlegalreform.com/research/do-class-actions-benefit-class-members> accessed 13 July 2015; LW Hensler, 'Class Counsel, Self-Interest and other People's Money' (2004) 35 *University of Memphis Law Review* 53; NS Ellis, 'The Class Action Fairness Act of 2005: The Story Behind the Statute' (2009) 35 *Journal of Legislation* 76; JR Macey and GP Miller, 'The Plaintiffs' Attorneys in Class Action and Derivative Litigation: Economic Analysis and Recommendations for Reform' (1991) 58 *University of Chicago Law Review* 1; JC Coffee, 'Understanding the Plaintiff's Attorney: The Implications of Economic Theory for Private Enforcement of Law through Class and Derivative Actions' (1986) 86 *Columbia Law Review* 669.

and deter wrongdoing.[49] Some US commentators have gone so far as to suggest that class actions deprive individual class members of their due process rights,[50] while imposing extortionate demands upon hapless businesses that find it cheaper to settle nuisance claims rather than defend them on the merits.[51] Accompanied by the belief that US attorneys file disproportionately high numbers of frivolous suits,[52] data indicates that US class-action settlements, particularly those in securities class actions amount to only a very small proportion of class member losses,[53] whereas attorney fees and expenses remain high.[54]

In Australia a much lower proportion of class actions are dismissed[55] and settlements are far more generous to class members. While definitive figures for the amount received by class members from settlements after deducting solicitor fees and litigation funding commission are not available, class members generally receive more than two-thirds of the total settlement funds available. Mean and median settlements for federal class actions filed between March 1992 and March 2014 listed below demonstrate that funded class settlements are much higher than non-funded settlements. If a large number of non-meritorious funded suits were filed, we would expect much lower settlement amounts. Comparison between the mean and median settlement amounts below also demonstrates that there are few outlier 'low ball' settlements for funded actions.

As we note above, Australian class actions are actually few and far between. There is no evidence that unmeritorious class actions are being pursued by unscrupulous law firms and funders to leverage unfair settlements that undermine legitimate business interests.[56]

49 E.g. LS Mullenix, 'Ending Class Actions as We Know Them: Rethinking the American Class Action' (2014) 64 *Emory Law Journal* 399, 420–421; L Sandstrom Simard, 'View from within the Fortune 500: An Empirical Study of Negative Value Class Actions and Deterrence' (2014) 47 *Indiana Law Review* 739, 772 (concluding from survey evidence that corporations generally do not invest sufficiently in learning from earlier class action litigation); JC Coffee, 'Reforming the Securities Class Action: An Essay on Deterrence and its Implementation' (2006) 106 *Columbia Law Review* 1,534. However, see contra JN Jennings, S Kedia and S Rajgopal, 'The Deterrent Effects of SEC Enforcement Action and Class Action Litigation' (2011) <http://ssrn.com/abstract=1868578SSRN> accessed 14 July 2015, concluding that the threat of a class action is more of a deterrent to corporate wrongdoing than SEC enforcement action.

50 M Redish, *Wholesale Justice: Constitutional Democracy and the Problem of the Class Action Lawsuit* (Stanford: Stanford University Press 2009).

51 Coffee (2015) above n 1, 133.

52 Most of the studies related to frivolous suits concern securities class actions, e.g., R Comolli and S Starykh, *Recent Trends in Securities Class Action Litigation: 2014 Year Review* (New York: NERA Economic Consulting 2015) 24, noting that between 2008 and 2013, 22%–48% of securities class actions were dismissed (including dismissals without prejudice and dismissals under appeal). See further J Cooper Alexander, 'Do the Merits Matter? A Study of Settlements in Securities Class Actions' (1991) 43(3) *Stanford Law Review* 497.

53 According to the Stanford Securities Class Action Clearinghouse, *Securities Class Action Settlement Report 2014* (Stanford Law School 2014) <http://securities.stanford.edu/clearinghouse-research.html> accessed 13 July 2015, between 2005 and 2014, securities class action settlements as a percentage of estimated damages varied between 1.8 and 3.1%. See also Comolli and Starykh (2015) above n 52, 33 estimating that between 2010 and 2014 securities class-action median settlements as a percentage of estimated damages varied between 1.8–2.4%.

54 Comolli and Starykh (2015) above n 52, 34 – noting that median attorney fees for securities class-action settlements of less than $5 million represented 30% of the settlement. However, attorney fees decreased with settlement size and reach 9.6% of settlement for settlement amounts above $1 billion. However, for a contra view, see BT Fitzpatrick, 'Do Class Action Lawyers Make Too Little?' (2010) 158 *University of Pennsylvania Law Review* 2043.

55 Morabito (2014) above n 21, 13 noting that between 1992 and 2014, 22% of class actions were dismissed or discontinued by the Federal Court.

56 D Grave, K Adams and J Betts, *Class Actions in Australia* (2nd edn, Pyrmont, NSW: Lawbook Co Ltd 2012) 802.

Table 8.2 Funded vs non-funded class actions

Non-funded class actions	*Funded class actions*
Mean gross settlement fund = $10,454,467.	Mean gross settlement fund = $48,831,954.
Median gross settlement fund = $2,529,880.	Median gross settlement fund = $39,250,000.

3. The class-action project

Class actions are resource intensive, requiring substantial input of time, money and intellectual capital from the class-action law firms and the litigation funders that develop, initiate and prosecute them.[57] From their perspective, therefore, the class action is a joint venture project requiring collaborative end-to-end management.[58] The law firm and funder must understand the project's risks and allocate them, estimate the project's costs and the length of time required to see the project through to successful completion, manage project staffing, identify stakeholders and manage their interests, establish communication and engagement protocols between themselves and with their stakeholders, marshal and manage an array of project assets such as communication and database management software, discovery documentation, witness statements, counsel briefs and expert witnesses, monitor scheduling and costs to ensure the project keeps to budget and manage their relationship with external entities such as the Court, opposing parties and their legal representatives.[59] All these activities can be broken down into multi-sequenced stages.[60] However, before modelling the various stages of the class-action project, it is useful to outline the role of each of the project's participants.

4. The players

4.1 Class action law firm

In US federal class actions, the Court is required to affirm the appointment of class counsel, taking account of the work undertaken by the proposed counsel in identifying

57 Australian Productivity Commission, *Access to Justice Arrangements Inquiry Report, Vol 2* (Canberra: Commonwealth of Australia 2014) <www.pc.gov.au/inquiries/completed/access-justice> accessed 16 July 2015, at p 620; E Chamblee Burch, 'Financiers as Monitors in Aggregate Litigation' (2012) 87 *New York University Law Review* 1,273, 1,286–1,287; Murphy and Cameron (2006) above n 14, 410.

58 M Steinitz, 'The Litigation Finance Contract' (2012) 54 *William & Mary Law Review* 455, 479–483. This view of the class-action project is consistent with the decision of the Full Federal Court in *Brookfield Multiplex Ltd v Litigation Funding Partners Pte Ltd* (2009) 180 FCR 11, which determined that funded class actions were managed investment schemes for the purposes of the Corporations Act 2001 (Cth) Part 5C because the class members 'pooled' their rights of recovery into a common enterprise managed by the class law firm, the class plaintiff and the funder. Although that decision has been superseded by *International Litigation Partners Pte Ltd v Chameleon Mining NL (recs and mgrs apptd)* (2012) 246 CLR 445, which held that litigation funding arrangements were credit facilities and thus exempt from Part 7 Corporations Act (and thus implicitly 5C), the reasoning around the common enterprise nature of funded class actions has not been overruled.

59 Slater & Gordon's web page on Litigation Funding illustrates this approach. It refers to matching client needs with appropriate litigation funding 'depending on the size and nature of the project and risk-return paradigm' and promotes their experience in project managing litigation, including 'dealing with activity authorisation, reporting and litigation funder involvement.' See <www.slatergordon.com.au/dispute-resolution/litigation-funding> accessed 9 August 2015.

60 Steinitz (2012) above n 58, 504–507; G Halfteck, 'The Class Action as a Financial Call Option' (2004) Harvard Law and Economics Discussion Paper No 466 <http://papers.ssrn.com/sol3/papers.cfm?abstract_id=528043> accessed 9 August 2015.

or investigating the class claims, the proposed counsel's prior experience of class actions, counsel's knowledge of the applicable law and the resources that counsel will commit to prosecuting the class claims.[61] Unethical dealings, conflicts of interest, misleading communications to potential class members and other forms of professional misconduct are likely to lead to a finding that the proposed class counsel should not have carriage of the proceedings.[62]

No such explicit requirements regarding the requisite level of experience and expertise apply in Australian class proceedings. However, it appears that the complexity and risk associated with running class actions has led to specialisation and a high degree of concentration in the market for the provision of class-action legal services anyway.[63] Class-action proceedings initiated in the Federal Court of Australia are dominated by two law firms that specialise in collective redress. From March 2009 to March 2014, 43 per cent of filings involved either Maurice Blackburn or Slater & Gordon.[64] In their scan of class actions filed throughout Australia,[65] Allens Linklaters confirmed the dominance of Maurice Blackburn, but also found that between 2012 and 2014 a small number of other Australian law firms, including Piper Alderman and Maddens, had emerged, with up to a third of class actions filed by firms new to class-action practice during that two-year period.

Coupled with the relatively small number of active funders, the highly concentrated nature of Australian class law firms means that there are a significant number of repeat transactions between the firms and funders. The implications for class-action governance are discussed further below. Arguably, the concentrated nature of the class-action market may also lead to less innovation in funded class-action design, and allow funders and class law firms to charge non-competitive commissions and fees. Nonetheless, crowded third-party funding markets are not necessarily more advantageous for consumers. For example, notwithstanding licensing and regulatory oversight there are high numbers of consumer complaints concerning the thousands of claims management companies that underwrite and manage personal injury and financial services claims in the United Kingdom.[66] Claims management companies' commissions that are typically about 25 per cent are comparable with those charged by Australian litigation funders that undertake far more risk.[67] More disturbingly, a sizable amount of malpractice within the United Kingdom's claims management market has been uncovered.[68] If voracious, competition can thus be more harmful to consumers particularly where they are not advised by an independent law firm.

61 Federal Rules of Civil Procedure (US), Rule 23 (g) (1) (A).

62 *Reliable Money Order Inc v McKnight Sales Co Inc* 704 F 3d 489 (2013). Sometimes, these findings are made by an appellate court following the filing of an appeal by class members dissatisfied with the settlement executed by the lead plaintiffs on their behalf and approved by the trial judge, see, for example: *Eubank v Pella Corporation* 753 F 3d 718 (7th Cir 2014).

63 See further *Kirby v Centro Properties Ltd* (2008) 253 ALR 65 at [24] per Finkelstein J – describing a dispute regarding representation of a proposed merger of competing classes as reflective of the competitive market for class-action legal services and for litigation funding.

64 Morabito (2014) above n 21, 10.

65 Allens Linklaters (2015) above n 23, 2.

66 A McVeigh, 'Claims Management Companies Face Thousands of Complaints' *BBC News* (London, 5 November 2015) <http://www.bbc.com/news/business-34730557> accessed 10 December 2015.

67 *Which?*, 'Claims Management Companies: Claims Made by CMCs' (2015) *Which?* <www.which.co.uk/money/insurance/guides/claims-management-companies/claims-made-by-cmcs/> accessed 11 December 2015.

68 For example in 2014–2015, 105 claims management company licenses were cancelled: United Kingdom Ministry of Justice, *Claims Management Regulation Annual Report 2014–2015* (Ministry of Justice 2015) 29.

US courts are empowered to propose attorney fees and non-taxable costs.[69] However, Australian courts do not propose the class-action law firm's fees. This is a matter for review once the class action has settled or judgment is given. As noted above, Australian lawyers are currently prohibited from charging contingency fees or damages-based fees[70] as they are known in the United Kingdom. Absent third-party funding, it is common for class-action law firms to enter into retainer agreements with class members on a 'no win – no fee' basis[71] that make provision for a success premium capped at 25 per cent of regular legal fees[72] in the event that the claim is successfully determined.[73] 'No win – no fee' retainers are also a feature of funded proceedings, however since it is the funder who bears the litigation risk, it is the funder who charges a success fee.[74]

That position may change as a result of recommendations made by the Australian Productivity Commission to permit damages-based funding where lawyers can charge a percentage of the claim recovered on a contingent no–win, no–fee basis. The recommendation applies to all claims excluding those arising in family or criminal law and therefore implicitly includes class-action claims. If the recommendation is implemented, it would align the position of Australian class-action law firms with those in Canada and the United States. However, the Productivity Commission notes that unlike the United States, class representatives (and potentially law firms and funders) would still be liable for disbursements and, more importantly, adverse costs in the event that the proceedings were unsuccessful. The Commission believes that the retention of the cost-shifting rule would act as a sufficient deterrent against unmeritorious claims, and referred to the experience in Ontario, Canada and the United Kingdom where damages-based funding applies in conjunction with cost shifting, as evidence that a loosening of the belt buckle around the supply of funding for class actions will not necessarily lead to the instigation of frivolous litigation.[75]

To address the information asymmetry affecting consumers with little experience of the law, the Commission recommended that the permissible fee that law firms should charge be capped on a sliding scale where the fee decreases proportionally to claim size.[76] Reference was made to sliding scales already used in jurisdictions such as California and New York. In New York, for example, attorneys are permitted to recover fees up to 30 per cent of claims valued under $US 250,000 but only 10 per cent of claims valued over $US 1.25 million.[77] The caps on law firm fees envisaged by the Productivity Commission are thus lower than the success fees currently charged by litigation funders, which average 31 per cent of the

69 Federal Rules of Civil Procedure (US) Rule 23 (g) (1) (C) & Rule 23 (h).

70 Note that damages-based agreements are not permitted in UK competition class actions, see: Competition Act 1998 (UK), s 47C (8).

71 Occasionally, class actions have been funded by the class members themselves. See, for instance, *Milfull v Terranora Lakes Country Club Ltd* [2006] FCA 801. The other types of funding strategies that have been implemented in Australia are set out in Waye and Morabito (2012) above n 2, 24–25.

72 E.g. Legal Profession Uniform Law (NSW), s 182; Legal Profession Act 2007 (Qld), s 324; Legal Profession Uniform Law Application Act 2014 (Vic), Sch 1, s 182; Legal Practitioners Act 1981 (SA), Sch 3, s 26 (4) (b).

73 Grave, Adams and Betts (2012) above n 56, 764.

74 Grave, Adams and Betts (2012) above n 56, 821–822.

75 Australian Productivity Commission, *Access to Justice Arrangements Inquiry Report, Vol 2* (Canberra: Commonwealth of Australia 2014) <www.pc.gov.au/inquiries/completed/access-justice> accessed 16 July 2015, 612–613.

76 Ibid. 625–629. However, note that the Commission also recommended that sophisticated clients should be exempt from such limits.

77 New York Judiciary Law §474 (a).

settlement/judgment,[78] although the Productivity Commission has recommended that the caps should not incorporate a requirement that lawyers fund disbursements or indemnify clients for adverse costs.[79] If class representatives or class members are unable to bear the risk of liability for these expenses, the class-action law firm may choose to fund them itself on a contingency basis[80] or else purchase ATE insurance which it can later pass on to class members at settlement. In *Creigton v Australian Executor Trustees Ltd ACN 007 869 794*[81], for example, Middleton J of the Federal Court authorised a notice to group members advising them that a class action had been commenced on their behalf where the solicitors on record, Slater & Gordon, were acting on a no–win, no–fee basis. The notice went on to provide that if the class action was successful, Slater & Gordon would be entitled to recover a 25 per cent uplift on their professional fees plus recoup disbursements from the compensation pool awarded to the class. The disbursements incorporated the cost of providing an adverse costs indemnity for class representatives and the provision of ATE insurance to underwrite the indemnity. According to the notice, Slater & Gordon claim that the combination of conditional fees and ATE insurance will result in much lower transaction costs for class members than commission-based litigation funding. Mixing damages-based fees or conditional-based fees and ATE insurance to indemnify class representatives against adverse cost orders may thus provide potential competition for litigation funders and drive funder commissions downwards, depending on the capacity of class-action law firms to sign up a critical mass of class members to retainer agreements.[82] Alternately, if damages-based fees are introduced funders may engage in more widespread litigation risk sharing with law firms than is currently practised.[83]

4.2 Litigation funder

Consistent with practice in the United Kingdom,[84] Canada,[85] New Zealand[86] and in most of the United States[87], the regulatory barriers to entry for Australian litigation funding of class actions are low.[88] Currently, litigation funders are exempted from the requirement of

78 V Morabito and V Waye, 'Reining in Litigation Entrepreneurs: A New Zealand Proposal' (2011) *New Zealand Law Review* 323.

79 However, the Australian Productivity Commission recommended that if law firms charge damages-based fees that they should be subject to orders for security for costs and adverse cost orders as warranted on a case-by-case basis.

80 See *Sibthorpe v Southwark LBC* [2011] EWCA Civ 25 – English Court of Appeal held that an agreement to indemnify a client against adverse costs and pay disbursements on a contingent basis was not champertous.

81 Case No. VID790/2014. Order made 26 June 2015.

82 The book-building phase of the class-action project is discussed further below.

83 Currently, it is common for class law firms to receive 75% of their professional fees from the funder during the course of the class action, and the remainder in the event of a successful outcome. See, for example, *Blairgowrie Trading Ltd v Allco Finance Group Ltd (Receivers & Managers Appointed) (In Liq)* [2015] FCA 811 at para [39] per Wigney J.

84 R Mulheron, 'England's Unique Approach to the Self-Regulation of Third Party Funding: A Critical Analysis of Recent Developments' (2014) 73 *Cambridge Law Journal* 570.

85 Kalajdzic, Cashman and Longmoore (2013) above n 5, 122.

86 A Wicks, 'Class Actions in New Zealand: Is Legislation Still Necessary?' (2015) *New Zealand Law Review* 73.

87 V Shannon, 'Harmonizing Third-Party Litigation Funding Regulation' (2015) 36 *Cardozo Law Review* 861, 884.

88 The Australian Productivity Commission believes that the threshold for entry is in fact too low and has recommended the introduction of a licensing regime to ensure that funders are reputable, financially sound and capable: Australian Productivity Commission, *Access to Justice Arrangements Inquiry Report, Vol 2* (Canberra: Commonwealth of Australia 2014) <www.pc.gov.au/inquiries/completed/access-justice> accessed 16 July 2015, 631–632.

an Australian Financial Services License, Credit Providers License as well as the requirements governing managed investment schemes provided they appropriately manage conflicts of interest between themselves, the class law firm and the class members.[89] Failure to appropriately manage conflicts of interest will expose the funder to criminal penalties.[90] The Australian Securities & Investments Commission (ASIC), which regulates financial and credit service providers, has issued a Regulatory Guide to assist funders to meet their obligations, discussed below apropos the various stages of the class-action project and tension points for claim governance.[91]

Subject to a number of exceptions, in Australia it is not possible to assign claims *in personam* to third-party litigation funders.[92] Consequently, litigation funding is usually arranged as an agreement between the class members and the funder for the funder to underwrite the cost of proceedings in exchange for a share of the compensation pool. The terms of litigation funding agreements vary:[93]

1. Funders may underwrite all costs associated with conducting the class action, including law firm fees and disbursements and provide indemnification against advance cost orders.
2. Funders may underwrite a proportion of the law firm's fees and provide indemnification against adverse cost orders.
3. Funders may underwrite a proportion or all of the law firm's fees but not provide indemnification against adverse cost orders.
4. Funders may underwrite disbursements and provide indemnity for adverse costs but not fund the law firm's fees.

Should a funding agreement not require an indemnification for adverse costs orders, this will not insulate the funder from costs liability. Australian courts generally have broad powers to make costs orders against third parties that have been involved in the instigation and management of proceedings or that otherwise stand to financially benefit from them.[94] Consequently, funders who do not provide costs indemnification may well arrange for ATE insurance cover equivalent to any potential adverse cost order that they may recover from class members if the claim is successful, or insist that the class law firm or class representative arrange for ATE cover.[95]

89 Corporations Regulations 2001 (Cth), Regs 5C.11.01; 7.1.04N; 7.1.06 (2A); 7.1.06 (2B); 7.6.01AB; 7.8.26; 7.9.98A.

90 Corporations Act 2001 (Cth) s 1311.

91 ASIC, Regulatory Guide 248, *Litigation Schemes and Proof of Debt Schemes: Managing Conflicts of Interest* (2013).

92 *Equuscorp Pty Ltd v Haxton* (2012) 246 CLR 498; *Poulton v Commonwealth* (1953) 89 CLR 540. The assignment of a bare right to litigate is invalid unless a pre-existing genuine commercial interest can be established between the parties.

93 Law Council of Australia/Federal Court of Australia, *Law Council of Australia's Case Management Handbook* (Federal Court of Australia 2014) <http://www.fedcourt.gov.au/law-and-practice/case-management-handbook> accessed 11 December 2015, 341.

94 See, for example, *Gore v Justice Corporation* (2002) 119 FCR 429 – where a commercial funder was ordered to pay the costs of a successful defendant. NB the R 42.3 (2) (c) Uniform Civil Procedure Rules 2005 (NSW) that previously prevented a costs award against third-party funders discussed by the High Court in *Jeffery & Katauskas Pty Ltd v SST Consulting Pty Ltd* (2009) 239 CLR 75 has been repealed.

95 In *Wepar Nominees Pty Ltd v Schofield (No 2)* [2014] FCA 225 at [46], for example, the class representatives were required by the funder to pay the premium for insurance against adverse costs orders that the funder had agreed to indemnify. See further N Rowles-Davies, *Third Party Litigation Funding* (Oxford: Oxford University Press 2014) at [5.90].

However, contrary to non-binding recommendations emanating from the European Union,[96] there is no hard and fast rule that parties to funded proceedings or funders must provide security for costs. Security for costs is a discretionary matter for the Court. Nonetheless, the general trend of Australian authority is to require class representatives to arrange for the litigation funder to provide such security.[97] Given the decision in *Matthews v SPI Electricity Pty Ltd (No 9)*,[98] where the Court found that it had the power to order security for costs against third-party insurers of group members, in the future it is likely that security for costs may also be awarded directly against funders.

Any litigation funding agreement between the funder and the class members must be disclosed to the Court.[99] Additionally, in the Victorian and New South Wales jurisdictions, explicit overarching duties have been imposed upon litigation funders to behave honestly and reasonably, and to ensure that proceedings are conducted as efficiently as possible.[100] Insurers, parties and their lawyers are also required to abide by these duties.

4.3 Class representatives

Unlike many European jurisdictions,[101] class representatives in Australia are required to have individual standing to sue the respondent to lead class proceedings.[102] This precludes public interest organisations such as conservation groups or consumer associations from initiating class actions, underscoring the entrepreneurial character of the Australian class action. However, while the lead plaintiffs must have standing to sue, it is not necessary for them to have been individually harmed by the conduct challenged in the class

96 European Commission, Recommendation of 11 June 2013 on common principles for injunctive and compensatory collective redress mechanisms in the Member States concerning violations of rights granted under Union Law (2013/396/EU), Cl 15 (c).

97 *Bufalo Corp Pty Ltd (recs and mgrs apptd) (in liq) v Lendlease Primelife Ltd* (No 3) [2010] VSC 263 at [65–66] per Judd J; *Canberra Residential Developments Pty Ltd v Brendas* [2009] FCA 745; *Green (as liquidator of Arimco Mining Pty Ltd) v CGU Insurance Ltd* (2008) 67 ACSR 105 [51–53] per Hodgson JA stating that: 'the existence of the funder and the funding agreement is a matter that favours an order for security which, according to the funding agreement, the funder would be obliged to comply with'. But compare with *Traderight (NSW) Pty Ltd v Bank of Queensland* [2010] NSWSC 1502 where held that existence of litigation funding agreement with indemnity for adverse costs rendered security for costs unnecessary.

98 [2013] VSC 671.

99 Federal Court of Australia, Practice Note CM17, Representative proceedings commenced under Part IVA of the Federal Court of Australia Act 1976 (Cth), Cl 3.6; Supreme Court of Victoria, Practice Note 10 of 2015, Conduct of Group Proceedings (Common Law Division), Cl 3.6; New South Wales, Supreme Court, Practice Note SC GEN 17, Representative Proceedings (2014), Cl 7.2.

100 Civil Procedure Act 2010 (Vic), s 10 (1) (d) (ii); Civil Procedure Act 2005 (NSW), s 56(4).

101 For example, in Sweden class actions may be initiated by consumer or worker organisations: Förordning 2007:1041 med Instruktion för Allmänna reklamationsnämnden, s 5. Other examples include Italy and Spain. See Codice del consumo (Decreto legislativo 6 settembre 2005, n. 206), Art 140 bis, s 1 and Ley Orgánica 6/1985, de 1 de julio, del Poder Judicial, Art 7.3 respectively. In France, consumer associations are the only parties that may instigate class proceedings for breach of competition and consumer laws, see: Code de la Consommation, Art R423-3. These provisions align with the EU Commission's Recommendation of 11 June 2013 on common principles for injunctive and compensatory collective redress mechanisms in the Member States concerning violations of rights granted under Union Law (2013/396/EU), Preamble, Cl 18.

102 Federal Court of Australia Act 1976 (Cth), s 33D; Supreme Court Act 1986 (Vic), s 33Ds; Civil Procedure Act 2005 (NSW), s 158 (1). See further *Melbourne City Investments Pty Ltd v WorleyParsons Ltd* [2014] VSC 303 – class plaintiff refused standing in proposed securities class action on the basis that the relevant shares were purchased prior to the alleged misleading and deceptive conduct giving rise to the action.

proceedings.[103] Consequently, entities such as trade unions[104] and Australia's consumer 'watchdog', the Australian Competition and Consumer Commission, have also been able to assume the role of lead plaintiff in federal class actions.[105] But the vast majority of Australian class representatives have been individual volunteers who rarely epitomise political or community interests.[106] While Australian class actions may strengthen public law enforcement through the deterrent impact of compensation, the pursuit of community interest is largely a matter of regulatory enforcement.[107] As a result, compared with jurisdictions like Brazil[108] and India,[109] typically Australian class actions are less focused upon pursuing socio-economic goals and more focused upon the pragmatic task of securing compensation.[110]

Those in favour of allowing private individuals backed by entrepreneurial law firms and litigation funders to initiate class actions argue that limiting the instigation of class actions to 'ideological plaintiffs' such as consumer or environmental organisations or to public bodies such as Ombudsmen will have a chilling effect on the number of actions that will be brought.[111] Others have noted that despite their lack of profit motives,[112] that ideological plaintiffs are not necessarily better class representatives.[113] The diffuse and expansive natures of their mission and membership base as well as the competing demands upon their funds may make them poor substitutes for a well-resourced tripartite of class representative,

103 Some of the statutory requirements surrounding standing in class actions are reviewed in V Morabito, 'Ideological Plaintiffs and Class Actions – An Australian Perspective' (2001) 2 *University of British Columbia Law Review* 459, 470–482.

104 See J Caruana and V Morabito, 'Australian Unions – The Unknown Class Action Protagonists' (2011) 30 *Civil Justice Quarterly* 382.

105 A total of six Part IVA proceedings have been filed by the ACCC on behalf of consumers. See V Morabito, *An Empirical Study of Australia's Class Action Regimes, First Report: Class Action Facts and Figures* (2009) <http://globalclassactions.stanford.edu/content/empirical-study-australias-class-action-regimes-first-report-class-action-facts-and-figures> accessed 10 December 2015, 28.

106 See J Caruana and V Morabito, 'Turning the Spotlight on Class Representatives – Empirical Insights from Down Under' (2012) 30 *Windsor Yearbook of Access to Justice* 1, 7 for the empirical finding that during the first 17 years of class actions in the Federal Court of Australia approximately 86% of class representatives were individuals.

107 E.g., Australian Consumer Law, ss 237 and 277.

108 See discussion in A Pellegrini Grinover, 'Brazilian National Report' in D Maleshin (ed.), *Civil Procedure in Cross-Cultural Dialogue: Eurasia Context* (Moscow: IAPL World Conference on Civil Procedure 2012).

109 S Deva, 'Public Interest Litigation in India: A Critical Review' (2009) 28(1) *Civil Justice Quarterly* 19.

110 This is not to say that there have never been Australian class actions where predominantly non-monetary legal redress and/or socio-economic goals were pursued. See, for instance, V Morabito and J Ekstein, 'Class Actions Filed for the Benefit of Vulnerable Persons – An Australian Study' (2016) 35(1) *Civil Justice Quarterly* 61, 87 where it is revealed that approximately one in every four federal class actions filed in the first 22 years of the operation of this class-action regime were non-investor actions filed for the benefit of vulnerable claimants.

111 E.g., R Van Den Bergh, 'Private Enforcement of European Competition Law and the Persisting Collective Action Problem' (2013) 20 *Maastricht Journal* 12, 23 observing that experience in Sweden, France and the United Kingdom demonstrates that where consumer associations have standing to bring actions for compensation that the number of cases and participation rates are low.

112 According to commentators, when non-profit associations initiate class actions their focus is upon the class as a whole rather than upon their personal claims: e.g., S Voet, 'Consumer Collective Redress in Belgium: Class Actions to the Rescue?' (2015) 16 *European Business Organization Law Review* 121, 127.

113 E.g., S Isssacharoff, 'The Governance Problem in Aggregate Litigation' (2013) 81 *Fordham Law Review* 3,165, 3,184–3,185; S Issacharoff and GP Miller, 'Will Aggregate Litigation Come to Europe' (2009) 62 *Vanderbilt Law Review* 179, 192–197. See, however, Morabito (2001), above n 103, 496–497 for references to law reform commissions and scholars that have endorsed the opposite view.

law firm and funder with the latter two having a hard-nosed focus upon claim maximisation.

In the majority of cases, class representatives in Australia are recruited by class-action law firms and chosen for their appeal, their ability to provide legal instructions, their capacity to represent the class members, and their ability to provide compelling testimony.[114] If a funder is involved the funder will also require that the class representative be able to work productively with them.[115] Due to exposure to adverse costs orders, there is significant financial risk associated with being a class representative if there is no funder indemnifying the representative for these costs.[116] Nonetheless, class representatives are not necessarily impecunious, coming from a variety of occupations and socio-economic backgrounds.[117] Accordingly, they will require reassurance from the law firm that the proposed proceedings have a reasonable prospect of success.

Although subject to review for the adequacy of their representation,[118] in Australia there are no upfront hurdles that must be met to qualify as a class representative. It is not necessary for the class representative to have a substantial stake in the proceedings,[119] for the representative to be in a sufficient financial position to pay potential adverse costs orders,[120] for the representative's claims to coincide with class members' claims[121] or for the class representative to actually be entirely representative of class members. Typicality is not a requirement for being a class representative.[122]

114 *Cook v Pasminco Ltd [No 2]* (2000) 107 FCR 44, 49 – 50 per Lindgren J. See also Caruana and Morabito (2012) above n 106, 14–15.

115 Walker, Khouri and Attrill (2009) above n 40, 1045.

116 Federal Court of Australia Act 1976 (Cth) s 43 (1A); Supreme Court Act 1986 (Vic) s 33ZD (a); Civil Procedure Act 2005 (NSW) s 181 all provide that the Court may not award costs except against the representative parties. See further comments of Wigney J in *Blairgowrie Trading Ltd v Allco Finance Group Ltd* [2015] FCA 811 at [21].

117 Caruana and Morabito (2012) above n 106, 28–35; V Morabito, *An Empirical Study of Australia's Class Action Regimes, Second Report: Litigation Funders, Competing Class Actions, Opt Out Rates, Victorian Class Actions and Class Representatives* (2010) <http://globalclassactions.stanford.edu/empirical> accessed 10 December 2015, 45–48.

118 See discussion below.

119 E.g. *Earglow Pty Ltd v Newcrest Mining* [2015] FCA 328 – although 80% of the respondent shareholders were large institutional investors, small individual retail investors were still permitted to act as the class representatives. Compare with Private Securities Litigation Reform Act 1995, 15 USCA §78u -4 (a) (3) that empowers the Court to appoint the lead plaintiff based on a rebuttable presumption that the most adequate plaintiff has the largest financial interest in the relief sought by the class.

120 *Cook v Pasminco Ltd (No. 2)* (2000) 107 FCR 44 at [29–30] per Lindgren J; *Kelly v Willmott Forests Ltd (in liq)* [2012] FCA 1446 at [129] per Murphy J. Nonetheless, deliberately choosing impecunious class representatives to avoid cost liabilities may attract an order for security for costs: *Bray v F Hoffman-La Roche Ltd* (2003) 130 FCR 317 at [252] per Finkelstein J; *Matthews v SPI Electricity Pty Ltd & Ors (No 9)* [2013] VSC 671 at [122] per Derham AsJ.

121 For example, in *Matthews v SPI Electricity Pty Ltd (Ruling No 5)* (2012) 35 VR 615, a case arising out of the Black Saturday Kinglake and Kilmore East bushfires, the lead plaintiff's claim did not include claims for pure economic loss or dependency whereas other class members' claims did. Moreover, because the parameters of the duty of care and causation depended upon the geographical location of class members apropos the fire ignition point, the merits of class member claims and the plaintiff's claim varied considerably. To overcome this problem, Forrest J held that four sample group members should be permitted to give evidence at the trial to represent some of these differences.

122 Ibid. *Earglow Pty Ltd v Newcrest Mining* [2015] FCA 328. However, compare with the US where strict typicality and commonality requirements often lead class actions to falter at the certification stage, e.g., *Wal-mart v Dukes* 131 S Ct 2541 (2011).

4.4 Class members

As a result of the low value of their individual stakes, class members may have little incentive to monitor or participate in class proceedings.[123] Consequently, class members are often characterised as unknown individuals and entities whose role in proceedings is mostly passive.[124] However, as elsewhere, Australian experience has demonstrated that this is not always the case. While they may avoid acting as class representatives,[125] institutional investors and wealthy or activist individuals do sometimes play an active role in class governance.[126]

Class members are not parties to class proceedings.[127] Rather, they are the potential beneficiaries of actions taken on their behalf by the class representatives, their lawyers and funders. Although they are not liable for adverse costs,[128] class members, particularly active class members, may be called upon to contribute security for costs.[129] They may also incur legal expenses by being required to undertake discovery[130] and to provide particulars of their claims.[131] More importantly, as a result of the class settlement's binding nature, class members may suffer detriment if the proceedings are settled too cheaply or in a manner that unfairly discriminates against their interests. Arguably, therefore, their vulnerability to cost and detriment together with their position as a potential recipient of a class-action windfall provides a basis for imposing fiduciary obligations on those who purport to represent them.

Clearly, where class members enter into retainer agreements with the class-action law firm fiduciary obligations will apply.[132] Otherwise, so far, judicial commentary in Australia has largely been limited to considering the fiduciary obligations of class-action lawyers apropos class members who have not entered into retainer agreements, with a number of judges stating that class members collectively are owed fiduciary duties by the law firms having carriage of the class proceedings.[133]

123 *P Dawson Nominees v Brookfield Multiplex Limited (No 2)* [2010] FCA 176, [16]–[17] per Finkelstein J and *Timbercorp Finance Pty Ltd (In Liq) v Collins and Tomes* [2015] VSC 461, [528] & [542] per Robson J. See further Samuel Issacharoff, 'Governance and Legitimacy in the Law of Class Actions' [1999] *Supreme Court Review* 337, 371–372; Macey and Miller (1991) above n 48, 19–21.

124 E.g. JC Coffee (2015) above n 1, 5.

125 See Caruana and Morabito (2012) above n 106, 9, fn 25 where it was revealed that in the first 17 years of operation of the federal regime only four institutional investors acted as lead plaintiffs.

126 V Morabito, 'An Empirical and Comparative Study of Reimbursement Payments to Australia's Class Representatives and Active Class Members' (2014) 33 *Civil Justice Quarterly* 175, 186–187 – discussing judicial awards of reimbursements for active class members; M Legg, 'Entrepreneurs and Figureheads – Addressing Multiple Class Actions and Conflicts of Interest' (2009) 32 *University of New South Wales Law Journal* 909, 918 – discussing active role of institutional class members in securities proceedings.

127 *Wotton v State of Queensland* (2009) 109 ALR 535 at [33] per Rares J; *Mobil Oil Australia Pty Ltd v The State of Victoria* (2002) 211 CLR 1 at [5] per Gaudron, Gummow and Hayne JJ; *Johnson Tiles Pty Ltd v Esso Australia Ltd* (1999) 94 FCR 167 at [31] per Muirhead J.

128 E.g. Federal Court of Australia Act 1976 (Cth), s 43 (1A); Supreme Court Act 1986 (Vic), s 33ZD (b); Civil Procedure Act 2005 (NSW), s 189.

129 *Madgwick v Kelly* (2013) 212 FCR 1.

130 *Regent Holdings Pty Ltd v State of Victoria* (2012) 36 VR 424; *Jarra Creek Central Packing Shed Pty Ltd v Amcor Ltd* [2011] FCA 671; *Thomas v Powercor Australia Ltd (No 1)* (2010) VSC 489.

131 *Lam v Rolls Royce Plc (No 3)* [2015] NSWSC 83; *Meaden v Bell Potter Securities Ltd* [2011] FCA 136; *Thomas v Powercor Australia Ltd (No 1)* (2010) VSC 489.

132 Grave, Adams and Betts (2012) above n 56, 232.

133 E.g. *Kelly v Willmott Forests Ltd (in liq) No. 4* (2016) 112 ACSR 584 at [308–309] per Murphy J.; *King v AG Australia Holdings Ltd* (2002) 121 FCR 480 at [24] per Moore J; *Courtney v Medtel Pty Ltd* (2002) 122 FCR 168 at [57] per Sackville J; *Williams v FAI Home Security Pty Ltd (No. 4)* (2000) 180 ALR 459 at [22] per Goldberg J. See further S Degeling and M Legg, 'Fiduciary Obligations of Lawyers in Australian Class Actions: Conflicts between Duties' (2014) 37 *University of New South Wales Law Journal* 914.

Given that some class members may not be identifiable and that many are unlikely to have communicated with the class law firm, these judicial statements appear to rest upon the law firm's relatively untrammelled authority over the conduct of the class proceeding and settlement negotiations as well as the lawyer's duties as an officer of the court more than upon any repose of trust and confidence that would underpin the traditional lawyer–client relationship.

By comparison, the nature of the legal relationship of the class representative apropos class members remains unclear.[134] Although they are categorised as 'class representatives' they do not receive instructions from or act on behalf of class members. Class representatives play an emblematic role.[135] Consequently, under Australian law it seems unlikely that they will be characterised as fiduciaries of class members.[136] Nonetheless, they must instruct the class-action law firm regarding acceptance of settlement offers, withdrawal, and other strategic decision making in the proceedings.[137] Thus, even if they do not overtly act on behalf of class members, their instructions will ultimately affect their interests. How Australian legislation and case law addresses potential conflicts of interest that might arise between class representatives and class members is discussed further below.

5. Stages in the class-action project

As outlined, the class-action project composes a multi-sequenced joint venture arrangement between the class law firm and the funder. The various stages are illustrated in the following diagram and elaborated upon further below.

For reasons of space, this paper will examine the various stages of the class-action project up until the point of settlement and court approval. The various issues that arise between the funder, class law firm, class representatives and class members during the administration of the settlement distribution scheme warrant detailed treatment in a future publication.

6. Ideation and claim formulation

All forms of entrepreneurship commence with ideation, that is, the creative process of generating, developing and articulating new business ideas.[138] The class-action project is no

134 V Morabito, 'Replacing Inadequate Class Representatives in Federal Class Actions: Quo Vadis?' (2015) 38 *University of New South Wales Law Journal* 146, 170; Grave, Adams and Betts (2012) above n 56, 175.

135 However, as we note above, typicality is not a mandatory requirement.

136 *Darwalla Milling Co Pty Ltd v F Hoffman-La Roche Ltd [No 2]* (2006) 236 ALR 322 at [75] per Jessup J and *Timbercorp Finance Pty Ltd (In Liq) v Collins and Tomes* [2015] VSC 461, [573] per Robson J. See, however, *Blairgowrie Trading Ltd v Allco Finance Group Ltd* [2015] FCA 811 at [176]-[177] per Wigney J; *Matthews v SPI Electricity Pty Ltd; SPI Electricity Pty Ltd v Utility Services Corporation Ltd (Ruling No 1)* [2011] VSC 167 at [119] per J Forrest J; and *Tomlinson v Ramsey Food Processing Pty Ltd* [2015] HCA 28 at [40] per French CJ, Bell, Gageler and Keane JJ. As to Australian law regarding the imposition of fiduciary obligations generally see *John Alexander's Clubs Pty Ltd v White City Tennis Club Ltd* (2010) 241 CLR 1 at [86] – [95] holding that an undertaking to act on behalf of another's interests and/or an entrustment with the protection of property are critical indicators of fiduciary obligation.

137 As succinctly explained by a Canadian court, a lead plaintiff is expected to 'generally act as any private client would in supervising his or her own litigation': *Baker Estate v Sony BMG Music (Canada) Inc* [2011] OJ No. 5781 at [95]. British Columbia's Court of Appeal has drawn attention to 'other intangible costs (that) are .... borne by such a plaintiff, including the sometimes not inconsiderable weight of being the leader of the claimants': *Parsons v Coast Capital Savings Credit Union* [2010] BCJ No. 1184 at [20].

138 J Kim and LA Fish, 'From Nothing to Something: An Experiential Entrepreneurship Exercise' (2010) 8(1) *Decision Sciences Journal of Innovative Education* 241; TB Ward, 'Cognition, Creativity and Entrepreneurship' (2004) 19(2) *Journal of Business Venturing* 173.

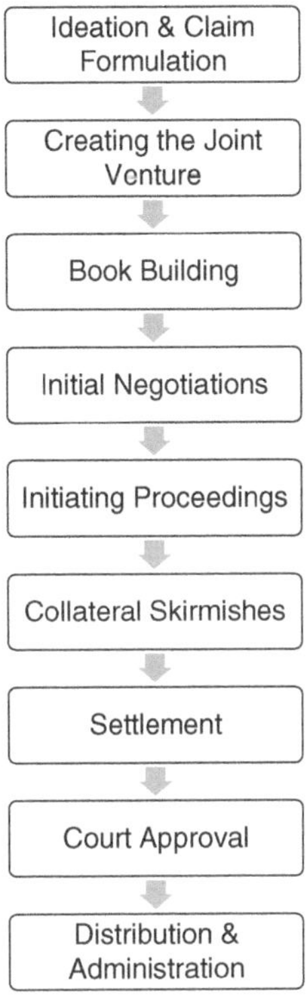

Figure 8.2 Stages in the class-action project

exception. In this instance, ideation revolves around the identification of systematic harm that gives rise to opportunities for seeking collective redress. Australia has a large array of regulation governing systematic harm, covering areas such as the marketing of securities, defective products, unfair consumer practices, faulty building construction, food safety, defective therapeutic goods and cartel conduct. The activities of regulators and media reports of breach provide a basis for exploring whether these potential opportunities can be developed into class-action investments.

Characteristically, it is the class law firm that identifies and first develops class-action opportunities rather than the funder,[139] but there have been a few instances in the past where the funder has detected and identified the class-action investment opportunity, appointed the class law firm, recruited members, and managed how the claim will be conducted.[140]

139 *Melbourne City Investments Pty Ltd v Treasury Wine Estates Limited (No 3)* [2014] VSC 340 at [63] per Ferguson J; *Matthews v SPI Electricity Pty Ltd (Ruling No. 1)* (2011) 34 VR 560 at [122] per J Forrest J; *Kirby v Centro Properties Ltd* (2008) 253 ALR 65 [4–6] per Finkelstein J; *Mobil Oil Australia Pty Ltd v The State of Victoria* (2002) 211 CLR 1 at [183] per Callinan J.

140 V Waye, *Trading in Legal Claims: Law, Policy & Future Directions in Australia, UK & US* (Adelaide: Presidian Publishing 2008) 238.

7. Creating the joint venture between the class law firm and the funder

While class law firms may have commercial agreements with the funder related to project planning, payment of invoices and so on, they are not usually retained by the funder to act on the funder's behalf apropos the class action.[141] However, this does not mean that the funder simply acts as a passive banker to the class law firm and class members.

In the traditional lawyer–client setting involving individual claims there would commonly be a frank and full-ranging discussion to determine whether to pursue the claim. The discussion between lawyer and client would normally encompass: the range of potential outcomes arising from the pursuit of the claim and the likelihood that they might be achieved; advice on the overall cost of how much might be involved to take the case to a particular stage such as entering into initial negotiations or going to trial; the effect of the cost-shifting rule; whether pursuit of the claim is justified given the cost of claim prosecution; the method for charging legal costs; options for the payment of legal fees; as well as funding options.[142] As the lawyer is required to act in the client's best interests, the discussion should explore each funding option's suitability and their advantages and disadvantages apropos the client's needs.[143] For example, is the client better off with a damages-based agreement where the lawyer agrees to take responsibility for adverse costs and disbursements or is the client better off seeking independent ATE insurance and a conditional fee agreement? Will a commercial funder who might charge a higher rate of commission than a law firm, nonetheless be the better choice if the commercial funder agrees to pay for disbursements and indemnify against adverse costs?

Insofar as individual commercial claims are concerned, the funder does not proactively seek out investment opportunities. Following discussions between the client and lawyer, typically an approach is made to the funder with an initial funding proposal (incorporating a legal assessment of the case) together with submission of key documents.[144] The funder then assesses the value of the case (less any estimate of legal fees and adverse costs), the

141 See J Walker, 'Policy and Regulatory Issues in Litigation Funding Revisited' (2014) 55 *Canadian Business Law Journal* 85, 100, 107. However, there have been previous exceptions to this general trend in the class-action context. In *Campbells Cash & Carry Pty Ltd v Fostif Pty Ltd* (2006) 229 CLR 386, for example, the funder Firmstones retained the solicitors in the proceedings and exercised almost complete control over the conduct of the action. See further Corporations Regulations 2001 (Cth) 7.6.01AB (4) (d) (v) – imposing a requirement that procedures are documented for addressing conflicts that might arise where the class law firm is retained by the funder as well as the class members.

142 There are no specific professional conduct rules governing lawyers and the funding of matters in Australia. However, arguably the duty to discuss funding options falls within the client care rule: see Australian Solicitors Conduct Rules 2011, 4.1.1. See, for example, Queensland Law Society, *Guide to Client Care: Communication and Service* available at <www.qls.com.au/Knowledge_centre/Practising_resources/Client_Care_Guide> accessed 13 December 2015, 35, exhorting solicitors to discuss funding options with their clients. For a discussion of how the client care rule has been interpreted apropos litigation funding in the United Kingdom by its Law Society, see J Popperwell, 'Litigation Funding and the SRA Handbook' in R Pirozzolo (ed.), *Litigation Funding Handbook* (London: Law Society 2014).

143 Ibid.

144 E.g., IMF Bentham, Funding, The Funding Process, available at <www.imf.com.au/funding#the-funding-process> accessed 9 August 2015; Litigation Lending Services, Our Funding Criteria, available at <www.litigationlending.com.au/our-funding-criteria.html> accessed 9 August 2015. See further Rowles-Davies (2014) above n 95, 5.03.

strength of the claim and the capacity to recover compensation from the defendant(s).[145] If the claim is sufficiently viable the funder will enter discussions with the client's lawyer and/or client to determine the level and terms of funding it is prepared to provide. Once agreement is secured, the matter can proceed. The funder maintains a strong monitoring role over the claim, including activity authorisation, budgetary control and regular reporting on claim progress, and in some cases may help to drive litigation strategy.[146]

While funding options and the terms and conditions of funding agreements must still be canvassed between the class law firm and class representative, in the class-action setting often the basic terms of funding arrangements have already been negotiated by the class law firm, commercial funder and possibly large institutional investor or other potential active class member before or in parallel with the identification of a suitable candidate for lead plaintiff.[147] Funders of class actions are usually consulted by class law firms at an early stage for seed capital or project management assistance to aid the investigation and evaluation of the claim and the identification and recruitment of class members. For their part, funders will be seeking profits that take account of their overheads, the costs they bear in obtaining finance, specific project costs and, where the funder is a hedge fund, the returns that may have been promised to their investors.[148] As a rule, before committing substantial funds, funders will require a preliminary indication of the extent, strength, nature and quantum of the claim and whether the claim meets the statutory requirements to initiate class proceedings.[149] During their initial discussions, early decisions will need to be made between the funder and the class law firm as to how they will work together and underwrite their preliminary investigations so as to reach the stage where a critical mass of claimholders is engaged and class representatives identified. The funder is thus a joint venturer in the class-action project quite some time before settlement negotiations with respondents are undertaken or class proceedings are instituted, and in some cases, before a class representative is identified and able to provide instructions regarding funding arrangements.

The mismatch in timing between funder and class law firm engagement and the provision of instructions from class representatives is not necessarily problematic if the funding agreement is appropriately staged, and the law firm discharges its fiduciary duty and ensures that the full array of funding options is rigorously examined and that negotiations with the chosen funder(s) are robust.[150] On the other hand, given the reliance of the law firm on the funder for the payment of its fees and the small number of Australian class law firms and funders willing to underwrite class actions resulting in many repeat interactions between them, expecting the class law firm to behave in a robust, arm's length manner

145 E.g. IMF Bentham, ibid.

146 Waye (2008) above n 140, 236–240.

147 E.g. *Blairgowrie Trading Ltd v Allco Finance Group Ltd* [2015] FCA 811 at [26] per Wigney J outlining that the funder and the class law firm identify and investigate potential class actions and once determined to be meritorious, they then seek out claimholders; *Modtech Engineering Pty Ltd v GPT Management Holdings (No 2)* [2013] FCA 1163 at [39–42] per Gordon J – outlining the necessity of investigating the claim and potential funding prior to the identification of the lead plaintiff. See further *Kirby v Centro Properties Ltd* (2008) 253 ALR 65 at [4–6] per Finkelstein J.

148 Rowles-Davies (2014) above n 95, 5.78.

149 Walker, Khouri and Attrill (2009) above n 40.

150 In this regard, it would be helpful if Australia's legal professional conduct rules explicitly addressed the requirement to examine funding options and imposed a duty on practitioners to ensure that the best funding arrangements are offered to clients. A good example is: The Association of the Bar of the City of New York Committee on Professional Ethics, Formal Opinion 2011-2: Third Party Litigation Financing, Part B.

while in the initial stages of negotiating terms with a funder may be over-sanguine.[151] Once the law firm and the funder have commenced to investigate and develop the class-action project as joint entrepreneurs it may be hard for the law firm to step back from that position and carefully scrutinise the features of an arrangement that guarantees payment of its fees. Conversely, law firms themselves may be tempted to negotiate terms with the funder that may benefit their interests at the expense of the class, and funders seeking their business may be tempted to acquiesce. For example, the law firm may insist that the funder underwrite all preliminary investigation and due diligence costs incurred prior to the recruitment of class members and identification of the class representative and that these be passed on to the class as disbursements.[152]

Nonetheless, there is evidence that experienced and well-capitalised class-action law firms arrange a variety of litigation risk sharing tailored to the circumstances of the relevant class action, and that some have been innovators in developing particular funding options and in drawing new litigation funders to the Australian market. For example, Slater & Gordon claim that they maintain strong relationships with a number of domestic and international funders and that they will endeavour to fashion a funding solution that best meets the needs of their clients. They also claim that because they are a significant source of business for funders they are able to exercise leverage over funder pricing and the terms of funding agreements, using strategies such as tenders and syndication to drive prices down.[153] For their part, to minimise cost and maximise returns, funders also often insist that class law firms bear a portion of litigation risk.

Moreover, as funding agreements are typically divided into tranches with specified timeframes or milestones,[154] once a class representative has been identified and a critical mass of class members registered it is common for retainer and litigation funding agreements to be reviewed and amended to better suit the interests of all parties.[155] The fact that class members are required to affirmatively agree to the retainer and funding agreement fully informed of the relevant divergent interests involved and subject to the consumer protections such as cooling off periods also serves to deter against improper collusion between the funder and the class law firm.

As ASIC has noted,[156] problems can and have arisen where the funder and class law firm or some class members have a pre-existing commercial relationship. The first pronouncement on this issue by an Australian court, in the context of funded class actions, was handed down by Ferguson JA of the Supreme Court of Victoria in November 2014 in *Bolitho v*

151 P Puri, 'Profitable Justice: Aligning Third-Party Financing of Litigation with the Normative Functions of the Canadian Judicial System' (2014) 55 *Canadian Business Law Journal* 34, 48; Waye (2008) above n 140, 236.

152 *Modtech Engineering Pty Ltd v GPT Management Holdings (No 2)* [2013] FCA 1163 – Court refused to approve pre-retainer costs being passed onto class in the absence of a specific provision in the retainer/funder agreements.

153 See Slater & Gordon, Litigation Funding, available at <www.slatergordon.com.au/dispute-resolution/litigation-funding> accessed 19 August 2015.

154 See, e.g., LCM Litigation Fund, Case Assessment Process available at <www.lcmlitigation.com.au/case-assessment-process/> accessed 19 August 2015.

155 E.g. *Blairgowrie Trading Ltd v Allco Finance Group Ltd (Receivers & Managers Appointed) (In Liq)* [2015] FCA 811 at [35] per Wigney J.

156 ASIC Regulatory Guide 248, *Litigation Schemes and Proof of Debt Schemes: Managing Conflicts of Interest* (2013) (hereafter RG), 248.13 (b).

Banksia Securities Limited (No 4).[157] Following an application by the defendants in this Victorian class action, Her Honour restrained lawyers (both the senior counsel and the solicitor) from representing the lead plaintiff. This was done 'in the interests of the protection of the integrity of the judicial process and the due administration of justice, including the appearance of justice'.[158] Her Honour's conclusion was based on the fact that the solicitor in question, Mr Elliott, and the wife of the senior counsel were major shareholders in the litigation funder that was underwriting the proceedings. A similar order, against the lead plaintiff's solicitors, was sought by the defendant in *Moore v Scenic Tours Pty Ltd*,[159] a NSW class action. The application was based on the fact that the sole director and shareholder of the litigation funder was the son of the founding partner, Mr Somerville, of the law firm in question.[160] Whilst no longer a partner of the firm, Mr Somerville was still working in the firm as well as being a beneficiary of a trust that owned shares in the incorporated legal practice.[161] Justice Garling was not satisfied that any direct or indirect financial connection between the law firm and the funder had been shown.[162] In refusing the order sought by the defendant, reliance was also placed by His Honour on the fact that Mr Somerville had no involvement in the conduct of this class action.[163]

In *Bolitho* Ferguson JA noted that ASIC's Regulatory Guide on conflicts of interest, mentioned above, appeared to evince a belief, on the part of ASIC, that it is permissible for lawyers to assume the dual roles of lawyer and funder in a proceeding, as long as adequate measures are in place to address any conflicts that arise.[164] Her Honour queried whether this apparent view, on the part of ASIC, was consistent with the regulatory framework.[165] Maurice Blackburn sought to have this issue determined by the Full Federal Court in the equine influenza class action filed against the Federal Government. This class action, brought by Maurice Blackburn, was funded by Claims Funding Australia Pty Ltd, a litigation funder established by the principals of the firm and operated for their benefit as trustee. Maurice Blackburn withdrew this application in January 2014 because the Federal Attorney-General had indicated his opposition to litigation funding companies that are owned by the principals of law firms, funding proceedings in which that law firm is retained by the plaintiff.

8. Book building vs common fund

To realize a reasonable return on investment, the class law firm and/or funder will need to engage with sufficient potential class members prepared to enter retainer and funding agreements.[166] Unless class members affirmatively agree to conditional uplift fees or a

157 [2014] VSC 582. With respect to instances of actual or potential conflicts of interest in non-funded class actions, see Morabito (2015) above n 134, 167–169; *Treasury Wine Estates Limited v Melbourne City Investments Pty Ltd* [2014] VSCA 351; *Melbourne City Investments Pty Ltd v Leighton Holdings Ltd* [2015] VSCA 235; *Walsh v WorleyParsons Ltd* [2015] VSC 135; and *Walsh v WorleyParsons Ltd (No 2)* [2015] VSC 310.

158 [2014] VSC 582 at [5].

159 [2015] NSWSC 237 at [4] per Garling J.

160 Ibid. [59], [75] & [78–79].

161 Ibid. [25–26].

162 Ibid. [68].

163 Ibid. [69].

164 [2014] VSC 582 at [38].

165 Ibid. [39].

166 Walker, Khouri and Attrill (2009) above n 40, 1,044. See further *Blairgowrie Trading Ltd v Allco Finance Group Ltd* (2015) 325 ALR 539; [2015] FCA 811 at [27] per Wigney J.

funder's commission these are not otherwise recoverable from them. Applying the analogy of assessing investor demand for an initial public offering of securities, recruitment of class members to the class-action project is commonly referred to as 'book building'.[167] Interest in proposed class actions is generated using the media and web communications with a view to persuading potential class members to register their interest or to enter into retainer and funding agreements.[168] A critical mass of the right kind of claims is not only necessary to make the class-action commercially viable for funders, but is also a matter of importance for respondents, enabling them to accurately calculate the extent of their liability once negotiations between them and the class law firm commence. The more class members that sign up to the law firm and funder the more likely it is that the respondent will settle the class claim.

Book building is a necessary corollary of the entrepreneurial and essentially private nature of litigation funding in Australia. In other jurisdictions like Canada where litigation funding agreements are approved in advance and become effectively binding upon all group members[169] the risk of failing to recruit a sufficient number of claimholders is obviated as is the need to expend significant resources during the book build. Australian class-action law firms have attempted to persuade Australian courts to adopt the Canadian approach, arguing that such orders will enable the class action to proceed as an open class yet remain commercially viable for the law firm and funder while concurrently ensuring that the costs associated with maintaining the class action are spread equitably across class members. In *Pathway Investments Pty Ltd v National Australia Bank Ltd (No 3)*,[170] the Court approved a settlement where deductions were made from the compensation received by class members who had not entered into funding agreements equal to the amount they would have been required to pay the funder if a funding agreement was in place. At that stage the class members were all registered with the class law firm, had been notified of the terms of the settlement and none had raised an objection to the funder's commission. Similar orders were made in analogous circumstances in *Farey v National Australia Bank*.[171] However, it was a bridge too far, when orders were sought for payment of funder commissions ranging between 32.5 and 35 per cent from any future compensation that might be obtained from the respondent in *Blairgowrie Trading Ltd v Allco Finance Group Ltd (Receivers & Managers Appointed) (In Liq)*.[172] In *Blairgowrie*, the class representatives had already agreed to pay the funder a commission on compensation recovered by the class as a whole, and so they were seeking an order from the Court that they should be reimbursed these amounts in the event that the class action was successful. However, according to Wigney J, the proposed order effectively amounted to the creation of a security interest

167 See *Bonham v Iluka Resources Limited* [2015] FCA 713.

168 The following examples illustrate this phenomenon: Maurice Blackburn, GBE Class Action, available at <www.mauriceblackburn.com.au/legal-services/general-law/class-actions/current-class-actions/qbe-class-action/> accessed 18 August 2015; Slater & Gordon, Docklands Lacrosse Building Apartment Fire class action, available at <www.slatergordon.com.au/class-actions/current-class-actions/docklands-lacrosse-building-apartment-fire-class-action> accessed 18 August 2015; Maddens Lawyers, Grantham Floods class action available at <http://maddenslawyers.com.au/class-actions/2011-grantham-flood/> accessed 19 August 2015.

169 See, e.g., *Stanway v Wyeth Canada Inc* [2015] 3 WWR 628; *Musicians' Pension Fund of Canada (Trustee of) v Kinross Gold Corp* (2013) 117 OR 3d 150; *Dugal v Manulife Financial Corp* (2011) 105 OR 3d 364.

170 [2012] VSC 625.

171 [2014] FCA 1242.

172 [2015] FCA 811.

against an unknown compensation pool for an unknown total sum as, at the early stage of the proceedings when the order was sought, the final legal costs and total funder commission could not be calculated.[173] Although Wigney J acknowledged the Court's statutory power to reimburse class representatives for outlays incurred in undertaking the class action, he determined that such an order was only available once damages were recovered and legal costs were ascertained. At the outset of the proceedings, it was not appropriate to endorse the commercial bargain that the class representatives had made with the funder, and questions of equity among class members were more appropriately addressed at settlement. The Canadian authorities were distinguished on the basis that Canadian class actions require certification whereas Australian class proceedings do not. Consequently, the Court declined to make the order sought. Absent law reform, the Canadian 'common fund' approach is therefore unlikely to gain much traction in Australia.

The book-building phase has been earmarked by ASIC as a tension point, which may give rise to a conflict of interest between the class law firm, funder and prospective class members because of the temptation to exaggerate the claim's prospects.[174] *Bonham v Iluka Resources Ltd*[175] illustrates how the need to recruit sufficient class members may lead to less than desirable behaviour. The case arose as an application for preliminary discovery against the proposed respondent on the basis that the information acquired would assist to determine whether to institute class-action proceedings for failure to comply with continuous disclosure obligations. The respondent opposed the proceedings on the ground that there was no evidence that the proposed lead plaintiff had a reasonable belief that he had a right to relief. The Court agreed with the respondent finding that the facts and circumstances surrounding the alleged failure to comply with continuous disclosure requirements amounted to no more than mere speculation. During the course of its reasoning the Court was critical of the conduct of the class law firm, ACA Lawyers. Prior to seeking preliminary discovery, ACA Lawyers had issued a media release outlining that they had attained funding from a London-based litigation funder in order to commence the class proceedings. ACA Lawyers' website also listed the Iluka Resources matter as part of their class-action portfolio. The Court considered that the media release and website statements amounted to a representation that a decision had already been made to commence proceedings. The application for preliminary discovery was therefore inconsistent with that representation. Although the Court found that ACA Lawyers had not acted dishonestly, it did find that the media and website statements created false and misleading impressions.[176] Accordingly, the Court was concerned that there may have been a breach of ACA Lawyers' professional duties, and referred the matter to the Office of the Legal Services Commissioner (NSW) for further consideration.

Alternately, in an attempt to recruit members, class law firms and funders may be tempted to play down their prospective fees. In *Modtech Engineering Pty Ltd v GPT Management Holdings Ltd*, for example, the Court was disquieted by the fact that the class law firm's estimate of its professional fees in its initial retainer agreement was three times less the actual fees presented to the Court for approval at settlement.[177] This suggests that

173 Ibid. at [52–60] & [134].
174 ASIC RG 248.14 (a).
175 [2015] FCA 713.
176 [2015] FCA 713 at [163–165] per Kerr J.
177 [2013] FCA 626 at [42] per Gordon J.

the assumptions and contingencies underlying professional fee projections set out in retainer agreements should be clearly articulated so that later deviations are appropriately explained. Alternately, it might be wise for class law firms to include a range of scenarios with particularised costs estimates and incorporate these into their retainer agreements.

ASIC recommends that the book-building process be overseen by senior management[178] to prevent misleading marketing in respect of significant features, risks and returns. In particular, ASIC warns against representations about amounts prospective members might receive without ensuring that due allowance is made for deducting the class law firm's professional fees and disbursements along with the funder's proposed success fee. Prior to entering into the retainer and funding agreements, prospective members must be supplied with information that will assist them to understand how their interests might diverge from those of the funder and the class law firm.[179] Disclosure may occur electronically,[180] and to ensure that prospective members are protected from high-pressure sales tactics, ASIC recommends that they be provided with a cooling-off period to enable them to seek independent legal advice.[181]

9. The funding agreement with the class representative and class members

As we have seen, Australian courts[182] do not pre-approve funding agreements. That position flows from the courts' predisposition toward economic liberalism and associated reluctance to review the substantive components of private contracts unless well-recognised exemptions that undermine free bargaining, such as misrepresentation or unconscionability, apply. Nevertheless, the funding agreement may become a source of tension in claim governance, particularly in relation to (1) the size of the funder's commission, (2) the control that the funder exerts over the conduct of proceedings, including settlement and (3) termination of funding. As noted above, funders and class law firms are required to have documented processes in place for identifying and managing the conflicts of interest that may arise in respect of these matters.[183] The written procedures must incorporate how conflicts of interest will be disclosed to members and prospective members of the class action as and when they arise.[184] There is also a specific obligation for clear and full disclosure to class members of the terms of the agreement between the funder and the class law firm.[185]

178 RG 248.64–68.

179 RG 248.54–55.

180 RG 248.62. For example, prospective members of funding with IMF Bentham may apply for a copy of IMF Bentham's at the following: <www.imf.com.au/funding/how-we-manage-conflicts> accessed 16 August 2015.

181 RG 248.71 (b).

182 The New Zealand Court of Appeal has also come to the conclusion that '(i)t is not the role of the courts to act as general regulators of litigation funding arrangements'. However, it reserved its position in respect of representative proceedings, see *Waterhouse v Contractors Bonding* [2014] NZLR 91 at [28].

183 An example can be found here: Litigation Lending Services, Conflicts of Interest Policy available at <www.litigationlending.com.au/what-we-do.html> accessed 19 August 2015.

184 Corporations Regulations 2001 (Cth), Reg 7.6.01AB (4)(d)(ii). See further RG 248.51.

185 RG 248.71 (g).

10. Funder's commission

Although the success premium that can be charged by lawyers is capped at a 25 per cent premium over regular lawyer fees,[186] the size of litigation funding commissions is not regulated. Funders' fees are regarded as a matter of private contract between funders, class representatives and group members, and so there have been few class-action matters where the terms of funding agreements have been reviewed.[187] In *ASIC v Richards*,[188] the Full Federal Court refused to approve a proposed settlement where self-financed group members sought a 35 per cent uplift to be paid out of the class compensation pool, primarily because the prospect of a funding premium had not been raised until two years after litigation had commenced and the non-funded group members were therefore denied the choice to fund and receive a premium. The Court also considered that the funding premium, which amounted to a 525 per cent return on the funds provided, was disproportionate because none of the funded group members faced an adverse costs order. Moreover, as the premium was calculated on the basis of the funded members' claims rather than the funding they provided, there was a significant disconnect between the proposed premium and the risk they bore. The funders sought to justify the 35 per cent uplift by comparing it favourably to the uplift premium charged by commercial litigation funders, but the Court was unconvinced. The Court noted that unlike commercial litigation funders, group members were not in the business of investing in litigation for profit and there was no justification for the 35 per cent uplift of the kind commercial funders would normally undertake when deciding whether to fund a claim and the premium to be charged including an examination of 'the nature of the proceedings, the risk (legal, factual and commercial) of the specific litigation, competition between funders for the right to fund the litigation, negotiations with solicitors about the terms on which the funding will be advanced and the nature and composition of the overall business (or "book") of the litigation funder.'[189] These latter comments suggest that judges generally approve of the amounts that commercial litigation funders charge. There is also Productivity Commission[190] endorsement to the effect that the fees charged are commensurate with the services and litigation risk transfer that funders offer.

186 Australian superior courts fix a scale of costs for various items of legal work that govern disputes arising from adverse cost orders. These scales provide a benchmark for determining the reasonableness of costs but they are not determinative, see, e.g., Federal Court Rules 2011, Schedule 3.

187 In *Pharm-a-care Laboratories Pty Ltd v Commonwealth of Australia (No. 6)* [2011] FCA 277 at [39–43] Flick J opined that Federal Court of Australia Act 1976 (Cth) s 33ZF might provide the Court with power to approve the litigation funder's commission but he did not pursue to review it, noting that group members might prefer to receive very little compensation instead of nothing. Similar sentiments were expressed in *Wepar Nominees Pty Ltd v Schofield (No 2)* [2014] FCA 225 at [46] per Besanko J. In *Re Timbercorp Securities Ltd (Applications for the approval of compromises)* [2012] VSC 590, which was a non-class action group proceeding, the Court held that representative plaintiffs who had entered into funding agreements were entitled to be indemnified for the 25% uplift fee that had been contracted from the settlement funds held in trust on behalf of all claimholders party to the proceedings. The Court found that the amount of uplift was reasonable in the circumstances and consistent with funder fees in the class-action context.

188 [2013] FCAFC 89.

189 Ibid. at [52] per Jacobson, Middleton and Gordon JJ.

190 Australian Productivity Commission, *Access to Justice Arrangements Inquiry Report, Vol 2* (Canberra: Commonwealth of Australia 2014) <www.pc.gov.au/inquiries/completed/access-justice> accessed 16 July 2015, 635.

Consequently, compared with Canada,[191] Australia takes a relatively laissez-faire attitude to litigation funding commissions. While basic consumer protections apply to consumer class members, absent egregious over-reaching it seems unlikely that the funder's commission itself will be regarded as 'unfair' or 'unconscionable'.[192] Furthermore, as a result of their carve out from the provisions of the National Consumer Credit Code,[193] litigation funder's success fees are not subject to the control on usurious interest rates that the Code lays down.[194] The market is therefore the ultimate determinant of funding commissions, which in Australian class actions tend to range from 20 to 50 per cent of class members' compensation.[195]

Whether the market is working effectively is difficult to ascertain. It has been noted that despite the increasing number of litigation funders entering the Australian market that funding commissions have remained stable.[196] Australian funding commissions also seem comparatively high generating returns on investment (excluding overheads) of between 158 and 300 per cent.[197] In Canada, for example, funding commissions approved by the courts range between 5 and 10 per cent.[198] However, there is a substantial difference between Australian and Canadian practice. First, funders in Canada generally only fund disbursements and/or provide indemnity for adverse costs. There is no litigation risk transfer from the class law firm to the funder apropos the payment of the class law firm's professional fees, which are typically funded by the class on a contingency basis.[199] Second, in Ontario, there is a competing source of financial support in the form of the Class Proceedings Fund. This fund charges a 10 per cent levy.

191 See, e.g., *Schenk v Valeant Pharmaceuticals International Inc* [2015] ONSC 3215 – A litigation funding agreement where commission increased from 30 to 50% over a period of 20 months, and that included escalation clauses if the litigation budget was exceeded, was not approved and found to constitute maintenance and champerty. See also *Guiliani v Region of Halton* [2011] ONSC 5119 – Court refused to allow litigation funder's effective interest rate of approximately 60% to be recoverable as a disbursement on the basis that the interest rate was usurious and would bring justice into disrepute if allowed.

192 Funders must ensure that their funding agreements comply with consumer protections set out in the Australian Securities and Investment Commission Act 2001 (Cth): Corporations Regulations 2001 (Cth) Regs 7.6.01AB (4) (d) (vii) & (4) (e). See further *Nemeth v Australian Litigation Funders Pty Ltd* [2014] NSWCA 198.

193 Corporations Regulations 2001 (Cth), Reg 7.1.06 (2A) & (2B).

194 National Consumer Credit Protection Act 2009 (Cth), Schedule 1, National Credit Code, s 32A imposes a 48% limit on annual interest rate charges for consumer credit contracts.

195 US Chamber Institute for Reform, *Third Party Litigation Financing in Australia – Class Actions, Conflicts and Controversy* (2013) 3–4. Appendix to Submission to the Australian Productivity Commission, Access to Justice Arrangements Inquiry available at <www.pc.gov.au/inquiries/completed/access-justice/submissions> accessed 21 August 2015.

196 Ibid.

197 For example: IMF Bentham Ltd's Annual Report 30 June 2015 noted a 158% return on litigation investment; in 2014 IMF Bentham Ltd reported a 173% return on litigation investment; in 2013 IMF Bentham Ltd reported a 290% return on litigation investment; and in 2012 IMF Bentham reported a 310% return on litigation investment. See IMF Bentham Ltd, Shareholder Reports, available at <www.imf.com.au/shareholders/financial-reports> accessed 21 August 2015.

198 *Stanway v Wyeth Canada Inc* [2015] 3 W.W.R. 628; *Musicians' Pension Fund of Canada (Trustee of) v. Kinross Gold Corp* (2013) 117 OR (3d) 150; *Smith v Sino-Forest Corp* (2012) 34 C.P.C. (7th) 156; *Dugal v. Manulife Financial Corp* (2011) 105 OR (3d) 364.

199 CM Wright and A O'Brien, 'Third-Party Funding for Class Actions, And Control Over the Litigation' (2014) 55 *Canadian Business Law Journal* 165, 165.

Notwithstanding the lack of regulation, ASIC has identified the formulation of the funder's commission as a potential source of conflict of interest.[200] ASIC is particularly concerned with funding commissions that vary or escalate in a manner that unduly favours the litigation funder. ASIC cites the following example of a term that gives rise to a conflict of interest between the funder and the class:

> [T]he funding agreement may include terms that the funder is to be paid 30% of the amount recovered if proceedings are issued within one year or, if proceedings are not issued within one year, the funder is to be paid 45% plus a management fee of 5%.[201]

The above is clearly a one-sided example that bespeaks of collusion between the funder and class law firm to extract as much commission as possible with little exposure to risk. However, provided there is a connection between risk and return, escalating funding commissions can be commercially legitimate and, therefore, justifiable. The longer the funder's money is at risk, the higher the cost of that money to the funder. Lengthy matters generally incur higher legal fees and these sunk costs also increase risk by making it harder to walk away. The risk of trial and a potentially adverse outcome also increases the longer a matter goes on, as does the likelihood that the respondent's own sunk costs will entrench its defensive position, making it less likely to settle. Although refinement of the dispute through pleadings' amendments and increased access via discovery to documentation facilitate improved understanding of the strengths and weaknesses of a matter as it matures, it also allows the respondent to better defend the matter.[202] Accordingly, and consistent with practice elsewhere,[203] provided these are a proper reflection of increasing litigation risk, Australian courts are seemingly unperturbed by escalating commissions.[204]

Another example of potential conflict relates to differential funder fees between class-action members. In *Modtech Engineering Pty Ltd v GPT Management Holdings*[205] the funder fee varied between 25 and 30 per cent depending on the number of securities that the class members purchased within the relevant claim period. Similar variations were noted in *Blairgowrie Trading Ltd v Allco Finance Group Ltd (Receivers & Managers Appointed) (In Liq)*.[206] Even so, variation in funding commissions as between class members may also be commercially justifiable without amounting to unfair discrimination between class members. In a securities action like those considered in the *Modtech* and *Allco* cases, funding agreements with institutional investors with large-sized claims are likely to be less expensive to administer than agreements with small retail investors. Discounts for large institutional investors may also be necessary to attract them as class members and make the

200 RG 248.14 (b).

201 Ibid.

202 Rowles-Davies (2014) above n 95 at 5.82.

203 E.g. *In the Matter of the Valetta Trust* [2011] JRC 227 – Royal Court of Jersey upheld an agreement incorporating an escalating funding clause from 25 to 50% over the effluxion of time; *Musicians' Pension Fund of Canada (Trustee of) v. Kinross Gold Corp* [2015] ONSC 9329 – Court not concerned with escalating fee from 7.5% before certification and 10% after certification.

204 See, e.g., *Blairgowrie Trading Ltd v Allco Finance Group Ltd (Receivers & Managers Appointed) (In Liq)* (2015 325 ALR 539); [2015] FCA 811 at [45] per Wigney J; *Moore v Scenic Tours Pty Ltd* [2015] NSWSC 237 at [38] per Garling J – escalating commissions noted by the Court without negative comment.

205 [2013] FCA 626 at [20] per Gordon J.

206 [2015] FCA 811 at [45] per Wigney J.

class action commercially viable and credible to respondents, which indirectly benefits all class members.[207]

At this stage, it is unclear how ASIC would actually address a substantive matter such as escalating commissions or variable fees between class members. Under the regulations it is up to the funder and class-action law firm to demonstrate that they have processes in place for managing conflicts of interest. In other words, the emphasis in the regulations is upon the internal processes governing management of conflicts of interest rather than upon the fairness of the funding agreement terms. Provided the variations are disclosed (as they would be when set out in the litigation funding agreement) and provided a commercial justification is proffered, it is difficult to see what more might be required of funders.

11. Funder control

In light of the European Commission's position that funder control of class actions should be prohibited[208] and case law from jurisdictions such as Canada[209] and the United States,[210] the Australian[211] and New Zealand[212] view that accepts that a degree of funder control over class proceedings is inevitable may seem abhorrent. However, from the Australian perspective, while funder control could be inimical to the administration of justice or the interests of class members this is not always the case.[213] Because of the commercial rationality it brings to proceedings funder input is generally regarded as beneficial.[214] In particular, through their strict budgetary practices and project management of class claims, funders have been identified as effective monitors of class-action law firm performance.[215]

207 See A Watson and M Donelly, 'Financing Access to Justice: Third-Party Litigation Funding and Class Actions in Australia' (2014) 55 *Canadian Business Law Journal* 17, 31 – noting that in many securities actions retail investors may only be able to claim up 10–20% of total losses, making buy-in from institutional investors a necessity for the class action to proceed.

208 EU Commission Recommendation of 11 June 2013 on common principles for injunctive and compensatory collective redress mechanisms in the Member States concerning violations of rights granted under Union Law (2013/396/EU), Cl 16 (a). However, these recommendations are non-binding and are not widely implemented. In the United Kingdom, the Association of Litigation Funders of England and Wales Code Cl 9.3 provides that the funder must not influence the litigant's counsel to cede control or conduct of the dispute to the funder.

209 E.g., *Stanway v Wyeth Canada Inc* [2015] 3 WWR 628 at [14–15] per Gropper J; *Musicians' Pension Fund of Canada (Trustee of) v Kinross Gold Corp* (2013) 117 OR 3d 150 at [41] per Perell J; *Dugal v Manulife Financial Corp* (2011) 105 OR 3d 364 at [33 (c)] per Strathy J.

210 E.g., *Progressive Gaming Intern Inc v Venturi* 563 F Supp 2d 321 (2008) – funding agreement held not champertous partly because the funders exerted no control over the lawsuit; *Anglo-Dutch Petroleum International Inc v Haskell* 193 SW 3d 87 (2006) at 104 – noting the lack of any control over the conduct of the relevant lawsuit that might render the litigation funding agreement void as against public policy; *Osprey Inc v Cabana Ltd Partnership* 340 SC 367 (2000) at 383 noting that litigation funding agreement may be vitiated by funder's officious intermeddling in the lawsuit. See further *ABA Commission on Ethics 20/20, White Paper on ALF filed with the House of Delegates* (2012).

211 *Re Belinda International Pty Ltd (subject to deed of company arrangement)* [2011] NSWSC 1283 at [13] per Ball J; *Campbells Cash and Carry Pty Ltd v Fostif Pty Ltd* (2006) 229 CLR 386 at [91–93]; *Project 28 Pty Ltd v Barr* [2005] NSWCA 240.

212 *Waterhouse v Contractors Bonding Ltd* [2014] 1 NZLR 91 at [45–46].

213 See, e.g., *Project 28 Pty Ltd v Tim Barr Pty Ltd* [2005] NSWCA 240 at [64–77] per Ipp JA analogising with insurers and holding that the law condones delegation of complete control to a funder and of itself does not constitute an abuse of process.

214 *QPSX Limited v Ericsson Australia Pty Ltd* [2005] FCA 933 at [54] per French J.

215 See further Chamblee Burch (2012) above n 57 and Walker (2014) above n 141, 106–107.

Nevertheless, ASIC has characterised funder control as a point of tension in claim governance. It cites examples of funders determining whether they will fund interlocutory proceedings, appeals or some causes of action but not others that the class representatives and their class law firm might propose. However, putting aside questions about control over settlement, and dealing purely with litigation tactics, arguably ASIC's concerns over funder control are misplaced. If a funder determines that interlocutory proceedings, or an appeal or limiting the causes of action should not be pursued because these strategies would not be worthwhile, surely the exercise of objective commercial judgment would benefit rather than harm class members who would otherwise not be able to effectively monitor whether the class law firm was over-servicing. As ASIC notes, to the extent that funders and class members each want to minimize the legal costs associated with the action, their interests align.

ASIC recommends that apart from disclosing the potential for conflicts about these matters that the retainer and funding agreements incorporate an obligation for the class law firm to prioritise class member instructions.[216] Most Australian litigation funding agreements comply with ASIC's guidelines and provide that in the event of a conflict over litigation tactics that the class representative's instructions will prevail.[217] Although the funder may choose not to underwrite the pursuit of strategies it regards as inappropriate, it will not be able to prevent the class law firm and class representative from pursuing those strategies if they choose to bear this cost. ASIC does not explicitly address the appointment or veto of class counsel by the funder, although arguably this matter also falls within the obligation to prioritise class member instructions.

Control over settlement is probably the most contentious aspect of litigation funding agreements and is elaborated upon further below.

12. Termination of funding

Termination of funding is not identified by ASIC as an area giving rise to a conflict of interest. However, breakdown of the funding arrangement has certainly arisen as a tension point in claim governance in Australia[218] and elsewhere[219] in the context of funding for individual redress. Some Australian litigation funding agreements provide that the funder may terminate the agreement at its sole discretion.[220] When read in light of the constraints upon the

216 RG 248.71 (c).

217 Walker (2014) above n 141, 100; Litigation Lending Services, Conflicts of Interest Policy available at <www.litigationlending.com.au/our-funding-criteria.html> accessed 20 August 2015, Cls 6.1.4 and 6.1.5.

218 E.g., *International Litigation Partners Pte Ltd v Chameleon Mining NL* [2011] NSWCA 50 – claimholder terminated litigation funding agreement early and litigation funder sought to recover legal costs it had underwritten plus an agreed commission; *Domson Pty Ltd v Zhu* [2005] NSWSC 1070 – legality of litigation funding agreement terminated by claimholder upheld.

219 E.g., *Harcus Sinclair (a firm) v Buttonwood Legal Capital Ltd* [2013] EWHC 1193 – funder found to have validly terminated a funding agreement on the basis that it had reasonably reached a decision that the likelihood of success was less than 60%; *S & T Oil Equipment & Machinery Ltd v Juridica Investments Ltd* 456 Fed Appx 481 (2012).

220 E.g., IMF Bentham's litigation funding agreement provides that IMF can terminate in its sole discretion with seven days' notice, see Walker (2014) above n 141, 101. See further JustKapital Ltd Investor Presentation, March 2015 available at <www.asx.com.au/asxpdf/20150331/pdf/42xmd3btwf49nc.pdf> accessed 21 August 2015, 18 – reassuring investors that JustKapital Ltd's standard funding agreement allows termination by notice without cause.

termination of funding agreements in the Association of Litigation Funders of England and Wales[221] that limit termination on the basis of material breach or lack of merit or commercial viability, this may seem unduly favourable to the funder and therefore subject to potential attack as an 'unfair' contract term.[222] Conversely, as a result of the substantial sunk costs involved in investigating and mounting a class action, the likelihood of a funder pulling out arbitrarily is low.

13. Negotiations with respondent(s)

Prior to the initiation of proceedings, all applicants in Federal Court matters including class representatives must take steps to try to resolve their issues in dispute.[223] While pre-action protocols are not mandatory in Victoria and New South Wales, arguably the overarching duty each of these jurisdictions imposes upon parties, their lawyers and funders to facilitate the just and timely resolution of disputes also incorporates a duty to at least consider negotiation and possibly Alternative Dispute Resolution prior to filing suit.[224] Consistent with its role as joint venturer in the litigation enterprise, it is common for litigation funders to be party to pre-proceeding negotiations.[225]

The fact that a funder lies behind the class action brings significant leverage to inter-party negotiations.[226] Consequently, if the funder and class law firm have managed to recruit a sufficient number of class members, it may be possible to settle claims at a very early stage without the initiation of proceedings, and therefore without Court scrutiny.[227] Notwithstanding the lack of Court approval, ASIC still requires that conflicts of interest between class members, funders and the class law firm are appropriately managed.[228] At a minimum, ASIC recommends that the proposed settlement be reviewed by counsel to ensure that it is both reasonable and fair.

14. Initiation of proceedings – defining the class

Prior to initiating proceedings, the funder and the class-action law firm will need to decide whether the matter will proceed as an open or a closed class.

221 Association of Litigation Funders of England and Wales, Code of Conduct (2014), Cls 11.2 and 12, available at <http://associationoflitigationfunders.com/code-of-conduct/> accessed 21 August 2015.

222 Australian Securities and Investment Commission Act 2001 (Cth), ss 12BF, 12BG, 12BH. Section 12BH (1) (b) refers to unilateral rights to terminate as unfair terms rather than broad-based rights of termination and therefore termination at 'sole discretion' may not be unfair if the class members have the same right. Currently, these provisions only apply vis-à-vis consumer contracts and contracts with small businesses below a threshold of $40,000. However, from mid-2016 the protection will extend to small business contracts below an upfront threshold of $300,000 or if the contract is greater than 12 months duration up to $1,000,000: Treasury Legislation Amendment (Small Business and Unfair Contract Terms) Act 2015 (Cth).

223 Civil Dispute Resolution Act 2011 (Cth), s 6.

224 M King, A Freiberg, B Batasol and R Hyams, *Adversarial Justice* (Sydney: Federation Press 2014) 123.

225 Eg *Earglow Pty Ltd v Newcrest Mining Ltd* (2015) 106 ACSR 49 at [10] per Beach J.

226 Watson and Donelly (2014) above n 207, 27 arguing that litigation funding creates equality of arms between plaintiffs and defendants.

227 For actual instances of pre-filing settlements in Australia, see King & Wood Mallesons, *The Review – Class Actions in Australia 2013–2014,* available at <www.kwm.com/en/au/knowledge/downloads/the-review-class-actions-in-australia-2013-2014-20140701> accessed 13 December 2015, 10.

228 RG 248.91.

Open classes – Members of open classes are defined by description. For example, in a securities class action, the class members may be defined as all shareholders who purchased shares in X Ltd between Y date and Z date.

Closed classes – Members of closed classes are not defined by description alone. In addition to falling into a category of person who might seek a legal remedy from the respondent(s), members of closed classes are also identified by limiting elements such as entry into a litigation funding agreement or entry into a retainer agreement with a class law firm.[229] Closed classes are often but not exclusively[230] employed by litigation funders (with assistance from the class-action law firm) as a means of excluding free riders and increasing the attractiveness of entering into a funding agreement. The validity of closed classes was upheld in *Multiplex Funds Management Ltd v P Dawson Nominees Pty Ltd*[231] on the pragmatic basis that the protection of the funder's position was an appropriate means of making class actions financially viable.

Given the inability to recoup investment through a common fund, there are significant incentives for funders to prefer closed classes. Closed classes prevent a funder's investment being undercut by free-riding claimholders, and also make it easier and less costly for funders to project manage the class action.[232] However, closed classes may encourage the initiation of copycat proceedings by other litigation entrepreneurs seeking to ride on the coat tails of the initial closed proceedings. As a result, courts may be faced with multiple proceedings in respect of the same alleged harm, thus undermining judicial economy, one of the very matters the implementation of class actions was meant to promote. Examples include: (1) the *Centro* case;[233] (2) the *Oz Minerals* case[234] and (3) the *Nufarm* case.[235]

To deal with the multiplicity of proceedings generated by closed classes, in *Kirby v Centro Properties Ltd*[236] the Court floated the option of consolidating proceedings and commissioning an independent panel to appoint a single class law firm. It went on to state that in the event of competing class actions where a choice had to be made regarding whether a particular law firm and funder should act, that the class-action experience of the law firm, the amount and cost of funding and the legal fees charged were all relevant

229 For other types of limiting elements see V Morabito, 'Class Actions Instituted only for the Benefit of the Clients of the Class Representative's Solicitors' (2007) 29 *Sydney Law Review* 5, 13–20.

230 E.g., *Clurname Pty Ltd v Commonwealth Bank of Australia (No 1)* [2015] FCA 153 – a proceeding funded by International Litigation Partners No 5 Pty Ltd was commenced as an open class proceeding but later converted to a closed class proceeding. *Earglow Pty Ltd v Newcrest Mining Ltd* [2015] FCA 328 is an open securities class proceeding where several large institutional investors who comprise part of the class have entered into funding agreements. *Modtech Engineering Pty Ltd v GPT Management Holdings Ltd* [2013] FCA 626 was an open class proceeding funded by Comprehensive Legal Funding LLC where 92% of class members had entered into funding agreements.

231 (2007) 164 FCR 275.

232 *Blairgowrie Trading Ltd v Allco Finance Group Ltd (Receivers & Managers Appointed) (In Liq)* [2015] FCA 811 at [23] per Wigney J.

233 *Kirby v Centro Properties Ltd* (2008) 253 ALR 65 – two actions initiated by Maurice Blackburn and funded by IMF and one action initiated by Slater & Gordon and funded by CLF.

234 *Anthony Scott & Anor v Oz Minerals Ltd* NSD 1433 of 2010 & *Hobbs Anderson Investments Pty Ltd v Oz Minerals Ltd* NSD 1,127 of 2,009 – two class actions – one initiated by Maurice Blackburn and funded by IMF and the other initiated by Slater & Gordon and funded by Litigation Lending Services.

235 Two class actions – one initiated by Maurice Blackburn funded by International Funding Partners Pte Ltd and Slater & Gordon funded by CLF. The actions were consolidated and settlement approved in *Gaby Hadchiti & Ors v Nufarm* [2012] FCA.

236 (2008) 253 ALR 65 at [32] per Finkelstein J.

matters to take into account. This interesting innovation is redolent of the powers granted to US Courts to appoint class counsel best able to represent the interests of the class,[237] but mostly Australian class law firms and courts have tended to respond to these issues by consolidating proceedings and maintaining separate representation and funding.[238] Dealing with different sets of law firms, funders and class members albeit in consolidated proceedings increases cost and complexity, and may make it harder for actions to settle.

15. Collateral skirmishes

Although Australian class actions need not be certified, the legislation establishing class actions in Victoria, New South Wales and the Federal Court imposes constitutive requirements that are frequently raised by respondents in applications to discontinue the proceedings. Among other things respondents may claim that the class members are not appropriately identified,[239] that there are no substantial common questions of law and fact,[240] that the class action is not an efficient and effective means of dealing with the claims of the class members,[241] that the class representatives lack standing[242] or that the pleadings are inadequate.[243] Prior to the Australian government's decision to exempt litigation funding from Commonwealth financial regulation requirements,[244] these collateral skirmishes incorporated challenges to litigation funding arrangements that added considerable cost and delay to proceedings as well as increased litigation risk.[245]

Now that litigation funding is an accepted part of the class-action landscape and regulatory issues have been resolved,[246] these collateral skirmishes should diminish. Further the Law

237 Federal Rules of Civil Procedure (US), Rule 23g (2).

238 See V Morabito, 'Clashing Classes Down Under – Evaluating Australia's Competing Class Actions through Empirical and Comparative Perspectives' (2012) 27 *Connecticut Journal of International Law* 245, 314–315.

239 E.g., *Larsson v WealthSure Pty Ltd* [2013] FCA 926 – group criteria included entering retainer agreement with class law firm, Maddocks Lawyers. However, definition allowed persons who entered retainer agreements after proceedings commenced to become class members. Also class members changed solicitors. Therefore, no class member satisfied group criteria. Consequently, proceedings discontinued. See further *Bray v F Hoffman-La Roche Ltd* [2003] ATPR 41-906 at [57] where the initial group definition of persons who purchased vitamins over a seven-year period in a cartel case alleging price fixing for vitamins was criticised by Merkel J.

240 *Murphy v Overton Investments Pty Ltd* [1999] FCA 1123.

241 *Meaden v Bell Potter Securities Limited (No 2)* (2012) 291 ALR 482; *Australian Competition & Consumer Commission v Giraffe World Australia Pty Ltd & Ors* [1998] FCA 819.

242 *Revian v Dasford Holdings Pty Ltd* [2002] FCA 1119.

243 This argument was raised by the respondent but ultimately not accepted by the Court in *Pharm-a-Care Laboratories Pty Ltd v Commonwealth of Australia (No 3)* [2010] FCA 361. In *Auskay International Manufacturing & Trade Pty Ltd v Qantas Airways Ltd* [2008] FCA 1458, the class representative's statement of claim was struck out but leave was given to file a new statement of claim. Similar orders were made in *Pampered Paws Connection Pty Ltd (ACN 116 460 621) (on its own behalf and in a representative capacity) v Pets Paradise Franchising (Qld) Pty Ltd (ACN 054 406 272)* [2008] FCA 1606.

244 C Bowen, 'Government Acts to Ensure Access to Justice for Class Action Member' (Australia, The Treasury, 4 May 2010) <http://ministers.treasury.gov.au/DisplayDocs.aspx?doc=pressreleases/2010/039.htm&pageID=003&min=ceba&Year=&DocType> accessed 18 August 2015.

245 See Hon Justice K Lindgren, 'Some Current Practical Issues in Class Action Litigation' (2009) 32(3) *University of New South Wales Law Journal* 900, 901–903, lamenting the delay and cost involved in the numerous interlocutory disputes that beset class actions.

246 Note, however, that the Australian Productivity Commission has recommended that funders should be subject to a licensing regime to ensure that funders meet prudential requirements: Australian Productivity Commission, *Access to Justice Arrangements Final Report, Vol 2* (2014) 632–633.

Council of Australia and the Federal Court of Australia have published a Case Management Handbook, which among other things exhorts the parties and their legal teams to co-operate effectively in the conduct of the class action. Senior members of each legal team are expected to meet at an early stage to discuss engagement logistics; points of contact and communication protocols (including timing expectations for responses) should be established; the use of hyperbole and inflammatory tactics should be avoided; regular meetings between legal teams should be scheduled; and external mediators or facilitators should be considered to ensure that the class action is conducted as efficiently as possible.[247]

16. Settlement and Court approval

Provided they are not dismissed during collateral skirmishes, the majority of class proceedings are settled.[248] While funder and class interests in maximising returns are generally aligned, because of the 'lumpy' nature of litigation investment[249] and the lengthy time required to yield returns, there may be a temptation for the funder and class law firm to collude and accept a smaller but more certain settlement rather than continue to bear intensifying litigation risk.[250] Both litigation funders and corporatized law firms are accountable to investors, and the pressure for maintaining regular returns may be high. Although, class members unhappy with the settlement may 'opt out' or lodge an objection, there is concern that their lack of incentive or inability to actively participate in the proceedings[251] makes them poor monitors, and therefore the potential for litigation funder and class law firm aggrandizement at their expense is real.[252]

However, settlement cannot occur without Court approval.[253] The range of factors that the Court will consider are summarised in *Practice Note CM 17 — Representative Proceedings Commenced under Part IVA of the Federal Court of Australia Act 1976* (Cth), and include the stage of the proceedings when settlement is sought, the likely complexity and duration of the action should it not settle and proceed further, the reasonableness of the proposed settlement in light of best recovery, class member wishes and litigation risk. Oversight by the Court taking account of these factors thus tends to militate against cheap settlement.

247 Law Council of Australia/Federal Court of Australia (2014) above n 93, 13.45–13.49.

248 Morabito (2014) above n 21, 13.

249 IBIS World (2015) above n 29, 6.

250 Walker (2014) above n 141, 97. 'Lumpy' returns are likely to be more problematic for funders with smaller litigation portfolios. See, e.g., Hillcrest Litigation Services Ltd, Annual Report 2014, available at <www.hillcrestlitigation.com.au/financials/financial-2014/> accessed 21 August 2015, 4 noting that the company posted a loss in that year due to the 'lumpy' nature of income derived from its investment portfolio.

251 As recently noted by Justice Robson of the Supreme Court of Victoria, 'a group member must know that they are a group member, be following the conduct of the group proceeding, and most likely obtain legal advice in order to determine whether their interests are being adequately represented by the plaintiff': *Timbercorp Finance Pty Ltd (In Liq) v Collins and Tomes* [2015] VSC 461, [578] per Robson J.

252 *Mercedes Holding Pty Ltd v Waters (No 1)* (2010) 77 ACSR 265 at [9] per Perram J. Similar concerns related to the position of a class-action law firm in respect of non-funded proceedings were expressed by Jessup J in *Peterson v Merck Sharpe & Dohme (Australia) Pty Ltd (No. 6)* [2013] FCA 447 at [23]. In the latter case the Court refused to approve a proposed settlement that had been presaged by an agreement by the respondent not to seek its costs against the class representative who was largely unsuccessful on questions of liability where the risk factors governing other class members were substantially different.

253 Federal Court of Australia Act 1976 (Cth), s 33V; Supreme Court Act 1986 (Vic), s33V; Civil Procedure Act 2005 (NSW), s 173.

Nonetheless, existing judicial oversight is insufficient for one commentator, who argues that because of the lack of independent and objective advocacy representing the interests of absent class members during settlement hearings, the Court's perspective is less critical than it should be.[254] He argues that, despite added cost, a class guardian should routinely be appointed to assist the Court in properly evaluating the settlement proposal. Such contradictors have been appointed from time to time in Canada,[255] the US[256] and Australia[257] and on occasion court registrars[258] or masters[259] have been asked to assist the Court, although their main function has been to assess the propriety of the class law firm's professional fees or applications by the class members for compensation based upon their input into the class action rather than the reasonableness of the settlement itself.[260] Given the lack of evidence of cheap settlements, arguably the extra cost of a contradictor to assess the overall reasonableness of a settlement is not justified. There is no reason why a Court should not be able to assess the factors outlined in *Practice Note CM 17 — Representative Proceedings Commenced under Part IVA of the Federal Court of Australia Act 1976* (Cth) itself, especially if evidence of a robust and comprehensive independent assessment of the settlement is submitted.[261]

Apart from overall reasonableness, the structure of the settlement may also raise conflicts of interest between the funder, class law firm and the class. ASIC says nothing about these matters, largely relying upon court oversight to determine whether the structure of the settlement is in the best interests of the class. Australian courts will not approve a proposed settlement if they consider that the settlement involves an unfair compromise of some members' claims for the benefit of others.[262] In principle, the settlement should be structured in a way that objectively discriminates between class members according to the harm

254 M Legg, 'Class Action Settlements in Australia – The Need for Greater Scrutiny' (2014) 38 *Melbourne University Law Review* 590, 611–613. See also V Morabito, 'An Australian Perspective on Class Action Settlements' (2006) 69 *Modern Law Review* 347, 380.

255 E.g., *Killough v Canadian Red Cross Society* (2001) 91 BCLR (3d) 309; *Baxter v Canada (Attorney-General)* (2006) 83 OR (3d) 481 – Court appointed adjudicator to assess compensation scheme administration fees.

256 E.g. *Miller v Mackey International Inc* 70 FRD 533 (SD Fla 1976).

257 E.g. *King v AG Holdings Ltd* [2003] FCA 1420 at [15] – per Moore J and *Dorajay Pty Ltd v Aristocrat Leisure Ltd* [2008] FCA 1311 at [11] per Stone J – contradictor appointed to represent the interests of potential members of the class who had been excluded from settlement.

258 *Modtech Engineering Pty Ltd v GPT Management Holdings (No 2)* [2013] FCA 1163 at [8–11] per Gordon J.

259 *Roberts v Texaco Inc* 979 F Supp 185 at 187 (SD NY 1997).

260 A notable exception in the Australian context was witnessed in June 2015 when, with respect to the settlement of four federal class actions filed on behalf of investors in certain managed investment schemes, Justice Murphy notified the parties that it required separate counsel to be appointed to represent the interests of group members not represented by the lead plaintiff's solicitors. The role of this separate counsel was to act as 'contradictor' to the applications for settlement approval: see *Kelly v MIS Funding No 1 Pty Ltd,* 'Section 33V Application for Settlement Approval – Submissions of Contradictor' (16 July 2015). What prompted this judicial initiative was that the settlement contained an admission on behalf of the group members that certain loan agreements whose validity and enforceability was challenged in the proceedings were in fact valid and enforceable.

261 *Winterford v Pfizer Australia Pty Ltd* [2015] FCA 426 at [25] per Davies J – noting the potential for conflict of interest and recommending that an assessment of the fairness and the reasonableness of a settlement distribution scheme should be assessed by an independent panel. In the absence of an independent assessment and in light of restrictions on class members' rights of review, the Court was not prepared to approve the proposed settlement.

262 *Australian Securities and Investments Commission v Richards* [2013] FCAFC 89 at [6–8]; *Peterson v Merck Sharp & Dohme (Aust) Pty Ltd (No 6)* [2013] FCA 447; *Williams v FAI Home Security Pty Ltd (No. 5)* [2001] FCA 399; *Verschuur v Vynotas Pty Ltd* [2004] VSC 130.

suffered and the differential risks that might affect their recovery of compensation.[263] This is generally achieved by way of a settlement distribution scheme incorporating a methodology by which different categories of class member claims for compensation will be calculated. When assessing the settlement distribution scheme, the Court, assisted by expert evidence, will examine whether the methodology employed is both rational and fair.[264]

As noted above, as part of the settlement process the Court is required to approve the class law firm's professional fees and disbursements (including disbursements related to ATE insurance). By contrast, litigation funding commissions are not directly reviewed. Nonetheless, litigation funding and law firm arrangements may be indirectly scrutinised as a result of the orders sought by the class law firm to facilitate settlement or to ensure equity between funded and non-funded members of open classes. In terms of these ancillary orders, the appointment of a contradictor is more justified as will be seen from the commentary below.

17. Manipulating the class

Closed classes favoured by funders raise concerns for respondents who might be reluctant to settle proceedings if potential class members outside of the closed class are unknown. The typical way that this 'tail risk'[265] is managed is to seek a court order temporarily opening the closed class so that outstanding claimants can register by a specified deadline.[266] Failure to register within the deadline renders the outstanding claims *res judicata*, thus providing comfort to respondents seeking to accurately determine the full extent of their potential liability. However, using a closed-class vehicle to attract class members to enter funding agreements and then temporarily opening the class to deprive those who did not enter such agreements of their rights to participate in the settlement clearly raises difficult questions regarding conflicts of interest between funded and unfunded claimholders. For this reason, courts are reluctant to make such orders early on in proceedings.[267] Nonetheless, orders for class closure have been made prior to the determination of liability.[268] It is therefore extremely important to ensure that the impact of class closure is appropriately notified to all members of the open class, and that the interests of non-funded absent class members are adequately protected. In this regard, given the clear conflict of interest between the class representatives, funded class members and respondent(s) in ensuring a successful settlement, on the one hand, and the interests of absent members who may be excluded from the fruits of settlement on the other, the appointment of a contradictor may be warranted.[269] At the very least the Court, whether informed by a contradictor or by its own means, must

263 *Collin v Aspen Pharmacare Australia Pty Ltd [2013] FCA 1336*; *Darwalla Milling Co Pty Ltd v F Hoffmann — La Roche Ltd (No 2)* (2006) 236 ALR 322.

264 *Lee v Bank of Queensland* (2014) 103 ACSR 436 at [35–39] per Collier J; *Wepar Nominees Pty Ltd v Schofield (No 2)* (2014) 99 ACSR 234 at [13–17] per Besanko J.

265 See D Taylor and A Weeks, 'Mediation in Shareholder Class Actions: A Defendant's Perspective' (2015) 2(2) *Australian Alternative Dispute Resolution Law Bulletin* 34, 35.

266 See, e.g., *Blairgowrie Trading Ltd v Allco Finance Group Ltd* [2015] FCA 811 at [28] per Wigney J; *City of Swan v McGraw-Hill Financial Inc* (2014) 233 FCR 328; *Inabu Pty Ltd v Leighton Holdings Ltd* [2014] FCA 622 at [16–17] per Jacobson J.

267 E.g., *Camping Warehouse Australia Pty Limited v Downer Edi Limited* [2015] VSC 122; *Winterford v Pfizer Australia Pty Ltd* [2012] FCA 1199; *Thomas v Powercor Australia Ltd (No 1)* [2010] VSC 489.

268 *Lam v Rolls Royce Plc (No. 3)* [2015] NSWSC 83; *Matthews v SPI Electricity Pty Ltd (Ruling No. 13)* (2013) 39 VR 255.

269 See also Morabito (2006) above n 254, 381.

ensure that notification to absent class members is widespread and easily understood, that sufficient time is made available to object and if there are large numbers of unsophisticated absent class members who might have objected if properly advised and resourced that proper consideration is given to this factor in determining whether to approve the temporary opening of the class. Depending on the demography of the class, the court is likely to order that notice be given in traditional media such as newspapers and radio, through new media such as court and class law firm websites, Facebook and Twitter, and where communities are affected by posters in public areas, such as police stations, schools, medical practices and community centres.[270]

Apart from opening a closed class, the prospect of settlement particularly for large, complex proceedings has also led to tactics involving excision of certain categories of class member from settlement.[271] However, subject to the caveats outlined above, arguably Australian Courts are well armed to balance the competing interests that proposed amendments to narrow the class present, and strive to ensure that no such orders are made without notification to all parties affected so that objections may be made and heard. In *Clurname Pty Ltd v Commonwealth Bank of Australia (No. 1)*,[272] an open class action regarding synthetic collateralized debt obligations purchased by class members and marketed by the respondent was commenced in 2012. Following extensive negotiation and mediation, the matter settled in 2015 on condition that two substantial categories of investor, 'institutional investors' and 'settled investors', were excluded from the class. Two institutional investors and one settled investor objected to these terms, partly on the ground that they claimed to be contingently liable to the funder under agreements made prior to the initiation of proceedings. The funder denied that this was the case and indicated that it was prepared to enter into a covenant to waive any such rights. When considering the objections, the Court noted the conflict of interest that the situation created for the class law firm and the funder. Nonetheless, the Court approved the excision and the settlement. The Court was persuaded on the basis that the matter would otherwise not settle at all and that it was still open to the objectors to commence their own proceedings.

18. Equalisation orders in open class proceedings

To ensure equity between funded and non-funded class members regarding their share of the compensation pool in open class proceedings, it is common for the class representative to apply for an equalisation order. Equalisations orders are distinguishable from the 'common fund' orders made in *Pathway Investments Pty Ltd v National Australia Bank Ltd (No 3)* and *Farey v National Australia Bank* discussed above. Rather than deduct a commission from all class members regardless of whether they have entered into a funding agreement and pay those sums direct to the funder, an equalisation order requires the deduction of the funder's commission from each of the non-funded class member's claims, adding the deductions to the total compensation pool, and thereafter pro rata distribution

270 *Matthews v SPI Electricity Pty Ltd and SPI Electricity Pty Ltd v Utility Services Corporation Ltd (Ruling No 13)* (2013) 39 VR 255 at [100] per Forrest J.

271 This tactic has not been limited to funded class actions. See generally V Morabito, 'Judicial Responses to Class Action Settlements that Provide No Benefits to Some Class Members' (2006) 32 *Monash University Law Review* 75.

272 [2015] FCA 153.

to all class members. Such an order thus equalises the position of funded and non-funded class members apropos their share of the total compensation pool but does not add to the total return received by the funder.

One Federal Court judge has expressed the view that equalisation orders are preferable to common fund orders because the common fund order provides an unjustified boon to the funder, and is contrary to the notion of a freely made commercial bargain between the funder and class members.[273] Nevertheless, questions have been raised as to whether equalisation orders are just as incompatible with free bargaining.[274] Those opposed to equalisation orders argue that non-funded class members should not be compelled to contribute toward a funder's commission in which they have had no say, especially as the court does not vigorously examine the reasonableness of what might have been agreed to by a compliant class representative de facto appointed by the funder and class law firm.[275] They also question the rationale of making equalisation orders. Although the equalisation order is designed to prevent non-funded members from receiving a windfall, the windfall is not necessarily at the expense of funded members who have already agreed to pay a funder's commission regardless of the number of non-funded members in the class. They argue that a funder's interests can be adequately protected by pursuing the class action as a closed class.[276] Concerns have also been raised that while notification of proposals to open and closed classes or to excise class members are generally executed appropriately, the same cannot be said of equalisation orders,[277] where the impact on non-funded members' compensation is sometimes hidden within confidential and complex loss assessment formulae. These concerns suggest that a contradictor should be appointed or independent expert evidence adduced to examine the reasonableness of the funder's commission and the method that this conveyed to non-funded members to ensure that they are in an adequate position to object.

19. Law firm fees

While funders may be good monitors of law firm performance during the conduct of class proceedings, they may not be as rigorous in ensuring that professional fees and expenses are minimized during the settlement approval process. To recoup whatever amounts have been paid by the funder to the law firm to conduct the proceedings, the funder will want the court to approve as much of professional fees and disbursements claimed by the law firm as possible. That incentive is strengthened by the fact that under Australia's cost-shifting regime it is the respondent who is financially responsible for the payment of the fees and expenses approved by the court.

Generally, the approval of professional fees and disbursements is a matter considered independently of whether the compensation payable to class members is fair and reasonable.[278] Provided an independent assessment supports the fairness and reasonableness

273 *Modtech Engineering Pty Ltd v GPT Management Holdings Ltd* [2013] FCA 626 at [57] per Gordon J.
274 US Chamber Institute for Law Reform (2013) above n 195, 22–29.
275 Legg (2014) above n 254, 605.
276 US Chamber Institute for Law Reform (2013) above n 195, 22–29.
277 Ibid. 24–25.
278 E.g., *Sherwood v Commonwealth Bank of Australia (No 5)* [2015] FCA 688; *Lee v Bank of Queensland Ltd* (2014) 103 ACSR 436. See further *Jarra Creek Central Packing Shed v Amcor Ltd* [2011] FCA 671 at [129–130] per Jacobson J.

of the fees charged, the Court is likely to approve them.[279] To maintain independence, one commentator has recommended that the expert providing advice to the Court as to the reasonableness of the class law firm's professional fees be appointed by the Court rather than by the class law firm.[280] There is much merit to this recommendation as it appears that class law firms use the same experts to justify their fees on multiple occasions, thus undermining their independence.[281]

One Australian judge has suggested that legal retainers should be approved by the court prior to becoming binding on class members rather than on an *ex post facto* footing at settlement.[282] Usually the basis upon which professional fees and disbursements are calculated and submitted to the court for approval at settlement is confidential, and although class members must be notified of the terms of settlement these notices do not always record the exact amounts that will be deducted from individual compensation or explain how they might have been quantified. As a result, would-be objectors are provided with scant grounds for complaint. However, whether the answer to the lack of transparency is to submit the retainer to the court for *ex ante* approval is debateable.

Ex ante approval of attorney fees is possible at the point of certification and appointment of class counsel in the United States.[283] However, generally in the US fees are awarded at the end of litigation based on a percentage of the class recovery or the lodestar method, which subjects the attorney's reasonable hourly fees to a multiplier that takes account of litigation risk, complexity and other relevant matters.[284] At that stage, prior fee agreements may be relevant but they are not determinative.[285] Similar practice applies in Canada.[286]

Without the enforcement of strict cost budgeting, arguably the suggestion of *ex ante* approval in Australian courts will not assist matters very much. On an *ex ante* basis, the court will be merely providing its imprimatur to the standard method used to calculate fees (typically a variable hourly rate) as well as a pre-estimate of total legal costs that it is likely to be substantially different from the final sum at settlement. Given Australia's history of lengthy and complex class-action proceedings, the ability to accurately predict the total volume of professional fees and expenses in advance is significantly compromised. Moreover, unless there is evidence of strong arm's length bargaining or perhaps benchmarking with what a sophisticated class member might have agreed to, it is difficult to see what yardstick the Court would use to determine that a fee agreement struck prior to the initiation of proceedings with the class representatives and some class members should bind all class members. A pre-existing costs agreement is only one of the factors a court should

279 E.g., *Sherwood v Commonwealth Bank of Australia (No 5)* [2015] FCA 688 at [56] – [70] per Collier J; *Lee v Bank of Queensland* (2014) 103 ACSR 436 at [50] per Collier J; *Taylor v Telstra Corporation* [2007] FCA 2008 at [72] per Jacobson J. See, however, *Modtech Engineering Pty Ltd v GPT Management Holdings Ltd* [2013] FCA 626 and *Modtech Engineering Pty Ltd v GPT Management Holdings Ltd (No. 2)* [2013] FCA 1163 where the Court scrutinised the independent assessment of legal fees very carefully and found it wanting.

280 Legg (2014) above n 254, 608–610.

281 Ibid. 601–602.

282 *Modtech Engineering Pty Ltd v GPT Management Holdings Limited* [2013] FCA 626 at [27] per Gordon J.

283 Federal Rules of Civil Procedure (US), Rule 23(g) (1) (c).

284 M Hogan Greer, *A Practitioner's Guide to Class Actions* (Chicago: American Bar Association 2010) 216.

285 LA Baker, MA Perino and C Silver, 'Setting Attorneys' Fees in Securities Class Actions: An Empirical Assessment' (2013) 66(6) *Vanderbilt Law Review* 1677, 1,694–1,696 noting that *ex ante* fee agreements play a small role at the fee award stage of the class action.

286 E.g. *Labourers' Pension Fund of Central and Eastern Canada v Sino-Forest Corp* (2014) 237 A.C.W.S. (3d) 307, 12 C.B.R. (6th) 150.

take into account when considering the reasonableness of the total volume of claimed professional fees and expenses, and so requiring pre-approval will not alleviate much of the court's ultimate responsibility.

By contrast with funder's commissions, the common fund approach is not controversial with respect to professional fees and disbursements. Typically, law firm fees and disbursements are spread among the whole class by deducting them from the settlement sum that is then distributed according to the formulae embedded in the settlement distribution scheme.[287] Funders will naturally prefer that any deductions related to their commission will not be net of these amounts.[288]

20. Conclusion

Australia's comparatively liberal approach to its litigation entrepreneurs has created an environment that has allowed litigation funding to flourish. Newcomers, both domestic and international, have flocked to the Australian market, which has grown steadily since the Australian High Court provided its imprimatur for the litigation funding of class actions in 2006. As a result, class actions that had been in severe decline were revived.[289]

The symbiotic nature of the relationship between litigation funders and class law firms in engendering that revival has been acknowledged by Australian courts, which have generally been accommodating to funder interests by conceding to closed classes, class manipulation and a hands-off approach to funder commissions. While other jurisdictions such as Canada have confined the role of litigation funders in class actions to that of banker, Australian policy makers and courts have fully embraced the role of litigation funder as joint venturer in the class-action project. Apart from a requirement to properly manage conflicts of interest, Australia's financial regulator, ASIC, exerts minimal oversight over matters such as litigation funding commissions, the degree of funder control over the class action and the termination of funding. Similarly, aside from general norms related to misleading and deceptive conduct, the book-building stage of the class action proceeds relatively unconstrained by regulation.

ASIC's position is highly dependent upon the ethics and expertise of Australia's class-action law firm specialists, the financial probity and integrity of its litigation funders and judicial scrutiny of the class-action settlement. During the book-building stage of Australian class actions, so far, only minor non-intentional infractions of ASIC's disclosure and conflict of management provisions have been detected and addressed. Improvements in how clearly class law firms communicate with potential class members concerning their professional fees and the stage of the class-action project appear warranted. Nonetheless, Australian courts have been tested by instances of a financial relationship between a funder and the class law firm. In these cases, the ASIC guidelines regarding the management of conflicts of interest are not particularly helpful since they assume that disclosure and internal review are complete palliatives. However, Australian courts will restrain proceedings if the financial relationship between the class law firm and funder is sufficiently direct as to raise a

287 See, e.g., *Modtech Engineering Pty Limited v GPT Management Holdings Limited* [2013] FCA 626 at [22] per Gordon J; *Wepar Nominees Pty Ltd v Schofield (No 2)* (2014) 99 ACSR 234 at [31] per Besanko J.

288 See, e.g., *Wepar Nominees Pty Ltd v Schofield (No 2)* (2014) 99 ACSR 234 at [46] per Besanko J.

289 See commentary under the heading, 'Trends in Australian Class Actions' tracking the growth of funded class actions and the increase in the number of litigation funding firms operating in Australia.

reasonable belief that the professional judgment of the law firm vis-à-vis its duty to class members might be impaired. Yet, the potential impact of ongoing joint participation in class-action joint ventures has not been explored by the courts or the Australian Productivity Commission.

At the settlement stage of the project, Australian case law shows that conflicts of interest between funders, class lawyers, class representatives and class members do arise from time to time when the class membership is finalised, professional fees are determined and orders are sought to spread the cost of funding among class members. Australian courts take a ruthlessly pragmatic cost–benefit approach when it comes to assessing the overall reasonableness and fairness of the class settlement and the final composition of the class. If the settlement is reasonable and fair overall but otherwise unlikely without closing the class or excising certain categories of class member, Australian courts are still likely to approve settlement for the benefit of the majority of class members as well as the benefit of the class law firm and funder.

Curiously, Australian policy makers and its courts take an asymmetric approach to class-action transaction costs. Insofar as professional fees are concerned the courts will carefully scrutinise them, and provided there is independent evidence adduced to support the amount claimed they are likely to be approved. However, commercial funders' fees typically lie outside of the court's remit, and will continue to do so even if the Australian Productivity Commission's recommendations for the implementation of regulated damages-based professional fees are implemented. Proposals to approve funders' commission in advance and ensure that they are reasonable in terms of remuneration and litigation risk have been strongly rejected.

When they enter into litigation funding agreements, class representatives and class members enter a tripartite relationship where the other two parties' relationship has already been fully formed. Despite that the funder and class law firm are joint venturers who may even be subject to fiduciary-type obligations between themselves, Australian courts and policy makers adopt the position that class members' entry into this ongoing relationship is a voluntary, rational act. Accordingly, outside of over-reaching and patent financial conflicts between the class law firm and funder it is not a relationship that requires paternalistic management or intervention. To date, confidence in the assumption of rational free bargaining appears to be vindicated.

Bibliography

Alexander J. Cooper, 'Do the Merits Matter? A Study of Settlements in Securities Class Actions' (1991) 43(3) *Stanford Law Review* 497.

Allens Linklaters, *Class Actions: A Ten Year Survey* (May 2015) <www.allens.com.au/pubs/ldr/cuca28may15.htm> accessed 14 June 2015.

Australia, Attorney-General's Department, *A Strategic Framework for Access to Justice in the Federal Civil Justice System* (Barton, ACT: Commonwealth of Australia 2009).

Australian Law Reform Commission, *Grouped Proceedings in the Federal Court* (Sydney: Commonwealth of Australia 1988).

Australian Productivity Commission, *Access to Justice Arrangements Inquiry Report, Vol 1* (Canberra: Commonwealth of Australia 2014) <www.pc.gov.au/inquiries/completed/access-justice> accessed 16 July 2015.

Baker L.A., M.A. Perino and C. Silver, 'Setting Attorneys' Fees in Securities Class Actions: An Empirical Assessment' (2013) 66(6) *Vanderbilt Law Review* 1,677.

Berkovic N., 'Class Action "Main Threat" To Business' *The Australian* (Sydney, 15 May 2015).

Bowen C., 'Government Acts to Ensure Access to Justice for Class Action Member' (Australia, The Treasury, 4 May 2010) <http://ministers.treasury.gov.au/DisplayDocs.aspx?doc=pressreleases/2010/039.htm&pageID=003&min=ceba&Year=&DocType> accessed 18 August 2015.

Burch E. Chamblee, 'Financiers as Monitors in Aggregate Litigation' (2012) 87 *New York University Law Review* 1,273.

Caruana J. and V. Morabito, 'Australian Unions – The Unknown Class Action Protagonists' (2011) 30 *Civil Justice Quarterly* 382.

—— and V. Morabito, 'Turning the Spotlight on Class Representatives – Empirical Insights from Down Under' (2012) 30 *Windsor Yearbook of Access to Justice* 1.

Coffee J.C., 'Understanding the Plaintiff's Attorney: The Implications of Economic Theory for Private Enforcement of Law through Class and Derivative Actions' (1986) 86 *Columbia Law Review* 669.

—— 'Reforming the Securities Class Action: An Essay on Deterrence and its Implementation' (2006) 106 *Columbia Law Review* 1,534.

—— *Entrepreneurial Litigation: Its Rise Fall and Future* (Cambridge, MA: Harvard University Press 2015).

Comolli R. and S. Starykh, *Recent Trends in Securities Class Action Litigation: 2014 Year Review* (New York: NERA Economic Consulting 2015).

De Morpurgo M., 'A Comparative Legal and Economic Approach to Third-Party Litigation Funding' (2011) 19 *Cardozo Journal of International and Comparative Law* 343.

Degeling S. and M. Legg, 'Fiduciary Obligations of Lawyers in Australian Class Actions: Conflicts between Duties' (2014) 37 *University of New South Wales Law Journal* 914.

Deva S., 'Public Interest Litigation in India: A Critical Review' (2009) 28(1) *Civil Justice Quarterly* 19.

Ellis N.S., 'The Class Action Fairness Act of 2005: The Story Behind the Statute' (2009) 35 *Journal of Legislation* 76.

Federal Court of Australia, *Annual Report 2013–2014, Part 3 – The Work of the Court* (Commonwealth of Australia 2014) <www.fedcourt.gov.au/publications/annual-reports/2013-14/part-3> accessed 10 December 2015.

Fitzpatrick B.T., 'Do Class Action Lawyers Make Too Little?' (2010) 158 *University of Pennsylvania Law Review* 2043–2083.

Grave D., K. Adams and J. Betts, *Class Actions in Australia* (2nd edn, Pyrmont, NSW: Lawbook Co Ltd 2012).

Greer M. Hogan, *A Practitioner's Guide to Class Actions* (Chicago: American Bar Association 2010).

Halfteck G., 'The Class Action as a Financial Call Option' (2004) Harvard Law and Economics Discussion Paper No. 466 <http://papers.ssrn.com/sol3/papers.cfm?abstract_id=528043> accessed 9 August 2015.

Hensler D.R., N.M. Pace, B. Dombey-Moore, B. Giddens, J. Gross and E.K. Moller, *Class Action Dilemmas: Pursuing Public Goals for Private Gain* (Santa Monica & Arlington: RAND 2000).

Hensler L.W., 'Class Counsel, Self-Interest and other People's Money' (2004) 35 *University of Memphis Law Review* 53.

Hillcrest Litigation Services Ltd, *Annual Report 2014* (Perth: Hillcrest Litigation Services Ltd 2014) <www.hillcrestlitigation.com.au/financials/financial-2014/> accessed 21 August 2015.

IBIS World, *Litigation Funding in Australia: Industry Report OD5446* (IBIS World Pty Ltd 2015) <www.ibisworld.com.au> accessed 10 December 2015.

Issacharoff S., 'Governance and Legitimacy in the Law of Class Actions' (1999) *Supreme Court Review* 337.

—— 'The Governance Problem in Aggregate Litigation' (2013) 81 *Fordham Law Review* 3,165.

—— 'Litigation Funding and the Problem of Agency Cost in Representative Actions' (2014) 63 *DePaul Law Review* 561.

—— and G.P. Miller, 'Will Aggregate Litigation Come to Europe?' (2009) 62 *Vanderbilt Law Review* 179.

Jennings J.N., S. Kedia and S. Rajgopal, 'The Deterrent Effects of SEC Enforcement Action and Class Action Litigation' (2011) <http://ssrn.com/abstract=1868578SSRN> accessed 14 July 2015.

Kalajdzic J., P. Cashman and A. Longmore, 'Justice for Profit: A Comparative Analysis of Australian, Canadian and US Third Party Litigation Funding' (2013) 61(2) *American Journal of Comparative Law* 93.

Kim J. and L.A. Fish, 'From Nothing to Something: An Experiential Entrepreneurship Exercise' (2010) 8(1) *Decision Sciences Journal of Innovative Education* 241.

King & Wood Mallesons, *The Review– Class Actions in Australia 2013–2014* (King & Wood Mallesons 2014) <www.kwm.com/en/au/knowledge/downloads/the-review-class-actions-in-australia-2013-2014-20140701> accessed 13 December 2015.

King M., A. Freiberg, B. Batasol and R. Hyams, *Adversarial Justice* (Sydney: Federation Press 2014).

Law Council of Australia/Federal Court of Australia, *Law Council of Australia's Case Management Handbook* (Federal Court of Australia 2014) <http://www.fedcourt.gov.au/law-and-practice/case-management-handbook> accessed 11 December 2015.

Law Reform Commission of Western Australia, *Representative Proceedings: Discussion Paper* (Perth: Quality Press 2013).

Legg M., 'Entrepreneurs and Figureheads – Addressing Multiple Class Actions and Conflicts of Interest' (2009) 32 *University of New South Wales Law Journal* 909.

—— 'ADR and Class Actions Compared' in M. Legg (ed.), *The Future of Dispute Resolution* (Chatswood, NSW: LexisNexis 2013).

—— 'Class Action Settlements in Australia – The Need for Greater Scrutiny' (2014) 38(2) *Melbourne University Law Review* 590.

—— V. McBride and S.S. Clark, 'The Challenge of Class Actions in the Supreme Court of New South Wales' (2007) 45(8) *Law Society Journal* 56.

Lindgren K., 'Some Current Practical Issues in Class Action Litigation' (2009) 32(3) *University of New South Wales Law Journal* 900.

Macey J.R. and G.P. Miller, 'The Plaintiffs' Attorneys in Class Action and Derivative Litigation: Economic Analysis and Recommendations for Reform' (1991) 58 *University of Chicago Law Review* 1.

McVeigh A., 'Claims Management Companies Face Thousands of Complaints' *BBC News* (London, 5 November 2015) <http://www.bbc.com/news/business-34730557> accessed 10 December 2015.

Morabito V., 'Ideological Plaintiffs and Class Actions – An Australian Perspective' (2001) 2 *University of British Columbia Law Review* 459.

—— 'An Australian Perspective on Class Action Settlements' (2006) 69 *Modern Law Review* 347.

—— 'Judicial Responses to Class Action Settlements that Provide No Benefits to Some Class Members' (2006) 32 *Monash University Law Review* 75.

—— 'Class Actions Instituted only for the Benefit of the Clients of the Class Representative's Solicitors' (2007) 29 *Sydney Law Review* 5.

—— *An Empirical Study of Australia's Class Action Regimes, First Report: Class Action Facts and Figures* (2009) <http://globalclassactions.stanford.edu/content/empirical-study-australias-class-action-regimes-first-report-class-action-facts-and-figures> accessed 10 December 2015.

—— *An Empirical Study of Australia's Class Action Regimes, Second Report: Litigation Funders, Competing Class Actions, Opt Out Rates, Victorian Class Actions and Class Representatives* (2010) <http://globalclassactions.stanford.edu/empirical> accessed 10 December 2015.

—— 'Clashing Classes Down Under – Evaluating Australia's Competing Class Actions through Empirical and Comparative Perspectives' (2012) 27 *Connecticut Journal of International Law* 245.

—— 'An Empirical and Comparative Study of Reimbursement Payments to Australia's Class Representatives and Active Class Members' (2014) 33 *Civil Justice Quarterly* 175.

—— 'An Empirical Study of Australia's Class Action Regimes, Third Report, Class Action Facts and Figures Five Years Later' (2014) <http://papers.ssrn.com/sol3/papers.cfm?abstract_id=2523275> accessed 10 December 2015.

—— 'Replacing Inadequate Class Representatives in Federal Class Actions: Quo Vadis?' (2015) 38 *University of New South Wales Law Journal* 146.

—— and V. Waye, 'Reining in Litigation Entrepreneurs: A New Zealand Proposal' (2011) *New Zealand Law Review* 323.

—— and J. Ekstein, 'Class Actions Filed for the Benefit of Vulnerable Persons – An Australian Study' (2016) 35(1) *Civil Justice Quarterly* 61.

Moss G., 'Don't Miss Out on Class Action Payments' (September 2015) Investment & Pensions Europe Magazine <http://www.ipe.com/pensions/pensions/briefing/dont-miss-out-on-class-action-payouts/10009553.fullarticle> accessed 10 December 2015.

—— 'Justice Enhanced: Framing an Opt-out Class Action for England' (2007) 70(4) *Modern Law Review* 550.

Mulheron R., 'England's Unique Approach to the Self-Regulatin of Third Party Funding: A Critical Analysis of Recent Developments' (2014) 73 *Cambridge Law Journal* 570.

Mullenix L.S., 'Ending Class Actions as We Know Them: Rethinking the American Class Action' (2014) 64 *Emory Law Journal* 399.

Murphy B. and C. Cameron, 'Access to Justice and the Evolution of Class Action Litigation in Australia' (2006) 30(2) *Melbourne University Law Review* 399.

Papadakis M., 'ATE Insurance to Open Litigation Funding Market' *Australian Financial Review* (Melbourne, 7 November 2014).

Pellengrini A. Grinover, 'Brazilian National Report' in D. Maleshin (ed.), *Civil Procedure in Cross-Cultural Dialogue: Eurasia Context* (Moscow: IAPL World Conference on Civil Procedure 2012).

Popperwell J., 'Litigation Funding and the SRA Handbook' in R. Pirozzolo (ed.), *Litigation Funding Handbook* (London: Law Society 2014).

Puri P., 'Profitable Justice: Aligning Third-Party Financing of Litigation with the Normative Functions of the Canadian Judicial System' (2014) 55 *Canadian Business Law Journal* 34–53.

Queensland Law Society, *Client Care Guide* (Queensland Law Society 2015) <www.qls.com.au/Knowledge_centre/Practising_resources/Client_Care_Guide> accessed 13 December 2015.

Redish M., *Wholesale Justice: Constitutional Democracy and the Problem of the Class Action Lawsuit* (Stanford: Stanford University Press 2009).

Rowles-Davies N., *Third Party Litigation Funding* (Oxford: Oxford University Press 2014).

Sebok A.J., 'The Inauthentic Claim' (2011) 64 *Vanderbilt Law Review* 61.

Shannon V., 'Harmonizing Third-Party Litigation Funding Regulation' (2015) 36 *Cardozo Law Review* 861.

Simard L. Sandstrom, 'View from within the Fortune 500: An Empirical Study of Negative Value Class Actions and Deterrence' (2014) 47 *Indiana Law Review* 739.

Stanford Securities Class Action Clearinghouse, *Securities Class Action Settlement Report 2014* (Stanford Law School 2014) <http://securities.stanford.edu/clearinghouse-research.html> accessed 13 July 2015.

Steinitz M., 'The Litigation Finance Contract' (2012) 54(2) *William & Mary Law Review* 455.

Taylor D. and A. Weeks, 'Mediation in Shareholder Class Actions: A Defendant's Perspective' (2015) 2(2) *Australian Alternative Dispute Resolution Bulletin* 34.

United Kingdom Ministry of Justice, *Claims Management Regulation Annual Report 2014–2015* (Ministry of Justice 2015).

US Chamber Institute for Legal Reform, 'Do Class Actions Benefit Class Members? An Empirical Analysis of Class Actions' (2013) <www.instituteforlegalreform.com/research/do-class-actions-benefit-class-members> accessed 13 July 2015.

Van den Bergh R., 'Private Enforcement of European Competition Law and the Persisting Collective Action Problem' (2013) 20 *Maastricht Journal* 12.

Voet S., 'Consumer Collective Redress in Belgium: Class Actions to the Rescue?' (2015) 16 *European Business Organization Law Review* 121.

Walker J., 'Policy and Regulatory Issues in Litigation Funding Revisited' (2014) 55 *Canadian Business Law Journal* 85.

—— S. Khouri and W. Attrill, 'Funding Criteria for Class Actions' (2009) 32(3) *University of New South Wales Law Journal* 1,036.

Walsh K., 'Threat of Class Actions Scaring Companies' *The Australian Financial Review* (Melbourne, 15 May 2015).

Ward T.B., 'Cognition, Creativity and Entrepreneurship' (2004) 19(2) *Journal of Business Venturing* 173.

Watson A. and M. Donnelly, 'Financing Access to Justice: Third-Party Litigation Funding and Class Actions in Australia' (2014) 55 *Canadian Business Law Journal* 17.

Waye V., *Trading in Legal Claims: Law, Policy & Future Directions in Australia, UK & US* (Adelaide: Presidian Publishing 2008).

—— and V. Morabito, 'Collective Forms of Consumer Redress: Financial Ombudsman Case Study' (2012) 12(1) *Journal of Corporate Law Studies* 1.

—— and V. Morabito, 'Cultural Dimensions of Group Litigation: Australian National Report' in D. Maleshin (ed.), *Civil Procedure in Cross-Cultural Dialogue: Eurasia Context* (Moscow: International Association of Procedural Law Conference Proceedings 2012).

Wendel W.B., 'Alternative Litigation Finance and Anti-Commodification Norms' (2014) 63 *De Paul Law Review* 655–695.

Which?, 'Claims Management Companies: Claims Made by CMCs' (2015) *Which?* <www.which.co.uk/money/insurance/guides/claims-management-companies/claims-made-by-cmcs/> accessed 11 December 2015.

Wicks A., 'Class Actions in New Zealand: Is Legislation Still Necessary?' (2015) *New Zealand Law Review* 73.

Wright C.M. and A. O'Brien, 'Third-Party Funding for Class Actions, and Control over the Litigation' (2014) 55 *Canadian Business Law Journal* 165.

Wright E.W., 'National Trends in Personal Injury Litigation: Before and After "Ipp"' (2006) 33(7) *Brief* 6.

9 Funding of mass claims in Germany

Caught between a rock and a hard place?

Astrid Stadler

1. Setting the scene

The Member States of the European Union were given a certain period in which to implement the European Commission's Recommendation.[1] This period expired in the summer of 2015, and we can make a rather remarkable observation: not a single European government followed the Recommendation. Some have implemented or are going to implement new instruments of collective redress, but they have their own ideas. This came as no surprise! What *is* surprising is the fact that even in those Member States where class or group action legislation has been enacted, not much use has been made of that legislation. There are a couple of reasons for this development. One of these may be the lack of litigation funding.

Europe has not adopted the US or Australian "entrepreneurial" class action system[2] in which law firms are the driving force behind mass litigation. The German system offers a system of fixed lawyers' fees, which has the advantage that litigation costs are very predictable. Lawyers may be paid by their clients on an hourly basis, but this remuneration is not refundable under the "loser pays" rule (which is otherwise an almost full cost-shifting rule in Germany). Contingency fee arrangements with lawyers are allowed only if clients would not otherwise have access to justice.[3] As a result of the legal aid system, which provides support to all plaintiffs who do not have sufficient funds but have a meritorious claim, contingency fee agreements are a rare exception. Many households have legal expenses insurance, but such policies are not available for commercial cases. The number of mass-damages cases in Germany is limited as there can be no class actions, and personal injury cases are mostly covered by health insurance.[4] Mass litigation has gained some importance

1 Commission Recommendation of 11 June 2013 on common principles for injunctive and compensatory collective redress mechanisms in the Member States concerning violations of rights granted under Union Law (2013/396/EU).

2 For the historical development and a critical review of this system see JC Coffee, *Entrepreneurial Litigation: Its Rise, Fall and Future* (Cambridge: Harvard University Press 2015).

3 Sec 49b (2) Bundesrechtsanwaltsordnung (Federal Legal Profession Act). The provision replaces the former strict ban on contingency fees that the Federal Constitutional Court declared void in 2006 because it violated the guarantees of court access in the German Constitution, 1 BvR 2576/04, 12 December 2006: <www.bundesverfassungsgericht.de/SharedDocs/Entscheidungen/DE/2006/12/rs20061212_1bvr257604.html>.

4 Health insurance, however, normally covers only the direct expenses of a victim. There is no compensation for immaterial loss and of extraordinary expenses related to permanent damage. Loss of income of employees and workers will in most cases be covered – at least for a period of six weeks – by payments to be made by the employer or social security institutions, but for self-employed workers' compensation by the perpetrator is of great importance unless they have special insurance coverage.

in securities cases, but the KapMuG (Kapitalanleger-Musterverfahrensgesetz – Capital Market Test Case Act) has a very limited scope of application, and is not a very efficient instrument.[5] One of the most prominent recent cases is an action against VW in the context of its illegal manipulation of diesel car tests and the dramatic drop in the value of its shares as a consequence.[6]

In the absence of group or class-action instruments in Germany, claimants have come up with other solutions in order to benefit from the pooling of claims in a single piece of litigation. This paper will address the cases in which attempts have been made to pool together several claims by assigning them to a special-purpose vehicle, and will analyse why these failed. The attitude towards the assignment of accounts receivable for collection varies among legal systems. Whereas common-law countries – against the background of the old rules against maintenance, champerty and barratry, which have their roots in Roman law – are particularly reluctant to accept these assignments, continental law generally takes a more liberal attitude. However, German law has always been anxious to protect the monopoly of lawyers when it comes to legal advice and the enforcement of claims. Unlike US class actions, litigation in Europe seems not (yet) lawyer-driven and other protagonists need to take centre stage. Therefore, special-purpose vehicles are playing an increasingly important role in resolving mass disputes, but they meet considerable scepticism.

Claimants may reduce their litigation costs and procedural risks by assigning their claims, for a price, to companies specializing in the enforcement of damages claims – mostly on the basis of a profit-sharing agreement. There are two major fields where such transfers of claims are common for mass damages cases: securities cases and cartel damages cases. The bundling of claims in the hand of a single assignee can fill a gap where no real class or group action proceedings can exist. It can help to overcome an investment asymmetry that appears not only in consumer mass damages cases but also in cartel damages cases if there are wealthy repeat players on the defendants' side and small and medium-sized enterprises (SMEs) on the plaintiffs' side.

Despite the fact that calculating the damages arising from price-fixing cartels is a tricky issue,[7] cartel cases seem to be – at least at first sight – a rewarding field for mass damages claims once the cartel authorities have established that there *was* a cartel. Follow-on damages claims enjoy the privilege that it is not necessary to establish the defendants' wrongdoing, and the litigation can focus on the recovery of damages. Nevertheless, in practice there have not been many successful damage claims against cartelists – for a number of reasons. The fact that class-action proceedings or other instruments of collective redress are unavailable is only one of these. Preparing such actions and calculating damages

5 The Deutsche Telekom case, which started in 2003 and induced policy makers to enact the KapMuG in 2005, is, after more than 12 years, still in the stage of model case proceedings. The Federal High Court (*Bundesgerichtshof*) (21 October 2014, XI ZB 12/12 – *Neue Juristische Wochenschrift* [NJW] 2015, 236 = *BeckRS* 2014, 22871) granted an appeal by the claimants against the first model case decision of the Frankfurt Court of Appeal (*BeckRS* 2012, 10607) that the prospectus of Deutsche Telekom had been correct. The model case was remitted to the Frankfurt court.

6 On 15 October 2015 an action was filed by shareholders in the District Court of Braunschweig; other actions will follow.

7 In 2014, the European legislature enacted the Directive on certain rules governing actions for damages under national law for infringements of the competition law provisions of the Member States and of the European Union, 2014/104/EU, 26 November 2014. The period for transposition expires in December 2016. We will have to wait and see whether the new rules can indeed promote actions for the recovery of damages.

requires specialized experts, intensive work and expensive databases in order to simulate and to predict the development of prices with and without cartels. Pooling the claims in one party's name offers a number of advantages to claimants. Besides the obvious reduction of costs there is another, more psychological, effect: cartelists and their immediate buyers are business partners and quite often want to maintain their business relationships. Using an intermediary prevents a face-to-face meeting in the court, and seems to help them to do business as usual despite the litigation.

Fighting against cartels needs more than extraordinarily high administrative fines. Deterrent effects can be obtained only if the cartelists must fully internalize the damage caused. In contrast to the approach taken in the United Kingdom,[8] France[9] and the Netherlands,[10] the German courts have recently added another severe obstacle for claimants. The first reactions to this were entitled: "Cartel damage claims – Goodbye Germany?"[11]

2. Mass damages cartel cases and the role of special-purpose vehicles

2.1 Cartel Damage Claims (CDC) and the cement and hydrogen peroxide cartels

Cartel Damage Claims (CDC) is a company that has been incorporated in Belgium since 2002. Today, there is a holding S.A. and several subsidiaries that have been set up for different individual cartel cases. CDC's business model is based on the purchase of damages claims from companies whose suppliers have been found guilty of price-fixing, market sharing or similar violations of antitrust laws and who may be entitled to compensation. The purchase price paid by CDC has two components: a fixed one, which is more or less symbolic – in most cases 100 Euros, and a variable one that depends on the success of the claim. CDC pays to the former claimants between 65 per cent and 80 per cent of the damages it recovers. In other words, CDC works in return for a share of 20–35 per cent of the proceeds. Claimants fully assign their claims, to enable CDC to sue the cartelists on its own behalf, and the assignors are not involved in the litigation.

The cement cartel case[12] was the first and most famous case selected by CDC, and it dates back to the 1980s. Between 1988 and 2002 German producers of cement entered into several price-fixing cartels with respect to different regional markets in Germany. In

8 Sec 81 Schedule 8 Consumer Rights Act 2015 implements what is basically an opt-out group action for competition cases under Sec 47B Competition Act 1998. The Competition Appeal Tribunal has exclusive jurisdiction to try these cases.

9 The new French consumer class action (*loi* no 2014-344 rélative à la consommation, Journal officiel 18 mars 2014, 5400) grants legal standing to French consumer organizations in antitrust cases to sue for the recovery of damages in follow-on actions. The scope of application is limited to consumer claims arising from the violation of consumer contracts (contracts for the sale of goods and for services) and claims arising from the infringement of antitrust rules.

10 The Dutch Ministry of Justice published a draft for a new horizontal procedural instrument, a collective action to be initiated by representative entities. The draft met a great deal of criticism and is under consultation; for details see <www.internetconsultatie.nl/motiedijksma>; Tzankova, *Verbraucherrecht* (VbR) 2015, 106ff (part 1) and 178ff (part 2).

11 T Makatsch and V Abele, 'Kartellschadensersatz – Goodbye Deutschland?' (2015) *Wirtschaft und Wettbewerb* 461.

12 For details of the story see <www.carteldamageclaims.com/portfolios/cement-cartels/>.

2003, the German Federal Cartel Office imposed administrative fines totalling 702 million Euros on 12 companies and their representatives, including fines of 660 million Euros on the six largest German cement producers.[13] The administrative fines became res judicata for the defendants between 2003 and 2013. CDC bought claims from 36 companies allegedly damaged by the cartel for a total amount of approximately 131 million Euros, and in 2005 filed an action against six cartelists as joint debtors in the Regional Court in Düsseldorf. Because of some legal uncertainty about the validity of the assignments and as a precautionary measure, the assignments were repeated in 2008, 2009, and finally during the appeal stage of the proceedings in 2014. The whole proceedings ultimately lasted for 10 years, and none of the judges involved has dealt with the really important and central questions of the case: the causal link between the cartel and the damage, and the quantum of damage.

In the first round, the courts had to address a number of preliminary issues raised by the defendants. The cartelists challenged, in particular, the admissibility of the action and the assignment of the claims, arguing that CDC was only a litigation funder and was – from an economic point of view – acting on behalf of the former claimants. In 2008 and 2009 the Court of Appeals in Düsseldorf and the Federal High Court decided that the action was admissible. The question of whether the assignment of claims was actually legally valid was a matter of the merits of the case that had to be considered later. This court decision prompted CDC to rejoice on its website that its business model had been confirmed by the Federal High Court. CDC was pleased too quickly, as things turned out.

In December 2013, the Regional Court in Düsseldorf decided that the assignments were legally void, and the action was dismissed in its entirety.[14] The court held that the assignments completed before 2008 violated the strict rules of the German Act on Legal Advice.[15] The Act had been replaced by more liberal provisions in 2008 and from that time debt collectors simply had to obtain an official registration before they enforced foreign claims. As CDC had obtained such a registration, the assignments made after 2008 did not violate the new rules. However, the Düsseldorf Court held that all the assignments completed after the registration were void because they were contrary to public policy and *bonos mores* (Sec. 138 German Civil Code).[16] The main argument was based on the financial situation of CDC at the time of the assignments. In February 2015, CDC's appeal against the decision was dismissed.[17] The Court of Appeal of Düsseldorf shared the view that the assignments were invalid, and did not allow a further appeal to the Federal High Court, holding that the case did not raise questions of fundamental importance. As a result, and because of the "loser pays" rule, CDC had to pay the litigation costs not only for the six defendants, but also for several other companies that had become involved in the litigation as third-party interveners, based on a third-party notice by the defendants. The decision of the Düsseldorf Court of Appeal has thus created an extraordinary increase in the procedural

13 This amount was later reduced to 330 million Euros by the Federal High Court.

14 For a review of this judgment see A Stadler, 'Die Bündelung von gleichgerichteten Ansprüchen durch Inkassozession – Geschäftsmodelle zur Prozessfinanzierung auf dem Prüfstand' (2014) *Juristenzeitung* 613.

15 The primary objective of this Act was to preserve German lawyers' monopoly on any kind of legal advice, and as a consequence it prohibited any assignment of accounts receivable for collection on a repetitive and commercial basis unless there was an official licence.

16 District Court Düsseldorf (17 December 2013) *Juristenzeitung* 2014, 635.

17 Court of Appeals Düsseldorf (18 February 2015, IV-U Kart 3/14) *Juristenzeitung* 2014, 276.

risk for cartel damages claims and will not be without consequences for future cases.[18] One consequence will be even more intensive forum shopping across Europe.[19]

Courts in other parts of Europe, for example in Finland and the Netherlands, have taken a different approach and have accepted CDC's business model: in July 2013, the Helsinki District Court accepted the position of CDC as a plaintiff acting in its own name.[20]

CDC's action in Finland was based on a European-wide hydrogen peroxide price-fixing cartel confirmed by the European Commission in 2006. The group of cartelists included the Finnish company Kemira, who had to pay a fine of 33 million Euros for its infringement of the antitrust rules. Two of Kemira's customers transferred their right to compensation and damages to CDC, who sued Kemira in the Helsinki District Court for compensation of 21.4 million Euros. The court held that CDC was not in any shape or form a "dummy company", but that it had acquired the receivable damages with full ownership. It was therefore pursuing the action for damages on its own and at its own risk. The court did not even mention the financial situation of CDC.[21] In May 2014, Kemira settled the case with CDC and paid 18.5 million Euros in compensation.[22]

In the Netherlands, the Rechtbank Den Haag accepted an action by a CDC subsidiary[23] to bring damages claims against the participants in a price-fixing cartel regarding slack wax and paraffin wax (operating from 1992 to 2005). Despite the fact that the defendants referred to the decision of the Regional Court of Düsseldorf in the cement cartel case and the fact that German law was applicable to the assignment of the claims, the Dutch court did not declare the transfer of claims void. The allegations of the defendants with respect to the financial situation and resources of the CDC subsidiary were too vague and general to support an argument that there was a violation of public policy and *bonos mores*.[24]

2.2 *Air cargo case*

Another well-known cartel that keeps law firms and civil courts busy is the air cargo cartel established by 11 airfreight carriers operating around the world, who agreed to fix, among other things, a fuel surcharge that was imposed on contracting parties. The cartel, which operated between 1999 and 2006, resulted in a record fine of nearly 800 million Euros imposed by the European Commission. Only Lufthansa received complete immunity from the fines under the Commission's leniency programme. Several follow-on damages actions are pending across Europe (in the Netherlands, the UK and France), and again

18 CDC, however, did not give up. On 29 October 2015, CDC filed another action for damages based on the cement cartel. This time only *HeidelbergCement AG* was chosen as a defendant, with the claim, worth 138 million Euros, being filed at the District Court of Mannheim and CDC providing security for costs of 2.3 million Euros. The new action does not contradict the *res judicata* effect of the Düsseldorf judgments because the claims are now alleged to arise from a regional price-fixing cartel not from a cartel covering the federal territory of Germany as in the Düsseldorf case.

19 For an analysis of the consequences see A Stadler, 'Schadensersatzklagen im Kartellrecht – Forum Shopping Welcome!' (2015) *Juristenzeitung* 1,138.

20 District Court of Helsinki, Third Department, Interlocutory judgment 36492, 4 July 2013, 11/16750.

21 Even a non-assignment clause in the supply agreement between the original claimants and Kemira was held not to render the transfer ineffective.

22 E Wäktare, 'Private Enforcement: Settlement between Claimant CDC and Hydrogen Peroxide cartellist Kemira (Finland)' (2014) 5 *Journal of European Competition Law & Practice* 701.

23 *CDC Project 14 S.A*, founded by the CDC holding company.

24 Rechtbank Den Haag, Interlocutory decision 17 December 2014, C/09/414499/HA ZA 12-293.

intermediaries to whom the claims have been assigned by injured parties play a key role as plaintiffs. Two of these intermediaries are Equilib BV Netherlands, a private limited company with its registered office in Amsterdam, and CFE (Claims Funding Europe)[25] – a litigation funding company incorporated in Dublin and specializing in multi-party actions for the victims of corporate misconduct, in particular cartels, and in claims for shareholders. CFE is partially owned by an Australian class-action law firm (Maurice Blackburn Lawyers). The Amsterdam Court of Appeal had to decide an appeal lodged by Equilib against a judgment of the Amsterdam District Court to stay proceedings initiated by Equilib against several famous airlines. The Dutch courts did not apparently have any doubts with respect to the validity of the assignment of claims to Equilib, and set aside the District Court's decision.[26]

Another action that stems from the air cargo cartel is pending before the Regional Court in Cologne. The German railway operator Deutsche Bahn also allegedly suffered damage from the price-fixing cartel, and founded a wholly-owned subsidiary, Barnsdale Cartel Damage Solutions AG. This company is a special-purpose vehicle established to enforce not only the damages claims of Deutsche Bahn but also claims assigned to it by other companies. Shortly before the Court of Appeal in Düsseldorf dismissed CDC's appeal in the cement cartel case, Barnsdale extended its action and is now claiming compensation from several air cargo cartelists of 1.2 billion Euros plus 560 million Euros in interest.[27] This is the highest cartel damages claim ever filed in Germany, and we will have to wait and see how the court in Cologne deals with the assignments, and particularly whether it shares the strict position of the Düsseldorf judges.

In sum, the business model of an SPV specializing in the enforcement of foreign damages claims meets quite different legal assessments from different courts in Europe.

3. Assignment of claims – validity of the transfer?

German courts have traditionally been cautious about allowing manipulations of the person of the plaintiff by authorizing a third party to litigate on behalf of the original claimant. The former German Act on Legal Advice (originally enacted in 1936) did not allow formal authorization for the collection of a debt if the assignor remained, from an economic point of view, the claimant. Even a full assignment – although there are no particular restrictions under the substantive law – is subject to the court's scrutiny if the assignor maintains an economic interest in the pursuit of the claim. The business model of CDC and other special-purpose vehicles (SPVs) have in common that the assignor and the assignee share an economic interest in winning the case. Thus, it is not a "regular" assignment, but an assignment for the primary purpose of debt collection. However, even in the light of the existing case law the Düsseldorf courts took a surprisingly strict position without really balancing the interests of the parties. Some of the key factors are worth mentioning because they demonstrate that the existing rules do not set adequate criteria.

25 <www.claimsfundingeurope.eu>.

26 <www.barentskrans.nl/uploads/Judgment%20Equilib%20v%20KLM%20et%20al%2024%2009%202013.pdf>.

27 File no. 31 O 555/13; see also the report from 11 May 2015 in *Stuttgarter Zeitung* <www.stuttgarter-zeitung.de/inhalt.prozess-gegen-cargo-kartell-die-deutsche-bahn-verlangt-schadenersatz.a3b9d18a-339b-4867-8c2e-f89a4f2b4d82.html>.

3.1 Increased risks for the defendant?

It was beyond dispute that at the time of the original assignments CDC had a share capital of only 100,000 Euros, and would not have been able to reimburse the defendants for their litigation costs, even at the first instance, if CDC were to lose the case – even before considering the costs of an appeal. However, the courts' main argument against the validity of the assignment was not that CDC had no money, but that the assignment had *increased* the defendant's risk of not being reimbursed for its legal expenses. Would such a statement not require a comparison to be made of the defendant's risk with and without the assignment? If the original claimants themselves did not have sufficient resources, the assignment would not have increased or influenced the defendant's chances of receiving reimbursement. Although the judges speak about "shifting the risk", there is not a single word about the financial situation of the original claimants who would have been liable for the defendants' cost in case of an action without assignments in the same way as CDC.[28]

3.2 Obligation to provide security for costs?

German civil procedure rules do not grant any special protection for defendants' rights to reimbursement of litigation costs. Defendants do not enjoy any privilege of being sued only by "wealthy" plaintiffs.[29] The "loser pays" rule is generally viewed as a safeguard against abusive litigation, but one of its consequences is that a defendant generally bears the risk that the plaintiff is not in a position to reimburse him for his litigation costs. In contrast to other jurisdictions such as England[30] or Switzerland,[31] German courts do not have the discretion or option to ask the plaintiff for a guarantee. Security for legal expenses has always been a highly controversial political issue because imposing an obligation to provide security may generally hamper access to justice. Some Member States, therefore, have a rather strict attitude with respect to security for costs. In Italy in 1960, for example, the

28 As legal costs depend on the amount in controversy, however, the risk for a defendant that the claimant is able to meet an adverse cost order would be lower in individual actions. A consolidation of claims by CDC in a single piece of litigation leads to an increase in the amount in controversy and – up to a certain limitation by law – also increases the defendants' lawyers' fees.

29 Federal High Court (Bundesgerichtshof), *Neue Juristische Wochenschrift* (NJW) 1999, 1717, 1718; 1987, 2018.

30 Rule 25.12–25.14 Civil Procedure Rules. Rule 25.12: "Security for costs":

(1) A defendant to any claim may apply under this Section of this Part for security for his costs of the proceedings. (Part 3 provides for the court to order payment of sums into court in other circumstances. Rule 20.3 provides for this Section of this Part to apply to Part 20 claims.)

(2) An application for security for costs must be supported by written evidence.

(3) Where the court makes an order for security for costs, it will – (a) determine the amount of security; and (b) direct – (i) the manner in which; and (ii) the time within which the security must be given.

According to Rule 25.13 the court may ask for security if "(c) the claimant is a company or other body (whether incorporated inside or outside Great Britain) and there is reason to believe that it will be unable to pay the defendant's costs if ordered to do so;" or "(f) the claimant is acting as a nominal claimant, other than as a representative claimant under Part 19, and there is reason to believe that he will be unable to pay the defendant's costs if ordered to do so".

31 Art 99 Swiss Federal Code of Civil Procedure (2011): Courts can order security for costs if the plaintiff appears to be insolvent, particularly when bankruptcy proceedings have been commenced, or if there is any other substantial risk with respect to the reimbursement of litigation costs.

Constitutional Court declared a provision of the Italian Civil Procedure Code, which allowed courts to ask for security for legal costs and thus influenced access to justice, void.[32]

Even in jurisdictions in which the courts may impose such an obligation at the beginning of the proceedings, this possibility is often restricted to situations where the plaintiff's insolvency is imminent.[33] In Germany, even insolvent plaintiffs can file an action, because it is deemed unfair to deny them the chance of collecting a debt and thus ultimately escaping insolvency.[34] One of the strange consequences of the CDC case is that those plaintiffs who sue the defendant based on an assignment must actually now meet stricter requirements than normal claimants, as the assignment can be declared void by the court. Assignees are now more or less obliged to offer security for the defendant's legal expenses. CDC did so recently when it filed another action arising from the cement cartel,[35] and other SPVs have ensured that the assignor provides a default guarantee.[36]

3.3 Legitimate interests of assignors

German case law used to emphasize that an assignment is only void if it is the parties' *primary objective* to harm the defendant by using an intermediary without adequate resources. An assignee's lack of financial resources is not sufficient on its own to lead to the assignment being declared void. In any case, there must be a careful balancing of the interests of both parties. In the cement cartel case, the judges did not take into consideration that the use of a specialized company like CDC that was willing to make a considerable investment in the preparation of the litigation was probably the only realistic option for the claimants to obtain compensation. The defendants, on the other hand, were not particularly worthy of protection as they had clearly violated antitrust rules.

3.4 Validity of the assignment at a particular time?

As a general rule, the validity of an assignment must be assessed with respect to the point in time when the assignment was actually made. As a consequence, the Düsseldorf courts simply looked at CDC's financial situation at the time of the assignment – later assignments made while the proceedings were already pending were not taken into consideration for (some weak) procedural reasons. However, assignments for debt collection normally take place before litigation starts and often even before it is clear whether an action needs to be filed in the first place. Should the assignee be successful in negotiating an out-of-court settlement, no court will ever challenge the validity of the assignment – and CDC has demonstrated on several occasions that it prefers to settle disputes. Even if litigation is inevitable, the defendant's risk regarding his litigation costs is a theoretical one and lies (far) in the future. The assignee's financial situation can change considerably until the time when the costs become payable. In the cement cartel case it took exactly 10 years before the case

32 Corte costituzionale, 23–29 November 1960, n 67 (Gazz. Uff. 3 December 1960, n 297). According to art 98 of the Italian Civil Procedure Code, courts could order security for costs upon the defendant's application if there was reason to believe that the plaintiff might not be able to pay the defendant's costs at the end of the case.

33 Cf art 99 Swiss Federal Code of Civil Procedure (2011).

34 For actions filed by an insolvency administrator, the defendant's claim for reimbursement of his litigation costs is, however, privileged under insolvency law.

35 See fn 17.

36 Cf the assignment of claims by Deutsche Bank in a famous case decided by the Court of Appeal in Munich (14 December 2012) *BeckRS* 2013, 05349.

was finally lost, and CDC proved in the meantime to have sufficient resources. Even rich plaintiffs can become poor at the end of the day. German courts have applied different standards when examining whether the plaintiff has received a valid power of attorney, and have held that the closing of the trial is the decisive point in time when all requirements must be fulfilled.[37] An assignment and a power of attorney are, however, exchangeable in many situations. Questioning the validity of the transfer of a claim thus does not seem to be the right way to decide whether an assignee should be permitted to become a claimant party. There should also be much more flexible rules in relation to security for costs.

All told, a suspicion arises that the Düsseldorf courts of both instances were simply not inclined to accept CDC's business model. It would have been easy to find arguments in favour of a valid assignment. CDC – whether it likes it or not[38] – has meanwhile accepted the situation and is willing to provide security for costs, even if this amounts to millions of Euros. For newcomers, however, the decision of the Düsseldorf courts is a considerable handicap to entering the market.

4. Issues raised by special-purpose vehicles as claimant parties

There are a few lessons to be learned from the cement cartel case. The most important one is probably that third-party funding of litigation is such a critical and controversial issue that the courts – at least in Germany – are not able to solve the problem with their traditional instruments. Rules against immoral transactions, or public policy provisions, are far too broad to provide a reliable basis for funding mass litigation in antitrust cases and other mass damages situations. Some general questions raised in this context need to be decided by policy makers: Should special-purpose vehicles generally be excluded from bringing mass damages actions? Do defendants in collective redress proceedings need protection against "poor" claimants? If so, what kind of protection would be adequate?

4.1 Guidance from the EU Commission Recommendation 2013/396/EU or other legal systems?

The Commission's Recommendation 2013 provides rules on the legal standing of representative entities and on third-party funding of collective redress proceedings (Recommendations Nos. 4[39] and 15[40]), but it fails to address the problem of special purpose

37 Federal High Court (Bundesgerichtshof), *Neue Juristische Wochenschrift* (NJW) 1987, 2018; 1987, 313; 1960, 523.

38 The Court of Appeal in Düsseldorf did not allow a further appeal to the Federal High Court arguing that the case did not raise questions of fundamental importance (Sec 543 German Code of Civil Procedure). CDC refrained from an appeal against the non-admission by the Court of Appeal, Sec 544 German Code of Civil Procedure.

39 "Standing to bring a representative action: The Member States should designate representative entities to bring representative actions on the basis of clearly defined conditions of eligibility. These conditions should include at least the following requirements: (a) the entity should have a non-profit making character; (b) there should be a direct relationship between the main objectives of the entity and the rights granted under Union law that are claimed to have been violated in respect of which the action is brought; and (c) the entity should have sufficient capacity in terms of financial resources, human resources, and legal expertise, to represent multiple claimants acting in their best interest."

40 "Funding: The court should be allowed to stay the proceedings if in the case of use of financial resources provided by a third party: (a) there is a conflict of interest between the third party and the claimant party and its members; (b) the third party has insufficient resources in order to meet its financial commitments to the claimant party initiating the collective redress procedure; (c) the claimant party has insufficient resources to meet any adverse costs should the collective redress procedure fail."

vehicles clearly. CDC and other entities operating on the basis of the assignment of claims are in a technical or strictly legal sense neither "third-party funders" in the sense of the Recommendation nor representative entities.

4.2 England and Wales

In England and Wales, recent legislation has taken rather a strict position against SPVs as lead plaintiffs in collective redress actions. Since 2012[41] there has been an initiative of the Department for Business, Innovation & Skills (BIS) to implement new rules to govern collective proceedings and collective settlements in proceedings before the Competition Appeal Tribunal (CAT) for competition cases. In its consultation published in 2015, the BIS emphasizes – in this respect completely in line with the Recommendation – the importance of safeguards against misuse and the government policy that only meritorious cases should be brought. As part of this process, courts should apply a preliminary merits test to decide whether a case should proceed. In this context the consultation says:[42]

> 7.5 Government believes that only those who have a genuine interest in the case, such as genuinely representative bodies (for example, trade associations or consumer organisations) or those who have themselves suffered loss should be allowed to bring cases.
>
> 7.6 Government policy is therefore that claims should not be brought by law firms, third-party funders or special purpose vehicles. .... In order to achieve a balance between claimants and defendants, Government is minded to introduce presumption into the rules that organisations, that offer legal services, special purpose vehicles and third-party funders should not be able to bring cases.

Special-purpose vehicles are defined in the consultation as organizations created with the sole purpose of bringing a case. Thus there can be no doubt that CDC, Equilib and CFE are SPVs. The Consumer Rights Act 2015 finally chose a rather more diplomatic approach:[43] under Sec. 47B(8) of the Competition Act 1998 (as amended by the Consumer Rights Act 2015), the Competition Appeal Tribunal (CAT) may "authorise a person to act as the representative ... (a) whether or not that person is a person falling within the class ... but (b) only if the Tribunal considers that it is just and reasonable for that person to act as a representative in those proceedings." Rule 78 of the CAT Rules 2015[44] specifies the criteria for the appointment as a representative albeit without mentioning assignments explicitly:

41 <www.gov.uk/government/uploads/system/uploads/attachment_data/file/31528/12-742-private-actions-in-competition-law-consultation.pdf>. All responses to the consultation are available at: <www.gov.uk/government/consultations/private-actions-in-competition-law-a-consultation-on-options-for-reform>.

42 Competition Appeal Tribunal (CAT) Rules of Procedure, Review by the RT Honourable Sir John Mummery; in the same sense: Private Actions in Competition Law, Government Response: (January 2013) 5.30, 5.32.Cuk/government/consultations/competition-appeal-tribunal-rules-of-procedure-review.

43 CAT Rules of Civil Procedure, Government Response, September 2015, no 3.5: "No presumption will be included in the Rules to exclude certain organisations bringing cases. We believe that this flexibility is necessary as a presumption against legal firms, special-purpose vehicles and third-party funders is too prohibitive and could prevent for instance, a special-purpose vehicle that has been established to genuinely represent the class from being able to bring forward a case." Available at: <www.gov.uk/government/consultations/competition-appeal-tribunal-rules-of-procedure-review>.

44 The rules have been in force since October 2015.

78.—(1) The Tribunal may authorise an applicant to act as the class representative—

(a) whether or not the applicant is a class member, but

(b) only if the Tribunal considers that it is just and reasonable for the applicant to act as a class representative in the collective proceedings.

(2) In determining whether it is just and reasonable for the applicant to act as the class representative, the Tribunal shall consider whether that person—

(a) would fairly and adequately act in the interests of the class members;

(b) does not have, in relation to the common issues for the class members, a material interest that is in conflict with the interests of class members;

(c) if there is more than one applicant seeking approval to act as the class representative in respect of the same claims, would be the most suitable;

(d) will be able to pay the defendant's recoverable costs if ordered to do so; and

(e) where an interim injunction is sought, will be able to satisfy any undertaking as to damages required by the Tribunal.

English scholars expect the CAT to interpret the provision according to the Government's position taken during the consultation.[45] This rather strict handling of legal standing is in line with the old English rules against barratry, maintenance and champerty, which used to outlaw agreements by which strangers provided financial assistance to a litigant in return for a share in the recovery. In medieval England, these rules applied to protect the integrity of the legal process against misuse and to prevent "the sword of a baron, stalking into court with a rabble of retainers at his heels".[46] In an eighteenth-century case, Lord Loughborough explained the rule as follows: "parties shall not by their countenance aid the prosecution of suits of any kind; ... every person must bring [his action or suit] upon his own bottom and at his own expense".[47] The rationale for the prohibitions rested on public policy: individuals, particularly "gangster barons", should not stir up litigation at no risk to themselves, and the poor and weak were to be protected from exploitation by the rich and powerful.[48] Although for decades the rule against maintenance and champerty has appeared to be nothing but a historic relict with no practical importance in modern times and more or less a "dead letter", CDC and other SPVs now seem to be the "feudal gangster barons" of our modern times. In 2011, the English Court of Appeal emphasized: "the assignment of a cause of action for the purposes of enabling the assignee or a third party to make a profit out of the litigation will generally be void as savouring of champerty".[49] In other common-law countries, however, the attitude has changed. The New South Wales Law Reform Commission in Australia held in 1994:

45 R Mulheron, 'A Channel Apart: Why the United Kingdom has Departed from the European Commission's Recommendation on Class Actions' (2015) 17 *Cambridge Yearbook of European Legal Studies* 36, 53.

46 J Bentham, 'A Defence of Usury, Letter XII, Maintenance and Champerty' in J Bowring (ed.), *The Works of Jeremy Bentham* (Vol 3 Part 1, Edinburgh: William Tait 1843) 19, quoted by Lord Neuberger, 'From Barratry, Maintenance and Champerty to Litigation Funding' (Harbour Litigation Funding First Annual Lecture, Gray's Inn, 8 May 2013).

47 Wallis v. Duke of Portland, 3 Ves. Jun. 494 at 502.

48 Lord Neuberger (fn 46), para 33.

49 Simpson v. Norfolk & Norwich University Hospital (2011) EWCA Civ. 1149.

> The considerations of public policy which once found maintenance and champerty so repugnant have changed over the course of time. The social utility of assisted litigation is now recognized and the provision of legal and financial assistance viewed favourably as a means of increasing access to justice.[50]

Although English law has finally permitted conditional fee agreements (CFAs),[51] and a damages-based agreements regulation was enacted in 2013, there is still a deeply rooted aversion to "entrepreneurial litigation". Unlike the situation in the United States, lawyers (and courts) in Europe have never been regarded as the natural allies of citizens who, for their part, were dependent on self-help and individual action. Public enforcers in Europe are indeed reluctant to share their monopoly control over enforcement with "private attorney generals".[52] Whereas US courts abandoned the English rules against champerty and maintenance in the nineteenth century[53] (and further along the line even the "loser pays" rule), a kind of reactivation can be observed in some European countries. English litigation funders have meanwhile agreed on a Code of Conduct,[54] which includes an obligation on funders to maintain adequate financial resources in order to meet their obligations to fund all of the disputes they have agreed to fund.

4.3 Australia

Even Australia, the country where third-party funding originated, is struggling with the old restrictions inherited from English law. Bare rights of action (particularly rights to sue in tort and rights to sue for unliquidated damages in contract) are not assignable in Australia to this day.[55] Although maintenance and champerty have been abolished as tortious acts,[56] the rationale behind these restrictions survived in the shape of public policy considerations.[57] So-called "genuine commercial interests" of the assignor can prevail over the public policy objection if the genuine interests have existed before and do not stem from the assignment itself (which is normally the case with litigation funders).[58] In a 2006 decision of the High Court of Australia,[59] the question was raised whether the public policy objection also applies where litigation funders operate not on the basis of an assignment but under a power of attorney. The court accepted the litigation funder's role if the funder was not put in a position of full control of the litigation. Furthermore, it seems to be unclear whether the "genuine

50 New South Wales (Australia) Law Reform Commission, Barratry Maintenance and Champerty, Discussion Paper No 36 (1994), at para 2.55. For details see J Walker, 'Policy and Regulatory Issues in Litigation Funding Revisited' (2014) 55 *Canadian Business Law J.* 85ff.

51 CFA success fees are, however, not recoverable from the defendant.

52 Coffee (2015) 12ff.

53 Coffee (2015) 11.

54 Code of Conduct for Litigation Funders November 2011: <http://associationoflitigationfunders.com/code-of-conduct>.

55 Poulton v. Commonwealth [1953] 89 CLR (*Commonwealth Law Reports*) 540.

56 M Legg, E Park, N Turner and L Travers, 'The Rise and Regulation of Litigation Funding in Australia' (2011) 38 *Northern Kentucky Law Review* 625, 627f.; see also the statement of the New South Wales Law Reform Commission of 1994 (fn 50).

57 Sec 6 Maintenance, Champerty and Barratry Abolition Act 1993.

58 Tosich v. Tasman Investment Management, [2008] FCA (*Federal Court of Australia*) 377.

59 Campbells Cash and Carry Pty Ltd. v. Fostify Pty Ltd, [2006] 229 CLR (*Commonwealth Law Reports*) 386 = [2006] HCA (*High Court of Australia*) 41.

commercial interests" test also applies to bare rights in action. Assignments have a good chance of being accepted if the defendant's liability has already been established, because then claims for the recovery of damages are not deemed to be bare rights of action. Thus, follow-on actions like the ones brought by CDC would probably be accepted in Australia. The debate demonstrates, however, that it is not possible to draw a clear line between making an assignment and granting a representative a power of attorney if those concepts include a profit-sharing agreement with the assignor or the representative, respectively.

In a 2009 case,[60] the court held that the arrangement between the representative parties, the litigation funder and the solicitors to pursue the action constituted a so-called "managed investment scheme", which needed registration under the Australian Corporations Act.[61] The Australian Securities & Investments Commission (ASIC) had to step in, and issued an interim order that allowed for the "temporary operation of funded representative proceedings" without the need to comply with the Corporations Act.[62] Finally, in 2012, new legislation exempted litigation funders from the restrictions of the Corporations Act and the Australian financial services licence requirement,[63] but litigation funders must now put in place "adequate arrangements" for managing conflicts of interest. Interestingly, the Australian legislator did not seize the opportunity to impose capital adequacy requirements on litigation funders. Defendants are therefore left with no protection against the funder not being able to meet an adverse costs order. Courts provide some protection by ordering security for costs, but normally the security that is required is substantially lower than the costs actually incurred.[64]

In conclusion, legal systems with a longer tradition of litigation funding are also struggling to develop an adequate legal framework for funders. In continental Europe it is also up to policy makers to strike a balance between the interests of claimants who depend on litigation funding and the adequate protection of defendants.

5. Third-party funding, special-purpose vehicles and the necessary safeguards

5.1 Special-purpose vehicles as gap-filling entities

Mass litigation can be organized in various ways. Class or group actions are one such way, and allow for the pooling of claims through procedural instruments. Where such mechanisms do not exist in procedural law, a bundling of claims can be achieved under the substantive law, either by assignment or by granting a power of attorney to a

60 Brookfield Multiplex Limited v. International Litigation Funding Partners Pte Ltd (2009) 180 FCR (*Federal Court Reports*) 11.

61 In a similar case, a court in New South Wales interpreted a litigation funding agreement as a "financial product" as defined by the Corporations Act. As a consequence the funder was required to hold an Australian financial services licence: International Litigation Partners Pte Ltd v Chameleon Mining NL and Anor [2011] 276 ALR (*Australian Law Reports*) 138.

62 R McInnes, A Kennedy-Breit, 'Regulation of Litigation Funding – A Death Knell for Funders or a Bump in the Road?' (*Clayton Utz Insights*, 24 November 2011) <www.claytonutz.com/publications/edition/24_november_2011/20111124/regulation_of_litigation_funding-a_death_knell_for_funders_or_a_bump_in_the_road.page>.

63 Corporations Amendment Regulation 2012 (No 6) dated 12 July 2012.

64 M Legg, 'Regulation of Litigation Funding' (*UNSW Australia*, 2011) <www.clmr.unsw.edu.au/article//regulation-of-litigation-funding>.

"representative". SPVs should not generally be excluded from either type of collective redress proceedings, because complex mass damages cases may require the pooling of claims to enable an efficient preparation of the litigation and to shift the procedural risks from risk-averse individuals to entities with a risk-spreading portfolio of claims. The profit-making nature of those entities must not be mistrusted from the outset. If the private enforcement of damages claims is to be promoted as a supplement to or even a substitute for the public enforcement, we have to think about incentives, and it is not sufficient to build solely on "idealistic plaintiffs" such as consumer associations. Even organizations like these need financial support, either from members' fees or from state funds, as they typically attend to small claims that do not promise any profit. Furthermore, long-standing interest groups are mostly established to represent consumers or private investors, but they are not available for all kinds of mass damages claims. In particular, aggrieved parties who have suffered medium-sized monetary losses because of price-fixing cartels, the infringement of securities regulations or the violation of the contractual obligations of insurers, banks or other financial service providers have to organize the pursuit of their damage claims by themselves. Anybody who may be inclined to help them is not going to do so for free. This does not necessarily mean that we have to adopt the US philosophy of "justice for profit",[65] or to accept a more or less unregulated market of private enforcers. Safeguards are undeniably necessary, but the appropriate measures depend on the risks involved.

5.2 Are special-purpose vehicles representative entities or third-party funders?

The Commission's Recommendation allows associations that are founded ad hoc to represent claimants, without distinguishing situations where claims are assigned to the association from those where they are not. However, for very good reasons it requires that representative entities meet certain standards, to ensure the adequate representation of the claimants during the proceedings and any settlement negotiations. This becomes particularly important should a Member State decide on a system of opt-out proceedings. It is then not sufficient to establish the criteria for legal standing, but the courts seized must be given the power to supervise the representative entity and react if necessary. Where injured parties are free to select a representative entity and where there is even a competitive market for representatives, legislatures may be content with the implementation of some basic requirements for legal standing, such as adequate financial resources and sufficient experience in organizing the bringing of mass claims.

Litigation funding arrangements with potential litigants often do not include any assignments of claims to the funder, or a power of attorney.[66] Typically, funders agree to pay the costs and to accept the risk of an adverse costs order. SPVs do not differ in only this way from the representative entities that the Commission has in mind. SPVs also offer a special type of funding, by buying claims and assuming the part of the plaintiff themselves. This does not mean that the former claimants do not need any protection, but the situation is different and better resembles a contingency fee arrangement with the plaintiff's counsel. Claimants take up with SPVs inter alia to allow them to remain off stage during the

65 See J Kaladjdzic, P Cashman and A Longmoore, 'Justice for Profit: A Comparative Analysis of Australian, Canadian and US Third-Party Litigation Funding' (2013) 61 *American Journal of Comparative Law* 93.

66 See, for example, Legg, Park, Turner and Travers (2011) 631.

litigation. Although assignors and assignees are united by common economic interests, principal–agent conflicts, like those in client–attorney relationships, may appear. In this respect, more research is probably needed to analyse the complex triangle between the former claimants, who still retain an interest in the outcome of the litigation, the SPV, and the counsel who is closely connected to the assignee. Litigation funding by class counsels raises concern in Europe because lawyers are seen as part of the judicial system and as performing a semi-public role.[67] Thus, if class counsels have a personal interest in the outcome of the litigation, conflicts of interests between them and the class are almost inevitable. Lawyers operating on a contingency fee basis and representing a large number of unidentified class members will at some point in the proceedings not be inclined to invest more time and work in the litigation. This results in early settlement with the defendant. SPVs operating on a profit-sharing agreement may be similarly tempted, particularly if there is a close relationship with the representing lawyers. Member States that have strict rules against contingency fee agreements will therefore consider implementing safeguards to prevent law firms from establishing their own SPVs as a bypass.[68]

Claimants who sell their claims (which are sometimes worth several millions of Euros) to an (independent) SPV are aware of the profit-making character of the assignee and the risks involved. Whereas lawyers, as members of a regulated profession, must comply with ethical and professional standards and therefore legitimately enjoy public confidence, SPVs do not. The relationship is a purely contractual matter, like the relationship that exists when there is funding by ATE insurance.[69] If assignors are to be protected against unfair contract terms or inadequate performance by SPVs, this is a matter of substantive law regarding the contractual relationship between the parties to the assignment. Therefore, SPVs like CDC are different from representative entities like interest groups or consumer associations, and must be considered to be litigation funders.

5.3 Protection of claimants against special-purpose vehicles as litigation funders

The Commission's Recommendation is anxious to protect both claimants and defendants against the risks of (third-party) funding. Recommendation No. 16 requires Member States to ensure that third-party funders do not seek to influence procedural decisions. It would seem to be unrealistic to try to avoid any influence. However, if a third party assumes a procedural risk, she cannot be completely denied the right to have a voice in the conduct of the litigation. Typically, settlements are a major source of conflicts of interest between claimants and third-party funders. Litigation funders are interested in a return on their investment. Settlements are attractive for them only if the claimants (and thus they themselves) receive money. Therefore, unlike counsels who can always claim compensation for their legal representation, litigation funders are not interested in settlements under which the defendant offers only coupons to the class members or specified services like the repair or replacement of goods. Such conflicts of interest typically occur in consumer cases.

67 S Voet, 'The Crux of the Matter: Funding and Financing Collective Redress Mechanisms' in B Hess, M Bergström and E Storskrubb (eds), *EU Civil Justice, Swedish Studies in European Law* (Oxford: Hart Publishing 2015) 201.

68 The German courts have also declared an assignment of claims by a client to his lawyer to be void on the grounds that it violates the prohibition on contingency fee arrangements and professional ethics, Court of Appeals Frankfurt, *Neue Juristische Wochenschrift* (NJW) 2011, 3,724.

69 Voet (2015) 17.

In cartel damages cases, SPVs like CDC will normally only take on damages claims, and the assignments refer only to pecuniary claims.

In other cases – mainly consumer mass damages cases – in the absence of specific legal provisions on third-party funding it will often be the task of the courts seized to prevent at least any undue influence by third-party funders, for example by denying court approval to particular settlements. This requires, however, that the court is aware of the third-party funding. Where the involvement of litigation funders does not become obvious automatically (as in the case of an assignment or power of attorney), plaintiffs should be required by law to disclose the third-party funding; this is recommended by the Commission's Recommendation No. 4. However, the disclosure must be general in nature and details should be disclosed – if they are disclosed at all – only to the court. The defendant must not have access to the funding agreement or other details, because of the high potential for misuse. A defendant party who is aware of the limited financial resources of the plaintiff's side is likely to draw the proceedings out until the claimant runs out of money.

5.4 Protection of defendants against special-purpose vehicles

Collective redress proceedings involve high amounts in controversy and the litigation costs are often higher than in normal proceedings. Where cost-shifting rules apply, successful defendants face the risk of going away empty-handed, and the "loser pays" rule fails to prevent unmeritorious actions if plaintiffs do not bear a considerable risk because they do not have the resources to meet adverse costs orders in any way.

5.4.1 Abolition of the "loser pays" rule?

One option to get rid of the problem could be the abolition of cost shifting, although this would be done at the cost of raising other issues. European countries traditionally apply the "loser pays" rule,[70] in contrast to the American "rule of cost", and the German system is particularly generous in the handling of cost shifting. In principle, all adequate and necessary costs are reimbursable, and the recoverability gap is low compared to other countries. A system of clearly and legally fixed attorneys' fees and court fees, which both depend on the amount in dispute, makes litigation costs predictable,[71] and there is not much dispute over costs orders. Other Member States like the Netherlands[72] or England and Wales[73] do not promise the defendant a full reimbursement of his costs from the outset. Nevertheless,

70 C Hodges, S Vogenauer and M Tulibacka, 'The Oxford Study on Costs and Funding of Civil Litigation' in C Hodges, S Vogenauer and M Tulibacka (eds), *The Costs and Funding of Civil Litigation* (Oxford: Hart Publishing 2010) 3.

71 J Peysner, 'England and Wales' in C Hodges, S Vogenauer and M Tulibacka (eds), *The Costs and Funding of Civil Litigation* (Oxford: Hart Publishing 2010) 289, 302. For an example that compares the costs for a particular case in the US and in Germany see A Junker, 'Die Steuerung des Zivilprozesses durch das Kosten- und Streitwertrecht im anglo-amerikanischen System' (2015) 128 *Zeitschrift für Zivilprozess* 3ff, 19.

72 ML Tuil, 'The Netherlands' in C Hodges, S Vogenauer and M Tulibacka (eds), *The Costs and Funding of Civil Litigation* (Oxford: Hart Publishing 2010) 401, 415ff.

73 The rules in England and Wales have changed considerably with the Jackson review; for details, see Peysner in this volume, and also J Peysner, 'England and Wales' in C Hodges, S Vogenauer and M Tulibacka (eds), *The Costs and Funding of Civil Litigation* (Oxford: Hart Publishing 2010) 313ff; C Hodges, 'Settlement and Its Pitfalls in England and Wales' in C Hodges and A Stadler (eds), *Resolving Mass Disputes – ADR and Settlement of Mass Disputes* (Cheltenham: Edward Elgar 2013) 106ff.

there is widespread consensus in Europe (and beyond[74]) that the "loser pays" rule is an important instrument to prevent claimants from bringing bad claims.[75] Today, under German legal doctrine, a plaintiff whose case is dismissed is not considered to have acted wrongly by filing the action. Cost shifting is simply a matter of fairness between the parties.[76] A plaintiff who wins the case is simply put in a position as if his claim had never been denied. Vice versa the defendant who wins the case is in a position as if no claim had ever been made on him.[77] Each party who starts litigation or forces his opponent to do so runs the same risk of bearing the costs arising from the proceedings. Admittedly, where the outcome of the litigation is not easy to predict, claimants have to make a difficult decision before starting litigation, and cost-shifting rules may be an obstacle to access to justice. In the United States, the American rule of cost promotes private enforcement, but it is also one of the reasons why settlements can be extorted from defendants. As John Coffee[78] has explained, the abolition of the "loser pays" rule, unlike the adoption of contingency fees, was not primarily the result of an American "access to justice" movement in the eighteenth century. The shift from the English "loser pays" rule to the American rule was predominantly the result of the bar's attitude. Lawyers simply wanted to be paid by their clients on the basis of the terms of the agreement between them, and did not want to enforce a claim for their fees (in practice only part of their fees because cost-shifting rules did not allow full recoverability of fees) against the other party.

In Germany, there is virtually no debate on the "loser pays" rule. Problems with access to justice arising from the cost-shifting rule are mitigated by certain provisions that allow courts to reduce the amount of controversy in litigation and thus also to reduce court fees and lawyers' fees.[79] DG Competition's proposal in its White Paper of 2008[80] to abolish the "loser pays" rule in order to encourage private enforcement of cartel damages claims stoked fears in the business sector that the US class action system might finally find its way to Europe. The Commission's Recommendation of 2013 avoids this mistake and considers cost shifting as an important safeguard in collective redress proceedings.[81] The "loser pays" principle is, however, closely related, at least in Germany, to a rather formal definition of

74 For fee-shifting rules in Canada see ES Knutsen and J Walker, 'Canada' in C Hodges, S Vogenauer and M Tulibacka (eds), *The Costs and Funding of Civil Litigation* (Oxford: Hart Publishing 2010) 239, 251f; for Australia see C Cameron, 'Australia' in C Hodges, S Vogenauer and M Tulibacka (eds), *The Costs and Funding of Civil Litigation* (Oxford: Hart Publishing 2010) 195, 201; G Cazalet, 'Unresolved Issues – Costs in Public Interest Litigation in Australia' (2010) 29 *Civil Justice Quarterly* 108.

75 R Stürner, *Die Aufklärungspflicht der Parteien des Zivilprozesses* (Tübingen: Mohr 1976), 262 ("Filterwirkung"); G Wagner and R Harbst, 'Offers to Settle – ein Modell für das deutsche Zivilprozessrecht' (2007) 120 *Zeitschrift für Zivilprozess* 269ff, 270; for the history of the "loser pays" rule in Europe see G Kodek, 'Funktion und Dogmatik des Prozesskostenersatzes aus österreichischer Sicht' (2015) 128 *Zeitschrift für Zivilprozess* 29ff, 30ff, for the effect of filtering out unmeritorious claims, see 50ff; the control function of cost-shifting rule is also discussed by C Wolf, 'Steuerung des Zivilprozesses durch Streitwert- und Kostenrecht' (2015) 128 *Zeitschrift für Zivilprozess* 69ff.

76 Kodek (2015) 48 ("Gerechtigkeitsanliegen").

77 P Chvosta, *Prozesskostenrecht* (Vienna: Manz 2001) 14ff.

78 Coffee (2015) 23.

79 For example, Sec 89a Antitrust Act: a party must establish prima facie evidence that the full amount of litigation cost would place her economically in a difficult position.

80 COM (2008) 165 Final, para 2.8.:"National courts may therefore have to be empowered to derogate from this [loser pays rule] principle, for example by guaranteeing that an unsuccessful claimant will not have to bear the defendants' costs that were unreasonably or vexatiously incurred or are otherwise excessive."

81 Recommendation No 13.

who is liable for costs. An adverse costs order can address only a person who has formally become a party to the litigation. Thus, with respect to the claimant's side it makes a difference whether an SPV is acting on its own behalf on the basis of an assignment of claims (which makes only the SPV a party to the litigation) or is acting on a power of attorney that leaves the injured person as the claimant and potentially liable for the defendant's litigation costs. This is a consequence that needs to be reconsidered.

5.4.2 Safeguards to protect the defendant against poor claimants?

It does not follow automatically from the "loser pays" principle that defendants deserve protection against poor claimants. As mentioned above, the German legislature has so far taken the position that defendants cannot ask for security for costs unless the plaintiff is domiciled outside the European Union and does not have sufficient assets in Germany.[82] Thus defendants are left with a considerable risk in "normal" proceedings. It does not seem necessary to change the principle as such. Modifications should, however, be considered where the claimant's side increases the defendant's risk by bundling numerous claims into a single lawsuit. In the German system for legal fees, a higher amount in dispute through aggregated claims means higher fees and thus a higher risk that defendants will be left with a claimant who might be judgment-proof. Safeguards such as security for costs should apply equally to all plaintiffs, and must not depend on the involvement of third-party funders, representative entities or assignees.[83] A general legal obligation for claimants to provide security for the defendant's costs in collective redress proceedings will discourage private enforcement and thus prevent the necessary deterrent effect. Instead the court, upon application by the defendant, must have absolute discretion to decide, on a case-by-case basis, whether security is necessary. The plaintiff's ability to meet an adverse costs order can be taken into account, but his lack of resources – which is only one criterion among others – should become important particularly where he has taken steps in relation to his assets that would make it difficult to enforce an order for costs against him.[84] Where access to the courts depends on the pooling of claims in the hands of a special-purpose vehicle that specializes in preparing litigation of the relevant type, the courts must carefully balance the prospects of the claim (see below, 3), the public interest in the effective handling of mass damages claims and the defendant's need for protection. Further criteria may be as follows:

1. As it is difficult, if not impossible, to predict at the beginning of the proceedings what the financial situation of the claimant might be at the end, costs orders should be considered separately for each instance. Where an appeal is lodged, the situation must be re-considered.
2. Where an assignment of claims to an SPV has been made, the validity of the assignment must not depend on the financial situation of the SPV. SPVs should be allowed to operate on the basis of an assignment of claims or on a power of attorney. With respect to security for costs, the two situations should be treated equally, and a transfer of claims to an SPV must not, in general, relieve the assignors from any liability for the

82 Sec. 111 German Civil Procedure Code.

83 For a different attitude of some scholars in investment treaty arbitration see the contribution by E de Brabandere in this volume.

84 For a similar rule see Rule 25.13 CPR England and Wales.

defendant's costs. Requiring security from the plaintiff's side seems likely where the assignment to the SPV has been made by the assignor with a view to avoiding the possibility of a costs order being made against him.[85] In such a situation the courts should be free to make an order for security for costs directly against the assignor. However, where the claimants have legitimate reasons to seek the help of litigation funders, security orders should be the exception.

3. Courts must apply a preliminary merits test before making an order for security for costs. If the claimant party has a good chance of winning its case, no order for security should be issued. With respect to follow-on damages actions in cartel cases, in particular, security for legal costs should be the exception. Since, at the least, the defendant's liability on the merits is not in dispute, the proceedings cannot be deemed from the outset to be without merit. As a general rule, whenever the liability of the defendant as such has been established by an administrative or regulatory body or a court, the claimant party's interest in bringing damages claims prevails over the defendant's risk of ultimately being left with the costs.

6. Conclusion

Third-party funding and special-purpose vehicles acting as claimants in mass damages situation are a relatively new phenomenon in Europe. A new market is developing that lacks regulation, but it should not be banned from the outset. The courts in Germany have, in the cement cartel case, added new handicaps for the private enforcement of mass damages claims. In Germany, SPVs are in a difficult situation today, and cannot sue on their own behalf without facing obstacles that normal plaintiffs do not face. To be on the safe side, they have to offer security for costs more or less automatically, which is contrary to existing rules and makes litigation more expensive.

In order to provide a clear framework for litigation funding and the activities of special-purpose vehicles, legislative activities would be necessary in most Member States. But unsurprisingly policy makers are reluctant to come forward and, instead, often leave the field to self-regulation such as the English Code of Conduct or the Dutch Claimcode.[86] Such instruments are non-binding and their scope of application is often limited or unclear, and, in any case, non-compliance is without any sanctions. From a legal perspective, this type of "soft law" can provide some guidance, but no clear framework for the operation of third-party funders or SPVs. For some Member States another option could be establishing a quality control system for representative entities and/or third-party funders with a catalogue of requirements and a formal accreditation process. In such a system, a successful accreditation of SPVs or third-party funders could either be a requirement for legal standing before courts and for the permission to operate on the market, or by awarding a kind of certification provide at least orientation and guidance for claimants when seeking help in the enforcement of their claims. The European Commission seems to have in mind such a mechanism for long-standing representative entities. Of course, such quality control

85 For a similar rule see Rule 25.14 CPR England and Wales.

86 For details see I Tzankova and D Hensler, 'Collective Settlements in the Netherlands: Some Empirical Observations' in C Hodges and A Stadler (eds), *Resolving Mass Disputes – ADR and Settlement of Mass Claims* (Cheltenham: Edward Elgar 2013) 91. The text of the claimcode is available at: <http://stichtingservice.nl/wp-content/uploads/2014/07/claimcode-voor-claimstichtingen.pdf>.

systems could include certain requirements with respect to the financial resources of representative entities or third-party funders. Apart from that national legislatures may find it difficult to agree on the enactment of such terms, it might nevertheless be adequate to decide on the necessity of security for costs on a case-by-case balancing of party interests even though a basic financial strength of the claimant or third-party funder is guaranteed.

In Germany, comprehensive regulation of litigation funding would be premature and policy makers would first want to gain more experience of the new phenomenon. Nevertheless, a trend to drive SPVs away from Germany cannot be accepted, because they fill a gap in Member States in which no particular instruments of collective redress exist and no "idealistic plaintiffs" are available to represent claimants. SPVs and litigation funders should therefore be able to operate on the basis of assignments, but legislation must provide necessary safeguards for defendants. In the absence of comprehensive regulation of third-party funding in Germany, specific rules for security of cost orders are a minimum requirement. Such rules should provide safeguards to be used flexibly, and they need to be based on a careful balancing of interests. The general rule that plaintiffs must provide security for costs only in exceptional cases should be retained. Access to courts must not be restricted by a general requirement for such a guarantee in favour of the defendant. Collective redress proceedings that pool numerous claims into a single piece of litigation may require special protection for the defendant(s). Legislatures must provide guidance for the courts to make case-by-case decisions, and should particularly encourage follow-on actions and the enforcement of other meritorious claims.

Bibliography

Bentham J., 'A Defence of Usury, Letter XII, Maintenance and Champerty' in J. Bowring (ed.), *The Works of Jeremy Bentham* (Vol 3 Part 1, Edinburgh: William Tait 1843) 1–31.

Cameron C., 'Australia' in C. Hodges, S. Vogenauer and M. Tulibacka (eds), *The Costs and Funding of Civil Litigation* (Oxford: Hart Publishing 2010) 195.

Cazalet G., 'Unresolved Issues – Costs in Public Interest Litigation in Australia' (2010) 29 *Civil Justice Quarterly* 108.

Chvosta P., *Prozesskostenrecht* (Vienna: Manz 2001).

Coffee J.C., *Entrepreneurial Litigation: Its Rise, Fall and Future* (Cambridge: Harvard University Press 2015).

Hodges C., 'Settlement and its Pitfalls in England and Wales' in C. Hodges and A. Stadler (eds), *Resolving Mass Disputes – ADR and Settlement of Mass Disputes* (Cheltenham: Edward Elgar 2013) 106.

—— S. Vogenauer and M. Tulibacka, 'The Oxford Study on Costs and Funding of Civil Litigation' in C. Hodges, S. Vogenauer and M. Tulibacka (eds), *The Costs and Funding of Civil Litigation* (Oxford: Hart Publishing 2010) 3.

Junker A., 'Die Steuerung des Zivilprozesses durch das Kosten- und Streitwertrecht im angloamerikanischen System' (2015) 128 *Zeitschrift für Zivilprozess* 3.

Kaladjdzic J., P. Cashman and A. Longmoore, 'Justice for Profit: A Comparative Analysis of Australian, Canadian and US Third-Party Litigation Funding' (2013) 61 *American Journal of Comparative Law* 93.

Knutsen E.S. and J. Walker, 'Canada' in C. Hodges, S. Vogenauer and M. Tulibacka (eds), *The Costs and Funding of Civil Litigation* (Oxford: Hart Publishing 2010) 239.

Kodek G., 'Funktion und Dogmatik des Prozesskostenersatzes aus österreichischer Sicht' (2015) 128 *Zeitschrift für Zivilprozess* 29.

Legg M., 'Regulation of Litigation Funding' (*UNSW Australia*, 2011) <www.clmr.unsw.edu.au/article//regulation-of-litigation-funding>.

—— E. Park, N. Turner and L. Travers, 'The Rise and Regulation of Litigation Funding in Australia' (2011) 38 *Northern Kentucky Law Review* 625.

Lord Neuberger, 'From Barratry, Maintenance and Champerty to Litigation Funding' (Harbour Litigation Funding First Annual Lecture, Gray's Inn, 8 May 2013).

Makatsch T. and A. Volker, 'Kartellschadensersatz – Goodbye Deutschland?' (2015) *Wirtschaft und Wettbewerb* 461.

McInnes R. and A. Kennedy-Breit, 'Regulation of Litigation Funding – A Death Knell for Funders or a Bump in the Road?' (*Clayton Utz Insights,* 24 November 2011) <www.claytonutz.com/publications/edition/24_november_2011/20111124/regulation_of_litigation_funding-a_death_knell_for_funders_or_a_bump_in_the_road.page>.

Mulheron R., 'A Channel Apart: Why the United Kingdom Has Departed from the European Commission's Recommendation on Class Actions' (2015) 17 *Cambridge Yearbook of European Legal Studies* 36.

Peysner J., 'England and Wales' in C. Hodges, S. Vogenauer and M. Tulibacka (eds), *The Costs and Funding of Civil Litigation* (Oxford: Hart Publishing 2010) 289.

Stadler A., 'Die Bündelung von gleichgerichteten Ansprüchen durch Inkassozession – Geschäftsmodelle zur Prozessfinanzierung auf dem Prüfstand' (2014) *Juristenzeitung* 613.

—— 'Schadensersatzklagen im Kartellrecht – Forum Shopping Welcome!' (2015) *Juristenzeitung* 1138.

Stürner R., *Die Aufklärungspflicht der Parteien des Zivilprozesses* (Tübingen: Mohr 1976).

The Costs and Funding of Civil Litigation (Oxford: Hart Publishing 2010).

Tuil M.L., 'The Netherlands' in C. Hodges, S. Vogenauer and M. Tulibacka (eds), *The Costs and Funding of Civil Litigation* (Oxford: Hart Publishing 2010) 401.

Tzankova I. and D. Hensler, 'Collective Settlements in the Netherlands: Some Empirical Observations' in C. Hodges and A. Stadler (eds), *Resolving Mass Disputes – ADR and settlement of mass claims* (Cheltenham: Edward Elgar 2013) 91.

Voet S., 'The Crux of the Matter: Funding and Financing Collective Redress Mechanisms' in B. Hess, M. Bergström and E. Storskrubb (eds), *EU Civil Justice, Swedish Studies in European Law* (Oxford: Hart Publishing 2015) 201.

Wagner G. and R. Harbst, 'Offers to Settle – ein Modell für das deutsche Zivilprozessrecht' (2007) 120 *Zeitschrift für Zivilprozess* 269.

Wäktare E., 'Private Enforcement: Settlement between Claimant CDC and Hydrogen Peroxide Cartellist Kemira (Finland)' (2014) 5 *Journal of European Competition Law & Practice* 701.

Walker J., 'Policy and Regulatory Issues in Litigation Funding Revisited' (2014) 55 *Canadian Business Law J.* 85.

Wolf C., 'Steuerung des Zivilprozesses durch Streitwert- und Kostenrecht' (2015) 128 *Zeitschrift für Zivilprozess* 69.

10 Entrepreneurial motives in Dutch collective redress

Adding fuel to a 'compensation culture'?

Ilja Tillema

1. Introduction

A collective redress mechanism can be considered pointless without an initiator that pursues redress. To undertake such pursuits, the European Commission and many member states strongly rely upon non-profit representative bodies as a more trusted alternative to the US entrepreneurial lawyer.[1] This focus on consumer and other non-profit organizations has been incited by the fear that commerce-driven parties may lead to an 'American-style compensation culture', as entrepreneurial lawyers are believed to primarily pursue their own interests. On the other hand, literature suggests that a financial incentive (profit) for a (third) party to bring an action might be desirable, or even necessary, for a well-functioning collective redress mechanism.[2]

The debate on how to fulfil the goals of collective redress without also creating incentives for abuse mainly builds upon American experiences. While these experiences can obviously provide valuable information, caution is required given the difference between the legal systems and cultures in the USA and Europe. Therefore, it may be worthwhile shifting focus to the experience of a European jurisdiction with collective redress. Dutch law is a case in point. As the Dutch legislative framework seems to have opened a gateway to efficient and effective collective redress, useful material on the practical operation of the law can be collected from this jurisdiction. Notably, initiators with a more or less overt entrepreneurial objective have also entered the collective redress market in the last decade. To date, Dutch policy makers and courts have taken a rather liberal stance on the topic. So how has this approach shaped collective redress practice, and vice versa? This chapter maps the evolution of Dutch collective redress and the ensuing funding practices over recent years. In so doing, I aim to assess whether and to what extent entrepreneurial motives in collective redress have indeed – as some assume – fuelled a compensation culture. Is there an increase in the number of claims and, if so, is there evidence that entrepreneurial organizations cause this increase and/or bring frivolous claims?[3] These questions are relevant in light of a recent draft legislative proposal to further extend the current Dutch collective action regulation for claims for damages. This proposal has met with heavy criticism, including claims that it would only further develop a compensation culture. The data this

1 See Recommendations on common principles for injunctive and compensatory collective redress mechanisms in the Member States concerning violations of rights granted under Union Law (2013/396/EU), for instance, point 4, and Communication COM(2013) 401 final. Herewith, the EC focuses on private collective redress to complement public enforcement.

2 See para 3.

3 See para 4.1 for the scope of this assessment.

chapter provides may help clarify the role of entrepreneurial motives in creating or sustaining a collective redress 'compensation culture'.

The chapter is structured as follows. In Section 2, I give a brief overview of the Dutch regulatory framework of collective redress and its market. Section 3 provides some background information on compensation culture, including a definition, and frames it for the purpose of this chapter. The chapter continues by presenting and analysing data regarding (entrepreneurial motives in) collective redress in the Netherlands, gathered through case law and document analysis (Section 4). It indicates the number and types of collective claims that the courts dealt with, the types of initiators, and how the courts ruled on organizations' standing and cases' merits. The chapter closes with some concluding remarks in Section 5.

2. An overview of the Dutch legal framework for collective redress and its market

Dutch law provides for two legal proceedings that are designed specifically for collective redress: the collective action and the Collective Settlement of Mass Damage Act (WCAM).[4] These two legal proceedings can be summarized as follows.

First, since 1994, section 3:305a DCC has granted the authority to either a foundation (*stichting*) or an association (*vereniging*) with full legal capacity to bring a collective action to court. This representative action may concern any type of civil case and must represent similar interests of other persons. The organization's aim needs to be stated in its articles of association and should also be demonstrated in practice. Before bringing a claim, the organization must have made sufficient attempts to reach a settlement through consultation with the party held liable. If it has not done so, in general, the organization will be found inadmissible. This consultation requirement does not constitute a very high threshold to obtain standing: a two-week period after the defendant has received a request for such consultations is sufficient. Although the term might suggest otherwise, the actual degree of representativeness is not a requirement for a representative organization to obtain standing to bring a collective action. The collective action procedure does not allow the representative organization to claim for damages (no compensatory collective action). As mentioned, the 2014 draft to extend current regulation to allow representative organizations to claim for damages has endured heavy criticism, including that it would only further develop a compensation culture.[5] Currently, collective actions are primarily brought in order to obtain a declaratory judgment that states the

4 Section 3:305a Dutch Civil Code (DCC), and section 7:907-910 DCC and section 1013–1018 Dutch Code of Civil Procedure (DCCP). See for more information on various aspects of both instruments, for instance, IN Tzankova and D Lunsingh Scheurleer, 'The Netherlands' (2009) 622 *Annals of the American Academy of Political and Social Science* 149ff; T Arons and WH van Boom, 'Beyond Tulips and Cheese: Exporting Mass Securities Claim Settlements from the Netherlands' (2010) 21(6) *European Business Law Review* 857ff; F Weber and WH van Boom, 'Dutch Treat: the Dutch Collective Settlement of Mass Damage Act (WCAM 2005)' (2011) 1 *Contratto e Impresa/Europa* 69ff. This chapter focuses on collective redress through collective action and WCAM, but a few other roads may also lead to the settlement of mass claims in the Netherlands. See, for instance, N Frenk, 'Bundeling van vorderingen' (2003) *Tijdschrift voor Privaatrecht* 1,418–1,423; and I Tillema, 'Cessie als instrument ter afwikkeling van massaschadezaken' (2014) 12 *Maandblad voor Vermogensrecht* 333.

5 In 2014, a consultation document on the draft bill was issued. See *Kamerstukken II* 2011/12, 33 000-XIII, 14 (parliamentary motion) and the consultation document (including an English summary) <www.internetconsultatie.nl/motiedijksma>. For criticism, see, for instance, the responses to the consultation document from Dutch employers' organizations VNO-NCW and MKB-Nederland, and from the U.S. Chamber Institute for Legal Reform; <www.internetconsultatie.nl/motiedijksma/reacties>.

legal relationship between parties, such as the establishment that the defendant has committed a tort against the aggrieved parties (hereafter: class members). If the interests are suitable for bundling to provide an efficient and effective legal protection, the common points of law will be judged separately from the particular individual circumstances that may or may not actually lead to compensation, such as contributory negligence. The judgment has limited res judicata effect: it only binds the representative organization and the defendant, not the class members. Nevertheless, the verdict can provide a basis for settlement negotiations – possibly followed by a WCAM settlement – or for an individual proceeding to seek monetary compensation.

In addition to the collective action regulation, the WCAM was established in 2005. In short, this procedure provides for one or more representative organizations on the one hand, and the alleged liable party on the other, to submit a joint application to the Amsterdam Court of Appeal requesting it to declare legally binding a settlement that holds rights to compensation for the class members. A WCAM settlement may follow a previous test case or collective action, or may have arisen fully out of court. As part of the WCAM proceedings, the Amsterdam Court of Appeal assesses whether the interests of the class members are sufficiently guaranteed – for example, whether the amount of the compensation awarded is reasonable. During the proceedings, other representative organizations and individual interested parties have the right to bring forward objections against the settlement. If the court declares the settlement binding, all individuals affected by the mass damage event are bound by the settlement, unless they opt out within a certain period (of at least three months) following the announcement of the order.

Thus, both in collective actions and WCAM settlements, the pursuit of collective redress is undertaken by a representative organization that is legally structured as either a foundation or association. According to Dutch law, foundations and associations are legal entities established for a particular goal (usually but not exclusively a non-profit goal).[6] Although both entities are allowed to be driven by profits, profits cannot be paid out to founders or (board) members. Any profits made must be distributed in line with the goal of the foundation or association. The representative organizations that can bring a collective action or enter into a WCAM settlement are not otherwise regulated by law or bound by professional rules and rules of conduct, unlike Dutch practising attorneys. The organizations may complement or compete with attorneys' legal services in the field of collective redress, as attorneys may have a monopoly on legal representation in court-based civil litigation, but not on other legal services. However, an increase in the establishment of (ad hoc) representative organizations after mass damage events, combined with media criticism about the performance of certain organizations, led a group of practitioners to establish the *Claimcode*, a self-regulatory initiative on good governance that went into effect in July 2011.[7] Moreover, in 2013, an addition was made to the admissibility test of section 3:305a (2) DCC. This addition specified that a representative organization will also not obtain standing if its claim does not sufficiently guarantee the interests of the class members.[8] The aim of the provision is not to discourage representative organizations from entering the

6 Section 2:26ff DCC and 2:285ff DCC.

7 The *Claimcode* is available at <www.sbrd.nl/media/106/Claimcode.pdf>, 11ff. See also the Justification Document, JH Lemstra and RW Okhuijsen, 'Consultatiedocument zelfregulering claimstichtingen' (2010) 6 *Tijdschrift voor Financieel recht* 160ff. See, critical, E Bauw and T Bruinen, 'Slow Start of veeg teken?' (2013) 88(3) *NJB* 164.

8 See *Kamerstukken II* 2011/12, 33 126, 3, 4–5, and *Kamerstukken II* 2012/13, 33 126, 7, 10ff.

market in general, because they play a valuable role in the settlement of mass damage cases, but to discourage organizations that have a solely entrepreneurial objective. This entrepreneurial objective or motive is mainly expressed in the shape of a contingency fee. Although the opportunities for attorneys to engage in contingency fee arrangements are restricted,[9] this constraint does not apply to representative organizations. Such organizations may charge membership fees or ask for donations to fund their activities, but some (additionally) conclude contingency fee agreements with individual class members, and thus gain part of the damages in case of success. So far, within the context of collective redress, government policy has been to not further regulate these practices. On various occasions, the minister has attributed an important role to the aforementioned *Claimcode*, and to courts to assess the representative organization's standing; however, the minister explicitly stated that the court's assessment of a representative organization should not involve a test on the organization's business model, such as what contingency fee percentage is reasonable.[10] The upcoming legislative proposal to allow representative organizations to claim for damages will probably (re)boost this debate. This will also be the case in light of the European Commission's Recommendation 32, which states that for cases of private third-party funding of compensatory collective redress, it is prohibited to base remuneration on the amount of the settlement reached or the compensation awarded unless that funding arrangement is regulated by a public authority.

3. The fear of a compensation culture

Before presenting and analysing data regarding entrepreneurial motives in Dutch collective redress in Section 4, I will shed some light on the existence of a compensation culture in the Netherlands, or rather on the lack of proof thereof.

For decades, a reference to 'American situations' has provided an ominous motto, however ambiguous, to oppose the introduction of certain elements into the Dutch legal system.[11] One of the situations the expression refers to is the – alleged[12] – claim of compensation culture in the United States. Not infrequently, the picture is painted along the following lines. After any mishap, dollar-eyed individuals will rush to court to sue well-off modern-day Goliaths, with judges or juries awarding them sky-high damages, cheered on and assisted by relentless profit-seeking bounty hunters disguised as attorneys who then

9 An attorney's remuneration can be based on the outcome of litigation in the form of a success fee, that is, a fixed fee or hourly (cost-effective base) rate, which in case of success is increased with a 'bonus' rate or a percentage of the settlement or award upon judgment. In 2014, the government allowed a five-year pilot in personal injury cases that, under strict circumstances, lifts the ban on contingency fees; see Directive of the Dutch Bar Association, Stcrt. 25 July 2013, 20779.

10 For instance, in *Kamerstukken II* 2011/12, 33 126, 3 and 6, and *Kamerstukken II* 2012/13, 33 126, 7, 10ff and 19ff.

11 See, for instance, *Kamerstukken II* 2011/12, 33 126, 6. For comparable references to such situations in a European context, see some contributions in B Hess et al., *Evaluation of Contributions to the Public Consultation and Hearing*' (available at <http://ec.europa.eu/competition/consultations/2011_collective_redress/index_en.html>); S Wernicke, 'Von Sammelklagen und Kaperbriefen – Zum Kiobel-Urteil des US Supreme Court' (2013) 24(11) *Europäische Zeitschrift für Wirtschaftsrecht* 401ff; and <www.justicenotprofit.co.uk>.

12 See on myths and realities of US class action; for instance, DR Hensler, 'Revisiting the Monster: New Myths and Realities of Class Action and Other Large Scale Litigation' (2001) 11(2) *Duke Journal of Comparative and International Law* 179ff.

prompt most of the damages treasure to flow in their own coffers, leaving behind disillusioned Davids and bankruptcy-filing Goliaths. Unfortunately, such references to 'American situations', or compensation culture, are not always made with a solid basis, turning a possibly reasonable fear into little more than empty rhetoric. The more reliable arguments are also built largely on American experiences. According to opponents, collective redress and its funding by way of contingency fees will, among other things, contribute to a compensation culture by increasing the number and amount of claims, particularly frivolous ones.[13] Similarly, proponents have stated that the costs and risks of collective redress are decisive thresholds to access justice, and that the funding of litigation through third parties with a stake in litigation may diminish this threshold.[14] This will not only improve access to justice, but also better confront norm violators with the consequences of their behaviour. Law and economics scholars have stated that neither economic models nor empirical evidence support the conventional wisdom that a contingency fee system will lead to 'American situations' such as an increase of frivolous litigation.[15]

There is a practical lack of real evidence from the Netherlands concerning the existence of a compensation culture, as Haazen and Spier noted in their 1996 white paper on the expanding scope of liability law.[16] In 1998, following signs of an increasing appeal on liability law, the Dutch government commissioned a working group to study the development of a compensation culture in the Netherlands.[17] According to the government, the (further) development of a compensation culture was undesirable. This position was linked with the government's objective to solve conflicts within society as much as possible, rather than them ending up at a judge's plate. In its report, the working group defined compensation culture as a culture in which citizens claim for damages on a regular basis and for high amounts, without this necessarily leading to litigation.[18] The working group and, subsequently, the Dutch government[19] agreed that rather than discouraging the use of liability law or reducing the protection of aggrieved parties, policy should balance the negative and positive effects of a compensation culture and mainly aim to prevent excesses, such as extreme damages awards and an increasing demand for legal services instigated by providers

13 See, for instance, *Kamerstukken II* 2011/12, 33 126, 6, and certain – stakeholders' – responses to both Dutch and European consultation documents on collective redress; see nn 5 and 11.

14 S Keske, A Renda and R Van den Bergh, 'Financing and Group Litigation' in ML Tuil and L Visscher (eds), *New Trends in Financing Civil Litigation in Europe – A Legal, Empirical and Economic Analysis* (Cheltenham: Edward Elgar 2011); L Visscher and T Schepens, 'A Law and Economics Approach to Cost Shifting, Fee Arrangements and Legal Expense Insurance' in ML Tuil and L Visscher (eds), *New Trends in Financing Civil Litigation in Europe – A Legal, Empirical and Economic Analysis* (Cheltenham: Edward Elgar 2011); IN Tzankova, 'Funding of Mass Disputes: Lessons from the Netherlands' (2012) 8(3) *Journal of Law, Economics & Policy* 549ff.

15 See, for instance, HO Kerkmeester, 'Contingency Fees en letselschade: een rechtseconomische analyse' (1999) 47 *Verkeersrecht* 257ff; M Faure, T Hartlief and N Philipsen, *Resultaatgerelateerde beloningssystemen voor advocaten* (Maastricht: METRO 2006); M Faure, T Hartlief and N Philipsen, 'Funding of Personal Injury Litigation and Claims Culture. Evidence from the Netherlands' (2006) 2(2) Utrecht Law Review 1; M Faure and T Hartlief, 'Claimcultuur en beloningssystemen' in WH van Boom, I Giesen and M Smit (eds), *Civilologie: opstellen over empirie en privaatrecht* (Den Haag: Boom Juridische Uitgevers 2012).

16 OA Haazen and J Spier, 'Feitelijke ontwikkelingen en verzekerbaarheid' in A Bolt and J Spier (eds), *De uitdijende reikwijdte van de aansprakelijkheid uit onrechtmatige daad* (Preadvies NJV, Zwolle: WEJ Tjeenk Willink 1996).

17 *Kamerstukken II* 1998/99, 26 630, 1.

18 E Bauw and F van Dijk, *Naar een claimcultuur in Nederland?* (Den Haag: Ministerie van Justitie 1999).

19 *Kamerstukken II* 1998/99, 26 630, 1, 9.

of such services (ambulance chasing). The working group and government attributed such unwelcome negative effects to, inter alia, the use of contingency fees and no-cure-no-pay arrangements. Although the working group and government acknowledged possible positive aspects of these instruments, and stated that preventive measures should be carefully geared towards the type and severity of the excess, the working group concluded that these instruments should not be introduced in the Dutch legal system as they would strongly promote a compensation culture.[20] The working group also stated that it had noticed a change in claim behaviour, which it said required vigilance; however, it had not found direct proof of the existence of a compensation culture, as the available data were insufficient to accurately assess a change or development in claim behaviour. A number of quantitative reports have followed since, with the aim of curing the lack of data on dispute resolution.[21] For instance, in 2003, Eshuis conducted an empirical study specifically on the development in legal disputes that are brought to Dutch civil courts.[22] Eshuis found that the claim frequency had hardly increased between 1997 and 2000, and showed that although the amount of money claimed had risen in the given period, the awarded amounts had not grown to the same degree. According to various other reports, the number of civil cases rose steadily until 2009 and has started to decline since.[23] The causes for this decline are under debate,[24] but the aforementioned reports have not yet provided real evidence for the existence of a compensation culture. Moreover, the reports do not specifically address mechanisms of collective redress and their 'role' in (the development of) a compensation culture. Within this domain, real evidence is even more lacking.[25] In 2013, Tzankova and Hensler conducted case studies on four WCAM settlements. They concluded that the fear of compensation culture was ungrounded, and that improving the functioning of the instrument would not lead to frivolous litigation nor be likely to cause extensive litigation.[26] Nevertheless, it is clear that hard conclusions cannot be drawn from four case studies.

The lack of proof of the existence of a compensation culture may have shifted the government's aforementioned perception towards one of the instruments that 'would strongly promote a compensation culture': contingency fees. During the debate on the five-year pilot regarding contingency fees in personal injury cases, the minister stated that there is 'a relatively limited risk' of developing an excessive compensation culture in the Netherlands.[27] Hence, the experiment with contingency fees was allowed, albeit under

20 Recommendations 2 and 3.

21 Notably the multi-annual reports Dispute resolution delta (*Geschilbeslechtingsdelta*) of 2003, 2008, and 2014, based on the UK *Paths to Justice* Studies, and the report *Rechtspleging Civiel en Bestuur*, all available at www.wodc.nl.

22 RJJ Eshuis, *Claims bij de rechtbank* (Den Haag: Boom 2003).

23 Notably, RJJ Eshuis, AH Sprangers and BJ Diephuis, 'Civiele rechtspraak' in NE de Heer-de Lange, BJ Diephuis and RJJ Eshuis (eds), *Rechtspleging Civiel en Bestuur 2012* (Justitie in Statistiek) (Den Haag: Boom Lemma 2013). These reports are not directly aimed at investigating compensation culture, but do entail related elements.

24 See RJJ Eshuis and F Tulder (eds), *Daling instroom civiele zaken onderzocht* (Memorandum) (Den Haag: WODC 2014). See also para 4.3.1.

25 See for a plea for more empirical data on Dutch collective redress JH Lemstra, 'De claimstichting' in G van Solinge et al. (eds), *Relativering van de rechtspersoonlijkheid* (Deventer: Kluwer 2012).

26 Case studies on the Dexia, Shell, Vedior and Vie d'Or settlements: IN Tzankova and DR Hensler, 'Collective Settlements in the Netherlands: Some Empirical Observations' in C Hodges and A Stadler (eds), *Resolving Mass Disputes. ADR and Settlement of Mass Claims* (Cheltenham: Edward Elgar 2013) 91–105. See also para 4.4.

27 *Kamerstukken II* 2012/13, 31 753, 62, 3.

strict conditions and for a limited period. Moreover, as mentioned, within the context of collective redress, government policy so far has been to not further regulate the practices of entrepreneurial representative organizations. Nevertheless, the fear of a compensation culture remains a popular warning signal, also within the topic of collective redress.

4. Entrepreneurial motives in collective redress: Dutch data

4.1 The method and scope of the exploration

As the previous sections have shown, initiators with an entrepreneurial motive have entered the collective redress market, and Dutch policy makers and courts have taken a rather liberal stance on the topic. Nevertheless, the discussion on compensation culture remains present, also in the debate on the future of collective redress. In order to address the question of whether entrepreneurial motives in collective redress through contingency fee arrangements have contributed to a compensation culture, that is, to an increase in the number of (frivolous) claims, I have conducted an explorative (systematic) case law analysis. The data are presented and analysed in the three following sub-sections. First, I classify four types of representative organizations in order to help identify which types of initiators operate in the collective redress market and what types of claims they bring (Section 4.2). I then present and analyse the results of a case law study on collective actions from 1999 to 2015 (Section 4.3). I conducted searches in the court database (*rechtspraak.nl*)[28] using the following keywords: '3:305a', '305a', and '*collectieve actie*'.[29] In total, I found and analysed 400 collective action judgments (334 unique cases), supplemented with publicly available information on the cases and/or representative organizations.[30] Third, in Section 4.4, I examine the seven WCAM cases in which the settlements have been declared binding by the Amsterdam Court of Appeal from 2005 to 2015. I collected the data by analysing the WCAM orders and publicly available annexes such as the settlement agreement, and the case studies of Huls and Van Doorn (2007) and Tzankova and Hensler (2013).[31]

The research method has the following consequences for the scope of this chapter. First, it only discusses a part of the phenomenon of compensation culture, which is quite large and intangible.[32] Furthermore, only collective action judgments and WCAM settlements/orders have been studied. Alternative ways to achieve collective redress fall outside the scope,[33] as well as the darker numbers, such as out-of-court settlements and test cases that are under the name of individuals but funded by entrepreneurial third parties. It is also important to note that the consulted database does not inventory all existing case law on collective actions. However, it is said to contain the most important judgments assembled.[34]

28 In operation since 1999.

29 The database was last consulted on 19 January 2016.

30 For the specific variables and numbers, see paras 4.3 en 4.4.

31 NJH Huls and CJM van Doorne, 'De constructie van een massaclaim' (2007) 2 *RM Themis* 51ff; Tzankova and Hensler (2013).

32 See Bauw and Van Dijk (1999).

33 See n 4. Representative organizations that have based standing on both section 3:305a and (semi)assignments and/or powers of attorney do fall within the scope of the exploration.

34 For the selection criteria, see <www.rechtspraak.nl/Uitspraken-en-nieuws/Uitspraken/Paginas/Selectiecriteria.aspx>.

Therefore, although the analysed data might not fully reflect reality, the sample does reveal indicative trend lines and enables some tentative conclusions to be drawn.

4.2 Categorizing the market of representative organizations

When statements such as 'the proliferation of claim foundations, compensation culture and entrepreneurial lawyering' are used in the Netherlands, they usually refer to the more or less ad hoc organizations with their own financial interest that are established after a particular mass damage event to assemble a 'voice', increase leverage, and obtain some form of compensation for the represented individuals.[35] Such representative organizations are distinguished from interest groups such as Consumentenbond (consumers' organization), Milieudefensie (environmental protection organization), VEB (shareholders' organization), and FNV (employees' organization). The latter entities are considerably large and independent organizations that have established a track record of representing certain interests.[36] In the following, I have refined these two categories to better identify which types of initiators operate in the collective redress market, what types of parties they represent, and – to a certain extent – what types of claims they bring. The subdivision is based on the type of interest the organization aims to represent or protect.

First, I have distinguished representative organizations that pursue a public interest, such as the enforcement of environmental law, human rights or social security, for instance, Stichting Proefprocessenfonds Clara Wichmann and Milieudefensie. Hereafter, this type of organization is referred to as a 'public interest representative organization', or shortened to RO1. The second group comprises representative organizations that represent a private interest, such as consumers, retail investors, personal injury victims, tenants and employees. The claim will most likely have a pecuniary component and is often based on law that protects 'weaker' groups. Well-known Dutch examples of such organizations are Consumentenbond and FNV. This type of organization is referred to henceforth as a 'private interest representative organization', or shortened to RO2. The third category contains representative organizations that represent commercial or business interests, such as entrepreneurs' organizations (for instance, MKB), institutional investors, or lessors (for example, Fair Huur). This type of organization is referred to as a 'commercial interest representative organization', or RO3. These three types of organizations mainly operate by charging membership fees, contributions and/or receiving subsidies or donations. They may also have built up a war chest over the years in order to fund (future) collective redress.[37] The fourth and final category might cover all mentioned types of interests. In addition, regardless of the type of class members or law they protect, these organizations also have a financial interest of their own in the litigation: they gain a stake in litigation

35 See, for instance, *Kamerstukken II* 2011/12, 33 126, 3, 5; Lemstra (2012); N Trappenburg, 'Opkomst claimcultuur in Nederland dreigt' *FD* (Amsterdam, 9 December 2011); J Kleinnijenhuis, 'Nieuwe wet tegen malafide claimclubs' *Trouw* (Amsterdam, 8 December 2012); J Frederik, 'Waarom wij de Amerikaanse claimcultuur moeten importeren' *De Correspondent* (Amsterdam, 10 June 2014); C Driessen, 'Valt hier nog wat te claimen?' *NRC.nl* (Amsterdam, 10 October 2015) <www.nrc.nl/next/2015/10/10/valt-er-hier-nog-wat-te-claimen-1545303>; M van den Berg, 'Wildgroei aan claimstichtingen' *De Financiële Telegraaf* (Amsterdam, 20 October 2015); <www.jba.nl/nl/160/een-jaar-na-mh17-amerikaanse-toestanden-in-nederland>.

36 JMKP Cornegoor, 'Collectieve acties en belangenorganisaties in hun verschijningsvormen' in FMA 't Hart (ed.), *Collectieve acties in de financiële sector* (Zutphen: Uitgeverij Paris 2009) 26ff.

37 See para 4.4.2.

through contingency fee arrangements, since success will render them part of the proceeds. These organizations are mostly erected for a particular mass damage event, possibly in cooperation with individual attorneys or law firms. As mentioned, practising attorneys are not yet allowed to engage in contingency fee arrangements in the Netherlands, but this restriction does not apply to representative organizations, which are therefore free to choose their business model and funding arrangement. I refer to this type of organization as 'entrepreneurial representative organization' (RO4). According to opponents, this is the group that represents the feared and undesirable compensation culture.

4.3 Collective actions

4.3.1 The number and types of cases and representative organizations

In the following, I present the development of the number of collective actions in the research period and how the four types of organizations are represented in these actions. For this sub-section, I have listed 287 collective action judgments of first-instance courts (district and sub-district).[38] These judgments all concern unique cases. In each judgment/ case, I have identified which type of representative organization brought the particular collective action, based on the type of claimant(s), the type of aggrieved parties they represent, the way they fund their activities, and the type of case.[39]

Figure 10.1 shows the results.

Figure 10.1 demonstrates an upward trend of collective actions that have been dealt with by Dutch courts. It is important to reiterate that the searched database might not list all existing case law on collective actions. Therefore, although it is plausible that it has increased over time, the number of collective actions might be actually higher. However, the numbers remain modest. This prevents me from making strong claims, so I will restrict myself to some descriptive remarks.

The results indicate that the development of the number of public interest cases (RO1) is rather constant throughout the years. It seems unaffected by the presence of entrepreneurial representative organizations (RO4). This is to be expected, as a public interest case is not likely to entail pecuniary damage, meaning that an entrepreneurial business model will not be compatible with such action. The data clearly demonstrate that the initiators responsible for bringing most cases are those that represent the interests of 'weaker' parties, such as consumers and employees (RO2), and cases in which commercial interests were dealt with, such as those of branch organizations (RO3). Both curves also appear to move forward quite steadily. The curve that depicts the cases brought by entrepreneurial representative organizations starts to gradually climb as of 2008, but remains (well) under the level of the number of cases brought by all three other ROs. However, the relative size of cases of entrepreneurial organizations has grown. These findings do not necessarily support the claim that the development of entrepreneurial organizations (RO4) arose from a decrease in (financial means of) representative organizations such as the Consumentenbond

38 Not all 400 judgments were used, as they do not all concern unique cases and also include cases in which only the appellate judgment was published. Using only the judgments of the last instance (as I do in para 4.3.2) would create distortion due to the time interval between the first and last judgment.

39 If a representative organization was involved that represents two interests, both interests were counted as half. See, for instance, The Hague District Court 31 January 2001, ECLI:NL:RBSGR:2001:AA9729.

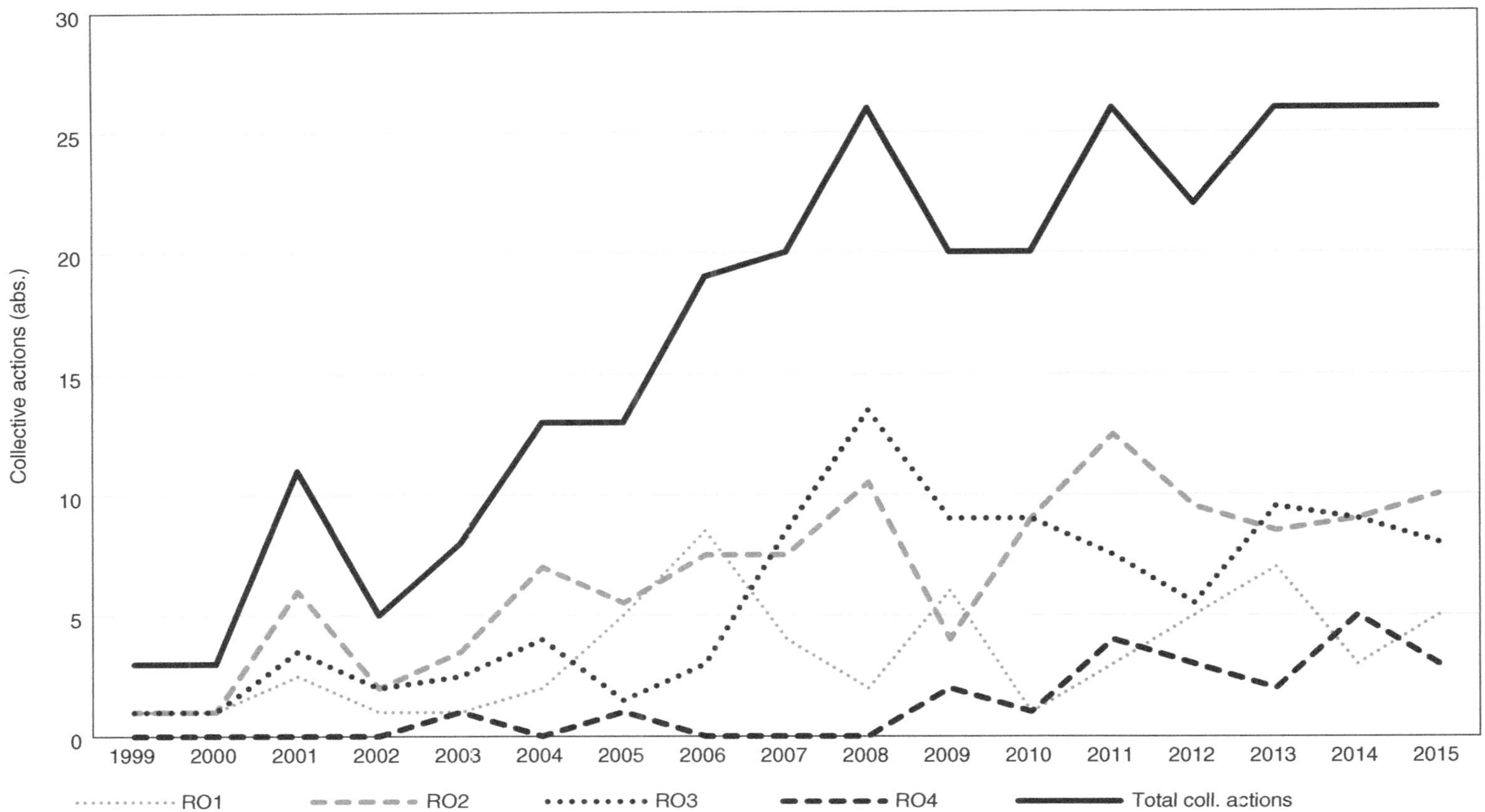

Figure 10.1 Output of collective actions in first instance courts per type of representative organization, in numbers (1999–2015) (ב=287)

(RO2). The findings do support the claim that there is an increased detection of mass wrongdoings,[40] although the number of collective actions appears to have remained modest. Nevertheless, the increase is not necessarily or merely instigated by entrepreneurial organizations.

The number of collective actions pales into insignificance compared to the development of output (judgments) of Dutch (sub-)district courts in 'regular' civil court cases.[41] As mentioned, reports show that the number of cases in the latter category has been declining since 2010. Eshuis et al. have mentioned and investigated various legislative changes as possible causes for this 'clear trend break', such as an increase in court fees or decrease in subsidized legal aid.[42] An observation that can be made from Figure 10.1 is that the number of collective actions does not seem to be affected by such legislative changes. This is not surprising, since court fees will most likely represent only a fraction of the total costs of a collective action,[43] and representative organizations will not be eligible for subsidized legal aid. It could perhaps also be argued that the rising popularity of collective action and WCAM mechanisms have also contributed to part of the decline in regular cases, but this would require further research.[44] I will return to this issue in Section 4.4.1.

4.3.2 Frivolous claims?

In order to address the question of whether the mushrooming number of representative organizations with an entrepreneurial agenda has led to an increase of abusive, unmeritorious or frivolous claims, I have identified elements in the collective action judgments that ***might*** point in that direction. However, I should note that judgments can only provide a certain degree of information about the underlying motives regarding claim behaviour.[45] Furthermore, the fact that Dutch law does not include an instrument such as a motion to dismiss can make it difficult to identify frivolous claims. I have attempted to do so by collecting data on the following elements: the admissibility of the representative organizations; whether the claim was approved/sustained or dismissed; and whether the court invoked a rule that aims to prevent or sanction unmeritorious claims. How these elements relate to (the possibility of) a frivolous claim will be explained under the respective headings. For this sub-section, I have listed 334 collective action judgments of all three instances: (sub-)district courts, courts of appeal and Supreme Court. These judgments all concern unique cases, for which only the last judgment was registered if an appellate judgment was issued.

40 Tzankova (2012) 559.

41 See NE de Heer-de Lange, BJ Diephuis and RJJ Eshuis (eds), *Rechtspleging Civiel en Bestuur 2012* (Justitie in Statistiek, Den Haag: Boom Lemma 2013), chapter 4, and, for 2013–2015, <http://wodc.nl/onderzoek/cijfers-en-prognoses/rechtspleging-civiel-en-bestuur>. These (periodical) reports contain data on, for instance, numbers and types of dispute resolution, and are compiled by the Research and Documentation Centre of the Ministry of Security and Justice (*WODC*), the Council for the Judiciary (***Raad voor de rechtspraak***), and – until 2012 – Statistics Netherlands (*CBS*).

42 See RJJ Eshuis, AH Sprangers and BJ Diephuis, 'Civiele rechtspraak' in NE de Heer-de Lange, BJ Diephuis and RJJ Eshuis (eds), *Rechtspleging Civiel en Bestuur 2012* (Justitie in Statistiek, Den Haag: Boom Lemma 2013) 85–86.

43 Currently, the maximum court fee for civil cases is capped at €3,903 (district court), €5,213 (court of appeal), or €6,519 (Supreme Court); see <www.rechtspraak.nl/Hoe-werkt-het-recht/Kosten-rechtszaak/Griffierecht>.

44 In many cases, the number of class members per collective action could not be extracted from the analysed judgments and/or available public information.

45 Cf Eshuis (2003) 19.

ADMISSIBILITY OF THE REPRESENTATIVE ORGANIZATIONS

If a party does not have capacity to litigate, a court will declare this party inadmissible (*niet-ontvankelijk*). Section 3:303 DCC entails a general restriction to standing. It applies to all civil cases and stipulates that a person has no right of action where he lacks sufficient interest. Unless contested, the court generally assumes this interest exists. As mentioned in Section 2, a specific limitation to standing applies for collective actions. Only a representative organization that meets particular criteria is allowed to bring a collective action; for instance, it is required to sufficiently represent the interests of the represented individuals. This requirement addresses the question of, first, to what extent class members will benefit from the collective action in case the claim is awarded, and, second, to what extent the representative organization has adequate knowledge and skills to litigate. For collective actions, it has been argued that a court can or should raise the representative organization's admissibility ex officio.[46]

Either way, in almost all of the analysed cases, the defendant(s) raised arguments against the admissibility of the representative organization. However, the number of cases in which the court actually found the representative organization inadmissible is relatively low. The results are presented in Figure 10.2.

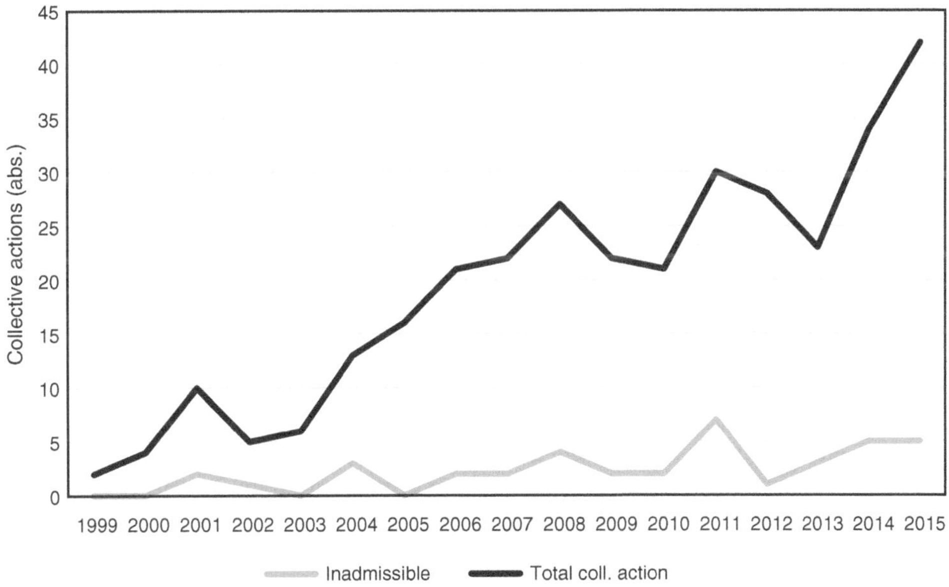

Figure 10.2 Number of collective actions in which the representative organization was found inadmissible, in numbers (1999–2015) (n=326)[47]

46 DF Lunsingh Scheurleer and FE Vermeulen, 'Collectieve acties en prejudiciële vragen in het financiële recht: revisie en integratie' in D Busch, CJM Klaassen and TMC Arons (eds), *Aansprakelijkheid in de financiële sector* (Deventer: Kluwer 2013) 265–268.

47 The total number of 3:305a cases is slightly lower than the total number of unique cases (334), as I have omitted interlocutory judgments that do not include a ruling on admissibility.

In reiteration, Figure 10.1 showed that the number of cases brought by entrepreneurial organizations started to climb gradually as of 2008. If the assumption that such organizations are responsible for 'bad' claims is true, the curve that represents the number of collective actions in which the representative organization was found inadmissible might have climbed more sharply than the curve that represents the total number of collective actions. This is not the case.[48] This could indicate either that few frivolous claims were brought (or, rather, resulted in a judgment) or that a court's main interest is to judge a claim's merits rather than an organization's admissibility. If a representative organization is found inadmissible, a judge might question what good that does for the aggrieved party that is affiliated with the representative organization. The aggrieved party will probably have already paid a fee or contribution and, after the organization is denied standing, might be left empty-handed. Therefore, the current test might merely be a paper tiger. Either way, this result confirms comments in the literature that standing in court is obtained relatively easily.[49] It might also support the minister's claim that an unimpeded access to justice has increased the number of collective actions.[50] The court's willingness, so far, to allow representative organizations standing might also be connected with the limitation to the collective action regulation in that it does not allow the representative organization to claim for damages. If the court also has to assess large amounts of damages, it may take a second or closer look at the organization that brings such claim. It is currently too soon to reach conclusion about the extent to which the 2013 raising of the bar for standing in collective actions has discouraged the mushrooming of entrepreneurial representative organizations from bringing collective actions. However, in light of the number of claims that the courts have found inadmissible so far, one could argue that the legislative amendment is not the most adequate way to prevent or discourage representative organizations from bringing collective actions.[51] At the time, the minister already suggested as much: 'I don't expect a considerable increase or decrease of legal entities that will be granted standing in court.'[52]

APPROVED CLAIMS

I have also recorded whether a claim was dismissed or approved. If a claim is dismissed, it does not necessarily render the claim unmeritorious. For instance, a claim might be difficult to prove, resulting in its dismissal. On the contrary, the number of claims approved signals the number of meritorious claims being brought. Although the idea of what is meritorious might change over time, it is unlikely that a judge will approve an unmeritorious or frivolous claim. Thus, an approved claim is unlikely to be unmeritorious. To clarify: if a claim is

48 The positive correlation between the variables 'inadmissible' and 'total number of collective actions' hardly changes after 2008. A first regression analysis (OLS) shows that there is no statistically significant effect between the lapse of time and percentage of claims in which the organization was found inadmissible. Similarly, no significant effect is discernible between the percentage of inadmissibility before and after 2008. However, the non-significance might also be attributed to the low number of observations (17; 1999–2015). Therefore, this paper is descriptive; for a more sophisticated statistical analysis, further research is required. The same applies to the analysis of the approved claims hereafter.

49 Tzankova and Lunsingh Scheurleer (2009) 153; MJ van der Heijden, 'Class Actions/les actions collectives' (2010) 14(3) *Electronic Journal of Comparative Law* 6. See also *Kamerstukken II* 2011/12, 33 126, 3, 5.

50 See para 2.

51 Cf MJ van der Heijden, 'Adempauze (II)' (2011) 61 *Nederlands Tijdschrift voor Burgerlijk Recht* 430; and I Tillema, 'De representatieve vordering: dekt de Europese vlag de Nederlandse lading?' (2014) 31(5) *NTBR* 194.

52 *Kamerstukken II* 2011/12, 33 126, 3, 5 and *Kamerstukken II* 2012/13, 33 126, 7, 9.

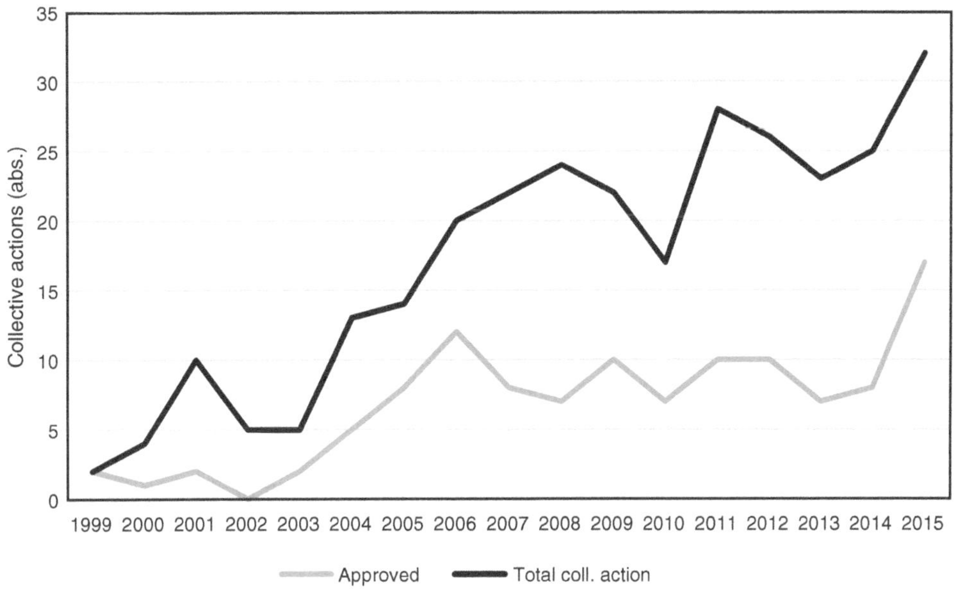

Figure 10.3 Number of collective actions in which the claim was approved, in numbers (1999–2015) (n=292)[53]

approved, the representative organization was not found inadmissible. The data regarding approved claims are presented in Figure 10.3.

As the curve that represents the approved cases rises in a rather parallel manner to that of the total number of collective actions, it is not likely that the amount of unmeritorious or frivolous claims filed has increased. It appears that the percentage of approved claims has not changed significantly over time,[54] thus, that organizations with an entrepreneurial motive are not necessarily responsible for an increase in the number of frivolous claims.

UNDUE LITIGATION CONDUCT OR ABUSE OF PROCEDURAL RIGHT

Third, I have registered whether the court found an infringement of rules that aim to prevent or sanction, among other things, frivolous claims and undue litigation conduct (section 21 DCCP, due process/*goede procesorde*, and section 3:13 DCC), and/or whether it compensated the opposing party after such claim or conduct (liability for litigation costs).[55]

53 The total number of 3:305a cases is slightly lower than the total number of unique cases (334), as I have omitted interlocutory judgments.

54 See n 50.

55 The Dutch fee-shifting system is based on the loser-pays rule: the losing party has to reimburse the winning party's litigation costs (section 237 DCCP). However, the cost award does not relate to the prevailing party's actual costs. Only in exceptional circumstances will all of its (reasonable) litigation costs be awarded. Such 'full indemnity' requires a substantive claim for damages: abuse of procedural right or tort.

I found 10 unique cases in which one of these grounds was invoked by the defendant (n=400).[56] In only one of these cases did the court indeed find an infringement. That case involved an entrepreneurial representative organization that had filed a claim that was the same as a claim that had been previously filed (and dismissed, due to a technicality). Given the close affinity between both claimants (the 'new' organization had changed its name slightly) and the fact that no new points of law were raised, the court of appeal found that the 'new' organization had abused its procedural right to litigate, and ordered it to pay the defendant's actual litigation costs of both instances for the 'second' claim (€25,853).[57]

4.4 WCAM settlements

4.4.1 The number and types of cases and representative organizations

In this and the following sub-section, I discuss the seven WCAM settlements that have been declared binding by the Amsterdam Court of Appeal from 2005 to 2015: DES, Dexia, Vie d'Or, Shell, Vedior, Converium, and DSB.[58] For this type of collective redress, as in the previous section, I observe what types of cases the court dealt with, which representative organizations were involved, and whether the involvement of entrepreneurial motives has led to an increase in (frivolous) claims.

Table 10.1 presents an outline of the WCAM settlements. As the 'Type of case' table row shows, the WCAM instrument mainly deals with financial products and securities cases. After the first WCAM settlement, in the DES case, no other settlement of personal injury claims followed, even though the WCAM was designed with this type of mass damage cases in mind.[59] As the settlements did not involve public interest litigation, no such representative organizations (RO1) are found in the outline [see the 'Representative organization (RO)' table row]. The organizations that were involved in the settlements can be qualified as those representing either private or commercial interests (RO2 or RO3). In addition, in both the Shell and Converium settlements, a US principal counsel was involved. Based on the manner in which these attorneys or law firms were remunerated (through contingency fee arrangements), they can be qualified as, or at least compared to, entrepreneurial representative organizations (RO4). I will return to these parties in Section 4.4.2.

With seven WCAM settlements concluded in over a decade, it is difficult to continue to insist that the instrument has given rise to an increase in litigation,[60] let alone an increase instigated by entrepreneurial organizations. Instead, it probably has the opposite effect, as it might – as intended – lead to a decline in 'regular' civil litigation. This assumes a certain interchangeability – that in each WCAM case, there would have been an outpouring of individual claims before Dutch courts had the WCAM not existed. This cannot be easily

56 Using the following keywords: '3:13', 'misbruik van recht', 'misbruik van proces', 'misbruik van procesrecht', 'misbruik van bevoegdheid', 'goede procesorde', 'proceseconomi*' and '21 Rv'.

57 The Hague Court of Appeal 21 April 2015, ECLI:NL:GHDHA:2015:827.

58 DES (1 June 2006, ECLI:NL:GHAMS:2006:AX6440), Dexia (25 January 2007, ECLI:NL:GHAMS:2007:AZ7033), Vie d'Or (29 April 2009, ECLI:NL:GHAMS:2009:BI2717), Shell (29 May 2009, ECLI:NL:GHAMS:2009:BI5744), Vedior (15 July 2009, ECLI:NL:GHAMS:2009:BJ2691), Converium (17 January 2012, ECLI:NL:GHAMS:2012:BV1026), and DSB (4 November 2014, ECLI:NL:GHAMS:2014:4560). See also I Tillema, 'Tien jaar WCAM: een overzicht' (2016) 4 *Maandblad voor Ondernemingsrecht*.

59 *Kamerstukken II* 2003/04, 29 414, 3, 2. See also Tzankova and Lunsingh Scheurleer (2009).

60 For a similar argument, see Tzankova and Hensler (2013).

Table 10.1 Overview of the WCAM cases (2005–2015)

	DES	*Dexia*	*Vie d'Or*	*Shell*	*Vedior*	*Converium*	*DSB*
Year of WCAM decision	2006 and 2014	2007	2009	2009	2009	2012	2014
Type of case	Product liability	Financial products and services	Financial products and services	Securities	Securities	Securities	Financial products and services
Class members	Personal injury victims	Retail investors (share leasing product)	Life insurance policy holders	Non-US shareholders	Shareholders worldwide	Non-US shareholders	Purchasers of various products
Size of the class (approximately)	Not quite clear. 17,000 persons registered in 2005	300,000, of which 25,000 persons (8.3%) opted out	11,000	500,000	2,000	12,000	345,000, of which 300 persons (0.1%) opted out
Representative organization (RO)	Stichting DES Centrum	Stichting Lease-verlies, Stichting Eegalease, VEB, and Consumentenbond	Stichting Vie d' Or	Shell Reserves Compensation Foundation, VEB, and two pension funds	VEB and Stichting uitvoering Vedior schikking (claim administrator)	Converium Securities Compensation Foundation and VEB	Stichting SSP, Stichting PAL, and Stichting SBRd (LEI)
(Alleged) liable party or parties	Pharmaceutical companies and insurers	Dexia (and Aegon)	Supervisor, state, auditors, and actuary	Shell	Human resources agency	Converium (reinsurer)	DSB's trustees plus insurers

(Continued)

Table 10.1 Overview of the WCAM cases (2005–2015) (Continued)

	DES	*Dexia*	*Vie d'Or*	*Shell*	*Vedior*	*Converium*	*DSB*
Funding of RO's activities prior to settlement	Subsidies and donations	Participants of ROs (or their LEI) paid a contribution of €45	Supervisor established and funded RO	Shell established and funded Foundation	Members VEB pay annual membership fee plus war chest VEB	US attorneys and (alleged) liable parties established & funded Foundation	Own resources, and defendants paid fees during negotiations
Settlement amount	€38 million	€1 billion	€45 million	$448 million	€4 million	$58 million (incl. compensation ROs)	max €500 million
RO compensated in settlement	Unknown	Dexia bears litigation and administration costs of ROs	Supervisor bears RO's costs ('voluntarily') to a maximum of €8.5 million	Shell bears costs of Foundation ($6 m), VEB ($6.2 m + attorney's fees) and US principal counsel ($47 m).	Randstad bears costs Stichting to a maximum of €212,000, plus the settlement costs	Converium bears costs Dutch litigation and administration (€1.6 million) plus US principal counsel fee (20% of settlement)	DSB bears the RO's costs, including annual amount to SSP and remuneration board SBRd
Compensation RO assessed?	No	No	No	Limited	Limited	Yes	No

tested, at least not with the study at hand. However, there is one case that hovered around both before and after the introduction of the WCAM, and although this is only one example, it does provide some evidence that the assumption is tenable. In the Dexia case (on the mis-selling of share leasing products), hundreds of individual cases flooded the courts of first instance, long before the WCAM instrument was implemented and a WCAM settlement was reached.[61] After the settlement was declared binding, the cases in court kept coming due to the many opt-outs. This lack of finality was probably caused by the following two factors. First, during the opt-out period, some courts issued more favourable judgments compared to the individual compensation that would be obtained through participating in the WCAM settlement. Second, this judicial buoyancy played directly into the hands of representative organizations that had already started to compete with the representative organizations who had realized the Dexia settlement.[62] The competitors claimed that they would help class members receive better compensation through individual litigation than through the WCAM settlement. In total, about 25,000 class members (approximately 8 per cent of the total) opted out. Although some individual Dexia cases are still pending, this number probably would have been larger in the absence of the WCAM. After this debacle, the WCAM regulation was amended. Nowadays, pending individual cases are suspended for the duration of the WCAM trajectory, including the opt-out period.[63] In the DSB case (on the mis-selling of various financial products, inter alia, endowment policies), at least one organization set out to help individuals obtain more advantageous results by rejecting and challenging the 2011 settlement as it was pending before the court of appeal to be declared binding. However, this did not lead to many opt outs; only 300 class members (approximately 0.1 per cent of the total) opted out. It could be that the legislative amendment helped to achieve such a low opt-out ratio; it could also be that the DSB settlement was more legitimate than the Dexia one, and DSB's bankruptcy undoubtedly played a role in the low opt-out ratio. In any event, apart from the Dexia case, all WCAM settlements achieved finality, which may have prevented an increase, however little or large, of regular cases to be dealt with by courts. To further substantiate this argument, I refer to Section 4.3.1, where I suggested that the rising popularity of the two Dutch collective redress mechanisms may have contributed to part of the decline in 'regular' civil cases. As mentioned, this would require further research, but as a start, I have presented the number of class members of each WCAM settlement in Table 4. As the 'Size of the class' table row shows, a substantial number of people were compensated on account of the settlements.

4.4.2 Frivolous claims?

I now return to the entrepreneurial organizations that were involved in the WCAM settlements. It is questionable whether entrepreneurial motives have increased the number of frivolous claims, as the WCAM instrument is designed to obtain a binding settlement.

61 See Huls and Van Doorne (2007).

62 NJH Huls and CJM van Doorne, 'De constructie van een massaclaim' (2007) 2 *Rechtsgeleerd Magazijn Themis* 56; and IN Tzankova, 'Funding of Mass Disputes: Lessons From the Netherlands' (2012) 8(3) *Journal of Law, Economics & Policy* 577ff.

63 See section 1015 DCCP.

Given the (active)[64] role of the WCAM judges, combined with the possibility for 'third' representative organizations and individuals to bring forward objections, a settlement is not likely to be declared binding if it concerns a frivolous claim. Moreover, it is important or even essential to reiterate that the defendant(s) act as co-initiator(s) of the request in order for the settlements to be declared binding. The power or position of a large corporation as a defendant, and its legal team, should not be overlooked or underestimated, especially given the high stakes involved (see the 'Settlement amount' table row). So far, although no hard conclusions can be reached based on this study, the cases show no signs of frivolous 'litigation', nor does it seem likely that industrious entrepreneurial organizations have encouraged this within the framework of WCAM, or will do so in the future.

Nevertheless, the following observations can be made within the context of 'American situations'. To fund their activities, most representative organizations charge contributions and/or receive donations (see the 'Funding of RO's activities prior to settlement' table row). In the Dexia case, for instance, the activities of the representative organizations were fuelled by class members that paid a contribution (€45) or an annual fee.[65] As part of the settlement that followed, Dexia[66] bore the representative organizations' costs. In the Shell, Converium and DSB cases, the defendants seem to have paid (also) the costs of the settlement negotiations. For parties such as the VEB, the recovery of costs 'and something' has turned into an important method of funding its activities; over the years, they have established a war chest for future activities.[67] In a way, defendants financially contribute to such activities. This is probably not done out of altruistic motives; more likely, given that the WCAM settlement will result in finality, these parties may want to reward the non-free-riders and the organization that 'helped' obtain this finality. Or it could just be that the representative organizations were good negotiators. However, the remuneration of parties such as VEB looks like pocket money compared to the US principal counsels' fees in the Shell and Converium case. As the 'RO compensated in settlement' table row shows, the fees were sizeable ($47 million in Shell and approximately $12 million in Converium). In literature, a lot of attention has been paid to these settlements due to their international character and (in Converium) the unfavourable settlement amount for non-US shareholders compared to that of US shareholders.[68] It is somewhat odd that the size of the attorneys' fees has hardly been discussed. Such a discussion is all the more pressing considering that the counsels also received a fee for their US activities. However, the representative organization's remuneration is not generally part of the court's assessment of the settlement's reasonableness (see the 'Compensation RO assessed?' table row). Based on the seven WCAM orders, it appears that the Amsterdam Court of Appeal always first considers

64 Notably, the WCAM settlement in the DSB case; see the annotations: F Oostlander in *JIN* 2014/220, I Tillema in *JA* 2015/1, and IN Tzankova in *JOR* 2015/10.

65 See, more elaborately on the Dexia case, Tzankova (2012); and Tzankova and Hensler (2013).

66 And, partially, Aegon.

67 See VEB's annual reports. In a number of settlements (Dexia, Shell, Vedior, Converium, but also in out-of-court settlements such as the Ahold settlement), VEB was remunerated and reimbursed for expenses and costs associated with realizing and implementing the settlement. See also ARJ Croiset van Uchelen, 'Handhaven of bijschaven? De effectiviteit van de WCAM' (2008) 6,772 *WPNR* 798.

68 See, for instance, J De Bie Leuveling Tjeenk and R Hermans, 'International Class Action Settlements in the Netherlands since Converium' in *International Comparative Legal Guide to: Class & Group Actions 2013* (London: Global Legal Group 2012) 6–12; and B Krans, 'The Dutch Class Action (Financial Settlement) Act in an International Context: The Shell Case and the Converium case' (2012) 31(2) *Civil Justice Quarterly* 141–150.

that the WCAM settlements should be assessed in light of the fact that, in most cases, an individual procedure would have been costly and time-consuming, and would have caused insecurity for the class members. As to the representative organizations' costs, in the Vie d'Or, Shell, and Vedior cases, the court also stated that these costs would not be deducted from the compensation for the class members and, therefore, the interests of the class members were sufficiently represented. The only case in which the amount of costs and fees was assessed explicitly is the Converium case. This assessment took place because the fees would be paid out of the settlement fund and would therefore reduce the class members' compensation considerably. Among other things, the 20 per cent fee for the US principal counsel was subject to the court's judgment. The court applied Dutch law, but took into account US documents and standards of reasonableness, since the legal activities mainly took place in the US and were performed by US law firms.[69] The court ruled that the costs and fees were not unreasonable and, therefore, did not render the remaining compensation unreasonable.

5. Conclusion

Fears of 'American situations', 'US-style class actions', 'compensation culture', or even 'piracy' have been expressed in the debate on funding collective redress. Unfortunately, these fears do not always have a solid basis and/or seemingly disregard the difference in legal system and culture between the USA and Europe, turning a possibly reasonable fear into an empty catchphrase. By describing the evolution of Dutch collective redress and its market, with this chapter and within its scope,[70] I have aimed to add some facts to the debate.

To signal the way entrepreneurial organizations have shaped collective redress, I have classified representative organizations into four types.[71] This has led to the finding that although there might have been a slow increase in the number of collective actions, this is not necessarily attributable to entrepreneurial organizations.[72] Although the relative size of cases brought by such organizations has grown, the case law study does not reveal a relative increase in frivolous claims, let alone one that can be linked to entrepreneurial parties. It has been suggested that organizations either bring few frivolous claims to court – that is, those that result in a judgment – or that a court's main interest is to judge a claim's merits rather than an organization's admissibility.[73] I found a couple of incidents that tie up with opponents' claims of 'American situations': an entrepreneurial organization that abused its procedural right, which the court sanctioned; and US counsels entering the WCAM market, including their sizeable fees, which the court disregarded in one settlement, and allowed in another.[74] I signalled that some representative organizations have set up a war chest for future litigation, and that the opt-out ratio of WCAM settlements has improved;

69 See considerations 6.5.1–6.5.8.

70 See para 4.1.

71 See paras 4.2 and 4.3.1.

72 See para 4.3.1.

73 See para 4.3.2.

74 See para 4.3.2, under '*Undue litigation conduct or abuse of procedural right*', and para 4.4.2, regarding the initiator's remuneration in the *Shell* and *Converium* case.

that is, the number of opt-outs has dropped. This has led to better finality and, possibly, prevented an increase of regular cases to be dealt with by courts.[75]

Past performance does not guarantee future results. Moreover, this exploration has not addressed those activities that are not subject to judicial oversight. Further research remains necessary. However, based on this exploration of Dutch collective redress output, I conclude that, incidents aside, claims that entrepreneurial motives create or sustain a collective redress compensation culture may very well lack merit.

Bibliography

Arons T. and W.H. van Boom, 'Beyond Tulips and Cheese: Exporting Mass Securities Claim Settlements from the Netherlands' (2010) 21(6) *European Business Law Review* 857.

Bauw E. and F. van Dijk, *Naar een claimcultuur in Nederland?* (Den Haag: Ministerie van Justitie 1999).

—— and T. Bruinen, 'Slow start of veeg teken?' (2013) 88(3) *NJB* 164.

Cornegoor J.M.K.P., 'Collectieve acties en belangenorganisaties in hun verschijningsvormen' in F.M.A. 't Hart (ed.), *Collectieve acties in de financiële sector* (Zutphen: Uitgeverij Paris 2009) 26.

Croiset van Uchelen A.R.J., 'Handhaven of bijschaven? De effectiviteit van de WCAM' (2008) 6772 *WPNR* 798.

De Bie Leuveling Tjeenk J. and R. Hermans, 'International Class Action Settlements in the Netherlands since Converium' in *International Comparative Legal Guide to: Class & Group Actions 2013* (London: Global Legal Group 2012) 6.

De Heer-de Lange N.E., B.J. Diephuis and R.J.J. Eshuis (eds), *Rechtspleging Civiel en Bestuur 2012* (Justitie in Statistiek, Den Haag: Boom Lemma 2013).

Driessen C., 'Valt hier nog wat te claimen?' *NRC.nl* (Amsterdam, 10 October 2015) <www.nrc.nl/next/2015/10/10/valt-er-hier-nog-wat-te-claimen-1545303>.

Eshuis R.J.J., *Claims bij de rechtbank* (Den Haag: Boom 2003).

—— A.H. Sprangers and B.J. Diephuis, 'Civiele rechtspraak' in N.E. de Heer-de Lange, B.J. Diephuis and R.J.J. Eshuis (eds), *Rechtspleging Civiel en Bestuur 2012* (Justitie in Statistiek, Den Haag: Boom Lemma 2013) 83.

—— and F. Tulder (eds), *Daling instroom civiele zaken onderzocht* (Memorandum) (Den Haag: WODC 2014).

Faure M., T. Hartlief and N. Philipsen, 'Funding of Personal Injury Litigation and Claims Culture. Evidence from the Netherlands' (2006) 2(2) *Utrecht Law Review* 1.

—— T. Hartlief and N. Philipsen, *Resultaatgerelateerde beloningssystemen voor advocaten* (Maastricht: METRO 2006).

—— and T. Hartlief, 'Claimcultuur en beloningssystemen' in W.H. van Boom, I. Giesen and M. Smit (eds), *Civilologie: opstellen over empirie en privaatrecht* (Den Haag: Boom Juridische Uitgevers 2012) 151–166.

Frederik J., 'Waarom wij de Amerikaanse claimcultuur moeten importeren' *De Correspondent* (Amsterdam, 10 June 2014).

Frenk N., 'Bundeling van vorderingen' (2003) *Tijdschrift voor Privaatrecht* 1,418.

Haazen O.A. and J. Spier, 'Feitelijke ontwikkelingen en verzekerbaarheid' in A. Bolt and J. Spier (eds), *De uitdijende reikwijdte van de aansprakelijkheid uit onrechtmatige daad* (Preadvies N.J.V., Zwolle: WEJ Tjeenk Willink 1996) 7–83.

Hensler D.R., 'Revisiting the Monster: New Myths and Realities of Class Action and Other Large Scale Litigation' (2001) 11(2) *Duke Journal of Comparative and International Law* 179.

75 See paras 4.3.1, 4.4.1 and 4.4.2.

Huls N.J.H. and C.J.M. van Doorne, 'De constructie van een massaclaim' (2007) 2 *Rechtsgeleerd Magazijn Themis* 51.

Kerkmeester H.O., 'Contingency fees en letselschade: een rechtseconomische analyse' (1999) 47 *Verkeersrecht* 257.

Keske S., A. Renda and R. Van den Bergh, 'Financing and Group Litigation' in M.L. Tuil and L. Visscher (eds), *New Trends in Financing Civil Litigation in Europe – A Legal, Empirical and Economic Analysis* (Cheltenham: Edward Elgar 2011).

Kleinnijenhuis J., 'Nieuwe wet tegen malafide claimclubs' *Trouw* (Amsterdam, 8 December 2012).

Krans B., 'The Dutch Class Action (Financial Settlement) Act in an International Context: The Shell Case and the Converium Case' (2012) 31(2) *Civil Justice Quarterly* 141.

Lemstra J.H., 'De claimstichting' in G. van Solinge et al. (eds), *Relativering van de rechtspersoonlijkheid* (Deventer: Kluwer 2012) 107–122.

—— and R.W. Okhuijsen, 'Consultatiedocument zelfregulering claimstichtingen' (2010) 6 *Tijdschrift voor Financieel recht* 158.

Lunsingh Scheurleer D.F. and F.E. Vermeulen, 'Collectieve acties en prejudiciële vragen in het financiële recht: revisie en integratie' in D. Busch, C.J.M. Klaassen and T.M.C. Arons (eds), *Aansprakelijkheid in de financiële sector* (Deventer: Kluwer 2013) 257.

Tillema I., 'Cessie als instrument ter afwikkeling van massaschadezaken' (2014) 12 *Maandblad voor Vermogensrecht* 333.

—— 'De representatieve vordering: dekt de Europese vlag de Nederlandse lading?' (2014) 31(5) *NTBR* 194.

—— 'Tien jaar WCAM: een overzicht' (2016) 4 *Maandblad voor Ondernemingsrecht.*

Trappenburg N., 'Opkomst claimcultuur in Nederland dreigt' *FD* (Amsterdam, 9 December 2011).

Tzankova I.N., 'Funding of Mass Disputes: Lessons from the Netherlands' (2012) 8(3) *Journal of Law, Economics & Policy* 549.

—— and D. Lunsingh Scheurleer, 'The Netherlands' (2009) 622 *Annals of the American Academy of Political and Social Science* 149.

—— and D.R. Hensler, 'Collective Settlements in the Netherlands: Some Empirical Observations' in C. Hodges and A. Stadler (eds), *Resolving Mass Disputes. ADR and Settlement of Mass Claims* (Cheltenham: Edward Elgar 2013) 91.

Van den Berg M., 'Wildgroei aan claimstichtingen' *De Financiële Telegraaf* (Amsterdam, 20 October 2015).

Van der Heijden M.J., 'Class Actions/les actions collectives' (2010) 14(3) *Electronic Journal of Comparative Law* 1.

—— 'Adempauze (II)' (2011) 61 *Nederlands Tijdschrift voor Burgerlijk Recht* 430.

Visscher L. and T. Schepens, 'A Law and Economics Approach to Cost Shifting, Fee Arrangements and Legal Expense Insurance' in M.L. Tuil and L. Visscher (eds), *New Trends in Financing Civil Litigation in Europe – A Legal, Empirical and Economic Analysis* (Cheltenham: Edward Elgar 2011) 7–32.

Weber F. and W.H. van Boom, 'Dutch Treat: The Dutch Collective Settlement of Mass Damage Act (WCAM 2005)' (2011) 1 *Contratto e Impresa/Europa* 69.

Wernicke S., 'Von Sammelklagen und Kaperbriefen – Zum Kiobel-Urteil des US Supreme Court' (2013) 24(11) *Europäische Zeitschrift für Wirtschaftsrecht* 401.

Index

For Product Safety Concerns and Information please contact our
EU representative GPSR@taylorandfrancis.com Taylor & Francis
Verlag GmbH, Kaufingerstraße 24, 80331 München, Germany